NAMING THE MULTIPLE

Critical Studies in Education and Culture Series

Culture, Politics, and Irish School Dropouts: Constructing Political Identities
G. Honor Fagan

Anti-Racism, Feminism, and Critical Approaches to Education
Roxana Ng, Pat Staton, and Joyce Scane

Beyond Comfort Zones in Multiculturalism: Confronting the Politics of Privilege
Sandra Jackson and Joseé Solís, editors

Culture and Difference: Critical Perspectives on the Bicultural Experience in the United States
Antonia Darder

Poststructuralism, Politics and Education
Michael Peters

Weaving a Tapestry of Resistance: The Places, Power, and Poetry of a Sustainable Society
Sharon Sutton

Counselor Education for the Twenty-First Century
Susan J. Brotherton

Positioning Subjects: Psychoanalysis and Critical Educational Studies
Stephen Appel

Adult Students "At Risk": Culture Bias in Higher Education
Timothy William Quinnan

Education and the Postmodern Condition
Michael Peters, editor

Restructuring for Integrative Education: Multiple Perspectives, Multiple Contexts
Todd E. Jennings, editor

Postmodern Philosophical Critique and the Pursuit of Knowledge in Higher Education
Roger P. Mourad, Jr.

NAMING THE MULTIPLE

Poststructuralism and Education

Edited by
Michael Peters

Critical Studies in Education and Culture
Edited by Henry A. Giroux

BERGIN & GARVEY
Westport, Connecticut • London

Library of Congress Cataloging-in-Publication Data

Naming the multiple : poststructuralism and education/ edited by
    Michael Peters.
        p.   cm. — (Critical studies in education and culture, ISSN
    1064–8615)
        Includes bibliographical references and index.
        ISBN 0–89789–485–5 (alk. paper). — ISBN 0–89789–549–5 (pbk. :
    alk. paper)
        1. Education—Philosophy. 2. Postmodernism and education.
    I. Peters, Michael (Michael A.), 1948–   . II. Series: Critical
    studies in education and culture series.
    LB41.N26   1998
    370'.1—dc21   97–22754

British Library Cataloguing in Publication Data is available.

Copyright © 1998 by Michael Peters

All rights reserved. No portion of this book may be
reproduced, by any process or technique, without the
express written consent of the publisher.

Library of Congress Catalog Card Number: 97–22754
ISBN: 0–89789–485–5
       0–89789–549–5 (pbk.)
ISSN: 1064–8615

First published in 1998

Bergin & Garvey, 88 Post Road West, Westport, CT 06881
An imprint of Greenwood Publishing Group, Inc.

Printed in the United States of America

The paper used in this book complies with the
Permanent Paper Standard issued by the National
Information Standards Organization (Z39.48–1984).

10 9 8 7 6 5 4 3 2 1

Copyright Acknowledgments

The editor and publisher gratefully acknowledge permission to use extracts from the following materials:

Jacques Derrida. (1998). *Du droit a la philosophie*. S. Winnett (Trans.). Minneapolis: University of Minnesota. Copyright © 1998 by the University of Minnesota.

Sexes and Genealogies by Luce Irigaray. Copyright © 1953 by Columbia University Press. Reprinted with permission of the publisher.

Luce Irigaray. (1996). *I love to you*. New York: Routledge. Copyright © 1996 by Routledge.

Contents

Series Foreword   ix
Acknowledgments   xiii

    Introduction — Naming the Multiple: 1
    Poststructuralism and Education
    Michael Peters

1   Jacques Lacan: Ideal-I and Image, Subject, and   25
    Signification
    Stephen Appel

2   Louis Althusser: Poststructural Materialist   49
    J. M. Fritzman

3   Michel Foucault: Philosophy, Education, and Freedom   65
    as an Exercise upon the Self
    James Marshall

4   Julia Kristeva: Intertextuality and Education   85
    Lucy Holmes

Contents

5   Jacques Derrida: The Ends of Pedagogy — From the   103
   Dialectic of Memory to the Deconstruction of the
   Institution
   Peter Trifonas

6   Gilles Deleuze: Practicing Education through   149
   Flight and Gossip
   Mary Leach and Megan Boler

7   Jean-François Lyotard: Education for Imaginative   173
   Knowledge
   A. T. Nuyen

8   Luce Irigaray: One Subject Is Not Enough — Irigaray   183
   and Levinas Face-to-Face with Education
   Betsan Martin

9   Jean Baudrillard: From Marxism to Terrorist Pedagogy   215
   Peter McLaren and Zeus Leonardo

10   Chantal Mouffe: Pedagogy for Democratic Citizenship   245
   Majia Holmer Nadesan and C. Alejandra Elenes

Index   265
About the Contributors   271

Series Foreword

Educational reform has fallen upon hard times. The traditional assumption that schooling is fundamentally tied to the imperatives of citizenship designed to educate students to exercise civic leadership and public service has been eroded. The schools are now the key institution for producing professional, technically trained, credentialized workers for whom the demands of citizenship are subordinated to the vicissitudes of the marketplace and the commercial public sphere. Given the current corporate and right wing assault on public and higher education coupled with the emergence of a moral and political climate that has shifted to a new Social Darwinism, the issues which framed the democratic meaning, purpose, and use to which education might aspire have been displaced by more vocational and narrowly ideological considerations.

The war waged against the possibilities of an education wedded to the precepts of a real democracy is not merely ideological. Against the backdrop of reduced funding for public schooling, the call for privatization, vouchers, cultural uniformity, and choice, there are the often ignored larger social realities of material power and oppression. On the national level, there has been a vast resurgence of racism. This is evident in the passing of anti-immigration laws such as Proposition 187 in California, the dismantling of the welfare state, the demonization of black youth that is taking place in the popular media, and the remarkable attention provided by the media to forms of race talk that argue for the intellectual inferiority of blacks or dismiss calls for racial justice as simply a holdover from the "morally bankrupt" legacy of the 1960s.

Poverty is on the rise among children in the United States, with 20 percent of all children under the age of eighteen living below the poverty line. Unemployment is growing at an alarming rate for poor youth of color, especially in the urban centers. Although black youth are policed and disciplined in and out of the nation's schools, conservative and liberal educators define education through the ethically limp discourses of privatization, national standards, and global competitiveness.

Many writers in the critical education tradition have attempted to challenge the right wing fundamentalism behind educational and social reform in both the United States and abroad while simultaneously providing ethical signposts for a public discourse about education and democracy that is both prophetic and transformative. Eschewing traditional categories, a diverse number of critical theorists and educators have successfully exposed the political and ethical implications of the cynicism and despair that has become endemic to the discourse of schooling and civic life. In its place, such educators strive to provide a language of hope that inextricably links the struggle over schooling to understanding and transforming our present social and cultural dangers.

At the risk of overgeneralizing, both cultural studies theorists and critical educators have emphasized the importance of understanding theory as the grounded basis for "intervening into contexts and power . . . in order to enable people to act more strategically in ways that may change their context for the better."[1] Moreover, theorists in both fields have argued for the primacy of the political by calling for and struggling to produce critical public spaces, regardless of how fleeting they may be, in which "popular cultural resistance is explored as a form of political resistance."[2] Such writers have analyzed the challenges that teachers will have to face in redefining a new mission for education, one that is linked to honoring the experiences, concerns, and diverse histories and languages that give expression to the multiple narratives that engage and challenge the legacy of democracy.

Equally significant is the insight of recent critical educational work that connects the politics of difference with concrete strategies for addressing the crucial relationships between schooling and the economy, and citizenship and the politics of meaning in communities of multicultural, multiracial, and multilingual schools.

Critical Studies in Education and Culture attempts to address and demonstrate how scholars working in the fields of cultural studies and critical pedagogy might join together in a radical project and practice informed by theoretically rigorous discourses that affirm the critical but refuse the cynical, and establish hope as central to a critical pedagogical and political practice but eschew a romantic utopianism. Central to such a project is the issue of how pedagogy might provide cultural studies theorists and educators with an opportunity to engage pedagogical practices that are not only transdisciplinary, transgressive, and oppositional, but also connected to a wider project designed to further racial, economic, and political democracy.[3] By taking seriously the relations between culture and power, we further the possibilities of resistance, struggle, and change.

Critical Studies in Education and Culture is committed to publishing work that opens a narrative space that affirms the contextual and the specific while simultaneously recognizing the ways in which such spaces are shot through with issues of power. The series attempts to continue an important legacy of theoretical work in cultural studies in which related debates on pedagogy are understood and addressed within the larger context of social responsibility, civic courage, and the reconstruction of democratic public life. We must keep in mind Raymond Williams's insight that the "deepest impulse (informing cultural politics) is the desire to make learning part of the process of social change itself."[4] Education as a cultural pedagogical practice takes place across multiple sites, which include not only schools and universities but also the mass media, popular culture, and other public spheres, and signals how within diverse contexts, education makes us both subjects of and subject to relations of power.

This series challenges the current return to the primacy of market values and simultaneous retreat from politics so evident in the recent work of educational theorists, legislators, and policy analysts. Professional relegitimation in a troubled time seems to be the order of the day as an increasing number of academics both refuse to recognize public and higher education as critical public spheres and offer little or no resistance to the onging vocationalization of schooling, the continuing evisceration of the intellectual labor force, and the current assaults on the working poor, the elderly, and women and children.[5]

Emphasizing the centrality of politics, culture, and power, *Critical Studies in Education and Culture* will deal with pedagogical issues that contribute in imaginative and transformative ways to our understanding of how critical knowledge, democratic values, and social practices can provide a basis for teachers, students, and other cultural workers to redefine their role as engaged and public intellectuals. Each volume will attempt to rethink the relationship between language and experience, pedagogy and human agency, and ethics and social responsibility as part of a larger project for engaging and deepening the prospects of democratic schooling in a multiracial and multicultural society. *Critical Studies in Education and Culture* takes on the responsibility of witnessing and addressing the most pressing problems of public schooling and civic life, and engages culture as a crucial site and strategic force for productive social change.

Henry A. Giroux

NOTES

1. Lawrence Grossberg, "Toward a Genealogy of the State of Cultural Studies," in Cary Nelson and Dilip Parameshwar Gaonkar, eds., *Disciplinarity and Dissent in Cultural Studies* (New York: Routledge, 1996), p. 143.

2. David Bailey and Stuart Hall, "The Vertigo of Displacement," *Ten 8* 2:3 (1992), p. 19.

3. My notion of transdisciplinary comes from Mas'ud Zavarzadeh and Donald Morton, "Theory, Pedagogy, Politics: The Crisis of the 'Subject' in the Humanities," in Mas'ud Zavarzadeh and Donald Morton, eds., *Theory Pedagogy Politics: Texts for Change* (Urbana: University of Illinois Press), p. 10. At issue here is neither ignoring the boundaries of discipline-based knowledge nor simply fusing different disciplines, but creating theoretical paradigms, questions, and knowledge that cannot be taken up within the policed boundaries of the existing disciplines.

4. Raymond Williams, "Adult Education and Social Change," in *What I Came to Say* (London: Hutchinson-Radus, 1989), p. 158.

5. The term "professional relegitimation" comes from a personal correspondence with Professor Jeff Williams of East Carolina University.

Acknowledgments

An edited collection of this nature, involving numerous contributors from a number of countries and also a number of partnerships or jointly authored chapters, always seems to take a long time to assemble, edit, and prepare for production. This task has been made immeasurably easier for me by my colleagues and students in Cultural and Policy Studies in Education at the University of Auckland, New Zealand: James Marshall, Megan Boler, Stephen Appel, and Betsan Martin. In addition, Lucy Holmes, who studied for a graduate degree in literature and now is teaching art theory, is completing her doctorate on the work of Julia Kristeva at the University of Auckland. Martin also is completing a doctorate; she is investigating the philosophy of Lucy Irigaray.

J. M. Fritzman, who teaches philosophy at Saint Xavier University; Peter McLaren, who teaches education at the University of California–Los Angeles; and A. T. Nuyen, who teaches philosophy at the University of Queensland, are colleagues who contributed to a collection I edited in 1995 on the educational significance of Jean-François Lyotard's work, *Education and the Postmodern Condition*. It was with great pleasure that I invited them to contribute to this collection. I had originally contacted Fritzman and McLaren to make a contribution. (McLaren is an old friend and mentor; my thanks to him for his continued support.) Given my academic interests and history, I originally had planned to contribute a chapter on Lyotard and had written a paper entitled "Jean-François Lyotard: From Language Games to *The Differend*." It was only after listening to Nuyen's paper at the annual conference of the Philosophy of

Education Society of Australasia, held in Brisbane in 1996, that I decided to ask him whether I could include his paper as a chapter of the present collection. Nuyen's paper on Lyotard seemed to me to face squarely important educational questions, more so than the paper I had written.

There are a number of women who have contributed to the collection. I already have mentioned Martin and Holmes; Mary Leach and Boler, feminist philosophers of education from the United States, have authored a chapter on the work of Gilles Deleuze; and Majia Holmer Nadesan and C. Alejandra Elenes have authored a chapter on Chantal Mouffe's theory of democratic citizenship. Nadesan teaches Communication Studies and Elenes teaches Women's Studies, both at Arizona State University West. It is, perhaps, part of the politics of discourses that traverse "poststructuralism" that forms of feminism figure prominently. Many — some would even argue, "the most important in recent years" — of the leading theoretical contributions come from women and feminists. I am very pleased that this collection contains chapters by feminist theorists about theorists who are feminist.

I also am indebted to Peter Trifonas, who allowed me to include at short notice a version of an essay on the work of Jacques Derrida he already had published in *Educational Theory*, when one of my original contributors could not deliver.

The result is, I think, a balanced work that, as an introduction, provides a beginning to the serious study in education of the work of French poststructuralist philosophers. I acknowledge the institutional support of both the School of Education and the University of Auckland, New Zealand, and the word processing and editorial help of Julie Bradley. I acknowledge also the work of Ellen Dorosh at Antietam Press for the preparation and production of the manuscript. Finally, I acknowledge the ongoing support of my wife, Tina Besley, who, over the years, has provided me with the encouragement to write.

Introduction — Naming the Multiple: Poststructuralism and Education
Michael Peters

> Becoming isn't part of history; history amounts only the set of preconditions, however recent, that one leaves behind in order to "become," that is, to create something new. This is precisely what Nietzsche calls the Untimely.
> — Deleuze, 1995: 171

> Assuming one thinks of a philosopher as a great educator, powerful enough to draw up to his lonely height a long chain of generations, then one must also grant him the uncanny privileges of the great educator. An educator never says what he himself thinks, but always only what he thinks of a thing in relation to the requirements of those he educates. He must not be detected in this dissimulation; it is part of his mastery that one believes in his honesty. He must be capable of employing every means of discipline: some he can drive toward the heights only with whips of scorn; others, who are sluggish, irresolute, cowardly, vain, perhaps only with exaggerated praise. Such an educator is beyond good and evil; but no one must know it.
> — Nietzsche, 1968: 512–13

ANSWERING THE QUESTION: WHAT IS POSTSTRUCTURALISM?

> Poststructuralism . . . is not oriented simply toward the negation of theoretical foundations, but rather toward the exploration of new grounds for philosophical and political inquiry; it is involved not simply in the rejection of the tradition of political and philosophical

discourse, but more importantly in the articulation and affirmation of alternative lineages that arise from within the tradition itself.
— Hardt, 1993: ix–x

All too often, the term "poststructuralism" — sometimes hyphenated and capitalized — is used to convey a sense of homogeneity, singularity, and unity. Some scholars and commentators tend even to talk of poststructuralist theory, implying a common method or approach. Others, in addition, conflate poststructuralism and postmodernism. Still others talk of French poststructuralism, configuring the movement in national, even nationalistic, terms. Clearly, the term "poststructuralism" — its cognates and associated terms — is problematic in certain ways. It is problematic because the identification of poststructuralism does not take account of the multiple: multiple formations of thought, multiple sources of inspiration, multiple differences and lines of influence between thinkers. It is also problematic precisely because of the multiple uses and meanings of the term as they have been applied to different thinkers. The first part of the title of this collection — *Naming the Multiple* — is meant to convey with a sense of irony something of these interpretive difficulties.

It is also to suggest at the outset that poststructuralism cannot simply be reduced to a set of shared assumptions, a method, or a body of theory. The term "multiple" mitigates against a kind of approach to contemporary intellectual history that proceeds chronologically, charting shifts by tracing lines of influence from one generation to another and by identifying intellectual origins. On this model of intellectual history, poststructuralism is restricted to one generation defined in terms of geography and confined to a national culture. Yet, one of the significant features of poststructuralism is its intercultural reception, translation, and development. The second part of the title — *Poststructuralism and Education* — signals the strategy guiding this collection of devoting each chapter to a different thinker. The overall aim is one of both resisting the temptation to render the complex skein of a movement of thought, characterized as much by its differences as its similarities and continuities, into a single methodology, philosophy, or body of theory and exploring the significance of poststructuralism for educational theory.

I previously have noted the way the uses of the terms "postmodernism" and "poststructuralism" are now commonly conflated and the way in which the matter is further complicated by the fact that a number of poststructuralists, including both Jean-François Lyotard and Jean Baudrillard, have systematically engaged the term "postmodernism," while others, such as Michel Foucault, have confessed that they do not know what the term or its associated notion postmodernity means or what problems they are expected to address (Peters, 1996). Lyotard, for example, originally adopted the most highly charged word postmodern from its current use among U.S. sociologists and literary critics dating from the late 1960s. In the very first footnote to *The Postmodern Condition*, Lyotard (1984: 85) acknowledges the contemporary sources of the usage of this term, which since has become embedded in so many different phrase regimes — the sociology of postindustrialism, mentioning the work of both Alain Touraine and Daniel Bell, and, loosely speaking, the literary theory of Ihab Hassan, together with the emphasis on performance in postmodern culture by Michel Benamou and Charles Caramello. He mentions, in addition, the now classic essay by M. Köhler. Yet, Lyotard (1984) is careful in his use of the term "postmodern": he applies it to a condition and defines it as "incredulity toward metanarratives." By defining it such, he is using the term to describe an ethos, attitude, or style rather than a period. In fact, he clearly rejects the sociological term that implies a periodizing. He writes: "I have said and will say again that 'postmodern' signifies not the end of modernism, but another relation to modernism" (Lyotard, 1988: 277). When Lyotard (1984) uses the term "postmodernism" in the essay "Answering the Question: What is Postmodernism?", he does so in terms of a Kantian account of the sublime in which art classified as modern is distinguished by its attempt to present the unpresentable. On this basis, he argues that the postmodern is undoubtedly part of the modern: "A work can become modern only if it is first postmodern. Postmodernism thus understood is not modernism at its end but in the nascent state, and this state is constant" (Lyotard, 1984: 79).

By contrast, Foucault (1983, 1991), when asked in interviews about the meanings of the terms "modernity" and "postmodernity," confessed that he did not understand clearly what they meant, what kind of problems were intended by the terms, or how they were common to postmodernists. He commented: "While I see clearly that behind what was known as structuralism, there was a certain problem — broadly speaking, that of the subject and the recasting of the subject — I do not understand what kind of problem is common to the people we call post-modern or post-structuralist" (Foucault, 1983: 205). Foucault makes it clear that structuralism was not a French invention and that the French movement of structuralism during the 1960s properly should be viewed against the background of European formalism, starting with the impulse of Russian modernism, focused around the forces of the combined movements of futurism and formalism. Asked the origin of the global term "structuralism," Foucault responds by saying that "none of the protagonists in the structuralist movement ... knew very clearly what it was all about" (1983: 190). He qualifies this statement by exempting those applying structural methods in linguistics and comparative mythology and then goes on to relocate French structuralism within the broad current of formalism that runs through twentieth-century Western culture. Foucault understood structuralism and its developments in France as intimately connected with the desire to bring to an end traditional Marxist intellectual culture (of the Stalinist kind that dominated postwar France) and to develop an alternative left culture (see Peters, 1996: 21–43).

In general, I follow Lyotard in regarding the term "postmodernism" as a broad cultural and aesthetic phenomenon with its original home in the European and U.S. avant-gardes, in discourses of poetics, literary criticism, and architecture. Both Irving Howe (1959) and Harry Levin (1966), for instance, used the concept postmodern in a derogatory sense to indicate the shift to "mass society" and to detect an anti-intellectual undercurrent threatening the humanism and enlightenment characteristics of the culture of modernism. The use of the term has been expanded considerably since its early use in the 1950s to apply more broadly to a set of sociocultural changes. By contrast, the genealogy of the poststructuralist movement, at least in its initial formations, is clearly a distinctively French phenomenon, tied closely to innovations in structural linguistics and closely related to the Nietzschean critique of both Georg Hegel and occidental rationality. The term "poststructuralism" (as opposed to the actual movement), as Mark Poster (1989: 6) remarks, is American in origin: "'poststructuralist theory' is a uniquely American practice. Americans have assimilated Foucault, Derrida, and the rest by turning their positions into 'poststructuralist theory.'"

Yet, even poststructuralism, itself, is not uncontested. Manfred Frank (1988), for instance, prefers neostructuralism, emphasizing a continuity with structuralism, while Richard Harland (1987) coins superstructuralism as a single umbrella based on an underlying framework of assumptions common to "Structuralists, Poststructuralists, (European) Semioticians, Althusserian Marxists, Lacanians, Foucauldians, et al" (Harland, 1993: ix–x). All three locutions — poststructuralism, neostructuralism, and superstructuralism — entertain as central the movement's proximity to structuralism.

It is a common strategy, especially in the literary reception of poststructuralism and in accounting for its theoretical innovations, to locate the movement in relation to its parent predecessor. Thus, for instance, John Sturrock (1986: 137) christens Jacques Derrida a "Post-Structuralist" — indeed, "the weightiest and most acute critic Structuralism has had" — and discusses the "post" in "post-Structuralism" in terms of "coming after and of seeking to extend Structuralism in its rightful direction." He continues: "Post-Structuralism is a critique of Structuralism conducted from within: that is, it turns certain of Structuralism's arguments against itself and points to certain fundamental inconsistencies in their method which Structuralists have ignored." This is part of a now standard literary reception of poststructuralism. Generally, it returns to Russian formalism and futurism to trace the interconnectedness and development of modern structuralist linguistics, often beginning with Ferdinand de Saussure's *Course in General Linguistics* and, later, Roman Jakobson's (who coined the term "structuralism") innovations to focus upon the so-called French structuralists (nominated as Claude Lévi-Strauss, Jacques Lacan, Louis Althusser, Roland Barthes, and the early Foucault), before investigating poststructuralism, characterized primarily in the figure of Derrida.[1]

Terry Eagleton's (1983) influential *Literary Theory: An Introduction*, for example, begins his chapter "Post-Structuralism" with an account of Derrida's deconstruction investigated in relation to Saussure's theory of meaning. Eagleton's account of poststructuralism is really an account of Derrida's deconstruction. However, he does locate the development of poststructuralism in relation to the specifically French politics prevailing immediately after 1968. Poststructuralism, for Eagleton (1983: 144), "smacks of a jaded resignation to the impossibility of truth," a resignation that he maintains also characterizes the Yale school of deconstruction (Paul de Man, Hillis Miller, Geoffrey Hartman). For the early Eagleton, one form of poststructuralism (read "deconstruction") represents "a hedonist withdrawal from history, a cult of ambiguity or irresponsible anarchism" (1983: 150), while another form — that associated with Foucault — is seen to point in a more positive direction. Steven Connor's (1991: 736) description of the passage from structuralism to poststructuralism as "a passage from centred to decentred or centreless structures" is more overtly sympathetic to Derrida.

Certainly, the U.S. reception of deconstruction takes its inauguration and institutionalization from the point at which Derrida delivered his essay "Structure, Sign and Play in the Discourse of the Human Sciences" to the International Colloquium on Critical Languages and the Sciences of Man at John Hopkins University in October 1966. It was a prestigious event involving the participation of reknowned French thinkers such as Jean Hyppolite, Lacan, Barthes, Tzvetan Todorov, Lucien Goldman, Georges Poulet, and others. In the preface to the proceedings the editors, Richard Macksey and Eugenio Donato (1970: x), describe the conference as "the first time in the United States that structuralist thought had been considered as a cross-disciplinary phenomenon." Of the proceedings, only a paragraph in Macksey's concluding remarks signals the importance of Derrida's "radical reappraisals of our [structuralist] assumptions" (1970: 320).

In the now classic essay "Structure, Sign and Play in the Discourse of the Human Sciences," Derrida (1978: 279–80) questions the "structurality of structure" or notion of "center" that has served to limit the play of structure. He writes:

The entire history of the concept of structure ... must be thought of as a series of substitutions of center for center, as a linked chain of determinations of the center.

Successively, and in a regulated fashion, the center receives different forms or names. The history of metaphysics, like the history of the West, is the history of these metaphors and metonymies. Its matrix . . . is the determination of being as *presence* in all senses of this word. It could be shown that all the names related to fundamentals, to principles, or to the center have always designated an invariable presence — *eidos, arche, telos, energeia, ousia* (essence, existence, substance, subject) *aletheia*, transcendentality, consciousness, God, man, and so forth.

He suggests that conceptual resources for the decentering of structure, of the transcendental signified, can be found in Friedrich Nietzsche, Sigmund Freud, and Martin Heidegger, and he distinguishes two interpretations: one Hegelian in origin and exemplified in Lévi-Strauss's work, "dreams of deciphering a truth or an origin which escapes play and the order of the sign" and seeks the "inspiration of a new humanism"; the other, based on "Nietzschean *affirmation*, that is the joyous affirmation of the play of the world and of the innocence of becoming, the affirmation of a world of signs without fault, without truth, without origin which is offered to an active interpretation," passes beyond man and humanism (Derrida, 1978: 292). As he explains "The *paradox* is that the metaphysical reduction of the sign needed the opposition it was reducing. The opposition is systematic with the reduction" (Derrida, 1978: 281). By defining itself against the philosophies of consciousness (e.g., existentialism), structuralism participates in shaping itself in relation to those philosophies and can never succeed in surpassing them (see Poster, 1975).

NIETZSCHE AND POSTSTRUCTURALISM

> Of ourselves we are not "knowers."
> — Nietzsche, 1956: 149

> The confrontation with Nietzsche has not yet begun, nor have the prerequisites for it been established. For a long time Nietzsche has been either celebrated and imitated or reviled and exploited. Nietzsche's thought and speech are still too contemporary for us. He and we have not yet been sufficiently separated in history; we lack the distance necessary for a sound appreciation of the thinker's strength.
> — Heidegger, 1991: vol. 1, 4

The history of contemporary French philosophy often is portrayed, following Vincent Descombes (1980: 3), as the passage from one generation dominated by the so-called three Hs — Georg Hegel, Edmund Husserl, and Heidegger — to a subsequent generation dominated by the so-called three masters of suspicion — Nietzsche, Freud, and Karl Marx.[2] Such a view tends to position historically Hegel and Nietzsche in opposition to each other as alternate sources of inspiration for different generations. That we should understand poststructuralism, in its specific French historical development, essentially as both a reaction against and an escape from Hegelian thought is a view for which I have argued elsewhere (see Peters, 1996). I characterized this reaction to or escape from Hegel in Deleuzian terms as "the play of difference" against "the labour of the dialectic." Gilles Deleuze's *Nietzsche et la Philosophie*, originally published in 1962, is, I argued, an inaugurating moment of French poststructuralism. Deleuze develops the Nietzschean play of difference as a polemic attack on the Hegelian dialectic, questioning its negative power and its purely reactive predisposition. The positive in Hegelian terms is achieved only through the double action of negation — the famous "the negation of negation." This is to be contrasted with the purely positive power of affirmation inherent in difference as the basis of a radical thought and philosophical movement that is neither Hegelian nor Marxist.

In support of this interpretation, I referred to Deleuze's summary of the Hegelian dialectic. I think it is worth repeating here:

Three ideas define the dialectic: the idea of a power of the negative as a theoretical principle manifested in opposition and contradiction; the idea that suffering and sadness have value, the valorisation of the "sad passions," as a practical principle manifested in splitting and tearing apart; the idea of positivity as a theoretical principle and practical product of negation itself. It is no exaggeration to say that the whole of Nietzsche's philosophy, in its polemic sense, is the attack on these three ideas. (Deleuze, 1983: 195)

The Hegelian dialectic reflects a false image of difference. Deleuze maintains: "The Hegelian dialectic is indeed a reflection on difference, but it inverts its image. For the affirmation of difference as such it substitutes the negation of that which differs; for the affirmation of the self it substitutes the negation of the other, and for the affirmation of affirmation it substitutes the famous negation of negation" (Deleuze, 1983: 196).

I argued that Deleuze's interpretation of Nietzsche and his Nietzschean critique of Hegel serves as the conceptual grounding for poststructuralism and that Deleuze's Nietzschean critique of the Hegelian dialectic should be acknowledged more fully as both one of the major keys to understanding French poststructuralism and a basis and starting point for an alternative radical theorizing: "Deleuze's 'manufacture' of Nietzsche effectively becomes the turning point for French philosophy, opening new spaces for philosophizing, helping to reinstate an outlaw tradition, and providing the basis for an alternative mode of critical thought both inside France and beyond" (Peters, 1996: 38).

This interpretation coheres with comments made by both Foucault and Deleuze. Foucault (1989), in an interview with Gerard Raulet in 1983, comments upon the importance of Nietzsche for himself, Deleuze, and others during the 1960s as a means of expressing a certain dissatisfaction with the theory of the subject articulated by phenomenology. He remarks how he read Nietzsche because of Georges Bataille and Bataille because of Maurice Blanchot. Yet, he denies that his relationship to Nietzsche was "historical" in any sense and that what he owed to Nietzsche centered on Nietzsche's critique of truth and its relation to the problem of self. This is also the line of argument pursued by Michael Mahon (1992: 2), who suggests that it is Nietzsche the genealogist, first and foremost, who is so important to Foucault: "The one who problematized truth as intimately entwined with relations of power, who sought a multiplicity of relations of forces at the origin of our taken-for-granted values and concepts and even the things that we experience. Foucault's Nietzsche, secondly, is the one who saw our prized and apparently given individuality as a historical product profoundly influenced by the falsifying grammatical structure of our language."

Deleuze, in conversation with Claire Parnet in 1986, makes the following remark clarifying the relationship of Foucault to Nietzsche:

Foucault and Nietzsche have three main things in common. First is their conception of force. Power in Foucault, like power in Nietzsche isn't just violence, isn't just the relation of a force to a being or an object, but corresponds to the relation of a force to the other forces it affects, or even to forces that affect it (inciting, exciting, inducing, seducing, and so on, are effects). Secondly, there's the relation between forces and form: any form is a combination of forces.... The third common point, finally, has to do with processes of subjectification: once again, this has nothing to do with constituting a subject, it's about creating ways of existing, what Nietzsche called inventing new possibilities of life. (Deleuze 1995: 117–118)

Clearly, the relationship of Foucault and Deleuze to Nietzsche differed greatly. For Deleuze, by contrast to Foucault, the elaboration of Nietzsche's will to power as the play of difference is an absolute antidialectic. For him, the dialectic expresses the triumph of reactive forces and nihilism. Only a philosophy that develops itself for itself through the will to power, which is the principle of multiple affirmation, can avoid negation and reaction to provide an active point of transmutation or transvaluation.

Derrida, by contrast, is reluctant to specify his Nietzsche inheritance because, as he says, at the heart of Nietzsche's *oeuvre* is an irreducible multiplicity that resists the stabilization of his work within a particular configuration:

The diversity of gestures of thought and writing, the contradictory mobility (without possible synthesis or sublation) of analytical incursions, the diagnoses, excesses, intuitions, the theatre and music of the poetic-philosophical forms, the more than tragic play with masks and proper names — these aspects of

Nietzsche's work has always appeared to me to defy, from the very beginning and to the point of making them somewhat derisory, all the "surveys" and accounts of Nietzsche (philosophical, meta-philosophical, psychoanalytic or political). (Derrida, 1994: 20)

In face of this multiplicity, Derrida invokes the concept of respect, and in response to the charge of "Nietzscheanism" leveled against his own writings, Derrida simply replies that it makes no sense. As he suggests "'To be Nietzschean' is a journalistic slogan which cannot cope with the names and pseudonyms of Nietzsche; its *raison d'etre* is, ultimately, to conjure away anxiety" (Derrida, 1994: 22). Derrida states: "I am neither able to, not want to save Nietzsche. My relation in general to thinkers just doesn't follow this kind of logic. Deconstruction cannot pose the problem of a proper name in terms of levels of allegiance or non-allegiance" (p. 25).

Ernest Behler in his Preface to the English edition of his *Confrontations* suggests that the image of the "new Nietzsche" as it has emerged since the 1960s finds its most characteristic expression in Derrida's work. In his study, Behler suggests that Derrida "highlights Nietzsche's turn toward infinite interpretation, or the affirmation of a view of the world as play, and shows how the style in which such thinking manifests itself must be plural" (Behler, 1991: vii). Such a view of Nietzsche contrasts sharply with Heidegger's interpretation of Nietzsche "as the thinker of the most condensed notion of modern metaphysics, the 'will to power.'" As Behler argues, Heidegger's Nietzsche is the last metaphysician, the one who inverts Platonism and seeks in the will to power a metaphysics of the subject that discloses the truth of the Being of beings. In confrontation with Heidegger, "Derrida views Heidegger's reading of Nietzsche as an extreme type of truth-oriented, unifying, and systematizing hermeneutics that, because of its own attachments to metaphysics, misconstrues the subtleties of Nietzsche's text in a highly reductionistic manner" (Behler, 1991: vii).

In an interview with Lyotard (1994: 67), Richard Beardsworth begins with the question of the importance of Nietzsche in Lyotard's work of the 1970s and the turn to Immanuel Kant and Ludwig Wittgenstein, together with the sudden absence of Nietzsche thereafter. Lyotard fiercely resists this interpretation, suggesting that the *Libidinal Economy* is predominantly a struggle with Freud, and although Lyotard acknowledges that he was greatly impressed by Pierre Klossowski's reading of Nietzsche in *Le Cercle Vivieux*, Beardsworth's attempt to "push Nietzsche" is misplaced. Lyotard suggests that his relations with Nietzsche "have always been a series of beginnings" (p. 90) and signals the difference of his relation to Nietzsche compared with Deleuze, who as "a metaphysician of energy," is truly inspired by Nietzsche.

Clearly, although not underestimating the importance of Nietzsche to poststructuralism, it is necessary to understand the differences and nuances of the relations of various poststructuralist thinkers to Nietzsche. This is as much a matter of intellectual autobiography — how individual thinkers perceive their relations to Nietzsche — as it is a matter of intellectual history and philosophical interpretation. It is easy to assume that the relations were one and the same and, consequently, to ignore not only the different ways in which thinkers such as Foucault, Deleuze, Derrida, and Lyotard (to name only an obvious group) formed their own specific relation to Nietzsche but also how these relations were (are) modulated through other thinkers — Blanchot, Bataille, and Klossowski, to name the most obvious examples — who are less familiar to the English-speaking community.

Duncan Large, in providing an introduction to a translation of Sarah Kofman's *Nietzsche and Metaphor*, discusses the intensification of interest in Nietzsche in the dozen years following the publication of Heidegger's *Nietzsche* in 1961 in terms of Deleuze's seminal work. Large writes:

In tracing the emergence of the new Nietzsche, one would undoubtedly have to consider the contributions of Georges Bataille and Maurice Blanchot, as well as of Jean Wahl, whose Sorbonne lectures series *La pensée philosophique de Nietzsche des annés 1885–1888* was published in 1959, the same year as *Nietzsche devant ses contemporains*, edited by Gèneviève Bianquis, the most outstanding Nietzsche translator and interpreter of the pre-war generation. Deleuze himself credits Pierre Klossowski with having rekindled interest in Nietzsche through two important essays, though it would be difficult to overestimate Deleuze's own definition of the new Nietzsche. (1993: x)

Bataille constitutes a special case requiring further comment. His *Sur Nietzsche* was published in 1945 (Bataille, Eng. trans. 1992), some 17 years before the publication of Deleuze's *Nietzsche et philosophie*. *Sur Nietzsche* constituted an early moment in the construction of a new philosophical (as opposed to a literary) French Nietzsche. Bataille's work on Nietzsche has had tremendous influence upon a wide range of scholars, including Klossowski, Foucault (who came to Nietzsche through Bataille), and Hélène Cixious, among many others. Sylvère Lotringer (1992: vii) claims that it was Nietzsche who "rescued" Bataille from Catholicism in 1920 when he was only 23, turning him against all religion. *Acéphale*, one of a number of journals (including the influential *Critique*) established by Bataille and the public face of the secret society of the same name, carried a number of articles by Bataille on Nietzsche in 1937. "Nietzsche and the Fascists" (Bataille, 1985a) attempted to reclaim Nietzsche from "the anti-Semitic falsifications" and interpretations of the fascists, including Nietzsche's sister Elisabeth Förster-Nietzsche, Richard Oehler (Nietzsche's cousin and his sister's collaborator), Benito Mussolini, Alfred Rosenberg, and Alfred Bäumler. (Bataille claims that Emmanuel Levinas also mistakenly identifies Nietzsche with the racist attitude.) Jean-Michel Besnier claims that: "One cannot understand Bataille well if one does not take his integral Nietzscheanism seriously, if one forgets, for example, that one of his essential political gestures was to want to "wrest Nietzsche from the grip of the Nazis" — that is to say, to preserve the symbol of the irreducibility (of heterogeneity) of thought against the totalitarian enterprise. If Nietzsche could be saved from Nazism then sovereignty is impossible" (1995: 18).

"Nietzschean Chronicle" (Bataille, 1985b) argues that the apogee of civilization is a crisis when sacred values lose their force and conventions begin to "decompose." The fascist solution for the recovery of the lost world consists of a restoration rather than a creation: it recomposes society on the basis of existing elements, developing the most closed form of organization (see also Bataille, 1985c).

In *Sur Nietzsche*, Bataille says that he thinks of Nietzsche as a philosopher of evil, rather than as the philosopher of the "will to power" (1945: xxiv) and it is clear that Nietzsche's work is used as a basis for Bataille's energetics and philosophy of transgression, where the practice of freedom is seen to lie within evil. Certainly, it is the posthumous *The Will To Power* that dominates *Sur Nietzsche*, rather than Nietzsche's *Genealogy of Morals* — a paradox, given Bataille's goal of resolving the problems of morality and its consistency with Nietzsche's own probings of the origin of morality in the *Genealogy* (see Lotringer, 1992: ix).

Large (1993: xi) mentions that François Ewald, in a recent edition of *Magazine Littéraire* devoted to "Les vies de Nietzsche," remarks that, without Deleuze, "Nietzsche would not be what he has become for us today." Deleuze's study of Nietzsche, Large maintains, "decisively breaks" with existentialist and, particularly, Hegelian readings to present Nietzsche's philosophy as both a continuation and a radicalization of the Kantian project of critique. Deleuze's reading, which emphasizes both the affirmation of difference and the play of active and reactive forces, was prefigured in Derrida's early work, and Deleuze continued "to set the agenda for French Nietzsche reception through the 1960s" (Large, 1993: xii).

Alan Schrift (1995: 3) provides some grounds to support an interpretation that accords Deleuze an influential place in the creation of a new French Nietzsche. He distinguishes poststructuralism from its structuralist and existentialist predecessors precisely in terms of the appeal to Nietzsche, and he acknowledges that "all of Nietzsche's French readers" — whether they came to Nietzsche directly or through Heidegger or Bataille — "were profoundly influenced by Deleuze's groundbreaking 1962 study *Nietzsche et la philosophie*" (p. 2).[3] He suggests that the importance of Deleuze's work for the French reception of Nietzsche that developed in the 1960s and 1970s "has been seriously underestimated by

Nietzsche's English-speaking readers, many of whom single out Derrida as the primary figure responsible for initiating the 'New Nietzsche'" (Schrift, 1995: 3).

In his study of the recent French legacy of Nietzsche, Schrift points out that poststructuralism is not a theory with a uniform set of shared assumptions; rather, it is, in his terms, "a loose association of thinkers" who draw upon a variety of sources, the most significant of which is Nietzsche:

Nietzsche's critique of truth, his emphasis on interpretation and the differential relations of power and knowledge, and his attention to questions of style in philosophical discourse have become central motifs within works of the poststructuralists, who have developed these Nietzschean themes in a number of ways: by attending to questions of language, power, and desire in ways that emphasize the content in which meaning is produced while making problematic all universal truth and meaning claims; by challenging the assumptions that give rise to binary, oppositional thinking, often opting to affirm that which occupies a position of subordination within a differential network; by questioning the figure of the humanistic human subject, challenging the assumptions of autonomy and transparent self-consciousness while situating the subject as a complex intersection of discursive, libidinal, and social forces and practices; by resisting the impulse toward claims of universality and unity, preferring instead to acknowledge difference and fragmentation. (Schrift, 1995: 6–7)

These Nietzschean *philosophemes* serve as a reference point for education theorists in seeking both to understand and to appropriate the insights of poststructuralism. They also serve as an interpretive basis for detecting and tracing the influence of poststructuralism in much recent educational theorizing: the critique of the Enlightenment subject of both liberal and Marxist perspectives, with the attendant development of more complex notions of student and teacher subjectivities; the challenge to simple-minded accounts of autonomy and agency; the reappraisals of models of interpretations of texts and their relations to various contexts — social, cultural, institutional, pedagogical; the reassessment of and consequent richer notions of reading and writing, considered as social practices; the intimate connections between power and knowledge in, for instance, not only classroom settings but also constructions of educational policies and the development of new pedagogical practices; the greater attention paid to the discursive power of "the languages of education" — those of educational administration, economics, management, measurement, and policy — in the constitution of education in the broadest sense; the utilization, in innovative ways, of forms of discourse analysis, deconstruction, archaeology, and genealogy as new means of analysis of educational institutions, practices, and policies; both an awareness and a political suspicion of the new communications and information technologies as, in part, the means for achieving globally what has been referred to as the information society, knowledge society, or information superhighway; the emphasis on notions and principles of becoming and process over questions of being and ontology in understanding educational practices; the critique of binary modes of thinking per se; the rehabilitation of desire as a set of cultural and educational forces; the acknowledgment of forces acting upon forces, individuals, and groups within educational settings; and the investigation and acknowledgment of the notion of difference, in its various conceptual manifestations, operating as a set of complex sociocultural and educational principles.

POSTSTRUCTURALISM AND EDUCATION: AFTER THE SUBJECT?

> The assumption of one single subject is perhaps unnecessary; perhaps it is just as permissible to assume a multiplicity of subject, whose interaction and struggle is the basis of our thought and our consciousness in general? A kind of aristocracy of "cells" in which domination resides? To be sure, an aristocracy of equals, used to ruling jointly and understanding how to command?
> *My hypothesis*: The subject as mulitplicity.
> — Nietzsche, 1968: 270

> It was in the 1950s and 1960s, at the moment when an interest in these difficulties [i.e., the dislocation of the absolute subject from the other and from time] developed in a very different way (Levinas, Tran-Duc-Thao, myself) and following moreover other trajectories (Marx, Nietzsche, Freud, Heidegger), that the centrality of the subject began to be displaced.... But if certain premises are found "in" Husserl, I'm sure that one could make a similar demonstration in Descartes, Kant, and Hegel.... This would have at least the virtue of de-simplifying, of "de-homogenizing" the reference to something like The Subject. There has never been The Subject for anyone.... The subject is a fable ... but to concentrate on the elements of speech and *conventional* fiction that such a fable presupposes is not to stop taking it seriously (it is the serious itself).
> — Derrida, 1995: 264

Schrift concludes his genealogy of poststructuralism by suggesting that "the page has been turned on French Nietzscheanism" (1995: 102). Both Foucault and Deleuze are dead; Derrida and Lyotard have turned away from Nietzsche. Lyotard, in particular, has turned away from Nietzsche to safer thinkers like Kant and Levinas. A new generation of thinkers has emerged who are explicitly anti-Nietzschean: Schrift cites Descombes and Luc Ferry and Alain Renaut. Yet, for Schrift, "the eclipse of Nietzsche" does not mean that one should give up on Nietzsche, nor does it mean that the poststructuralism is passé. He suggests that certain themes that first led the French to Nietzsche (e.g., the emphasis on interpretation, the critique of binary thinking, the attention to power differentials) are still worth recalling, and he maintains that other Nietzschean themes — the critique of both nationalism and fixed notions of self-identity — may be more relevant than ever. He also notes that "Nietzsche's *French* legacy is playing itself out more than anywhere else in the English-speaking philosophical and critical worlds" (Schrift, 1995: 123).

Certainly, Ferry and Renaut center their criticisms on the critique of subjectivity, arguing that "the philosophy of 68" eliminates and leaves no room for a positive rehabilitation of human agency necessary for a workable notion of democracy. Ferry and Renaut (1990: xvi), in their preface to the English translation of *La pensée 68*, referring to the philosophy of the 1960s as "Nietzschean-Heideggerian" antihumanism, state their argument in the following terms: "*Whether conducted in the name of a radiant future or a traditionalist reaction, the total critique of the modern world, because it is necessarily an antihumanism that leads inevitably to seeing in the democratic project, for example in human rights, the prototype of ideology or of the metaphysical illusion, is structurally incapable of taking up, except insincerely and seemingly in spite of itself, the promises that are also those of modernity.*" Yet, they conclude that "On the philosophical level it is impossible to return, after Marx, Nietzsche, Freud, and Heidegger, to the idea that man is the master and possessor of the totality of his actions and ideas. . . . Today it is a question of rethinking — *after this critique and not only against it* — the question of the subject" (Ferry and Renaut, 1990: xvi).[4] I am inclined to paraphase Ferry and Renaut, thus: it is impossible to innocently return to the Hegelian or phenomenological subject after Foucault, Derrida, Deleuze, and Lyotard (and, here, these proper names stand as emblems).

There is both the impulse and the temptation, perhaps, to run together Schrift's genealogy of poststructuralism and the (French) neoliberal rehabilitation of the subject. A gloss on this conjunction of thought might be framed, thus: both the critique of the subject and poststructuralism are, in some sense, over, and the combination of two events is not merely incidental, that is, "the eclipse of the French Nietzsche" (Schrift, 1995: 123) signals an "end" to poststructuralism, an end that can be specified in terms of an exhaustion of the critique of the subject: Now that the moment of French Nietzscheanism is completed or in some sense finished, so too the critique of the subject based upon Nietzsche's insights is over.

This is the kind of position, for instance, embraced by the most recent generation of French intellectuals who proclaim the end of one paradigm and the establishment of a new one. The officially designated shift is from poststructuralism to neoliberalism. Rational liberalism is fiercely anti-Nietzschean; its polemical target is both structuralism (Althusser, Lacan,

Lévi-Strauss) and poststructuralism (Foucault, Derrida, Lyotard, Deleuze, and Felix Guattari). Now that the philosophy of rebellion is dead or, at least, in its twilight, we can look forward to a renaissance of humanism, liberalism, individualism, and democracy. Such is said to be reflected in the new philosophical agenda: "the disappearance of historical teleology," the end of "nihilism, antihumanism, and the critique of identity and the subject" as viable alternatives for French thought, and a return to individualism and humanism, the recovery of human agency, intentionality, and consciousness (Pavel, 1989: 20).[5]

This conjunction of thought or line of argument can be resisted on a number of grounds. First, although not disputing the French legacy of Nietzsche, one might argue for a decentering of his centrality by multiplying the interpretations of his work, emphasizing the different relations each thinker displayed to Nietzsche and the way these relations have been modulated through other thinkers. The importance of Heidegger's (1991) *Nietzsche*, first published in 1961, and its mediated place in the forces of these relations comes to mind, as does the influence of Bataille's *Sur Nietzsche* (1992). It could be argued that the source of originality and power of French poststructuralism lies in the mediated relations (and reception) of Nietzsche's work or that, as in the case of Deleuze's philosophical position and development, it is not Nietzsche by himself that is important but, rather, Nietzsche in conjunction with other thinkers. For Deleuze, for example, the "other thinkers" must include Henri Bergson and Baruch Spinoza (see Hardt, 1993).

Second, and against Ferry and Renaut, one might resist the temptation, as Derrida (1994a) does, to conclude that Nietzsche is an enemy of democracy in general and has nothing to offer in the name of "a democracy to come." This strategy of argument would deny a simple-minded nihilism as it applies to the subject, to notions of political agency, and to the idea of democracy: "Since, in my eyes, Nietzsche criticises a particular form of democracy in the name of 'democracy to come', I don't consider Nietzsche to be an *enemy of democracy in general*." Derrida suggests that this move is to open up the difference between a notion of democracy, "which while having something in common with what we understand by democracy today . . . is reducible neither to the contemporary reality of 'democracy' nor to the ideal of democracy informing this reality or fact" (Derrida, 1994a: 41–42). It is this difference that Derrida indicates he has explored at length in *Spectres de Marx* (1994b). Although, as Derrida maintains, one cannot subscribe to all of what Nietzsche has written concerning the democracy of his day, he identified "particular risks in what he foregrounded under the name of 'democracy'" and "There are at the same time critical and genealogical motifs in Nietzsche which *appeal to a democracy to come*" (Derrida, 1994a: 41–42).[6] Certainly, the anti-Nietzscheanism of Ferry and Renaut does not rest upon or engage with

Nietzsche in any extended and critical sense, nor does it take into account the intercultural and transmission and development of the French Nietzsche legacy in the English-speaking world.[7]

Third, it is possible to argue that the anti-Nietzschean polemical attack on the critique of the subject is misplaced, that poststructuralism never liquidated the subject but, rather, rehabilitated it, decentered it, and repositioned it, in all its historical-cultural complexity. This line of argument also might draw attention to the fact that, although Ferry and Renaut talk of returning to the question of the subject, their critique of poststructuralism singularly lacks any resources for doing so. In other words, there is in Ferry and Renaut's work nothing that might suggest a reworking of the question of the subject in any guise except an innocent and unproblematic return to a (neoliberal) human agency. As Jean-Luc Nancy (1991: 3) comments in his "Introduction" to *Who Comes After the Subject?:* "I did not send my question ('Who comes after the subject?') to those who would find no validity in it, to those for whom it is on the contrary more important to denounce its presuppositions and to return, as though nothing had happened, to a style of thinking that we might simply call humanist, even where it tries to complicate the traditional way of thinking about the human subject."

For Nancy, the contributors (including Deleuze, Derrida, Blanchot, Lyotard, Levinas, Luce Irigaray, and Descombes) do not stand in a tradition or belong to a school, but rather "each entertains a complex rapport" to "the Husserlian, the Marxian, the Heideggerian, and the Nietzschean traditions" (1991: 3). When Nancy writes of "those who return, as though nothing had happened, to the humanist subject" (p. 3), clearly he has in mind Ferry and Renaut.[8]

In an interview with Nancy, originally published in *Who Comes After the Subject?*, Derrida (1995: 256) disputes Nancy's interpretation of the "liquidation of the subject" and, discussing the discourse concerning "the question of the subject" in France over the past 25 years, suggests instead the slogan, "a return to the subject, the return of the subject." Derrida briefly traces the place of the subject in Lacan (the decentering of the subject), in Althusser (its interpellation), and in Foucault ("a history of subjectivity" and "a return to a certain ethical subject"): "For these three discourses (Lacan, Althusser, Foucault) and for some of the thinkers they privilege (Freud, Marx, Nietzsche), the subject can be re-interpreted, re-stored, re-inscribed, it certainly isn't 'liquidated'. The question 'who', notably in Nietzsche, strongly reinforces this point. This is also true of Heidegger, the principle reference or target of the *doxa* we are talking about. The ontological questioning that deals with the *subjectum*, in its Cartesian and post-Cartesian forms, is anything but a liquidation" (Derrida, 1995: 257).

To these three discourses we might add those of Blanchot, Levinas, Deleuze, Guattari, Lyotard, Irigaray, and Julia Kristeva, not to mention Derrida's deconstruction of the subject and his recent interrogation of the subject of ethical, juridical, and political responsibility. What this tells us is that the problematic of the subject, as it has developed in France over the past 25 years, cannot be reduced to a homogeneity. The attribution of the liquidation of the subject to a Nietzschean poststructuralism — an attribution underlying the polemical attacks of Ferry and Renaut and also of a French kind of neoliberalism — operates polemically to identify its target only by ignoring the multiple: the time, place, and logical space of the subject, its multiple genealogy within the history of modern philosophy, and its active reinterpretation and reinscription.

Fourth, one might wish to disrupt the centrality of the French Nietzsche by pointing to a multiplicity of other sources of influence and reaction: Heidegger *and* de Saussure (Derrida); Kant *and* Hegel (Foucault); Kant, Wittgenstein, Levinas, Freud, *and* Marx (Lyotard); Spinoza, Bergson, David Hume, *and* Freud or Lacan (Deleuze). Why should we concentrate on influences when the importance of thought may be explained in terms of the combined forces of influence and reaction? We also should not underestimate forces of influence and reaction in the local French context: consider, for example, the importance of Jean-Paul Sartre, Althusser, Lévi-Strauss, Gaston Bachelard, and Georges Canguilhem in relation to Foucault.

Fifth, the notion of a pure poststructuralism — one uncontaminated, disrupted, or transformed that lends itself to a "taxonomic objectivization" or a "static tabularization" — discounts the way in which contemporary theory is a field constituted by plural forces (Derrida, 1990: 64–65). The principle of "taxonomic disorder" in "theory," as Derrida (1990: 67) maintains, can give rise to "reasoned and ordered translations or else to comic collapses," where "teratology is our normality." Each species of theory — for example, structuralism, psychoanalysis, neo- or poststructuralism, to say nothing of Marxist discourse — "constitutes its own identity only by incorporating other identities — by contamination, parasitism, grafts, organ transplants, incorporation, etc." (Derrida, 1990: 66). There are different modes of integration, transformation, combination, distortion, and appropriation, which makes it difficult to delimit movements into classifiable identities. This multiplicity cannot be reduced to a tabular order — fixed and stable — because of differences, on the one hand, between diverse cultural traditions and states and the opening of spaces among disciplines, on the other.

Sixth, a genealogy of poststructuralism that recognized it as a movement of thought that crossed national boundaries, cultural traditions, and, increasingly, in novel and unexpected ways, the North-South configuration of rich and poor nations would need to come to terms with poststructuralism's intercultural and international transmission, exchange, appropriation, and creative misappropriation. In these new contexts, the question of poststructuralism being over must be considered an absurdity and the question of Nietzsche's influence or legacy, perhaps less important.

Certainly, the chapters of this book are written on the assumption that poststructuralism — its genealogy, transmission, development, and application — has ongoing significance for educational theory. This book brings together a wide range of chapters by educationalists and philosophers. Each chapter is based around the work of a central poststructuralist philosopher and provides an introduction to his or her work, commenting upon its significance for education.

In Chapter 1, Stephen Appel provides a brief biography of Lacan before describing Lacan's project in terms of subjectivity; desire; the real, imaginary, and symbolic; and symbolization. Appel details the formation of the I, the now-famous "mirror stage," the path of the signifier, metaphor, and metonymy in Lacanian psychoanalysis. In commenting upon the implications of Lacan and Lacanian psychoanalysis for educational studies, Appel suggests a number of promising directions for scholarship and research: paranoic knowledge and its possible displacement of traditional epistemological emphases in philosophy of education and curriculum studies; the training of psychoanalysts; Lacan's critique of human agency; the concept of desire per se; and the Lacanian theory of subjectivity and its significance in understanding, for example, the teacher-student relationship. As Appel observes toward the end of his chapter: "From Lacan we learn about the unavoidable fragmentary nature of subjectivity, how the subject lives with the alienated confrontation with his or her lack. Not only is the subject lacking — so is the Other."

Although Lacan was born in 1901 and Althusser was born 17 years later, in 1918, both are commonly categorized as structuralists and important precursors to the generation of poststructuralist thinkers (see, for instance, Lechte, 1994). J. M. Fritzman resists this easy nomenclature and categorization to consider Althusser a poststructuralist materialist. Fritzman provides a brief account of Althusser's life and works. In the remainder of the chapter, as he says, "Given the need for brevity, the propositions in this chapter will be didactic and dogmatic, the theses schematic and provisional." Fritzman contrasts Althusser's position with those he opposes — economism and humanism — and traces the famous epistemological break that Althusser attributes to Marx's writings. He then proceeds to suggest ways in which Althusser's interventions may be useful to educationalists.

Foucault was a student of Althusser, and Foucault (1991: 56) himself suggests that one of the points of convergence between himself, Althusser, and Lacan was a matter of calling the theme of the subject into question once again. James Marshall in his chapter also takes up this great theme again to interpret Foucault's philosophy and its importance for education in terms of the practice of freedom as an exercise upon the self. He provides some biographical details on Foucault before examining his view of the point of philosophy as involving work on the self, a view that not only promotes freedom but also turns such a philosophy into an educational enterprise.

Lucy Holmes's chapter investigates "the material in theory," the inseparableness of the life and work of Kristeva, who was born in Bulgaria and arrived in Paris in 1965. She attended the seminars of Barthes and became a central member of the *Tel Quel* group, which included Philippe Sollers, Barthes, and Derrida. Kristeva, in particular, first became known as an interpreter of the work of the Russian formalist Mikhail Bakhtin and later as an important language theorist on her own account. Holmes traces Kristeva's involvement with psychoanalysis and the close relation between autobiography and theory in Kristeva's work. Holmes then discusses Kristeva's theory and critical practice of intertextuality and its relation to educational theory and practice.

The pedagogical path of Derrida's deconstruction is, in rough measure, the subject of Peter Trifonas's chapter. Trifonas claims that deconstruction offers "a resistance to the instruments of domination embedded within the praxeology of teaching-learning," illustrating his claim through a reading of Derrida's "The Age of Hegel." He investigates Derrida's contextualization of Hegel's "special report" on the pedagogy of philosophy in the Prussian education system of the early nineteenth century, reflecting on the ideology of the report, before discussing Derrida's recommendations to the Groupe de Researches sur l'Enseignement Philosophique for a critique of the pedagogical institution of philosophy.

In Chapter 6, Mary Leach and Megan Boler examine the work of Deleuze, providing a highly innovative and powerful feminist analysis. They provide an introduction to his work and then focus upon what they call "the Deleuzian project" and its quarrel with the Hegelian tradition. Leach and Boler use Deleuze's notion of rhizomatics to rehabilitate women's talk in the form of serious gossip and as an educational practice that "eludes the molarized discursive system which relies on the transmission model of communicating and learning." They also demonstrate how lines of flight can be used for the teaching of history and literature.

A. T. Nuyen argues that knowing-how should entail knowing-how-to-imagine, as well knowing-how-to-do, the technical skill, and knowing-how-to-think, the analytical skill. The end product, imaginative knowledge, helps to bring about a better world. It is the kind of knowledge required in the postmodern condition. Nuyen concentrates upon the differend in the work of Lyotard and the related phenomenon of the unpresentable to argue the case for imaginative knowledge. The kind of imagination we need to develop in order "to bear witness to *différends*" is given in Kant's account of the sublime, an account that Nuyen, following Lyotard, renders as presenting the unpresentable. Nuyen then considers the question of education for imaginative knowledge, describing some of the broad strategies that might be adopted.

In a chapter on the work of Irigaray, Betsan Martin considers the philosophical importance of the face-to-face relation as a basis for ethics, education, and sexual difference. Martin, in a complex and wide-ranging chapter, considers the influence of Levinas's ethics and the notion of ethical subjectivity conceived as an absolute alterity on Irigaray's philosophical position and development. Martin writes with considerable force when she considers Irigaray's approach to the question of sexual difference and of women becoming subjects, and she theorizes the importance of Irigaray's work for education on several grounds.

Peter McLaren and Zeus Leonardo, in a chapter subtitled "From Marxism to Terrorist Pedagogy," review the work of Baudrillard, which they consider vital to understanding the cultures of late capitalism. They contend that critical educators need to engage with the work of Baudrillard, even though it is flawed. His understanding and theorizations of capitalism as "part of a larger rationalization process associated with a new type of profileration of signs, a new type of dissemination of values, and a new type of radical semiurgy associated with cybernetic and semiotics systems, presents a serious challenge to educators working with students who often act as if modern values have been declared dead under the current conditions of hyperreality." In their chapter, McLaren and Leonardo trace Baudrillard's engagement with Marxism, his subsequent break with political economy, and his move to a revolutionary praxis. They appraise Baudrillard's ideas as they contribute to radicalizing social theory.

In the final chapter, Majia Holmer Nadesan and C. Alejandra Elenes consider the work of Chantal Mouffe as contributing to a pedagogy for democratic citizenship. Nadesan and Elenes begin the chapter by providing an overview of Mouffe's theoretical framework, commenting upon how articulation theory accounts for the ways "individual subjective identities emerge from social discourses." Next, they explain how Mouffe uses articulation theory to develop an ontology of democratic citizenship, and, finally, they discuss how Mouffe's theory of democratic citizenship might inform pedagogical practice.

NOTES

1. Part of the reason that deconstruction passed through literature rather than philosophy, especially in the U.S. context, clearly has to do with the way Derrida and deconstruction served to renew a focus upon the question of style

and the ways in which literary form impinges upon issues of philosophical content. Analytic philosophy is built upon the binary opposition of form and content. Analytic philosophers do not want to admit the question of style as a philosophical issue; yet, their rejection of the question is really a repressed preference for one style over all others. This deep-seated institutional preference for a particular group style, based on appeals to form, rigor, and clarity, not only has its roots in the evolving self-image of philosophy going back, at least, to Plato (who sought to ban poetry from *The Republic*) but also reflects the early scientization of philosophy in the nineteenth century and a kind of linguistic nationalism, where English — as an emerging metropolitan language — was seen as the most appropriate and transparent medium for the expression of thought.

2. "Nietzsche, Freud, Marx" is the title of a paper Foucault presented at the Colloquium at Royaumont in 1964. Schrift (1996: 340) suggests that, although French thought operated "within a conceptual field framed by the three so-called masters of suspicion," both Foucault and Deleuze privilege Nietzsche over Marx and Freud because "Marx operates primarily within the register of power and Freud operates primarily within the register of desire. . . . In privileging Nietzsche over Marx or Freud, both Foucault and Deleuze recognize the complicity between the poles of will and power."

3. I had not read Schrift's work until after my book *Poststructuralism, Politics and Education* had been published in 1996.

4. A similar kind of polemical critique of poststructuralism is carried out by Engel (1994). He calls poststructuralism "Nietzscheo-Structuralism" and advances six theses in characterizing it: there is no such thing as meaning, truth, epistemology (theses one, three, and four); nothing exists but forces; consciousness and subjectivity are just effects; philosophy creates concepts. Engel does distinguish between what he calls Heideggero-Nietzscheanism (Derrida) and Metaphysical Nietzscheanism (Deleuze).

5. See also Mark Lilla's (1994) introductory essay "The Legitimacy of the Liberal Age" to his edited collection *New French Thought: Political Philosophy*.

6. See also Mark Warren's (1988) study of *Nietzsche and Political Thought*. He interprets Nietzsche's philosophy as an extended answer to the following question: "How can humans be subjects of actions, historically effective and free individuals, in a world in which subjectivity is unsupported by transcendent phenomena or metaphysical essences?" (p. 7).

7. There are, I think, many trajectories one might attempt to trace in respect to intercultural transmission and development of Nietzsche's French legacy (a label that both homogenizes and is reductive — a very un-Nietzschean term). The following lines of scholarship point to some existing sites of inquiry within national contexts: the U.S. reception of Derrida or deconstruction (e.g., Haverkamp, 1995); the British reception of poststructuralism (e.g., Easthope, 1988); the German reception of Derrida (e.g., Behler, 1991); the U.S. reception of Nietzsche and the engagement with the French (e.g., Taubeneck, 1991); and the British Foucault (e.g., Gordon, 1996). In addition, one also might begin to trace the reception of the new French feminisms in the English-speaking world, a bewilderingly complex task (e.g., Marks and de Courtivron, 1981), and the redrawing of the lines between analytic philosophy, deconstruction, and literary theory (e.g., Dasenbrock, 1989).

8. Nancy reproduces a passage from his letter of invitation concerning the question, thus:

Who comes after the subject? This question can be explained as follows: one of the major characteristics of contemporary thought is the putting into question of the instance of the "subject", according to the structure, the meaning, and the value subsumed under this term in modern thought, from Descartes to Hegel, if not to Husserl. . . . A widespread discourse of recent date proclaimed the subject's simple liquidation. Everything seems, however, to point to the necessity, not of a "return to the subject" (proclaimed by those who would like to think that nothing has happened, and that there is nothing new to be thought, except maybe variations or modifications of the subject), but on the contrary, of a move forward toward someone — *some one* — else in its place (this last expression is obviously a mere convenience: the "place" could not be the same). Who would it be? How would s/he present him/herself. Can we name her/him? Is the question "who" suitable? (1991: 5)

I include such a long quote here because I think Nancy's questions concerning the subject provide a comprehensive starting point for educational theorists who are engaged in rethinking the educational subject.

REFERENCES

Bataille, G. (1985a). Nietzsche and the Fascists. In *Visions of Excess: Selected Writings, 1927–1939*, trans. A. Stoekl with C. Lovitt & D. Leslie, edited and with an introduction by A. Stoekl (Manchester: Manchester University Press) 182–196.

Bataille, G. (1985b). Nietzschean Chronicle. In *Visions of Excess: Selected Writings, 1927–1939*, trans. A. Stoekl with C. Lovitt & D. Leslie, edited and with an introduction by A. Stoekl (Manchester: Manchester University Press) 202–212.

Bataille, G. (1985c). Propositions. In *Visions of Excess: Selected Writings, 1927–1939*, trans. A. Stoekl with C. Lovitt & D. Leslie, edited and with an introduction by A. Stoekl (Manchester: Manchester University Press) 197–201.

Bataille, G. (1945). *Sur Nietzsche* (Paris: Gallimand). [English translation: *On Nietzsche*, trans. B. Boone (New York: Paragon House, 1992)].

Behler, E. (1991). *Confrontations: Derrida, Heidegger, Nietzsche*, trans. S. Taubeneck (Stanford, Calif.: Stanford University Press).

Besnier, J-M. (1995). Bataille, the Emotive Intellectual. In *Bataille: Writing the Sacred*, edited by C. Gill (London: Routledge) 12–25.

Connor, S. (1991). Structuralism and Post-Structuralism: From the Centre to the Margin. In *Encyclopedia of Literature and Criticism*, edited by M. Coyle, P. Garside, M. Kelsall, & J. Peck (London: Routledge) 736–749.

Dasenbrock, R. W., ed. (1989). *Redrawing the Lines: Analytic Philosophy, Deconstruction and Literary Theory* (Minneapolis: University of Minnesota Press).

Deleuze, G. (1995). *Negotiations, 1972–1990*, trans. M. Joughin (New York: Columbia University Press).

Deleuze, G. (1983). *Nietzsche and Philosophy*, trans. H. Tomlinson (New York: Columbia University Press). [Originally published 1962].

Derrida, J. (1995). "Eating Well," or the Calculation of the Subject. In *Points . . . Interviews, 1974–1994*, edited by E. Weber, trans. P. Kamuf & others (Stanford, Calif.: Stanford University Press) 255–287.

Derrida, J. (1994a). Nietzsche and the Machine: An Interview with Jacques Derrida by Richard Beardsworth, *Journal of Nietzsche Studies*, 7: 7–66.

Derrida, J. (1994b). *Specters of Marx: The State of Debt, the Work of Mourning, and the New International* (New York: Routledge).

Derrida, J. (1990). Some Statements and Truisms About Neologisms, Newisms, Postisms, Parasitisms, and Other Small Seismisms. In *The States of "Theory": History, Art, and Critical Discourse*, edited by D. Carroll (New York, Columbia University Press).

Derrida, Jacques (1978). Structure, Sign and Play in the Discourse of the Human Sciences. In *Writing and Difference*, trans. A. Bass (Chicago, Ill.: University of Chicago Press) 278–294.

Descombes, V. (1980). *Modern French Philosophy*, trans. L. Scott-Fox & J. Harding (Cambridge: Cambridge University Press).

Eagleton, T. (1983). *Literary Theory: An Introduction* (Oxford: Basil Blackwell).

Easthope, A. (1988). *British Post-Structuralism* (London: Routledge).

Engel, P. (1994). The Decline and Fall of Nietzscheo-structuralism. In *European Philosophy and the American Academy*, edited by B. Smith (LaSalle, Ill.: The Hegeler Institute).

Ferry, L., & Renaut, A. (1990). *French Philosophy of the Sixties. . . An Essay on Antihumanism*, trans. M. Cattani (Amherst: University of Massachusetts Press).

Foucault, M. (1991). *Remarks on Marx: Conversations with Duccio Trombadori*, trans. R. Goldstein & J. Cascaito (New York: Semiotext(e)).

Foucault, M. (1989). How Much Does It Cost for Reason to Tell the Truth? In *Foucault Live (Interviews, 1966–84)*, edited by S. Lotringer, trans. J. Johnson (New York: Semiotext(e)).

Foucault, M. (1983). Structuralism and Post-Structuralism: An Interview with Michel Foucault by G. Raulet, trans. J. Harding, *Telos*, 55: 195–211.

Frank, M. (1988). *What is Neostructuralism?* trans. S. Wilke & R. Gray (Minneapolis: University of Minnesota Press).

Gordon, C. (1996). Foucault in Britain. In *Foucault and Political Reason: Liberalism, Neo-Liberalism and Rationalities of Government*, edited by A. Barry, T. Osborne, & N. Rose (London: UCL Press) 253–270.

Harland, R. (1993). *Beyond Superstructuralism: The Syntagmatic Side of Language* (London: Routledge).

Harland, R. (1987). *Superstructuralism: The Philosophy of Structuralism and Poststructuralism* (London: Methuen).

Hardt, M. (1993). *Gilles Deleuze: An Apprenticeship in Philosophy* (Minneapolis: University of Minnesota Press).

Haverkamp, A., ed. (1995). *Deconstruction is/in America: A New Sense of the Political* (New York: New York University Press).

Heidegger, M. (1991). *Nietzsche*, trans. D. Krell (San Francisco, Calif.: Harper). [Originally published 1961].

Howe, I. (1959). Mass Society and Postmodern Fiction, *Partisan Review*, 26: 430–36.

Large, D. (1993). Translator's Introduction. In Sarah Kofman, *Nietzsche and Metaphor* (London: Athlone Press) vii–xl.

Lechte, J. (1994). *Fifty Contemporary Thinkers: From Structuralism to Postmodernity* (London: Routledge).

Levin, H. (1966). What Was Modernism? In *Refractions* (New York: Oxford University Press).

Lilla, M. (1994). The Legitimacy of the Liberal Age. In *New French Thought: Political Philosophy*, edited by M. Lilla (Princeton, N.J.: Princeton University Press).

Lotringer, S. (1992). Furiously Nietzschean. In *On Nietzsche*, edited by G. Bataille, trans. B. Boone (London: Athlone Press) vii–xv.

Lyotard, J.-F. (1994). Nietzsche and the Inhuman: Interview with Jean-François Lyotard by Richard Beardsworth. *Journal of Nietzsche Studies*, 7: 67–130.

Lyotard, J.-F. (1988). *The Differend: Phrases in Dispute*, trans. G. Van Den Abbeele (Manchester: Manchester University Press).

Lyotard, J.-F. (1984). *The Postmodern Condition: A Report on Knowledge*, trans. G. Bennington & B. Massumi (Minneapolis: University of Minnesota Press).

Macksey, R., & Donato, E., eds. (1970). *The Structuralist Controversy: The Languages of Criticism and the Sciences of Man* (Baltimore, Md.: Johns Hopkins University Press).

Mahon, M. (1992). *Foucault's Nietzschean Genealogy: Truth, Power, and the Subject* (New York: State University of New York Press).

Marks, E., & de Courtivron, I., eds. (1981). *New French Feminisms: An Anthology* (New York: Schocken Books).

Nancy, J.-L. (1991). Introduction. In *Who Comes After the Subject?*, edited by E. Cadava, P. O'Connor, & J.-L. Nancy (London: Routledge) 1–8.

Nietzsche, F. (1968). *The Will To Power*, trans. W. Kaufmann & R. J. Hollingdale, edited with commentary by W. Kaufmann (New York: Vintage Books).

Nietzsche, F. (1956). Preface. In *The Genealogy of Morals*, trans. F. Golffing (New York: Doubleday Anchor) 149.

Pavel, T. (1989). The Present Debate: News from France. *diacritics*, 19(1), 17–32.

Peters, M. (1996). *Poststructuralism, Politics and Education* (Westport, Conn.: Bergin & Garvey).

Poster, M. (1989). *Critical Theory and Poststructuralism: In Search of a Context* (Ithaca, N.Y.: Cornell University Press).

Poster, Mark (1975). *Existential Marxism in Postwar France: From Sartre to Althusser* (Princeton, N.J.: Princeton University Press).

Schrift, A. (1996). Nietzsche's French Legacy. In *The Cambridge Companion to Nietzsche*, edited by B. Magnus & K. Higgins (Cambridge: Cambridge University Press) 323–355.

Schrift, A. (1995). *Nietzsche's French Legacy: A Genealogy of Poststructuralism* (New York: Routledge).

Sturrock, J. (1986). *Structuralism* (London: Paladin).

Taubeneck, S. (1991). Translator's Afterword: Walter Kaufmann and After. In *Confrontations: Derrida, Heidegger, Nietzsche*, edited by E. Behler, trans. S. Taubeneck (Stanford, Calif: Stanford University Press).

Warren, M. (1988). *Nietzsche and Political Thought* (Cambridge, Mass.: MIT Press).

1

Jacques Lacan: Ideal-I and Image, Subject, and Signification
Stephen Appel

> We are split personalities sequentially, often simultaneously. We may turn our back in disgust on previous selves, but they hang around our neck like lovesick shadows.
> — Breytenbach, 1996

Jacques-Marie Émile Lacan was born in Paris in 1901, the eldest of three children in an upper–middle-class Catholic family. He studied medicine and received his doctorate in psychiatry before undergoing a training analysis with Rudolph Loewenstein. Lacan joined the Société Psychanalytique de Paris, which is officially recognized by the International Psychoanalytic Association (IPA) (a fact that becomes important later), in 1934. Before long, he became the major theorist of French psychoanalysis. Annually from 1954 to 1980, Lacan presented his famous and influential seminar, which was attended at one time or another by most major French intellectuals. (For the topics of the seminars, see Appendix.) The seminars are being translated and appear sporadically in English.

Always contentious, he developed alternative ideas about the training of analysts. This led to the first of several schisms in French psychoanalysis and also to his exclusion from the IPA. His election to president of the Société Psychanalytique de Paris in 1953 marked a division between medical and nonmedical factions on the question of training. Later that year, Lacan and others resigned to form the Société Française de Psychanalyse (SFP), thereby, apparently unwittingly, giving up IPA membership. In order to recognize the SFP, the IPA demanded the exclusion of

Lacan from training programs; this the SFP did, and in 1964 Lacan left to found the École Freudienne de Paris. *Écrits*, a major collection of his work, was published in 1966 to great interest in France, and a smaller collection appeared under the same title in English in 1977.

Ironically, then, as Lacan's star began to rise to great heights in the general intellectual milieu in France and beyond its borders, his official status as a psychoanalyst was first challenged, then under seige, then lost. In 1969, a Lacanian department of psychoanalysis was founded at the new Université de Paris-Vincennes; in 1974, he took charge of this department, naming his son-in-law, the philosopher Jacques-Alain Miller, as chair. Lacan unilaterally dissolved the École Freudienne de Paris in 1980 and founded the École de la cause freudienne, authorizing Miller as his successor. Lacan died of abdominal cancer the following year.

LACAN'S PROJECT

Lacan undertook a very ambitious endeavor to rethink Freudian developmental theory in terms of structural linguistics, and Lacanian social theory tries to account for the "humanization" (Althusser, 1964: 206) of biological individuals, the role of language and representation in positioning human subjects, and their interpellation in specific ideological discourses (Hall, 1980: 159).

The writing of Lacan is notoriously and purposely difficult. He wanted not only to persuade intellectually but also to affect the reader emotionally ("the function of language," he wrote, "is not to inform but to evoke" [1953: 86]). He did this by writing in an allusive and punning way, giving a feel for what, he argued, is the way the unconscious speaks. His early attraction to surrealism is evident in his use of language. Deeply interested in poetry and in mathematics, Lacan's writing is both lyrical and highly logical and complex in construction. It is easy to see why Stanley Leavy, for example, describes Lacan's work as "phenomenological," but he is wrong to call it "descriptive" (1990: 438). Lacan's work is nothing if not theoretical. The elements of his work are articulated with one another in a complicated system, although it should be pointed out before embarking on this journey that Lacan's work is impossible to recount in a linear fashion. Because he is "a builder of loosely moored conceptual mobiles" (Bowie, 1979: 122), his corpus should be considered whole. Unavoidably, therefore, concepts will be mentioned (signification, the Other, lack, desire) in what follows without proper introduction, only to be circled back upon later.

This chapter will not spend more time considering the developments, schisms, and loyaties of Lacan's career except to say that Lacan disputed the largely U.S. version of psychoanalysis ego psychology with its principle of a core, biologically given ego, and the attendant therapeutic attempts to strengthen the ego in order to enable people to become well-adjusted citizens (Roudinesco, 1990). Instead, like Sigmund Freud (Appel, 1992), as well as the early analysts, and later social commentators such as Jessica Benjamin, Christopher Lasch, and Joel Kovel, Lacan saw human beings in permanent conflict with their environment and with themselves. In French intellectual culture generally, of course, Lacan was part of the project of the "critique of the subject." To avoid confusion, it should be noted that the critique of the subject refers to a critique of the humanist, volitional agent: for Continental philosophy, the critical engagement with the Hegelian subject. When, for example, Agnes Heller (1990) speaks of the "death of the subject," she alludes to the fact that notions of both the transcendental Subject and the individual have been found wanting. Ernesto Laclau explains that "the death of *the* Subject (with a capital S) has been the main precondition of [the] renewed interest in the question of subjectivity" (1993: 1). The critique of the subject is perhaps better rendered for our purposes as the critique of subjectivism or identity. Things are, of course, never settled in philosophy; there is something of a backlash in France against antihumanism and the critique of identity (see Descombes, 1991; Peters, 1993).

Probably the most basic notion in Lacan's reading of Freud is that the subject is decentered. Rejecting traditional ideas of the self as a unified locus of thoughts and emotions, Lacan insisted that the human subject is split, without a center, and characterized by lack. Freud noted several times that poets and artists have intuitively known that the "I" of a sentence is split from the "I" who emits it. However, most of us most of the time accept as obvious and commonsensical that we each have an identity. Lacan's view is a counterintuitive one, then. It posits that, despite what we experience and what we like to believe, the commonsense self-image is *méconnaisance*, a misrecognition of ourselves. We are not to trust the ego, or conscious "I," because it "neglects, scotomizes, misconstrues" (Lacan, 1948: 22). "The ego for Lacan is thus formed on the basis of an *imaginary* relationship of the subject with his own body. The ego has the illusion of autonomy, but it is only an illusion, and the subject moves from fragmentation and insufficiency to illusory unity" (Benvenuto and Kennedy, 1986: 56). (It is worth noting here the sense in which Freud [1927] used the word "illusion" as being a belief motivated by an unconscious wish.) This imaginary relationship was to become an important element in Louis Althusser's theory of ideology-in-general (Appel, 1996).

SUBJECTIVITY

Lacan's central concerns can be put as follows: "*Who* are we talking to in the psychoanalytic situation?; and how does *speech* (and desire) function in this field?" (Hayes, 1990: 35). The first point to make about the human subject is that it is not the same as the ego. In contradistinction to René Descartes, Lacan did not say "I think, therefore I am"; rather, he said, "I think where I am not by thought, therefore I am where I do not think." "Furthermore," Anika Lemaire points out, "this formula leads us to see that I 'am' more surely there where 'I' do not 'think'" (1970: 123–124). Lacan is concerned principally with the subject who comes into being in the impossible attempt to express desire. As we shall see, the "I" exists in a "primordial form" (Lacan, 1968: 72), which, at the mirror stage, is constructed as the ego and which, upon the entry into language, becomes the human subject: "a psycho-social history" of "that tutelage of desire which we commonly call growing up" (Muller, 1985: 39). For Lacan, there was no final way to distinguish between biology, self, and society. The human subject always makes sense of, lives, and interprets biology. It is language that makes us social, or, rather, we become social when we enter language.

DESIRE

Psychoanalysis, for Lacan, is not a biological determinism. It is true that biological realities support the unconscious and its "basic category," desire "(exactly as biological existence supports historical existence) but neither *constitute*, nor *determine* it" (Althusser, 1964: 213n). Biology is always and only to be conceived of through the effects of drives, desire; psychoanalysis for Lacan deals with the configurational arrangements of desire.

Need, desire, and demand are related but are not synonymous. Need refers to biological needs like hunger, thirst, and sexual urges. Need, then, is nonrelational; it exists outside of any social relationship. Desire emerges out of need; in order to exist, it requires the self-awareness involved in thinking, for example, "I am hungry." Unlike need, "desire aims not so much toward gratification as towards *recognition*" (Leavy, 1990: 442). With Georg Hegel, Lacan said that, when one desires not a specific thing (food) but the desire of another, one has become human. Hegel saw human consciousness as being relational: the consciousness of the master being structured by the meaning he has for the slave, and vice versa. Similarly, for Lacan, the subject is structured in an intersubjective relationship with the Other. The Lacanian subject/Other relation should, however, not be thought of in the same terms as the upward spiral of the Hegelian dialectic. Malcolm Bowie makes this clear in his exegesis of the following of Lacan's ambivalent considerations of Hegel: "This is our personal *Aufhebung*, which transforms that of Hegel, which was his personal illusion, into an opportunity to pick out, instead and in place of the leaps of an ideal progress, the avatars of lack" (cited in Bowie, 1991:

97). (For a stimulating discussion of Lacan, Hegel, and dialectics, see Slavoj Zizek [1991a].)

The Other has several meanings in Lacan's work. It is the Other that creates an unfillable lack in the subject, thereby ensuring that desire will remain unsatisfied, because its aims perpetually are out of its reach. The Other sometimes refers to the whole domain of subject-Other interaction; sometimes, it refers only to the latter term. Lacan's term means variously "a father, a place, a point, any dialectical partner, a horizon within the subject, a horizon beyond the subject, the unconscious, language, the signifier" (Bowie, 1979: 136). This seeming potpourri can be made sense of if it is understood that, for Lacan, the abyss between desire and its object is introduced by the name of the father, language, the original Other. All of the inevitable alienations throughout life are manifestations of the "otherness" first put in place by the proto-Other. Language, "the complete tease" (Bowie, 1991: 83), is the medium through which the subject is constituted: "What I seek in speech is the response of the other. What constitutes me as a subject is my question. . . . I identify myself in language, but only by losing myself in it like an object" (Lacan, 1953: 86).

So, desire is understood by Lacan in more than one way. First, desire is not directed toward a thing (*objet petit a*) but toward yet another lacking desire, the desire of another. Second, objects are loved only if they appear to promise the filling in of the subject's lack; desire is, thus, narcissistic, the unachievable struggle for wholeness. Demand, in turn, is the address to a specific other person for a specific thing; it is a signification of desire. Desire, of course, cannot be specific; it is precisely what cannot be articulated by particularistic demand. The subject wants not only to have the object but also to be the object of another's desire to be desired or recognized. Because we have (biological) needs and desire (for love), every intersubjective act is ambiguous: is it aimed at satisfying a need or at displaying love? Because the reaction of the Other is always ambiguous, demand is perpetually repeated, forever incompletely addressed. Zizek uses the Hegelian phrase "loss of loss" with regard to *jouissance*, or pleasure-driven desire and its ever-changing goals: "by obtaining the object, we lose the fascinating dimension of loss as that which captivates our desire" (Zizek, 1991b: 86).

Desire, then, exists chronologically between need and demand. At (indeed, before) birth, the infant has certain biological needs. Later, the child realizes the incompleteness of the mother and of himself or herself and, so, desires what is missing. (The influence of the early Martin Heidegger on Lacan is apparent here. The subject is intentional in that he or she wishes to speak but, because his or her desire is always deflected, cannot.) This desire is expressed as demand or repression. Desire is analogous to Freud's *Wunsch*, which refers to directed drives as opposed to libido, the elemental energy as yet unconnected to specific images. Desire, though, does not refer to only specific acts of wishing but more to a "continuous force" (Sheridan, 1977: viii). All our demands are symbolic representations of our desire to be whole; our lack is in regard to an original state of oneness, of undifferentiated bliss. The subject-Other relationship is constituted by desire. In the encounter with the Other, the subject continually is remade; it is from the Other that the subject "receives even the message that he emits" (Bowie, 1979: 135).

So, it is the deficit between need and its articulation as demand that brings desire into being. At the entry into language, the infant becomes a subject, alienated from himself or herself, yet another lack. The model of desire and lack can be applied to make sense of the larger social scene.

REAL, IMAGINARY, SYMBOLIC

In the Rome Discourse, Lacan (1953) proposed three orders or planes of existence: the Real, the Symbolic, and the Imaginary. Again, their precise meaning is not easy to pin down. Lacan argued that psychoanalysis has not taken language seriously enough, getting lost in symbols. Not only is language the principal medium of psychoanalytic therapy; the unconscious itself, he said in a famous aphorism, is structured like a language. As usual, Lacan's startling formulation is precise here. Language, he meant, is prior to the unconscious. When the human subject enters language (*langue*, not *parole*), he or she is fitting into an extant Symbolic order that mediates the desire of said subject; drives are channeled by language. "The psychoanalytic experience has rediscovered in man the imperative of the Word as the law that has formed him in its image"; it is by way of "the gift of language" that "all reality has come to man and it is by his continued act that he maintains it" (p. 106). Truly, and at the risk of trivializing the issues here, for Lacan, in the beginning was the word.

The Real is that which is neither Imaginary nor Symbolic. Lying beyond language, it is the reality to which we cannot have direct access, although we must assume that it exists. Our experience of it is only via the mediation of the Imaginary and the Symbolic. Fredric Jameson (1977) says that the Real is history itself. One should read this as history plus nature plus the unconscious, our relation to which is always characterized by lack; desire is both historical and transhistorical. The Real is that which is unspeakable, "the ineliminable residue of all articulation" (Sheridan, 1977: x).

Lacan described the realm of the Imaginary as a preverbal (and, later in developmental, nonverbal) realm of alienated fantasy. The Imaginary is characterized by identification and duality; it is narcissistic and fusionary. Early on, the child's experience is disorganized and fragmentary, and the child is unable to distinguish between the inner and the outer world. The infant thinks essentially visually, in the Imaginary order; Imaginary for

Lacan derives from "image," not from "imagine." After entry into language, as we shall see, the child functions mainly in the Symbolic order of language, although the Imaginary remains "the enduring treasury of images" (Leavy, 1990: 439).

The Imaginary includes fantasies, images, and nonlinguistic structures. By contrast, the Symbolic is not narcissistic, it is social; it is not a duality but a triangularity. The Symbolic refers to language, the means through which desire is expressed; it is the domain of the signifier that continually restructures the subject. Coherent speech can occur only if the infant fully occupies a place in the Symbolic system of conventions. This involves, for example, being positioned by certain terms, for example, "boy," "girl," "son," "daughter." These terms are signifiers standing in particular relationships with a central signifier, the phallus, or desire for the Other.

Without suggesting that the three orders are coterminous with developmental stages, the entry of the child into language is the culmination of the journey from being a biological entity to being a human subject. This transition is achieved within "the Law of Culture," which has the same "formal essence" as language (Althusser, 1964: 209). To simplify a complex theory of an unstable manifestation, the Real, necessarily inaccessible to the subject, is represented by the ever-shifting Symbolic (language) and experienced in the constantly stabilizing Imaginary (images and illusion).

For Lacan, the psychical developmental sequence is as follows: drives (need), desire (lack), unconscious (repression). Clearly this is all subsumed under the workings of the id. The unconscious is continually voluble, demanding to be heard. However, the content of the unconscious is unacceptable to the subject and to the social order; when it reveals its existence in dreams, slips, symptoms, jokes, or fantasies, it is rejected as foolish, repugnant, or of little importance. The unconscious itself, that region of repressed tendencies and thoughts, is, to use another linguistic notion, the signifying chain along which desire passes; it is "the discourse of the Other," and language is an "endless tautology."

SYMBOLIZATION

Language not only represents desire, it also constitutes the subject. Moreover, it is not only the human mind that operates in and through language; human culture itself is representational, and these representational structures precede us and determine our fates.

> Symbols in fact envelop the life of man in a network so total that they join together, *before he comes into the world*, those who are going to engender him "by flesh and blood," so total that they *bring to his birth*, along with the gifts of the stars, if not with the gifts of the fairies, *the shape of his destiny*; so total that they give

the words that will make him faithful or renegade, the law of the acts that will follow him right to the very place *where he is not yet* and even beyond his death. (Lacan, 1953: 68, emphasis added)

Freud described in *Beyond the Pleasure Principle* (1920) a game played by his nephew. Holding onto a piece of string, the child would throw an attached cotton reel over the edge of his cot, uttering as he did so what sounded like the German word *fort* ("gone" or "away"). He then would pull back the cotton reel, joyfully saying what Freud understood to be *da* ("there"). The game, according to Freud, was an attempt by the infant to cope with the anxiety raised by the absence of his mother, the cotton reel acting as what D. W. Winnicott (1951) would come to call a transitional object for the mother. Lacan used this story to describe how language, at its very inception (or, rather, at the child's entry into language), and symbols remove the human subject from the Real. In this example, first the cotton reel and then language become substitutes for the mother. The story is, then, about self-alienation. The infant is both split off from his drives and subordinated to the Symbolic. From then on, the identity and the desire of the child are determined by the Symbolic. Again, it is important to keep in mind that subjectivity is not delusional (false consciousness) but illusional, "a *necessary* illusion whereby one lives, as it were, a story of one's life, of who one is" (Mitchell, 1988: 83).

Lacan spoke here of the letter. The letter refers first to the actualization of language: text, *parole*, be it in spoken words or symptoms. The second area to which the letter refers is the structure of language that preexists and determines the subject (*langue*), thus, his essay title, "The Agency of the Letter in the Unconscious or Reason since Freud" (1957). In an instance of his playfulness with language, he writes, "*lettre-l'être-l'autre*" (the letter implies being implies the Other). The subject is a "non-unitary ... field of effects produced by discourse; in other words ... a by-product of meaning" (Muller, 1985: 34).

LACANIAN PSYCHOANALYSIS

Importantly, for Lacan, the task of the psychoanalyst is not somehow to bring the patient in tune with reality. This is impossible. Of course, the patient wants or desires the answer from the analyst, but it is the task of the analyst to guide the patient to acknowledgment of his or her lack. The change required in the patient involves an awareness of the necessity of our incompleteness. "That is why the question *of* the Other, which comes back to the subject from the place from which he expects an oracular reply in some such form as '*Che vuoi*?,' 'What do you want?,' is the one that best leads him to the path of his own desire" (Lacan, 1960: 312). In the same way as Wilfred Bion's (1959) analyst acts as a container, the analyst for

Lacan reworks the patient's anxiety and projects back the question that indicates (in the sense of points to) the subject's lack. Although it is easy and almost overwhelmingly tempting to accept and cherish the ego, an image of unity, the patient's more difficult task is to come into contact with the discourse of desire. The conscious ego of the patient speaks empty speech. Empty speech is the expression by the patient of his or her desire without the patient knowing what it is that is being expressed. The patient talks about himself or herself as an object; free associations are addressed to the Other, the psychoanalyst. It is the task of the analyst to direct the patient to what lies beneath, namely, his or her impossible desire for wholeness. The analyst "takes the description of an everyday event for a fable addressed to whoever hath ears to hear, a long tirade for a direct interjection, or on the other hand a simple *lapsus* for a highly complex statement, or even the sigh of a momentary silence for the whole lyrical development it replaces" (Lacan, 1953: 44). Lacan rejected either optimism or pessimism and, like Freud, confronted "the irremediable" (Bowie, 1979: 151). The subject must come to know that "whatever his appetites may be, whatever his needs may be, none of them will find satisfaction in analysis, and that the most that he can expect of it is to organize his menu" (Lacan, 1964: 269).

THE FORMATION OF THE I

> If what Freud discovered and rediscovers with a perpetually increasing sense of shock has a meaning, it is that the displacement of the signifier determines the subjects in their acts, in their destiny, in their refusals, their blind spots, their end and fate, their innate gifts and social acquisitions . . . without regard for character or sex, and that willingly or not, everything that might be considered the stuff of psychology, kit and caboodle, will follow the path of the signifier.
>
> — Lacan, 1956: 60

So far, the outlines of Lacan's theoretical apparatus have been laid out. How, though, do the I and the subject come into existence? In "The Mirror Stage as Formative of the Function of the I as Revealed in Psychoanalytic Experience," Lacan (1949) can be said to follow Freud, who had said that the ego is a mental projection — a later construction, and not a hereditary entity (1923: 26).

The Mirror Stage

In the first months of life, the infant is largely autoerotic. Unable to distinguish between what is internal and what is external to its body, the infant does not perceive itself as a distinct or a unified being. Rather, it experiences itself as fragmented parts among surrounding objects. This imagery of a piecemeal body continues to manifest itself throughout life in dreams and in schizoid fantasy; the paintings of Hieronymus Bosch recreate it. Infancy is a time dominated by satisfied and frustrated needs. The infant experiences its helplessness and fragmentation. Not present from birth, the ego develops following a formative event in the early months of life, said Lacan. This is when, for the first time, the infant recognizes itself in a mirror. Of course, this does not necessarily have to occur literally before a mirror; the infant may recognize itself as reflected in the look or gaze of a person, typically the mother. Between 6 and 18 months, then, the child perceives itself, paradigmatically in the image in a mirror, as a whole and complete person, no longer as a fragmented collection of sensation, limbs, and affects. The infant experiences triumph when it perceives that it controls its body, every movement being reproduced in its reflected image, the "Ideal-I." Compared with the previous autoerotic stage, during which the child had an erotic relationship with its fragmented body, it now falls in love with the image of a *Gestalt*, a complete and autonomous image. However, this is in anticipation of the mastery yet to be achieved: "The mirror stage is a drama whose internal thrust is precipitated from insufficiency to anticipation" (Leavy, 1990: 442). Although the infant has poor control over its own body, it is able via the mirror stage to (mis)conceive itself as whole and self-controlled.

It is here that the self-alienation of the subject begins, alienation being fundamental to identification, because, for identification to occur, there must be a perceiving self and a perceived self. To put it in more accurate Lacanian terms, every act of identification constitutes, that is, brings into existence, the I and its Other. From the time of the mirror stage onward, reality is perceived as an image — an image, what is more, that tends toward completeness. Thus, unconscious desires are enmeshed with the Imaginary fantasies. This moment of self-identification is the original instance of a lifelong tendency to strive for and to cherish a unitary sense of self. "Alienating identity . . . will mark with its rigid structure the subject's entire mental development" (Lacan, 1949: 4) as well as all future social and cultural life. The relationship between the infant and the image is, indeed, an estranged one in which the child, not in control of its own movements, experiences as mastery what is, in fact, mastery of an image. This image has a double existence: as the actual image reflected on the surface of the mirror and as an I with "mental permanence," "it prefigures its alienating destination" (Lacan, 1949: 2).

It is crucial to remember that, although the I is certainly not in control of identification, the content of the subject is put into place by this identification. The mirror stage, in other words, is not something done to the infant by another but something the infant does, albeit not at all fully consciously in the active formation of the self. This activity is a form of human labor. All relationships with external objects will have an incongruous nature as a result of the imaginary and alienated experience of the ur-identification of the mirror stage. All identifications are, for Lacan, not only illusory but also ambivalent, aggressive, and narcissistic, being linked in a "correlative tension" in the "coming-into-being of the subject" (Lacan, 1948: 22). The infant has an ambivalent relation with his or her mirror image: it loves the complete oneness of the image, although it hates the fact that the image is external to it.

If identification is, as Lacan portrays it, alienated and ambivalent, it also is conflicted in another way; it stabilizes (by constituting the individual's I) at the same time as it fragments (alienating the subject from its desire). At the mirror stage, the infant comes to "see" both itself and the Other, to see itself *as* an Other. As the self is composed over the years of many such internalizations of misapprehensions, it is highly complex and conflictual. Although the "intersubjective dialectic" exists from the beginning, there is no possibility of the recognition necessary for full mutuality. (Indeed, Lacan said that his dog Justine was unique in that she was the only one who did not take him for someone else [Schneiderman, 1983: 130].)

The pre-Oedipal child lives in a dyadic, symbiotic relation with the mother; this is a time of the Imaginary. This relation is upset at the Oedipus stage with the entry of a third person, the father. The Oedipus complex positions the infant in language, in the family, and in gender. For Lacan, this did not mean the actual presence of the person of the father but, rather, the introduction of the father's name, establishing his absent presence. The father here is not this or that particular father but the symbolic father who powers the signifying chain of desire. The introduction of his name, the law, is the introduction of the Symbolic; the entry of the child into language marks the birth of the subject.

The Path of the Signifier

To illustrate how subjectivity fixes and shifts, Lacan (1956) used Edgar Allen Poe's story "The Purloined Letter," in which the prefect of police in Paris approaches Dupin for assistance in recovering a compromising letter apparently written to the queen and then stolen from her by Minister D. The queen had witnessed the theft but could not react for fear of implicating herself before the king. Although the police have thoroughly searched the minister's apartment, they have been unable to find the letter. Dupin discovers the letter, which lies, as he has reasoned, in full view. He steals the letter back, replacing it with a dummy letter. The story, Lacan argued, is structured in triads: the third person, the robber, and the loser. This structure is repeated with different characters filling the three positions. What is it that determines which position characters will occupy in the triad? The location of the letter. The letter moves along "a signifying chain." The robber (the minister and then Dupin) sees that the third person (the king and then the minister) has not detected the letter and has power as long as he possesses the letter. The place of the letter, and knowledge of that place, determines the possible actions of the subjects.

What does the letter signify? Pointedly, the contents of the letter are never revealed in Poe's story; we can never grasp the transcendant signifier. The letter, speech, the signifier, the demand — these all refer to the positioning function of the Symbolic, to interpellation, and to the impossibility of grasping Immanuel Kant's "thing-in-itself." The signifier determines the place of the subject without any need to invoke meaning or signification.

It is crucial to keep in mind that Lacan was not saying that anyone who comes into contact with the letter is automatically positioned in a particular way. Rather, he showed how positioning works in an overdetermined way: when one stands in a particular relation to the letter, one will be positioned by that letter. The reading of the letter — in other words, the specific meaning for and effect on the subject that the letter will have — is variable and unpredictable. This is, first, because the subject is already a subject of other letters and, second, because the letter or instance of interpellation itself has many possible meanings.

Lacan employed what structural linguistics says are the basic binary elements of all symbolic systems, signifier and signified. He found it useful here to extend Ferdinand de Saussure's (1915) classic formulation of the sign S/s, in which the signifier is not only arbitrarily and conventionally related to the concept or signified, as de Saussure would have it, but, rather Lacan saw the two parts of the sign as being related not in a stable and predictable way, but where the signified (lower case letter, italic script, bottom position) is separated from the signifier (upper case letter, roman type, top position) by the bar that indicates disjunction, repression. The autonomy of the signifier is dependant on the resistance of the bar. So, the concept and its name belong to different orders. Instead of a unity of signifier and signified (which de Saussure indicated by placing the above formulaic expression in an ellipse), Lacan postulated constant signification along a signifying chain, each signified capable of behaving as a signifier. Furthermore, a signifier always signifies another signifier in relation to other signifiers. The signifier "dog" has meaning only in relation to like signifiers, for example, "canine," "quadruped," "animal," and "pet," and to unlike signifiers, for example, "cat." Language is a system of differences, and it is nonrepresentational; there is no natural connection between concept and name. Lacan insisted upon the *glissement* or slippage between signifiers along the signifying chain. Even an emotion is a signifier, because it is an effect of desire. However, it is not the case that there is no relationship between signified and signifier or between signifiers; rather, the precise nature of the relationship is finally indecipherable.

The subject has no history, in that it is a "subject-for-discourse" (Morley, 1980: 169), but each instance of positioning or interpellation occurs in a particular way at a particular social-historical moment. Signifiers are not free-floating; they are linked in some way to each other and to the signified. The bar, in other words, is permeable. It is true, though, that we can never get at the signified. The only possible object of study, Lacan said, is the signifying chain itself. As Zizek puts it: "If we look for the 'deeper, hidden meaning' of the figures appearing in a dream, we *blind* ourselves to the latent 'dream-thought' articulated in it" (1991b: 51). The subject is represented by the signifier, and this process can provide representation only for another signifier; "the signifier represents the subject for another signifier" (Lacan, 1953: 83). This movement is not only linear. Over time, we construct a proliferation of chains of signification, continually substituting signifiers. Each instance of the letter has attached to it "a whole articulation of relevant contexts" (Lacan, 1957: 154): "In its symbolizing function speech is moving towards nothing less than a transformation of the subject to whom it is addressed by means of the link that it establishes with the one who emits it in other words, by introducing the effect of a signifier" (Lacan, 1953: 83). *Point de capiton* is the term Lacan used to describe the mechanisms of this articulation. It is wrong, then, to assume that Lacan was a textualist, one who believed that nothing exists but language. Rather, nothing for the subject exists separate from language. This distinguishes Lacan from "many more facile celebrations of the primacy of language" (Jameson, 1977: 359).

If Imaginary (mis)identification is an estrangement of the self, the Symbolic is a further alienation of the subject. Lacan produced a model of intersubjective relationships (see Benvenuto and Kennedy, 1986: 100) whereby the subject's movement toward the Other (or Real) is continuously diverted by the axis o o', the relationship between the ego and its mirror image; we experience the social world through the Imaginary. Whenever the subject attempts to speak, it is frozen and functions as a signifier. "The truth is thus always being 'purloined,' and the subject is constantly drawn to the four corners of the scheme. This duality of symbolic Other and imaginary other is basic to the structure of the subject" (Benvenuto and Kennedy, 1986: 101).

Metaphor and Metonymy

Although what is ultimately signified is desire, meaning cannot be more than the movement from one instance of signification to another. "Slips, failures, jokes and symptoms, like the elements of dreams themselves, became *signifiers*, inscribed in the chain of an unconscious discourse, doubling silently, i.e. deafeningly, in the misrecognition of 'repression,' the chain of the human subject's verbal discourse" (Althusser, 1964: 207–208).

Lacan again found it useful to use linguistic concepts in order to theorize representations of the unconscious. Of course, because he saw language as constitutive of human subjectivity (or, rather, saw language and subjectivity as being similarly structured), he intended for certain structural linguistic terminology to be more than just convenient ways of making his point. However, as opposed to the "purely formalist textualism" (Wexler, 1987: 152) of many critical theorists, it must be reemphasized that signification is not simply a closed complex of cross-referenced signs; signification is always the ultimately unsuccessful attempt to give expression to desire.

Signification, and, thus, also subject positioning, operates in one of two ways, analogous to the unconscious mechanisms of displacement and condensation that Freud postulated in *The Interpretation of Dreams* (1900). All signification operates, Lacan argued, like the linguistic tropes of metaphor and metonymy. He delved into the structural linguistics of Roman Jakobson (1956), who asserted that all connections between signifiers, all contiguity along the signifying chain, operate by these two linguistic tropes. Metonymy is the linguistic form in which words follow one another linearly, one element being conflated into another (for example, "Moscow said . . ."). This is like the splitting of the subject, where desire is always for that which is lacking. If metonymy is the desire for something else, then metaphor, the substitution of one word for another, from one signifier to another (for example, "the Iron Curtain"), is the mechanism by which that desire can be expressed. The object of desire is *le désir de l'Autre*, said Lacan. Bice Benvenuto and Roger Kennedy point out that this French expression can be translated into English as both the desire of the Other (metonymy) and the desire for the Other (metaphor) (1986: 130).

Because the infant's desire is unknown to it, it seeks to satisfy its lack in the Other by trying to identify with the mother's desire, thereby becoming the mother's object of desire. At the same time, the infant has possessive desires for her. Desire, in Lacanian theory, operates according to rules analogous to the linguistic rules of the signifier. Neurotic symptoms, being psychical condensations, are metaphorical; fetishism, by contrast, being a stoppage in the displacement functions of unconscious desire, is metonymic.

SOME IMPLICATIONS FOR EDUCATIONAL STUDIES

A recent critical study of schooling has overtly made the realm of the psyche relevant to sociological analysis. Wexler has theorized that social relations in the school are premised on "emotional dynamics of identification, attachment and caring" (1992: 36), and he has described three permutations of these relations: lack of care and withdrawal from interaction; desocialization and withdrawal from public life; and unintended assault on the self. Lacan's own work, though, has had very little impact on critical educational studies.

Lacan's work could conceivably be employed in many directions in educational studies. I will mention a few that come to mind. He spoke once of knowledge as "paranoiac" (1949: 2), a point that could instigate uncomfortable, but profitable, shifts in the epistemologies of philosophy of education and curriculum studies. One also could consider Lacan's ideas about the training of psychoanalysts *la passe* (Appel, forthcoming a) a practice that, together with his use of short analytic hours, led indirectly to his exclusion from the IPA. He spoke, too, of the lack of trust psychoanalysis places in aggression even in "the most Samaritan of aid" (Lacan, 1949: 6), including pedagogy (7); this is a warning to educationists when we are tempted to adopt high moral stances in relation to our own motives. An angle that I have found most useful is Lacan's critique of human agency; his anti-humanistic theory of the subject is an invigorating antidote to the humanistic agent of sociology of education (Appel, 1995).

It has been necessary to expand upon desire at some length, because it is an "unspoken" (Macherey, 1966) of poststructuralist accounts of education. Lacan's theorization of deep affective formation and form can be contrasted with, for example, Bronwyn Davies's ideas about desire. Acknowledging that "desire is spoken into existence," Davies explicitly turns her back on psychoanalysis, finding it to be "one more individualistic discourse" (1990: 504). In so doing, she loses the dynamic capacity of Lacan's theory of subjects that constitute each other through the evocation of necessary lack. If desire is a factor in social life, but it is not conceived of via psychoanalysis, what is it, what part does it play in subjectivity, and where does it come from? To show exactly how deep (or otherwise) desire is in her work, Davies says, "As a feminist I desire a world in which anyone's sex/gender is made relevant only in the process of biological reproduction" (1990: 501). Desire is "implicated in storyline," we are told; "it is through story that children can learn the patterns of desire appropriate for their gender" (Davies and Banks, 1992: 5). Clearly, what is called desire here is little more than learned preferences. It follows that such likes and dislikes can be unlearned; thus the exhortations to "write and speak utopias" (Davies, 1990: 515). "Positions" (Davies and Harré, 1990) thereby become personae or social character parts that we play in stories. Without the motivational trajectories of deeper, unsatisfiable desire, social life becomes no more than bad and good narratives, stories that we are at liberty to rewrite.

Can anything be learned from Lacan about the teacher-student relationship? If we leave aside overt skills and knowledge and concentrate upon areas of particular concern to critical sociology of education — the hidden curriculum, cultural capital, and socialization — it is clear that there is a realm of overlap with Lacan's notions of psychoanalysis. Although not the student's therapist, the teacher is involved in deep or transcendent change of students, and vice versa; schooling does make a difference. However, in the educational literature we see an exaggerated and ingrained trust in the possibility of insight leading to wholeness. Capitalism, patriarchy, and racism have cut us off from ourselves, the story goes, but it is possible, through consciousness-raising and social solidarity, to realize full selfhood and community, that is, democracy: "a space where the self and other can conjoin in a discourse of mutuality and respect" (McLaren, 1991: 34). Sydney Smith (1977) has called such "regressive reaction to separation anxiety," "the golden fantasy."

Like Melanie Klein (1946), Lacan saw aggression at work very early in development. Pre-Oedipal identifications are characterized by anxiety and aggression, while post-Oedipal identifications are troubled by aggression and guilt toward paternal authority. It is a crucial feature of identification that aggression is released "in any relation to the other, even in a relation involving the most Samaritan of aid" (Lacan 1949: 6). Contrast this vacillation with the unalloyed altruism portrayed in the fantasies of critical pedagogy; Peter McLaren, for example, wonders "as a critical educator . . . what love might mean at the level of the whole society" (1991: 34).

If Lacan's theory of subjectivity is valuable to social analysis and is to be useful in the study of education, it becomes necessary to grasp what is entailed in the study of the subject-Other relation. Although an emphasis on interpretation and signification is an advance, the focus on particular texts per se may produce readings that are asocial in that they take little account of the discursive context of each subject-text interaction. The "productivity of the text" must not come to refer only to the "capacity of the text to set the viewer 'in place' in a position of unproblematic identification/knowledge" (Hall 1980: 159). The reader or subject of any text is already constituted as a subject of various and changing positions in several intersecting chains of signification. This preconstituted subject is not freely available for interpellation by any discourse that happens along. The reader bears the marks of previous interpellations that play a part in whether and how interpellation will occur.

Extrapolating from Lacan's model of signification and subjectivity, one can say that no text has only one possible message. What any particular text can mean does not refer in any direct way to particular signifieds; rather, what a text signifies changes in the process of being read. There is, therefore, no moment when the text constitutes a subject in a way that could have been predicted. Other texts and discourses constantly act on subjects; Michel Pêcheux (1983) has introduced the term "interdiscourse" in this regard. The human subject is an interdiscourse, he says, marked throughout its life by several ideological discourses. Or, to use Freud's term again, the subject is "overdetermined." Accordingly, the appropriate object of study is not text-subject, but multiplicity of texts-subjects (Morley, 1980: 166). All depends, thus, on how reader and text, or subject and signifier, each in its complex historical and multiplicitous context, combine at a particular moment.

We must not try to deduce subject position from the text. The educational literature has many examples of subject positions being ascribed reductively from educational activities and texts. For example, Svi Shapiro says, "People whose time is spent in the often mindless tasks of the classroom will be prepared for the mindless activities of the office or shop floor" (1987: 145); and Jean Anyon says that the hidden curriculum provides a "tacit preparation for relating to the process of production in a particular way," a way qualitatively different for each social class (1987: 225). The nonreductive nature of subjectivity does not mean that we have to be content with a vision of a society as a systemic agglomeration of individually constituted subjects. Rather, every text has "preferred readings," and all readers and writers, "implicated as desiring bodies" (Wright, 1984: 5), are "preferred readers." Far from static ideology critique, Lacan's conceptualization of *glissement* of significations, which are in turn the demands of desire, is a dynamic, complex, theoretically coherent model of explanation. Critical educational studies are replete with ideology critique. For example, Heather Cathcart and Geoff Esland, after reviewing the "ideological substance of educational initiatives" for 14–16-year-olds, advocate remedying the distortions by a "fuller discussion in the context of a more rigorous and *less biased* social and political education" (1985: 191, emphasis added). Many neo-Marxists find it extremely difficult to transcend ideology critique. In the field of aesthetics, for instance, Terry Eagleton (1990) too quickly reduces movements in art and art theory to the historical state of economic production. Whether it is made explicit in each instance, ideology critique is underpinned by a notion of false consciousness. It should not be necessary to point out the untenability of this position. Believing in false consciousness assumes the existence, or at least the possibility, of a true consciousness held, no doubt, by the author.

There is an important distinction to be made between the constitution of the subject as an original potential space and the latter moments when this subject-in-general is interpellated into specific subject positions. As Morley (1980) says, we need to focus not on "the politics of the signifier," but on the moment when the constituted subject meets specific signification: the moment of interpellation. I have argued elsewhere that psychoanalysis has conceptual tools for coming to grips with the actual processes of interpellation (Appel, forthcoming b).

Johan Muller warns against letting the agency of subjects slip into the agency of discourse ("Clare uses her 'femininity' to ensnare Phil") (1985: 40). This is a useful reminder that any theory of the subject has as a basic postulate the notion that agency is the operation of subjects of and in ideological discourse. Discourse and ideology are concepts that refer to the totalizing function of the Symbolic tendency toward mystificatory closure and to the identifications of the Imaginary where the lacking subject sees itself as complete.

Although Lacan is best known for his work on language and the Symbolic, an indispensable part of his theory is the (Freudian pre-Oedipal) non-Symbolic realm of the Imaginary. If cultural practices are all those interactive practices of humans with their environment, then the very first practices of the infant are also cultural and, therefore, there are cultural practices that precede language. Although this point may not seem controversial at first glance, on reflection its implications for a theory of the subject and ideology in general become profound. Indeed, by in effect foregrounding the Symbolic and backgrounding the Imaginary, educational analysis tends to revert to a model of individuals adapting to society. Critical educational studies have been unable to theorize about the "structural resistance to identity . . . , the splitting of the ego and the inevitable mismatch of subject and culture." It cannot account for "those aspects of subjectivity 'beyond interpellation'" (Donald, 1991: 6). This resistance is, of course, not to be conflated with the conscious, rational resistance of actors so overstated in critical sociology of education. Rather, it is a resistance to closure that is inherent to all human practices, that is, it is structural.

Probably because Lacan himself was fascinated with the Symbolic order, and because of the place of the written word in the university, Lacanian cultural analysts have largely followed the tracks of signification and meaning. However, it is clear that the Imaginary, even if undeveloped theoretically, is a nondiscursive domain of culture that is usually ignored by word-drunk academia. There is, then, an aspect of human culture that is nonideological, nondiscursive. For example, the work of Foucault demonstrates that social power can act upon the body without being first mediated by consciousness. A writer who has developed the preverbal and nonverbal part of Lacan's work is Julia Kristeva (1980,

1986). Repression is necessary for signifying practice, "signifiance," and, says Kristeva, the "semiotic order" of channeled energy continues to challenge language and is, thus, kept at arm's length at the edges of discourse. The semiotic order has the force of negativity and reappears as rhythms, tone, and linguistic transformations. The playful fluidity of semiotic and symbolic constitute the field of human life, interpellations being temporary moments of anchorage within that unstable field. Perhaps Kristeva's work provides a way to transcend the fixation on ideology critique in educational studies.

While acknowledging a debt to Althusser, the theory postulated here is post-Althusserian: the starting point of inquiries is to be the necessary failure of ideology. The necessary failure of ideology, it can be argued, is the result of the nature of desire, the missing link of educational theory. Freud (1937) spoke of three impossible professions: psychoanalysis, government, and education. James Donald suggests that "this 'impossibility' is less a malfunction than a sign of the *necessary* failure of identity in the psyche and of closure in the social" (1991: 8).

From Lacan we learn about the unavoidably fragmentary nature of subjectivity, how the subject lives with the alienated confrontation with his or her lack. Not only is the subject lacking, so is the Other. The unconscious attempts to speak of what is forbidden *jouissance* and death; language, intonation, symptoms, dreams, and so forth, can only indirectly represent what is in the end inexpressible desire.

APPENDIX

Lacan's seminars (Bowie, 1991: 208–213).

Seminar I	(1953–54)	*Freud's Papers on Technique*
Seminar II	(1954–55)	*The Ego in Freud's Theory and in the Technique of Psychoanalysis*
Seminar III	(1955–56)	*The Psychoses*
Seminar IV	(1956–57)	*Object Relations and Freudian Structures*
Seminar V	(1957–58)	*The Formations of the Unconscious*
Seminar VI	(1958–59)	*Desire and its Interpretation*
Seminar VII	(1959-60)	*The Ethics of Psychoanalysis*
Seminar VIII	(1960-61)	*The Transference*
Seminar IX	(1961–62)	*Identification*
Seminar X	(1962–63)	*Anxiety*
Seminar XI	(1964)	*The Four Fundamentals of Psychoanalysis*
Seminar XII	(1964–65)	*Crucial Problems for Psychoanalysis*
Seminar XIII	(1965–66)	*The Object of Psychoanalysis*

Seminar XIV	(1966–67)	*The Logic of Phantasy*
Seminar XV	(1967–68)	*The Psychoanalytic Act*
Seminar XVI	(1968–69)	*From one Other to the other*
Seminar XVII	(1969–70)	*The Hidden Face of Psychanalysis*
Seminar XVIII	(1970–71)	*On a Discourse that wouldn't be Appearance*
Seminar XIX	(1971–72)	*... Or Worse*
Seminar XX	(1972–73)	*Again*
Seminar XXI	(1973–74)	*The Non-dupes Wander/The names of the father*
Seminar XXII	(1974–75)	*Real, Symbolic, Imaginary*
Seminar XXIII	(1975–76)	*The Sinthome*
Seminar XXIV	(1976–77)	*One knew that it was a mistaken moon on wings of love*
Seminar XXV	(1977–78)	*The Moment for Concluding*
Seminar XXVI	(1978–79)	*Topology and Time*
Seminar XXVII	(1980)	*Dissolution.*

REFERENCES

Althusser, Louis. (1964). Freud and Lacan. In L. Althusser (Ed.), *Lenin and philosophy and other essays*. New York: Monthly Review Press.

Anyon, Jean. (1987). Social class and the hidden curriculum of work. In E. Stevens and G. Wood (Eds.), *Justice, ideology, and education: An introduction to the foundations of education*. New York: Random House.

Appel, Stephen. (1996). *Positioning subjects: Psychoanalysis and critical educational studies*. Westport, Conn.: Bergin & Garvey.

Appel, Stephen. (1995). The unconscious subject of education. *Discourse, 16*(2), 167–189.

Appel, Stephen. (1992). Freud's "pessimism": Drives and civilization. *South African Journal of Philosophy, 11*(2), 41–43.

Benvenuto, Bice, & Kennedy, Roger. (1986). *The works of Jacques Lacan: An introduction*. London: Free Association.

Bion, Wilfred R. (1959). *Experiences in groups, and other papers*. New York: Basic Books.

Bowie, Malcolm. (1991). *Lacan*. London: Fontana.

Bowie, Malcolm. (1979). Jacques Lacan. In John Sturrock (Ed.), *Structuralism and since* (pp. 116–153). Oxford: Oxford University Press.

Breytenbach, Breyten. (1996). Writing the darkening mirror. In B. Breytenbach (Ed.), *The memory of birds in times of revolution*. New York: Harcourt Brace.

Cathcart, Heather, & Esland, Geoff. (1985). The compliant-creative worker: The ideological reconstruction of the school learner. In L. Barton and S. Walker (Eds.), *Education and school change* (pp. 173–192). London: Croom Helm.

Davies, Bronwyn. (1990). The problem of desire. *Social Problems, 37*, 501–516.

Davies, Bronwyn, & Banks, Charles. (1992). The gender trap: A feminist poststructuralist analysis of primary school children's talk about gender. *Journal of Curriculum Studies*, 24, 1–25.

Davies, Bronwyn, & Harré, Rom. (1990). Positioning: The discursive production of selves. *Journal for the Theory of Social Behaviour*, 20, 43–63.

de Saussure, Ferdinand. (1959). *Course in general linguistics*. New York: McGraw-Hill. [Original work published 1915]

Descombes, V. (1991). Apropos of the critique of "the subject" and the critique of the critique. In E. Cadava, P. Connor, and J. L. Nancy (Eds.), *Who comes after the subject?* New York: Routledge.

Donald, James. (1991). On the threshold: Psychoanalysis and cultural studies. In J. Donald (Ed.), *Psychoanalysis and cultural studies*. Basingstoke: Macmillan.

Eagleton, Terry. (1990). *Ideology of the aesthetic*. Cambridge, Mass.: Blackwell.

Freud, Sigmund. (1953a). The interpretation of dreams. In J. Strachey (Ed. and Trans.), *The standard edition of the complete psychological works of Sigmund Freud* (vol. 4). London: Hogarth. [Original work published 1900]

Freud, Sigmund. (1953b). Beyond the pleasure principle. In J. Strachey (Ed. and Trans.), *The standard edition of the complete psychological works of Sigmund Freud* (vol. 18). London: Hogarth. [Original work published 1920]

Freud, Sigmund. (1953c). The ego and the id. In J. Strachey (Ed. and Trans.), *The standard edition of the complete psychological works of Sigmund Freud* (vol. 19). London: Hogarth. [Original work published 1923]

Freud, Sigmund. (1953d). The future of an illusion. In J. Strachey (Ed. and Trans.), *The standard edition of the complete psychological works of Sigmund Freud* (vol. 21). London: Hogarth. [Original work published 1927]

Freud, Sigmund. (1953e). Analysis terminable and interminable. In J. Strachey (Ed. and Trans.), *The standard edition of the complete psychological works of Sigmund Freud* (vol. 23). London: Hogarth. [Original work published 1937]

Hall, Stuart. (1980). Recent developments in theories of language and ideology: A critical note. In S. Hall, D. Hobson, A. Lowe, and P. Willis (Eds.), *Culture, media, language: Working papers in cultural studies, 1972–1979*. London: Hutchinson.

Hayes, Grahame. (1990). Psychoanalysis, Lacan, and social theory, *Psychology in Society*, 14, 28–46.

Heller, Agnes. (1990). The death of the subject. *Thesis Eleven*, 25, 22–38.

Jakobson, Roman. (1956). Two aspects of language and two types of aphasic disturbances. In R. Jakobson and M. Halle (Eds.), *Fundamentals of language* (pp. 55–82). The Hague: Mouton.

Jameson, Fredric. (1977). Imaginary and symbolic in Lacan: Marxism, psychoanalytic criticism and the problem of the subject. *Yale French Studies*, 55–56, 338–395.

Klein, Melanie. (1946). *Envy and gratitude and other works, 1946–1963*. London: Hogarth.

Kristeva, Julia. (1986). *The Kristeva reader*. Oxford: Basil Blackwell.

Kristeva, Julia. (1980). *Desire in language: A semiotic approach to literature and art*. Oxford: Basil Blackwell.

Lacan, Jacques. (1977). *Écrits: A Selection*, A. Sheridan (Ed.). New York: Norton.

Lacan, Jacques. (1968). The mirror stage. *New Left Review*, 51, 71–77.

Lacan, Jacques. (1964). *The four fundamentals of psychoanalysis*. Harmondsworth: Penguin.

Lacan, Jacques. (1960). The subversion of the subject and the dialectic of desire in the Freudian unconscious. In J. Lacan, *Ecrits*, 292–325.
Lacan, Jacques. (1957). The agency of the letter in the unconscious or reason since Freud. In J. Lacan, *Ecrits*, 146–178.
Lacan, Jacques. (1956). The seminar on Poe's "Purloined letter." *Yale French Studies, 48*, 38–72.
Lacan, Jacques. (1953). The function and field of speech and language in psychoanalysis. In J. Lacan, *Ecrits*, 30–113.
Lacan, Jacques. (1949). The mirror stage as formative of the function of the I as revealed in psycho-analytic experience. In J. Lacan, *Ecrits*, 1–7.
Lacan, Jacques. (1948). Aggressivity in psychoanalysis. In J. Lacan, *Ecrits*, 8–29.
Laclau, Ernesto. (1993). Political frontiers, identification and political identities. Conference on ethnicity, identity and nationalism in South Africa: Comparative Perspectives, Grahamstown, South Africa.
Leavy, Stanley A. (1990). Lacan's words. *Psychoanalytic Quarterly, 59*, 437–443.
Lemaire, Anika. (1970). *Jacques Lacan*. David Macey (trans.). London: Routledge & Kegan Paul.
Macherey, Pierre. (1966). *A theory of literary production*. London: Routledge & Kegan Paul.
McLaren, Peter. (1991). Critical pedagogy: Constructing an arch of social dreaming and a doorway to hope. *Journal of Education, 173*, 9–34.
Mitchell, Juliet (Ed.), (1988). An interview, by Angela McRobbie. *New Left Review, 170*, 80–91.
Morley, Dave. (1980). Texts, readers, subjects. In S. Hall, D. Hobson, A. Lowe, and P. Willis (Eds.), *Culture, media, language: Working papers in cultural studies, 1972–1979* (pp. 163–173.). London: Hutchinson.
Muller, Johan. (1985). The end of psychology: Review of Henriques et al., *Changing the Subject*. *Psychology in Society, 3*, 33–42.
Pêcheux, Michel. (1983). *Language, semiotics and ideology: Stating the obvious*. London: Macmillan.
Peters, Michael. (1993). Against Finkielkraut's *La Défaite de la Pénsee*: Culture, postmodernism and education. *French Cultural Studies, 4*, 91–106.
Roudinesco, Elizabeth. (1990). *Jacques Lacan and co.: A history of psychoanalysis in France*. Chicago, Ill.: University of Chicago Press.
Schneiderman, Stuart. (1983). *Jacques Lacan: The death of an intellectual hero*. Cambridge, Mass.: Harvard University Press.
Shapiro, Svi. (1987). If you won't work Sunday, don't come in on Monday. In E. Stevens and G. Wood (Eds.), *Justice, ideology, and education: An introduction to the foundations of education* (pp. 141–145). New York: Random House.
Sheridan, Alan. (1977). Translator's note. In J. Lacan, *Ecrits*, vii–xii.
Smith, Sydney. (1977). The golden fantasy: A regressive reaction to separation anxiety. *International Journal of Psycho-Analysis, 58*, 311–324.
Turkle, Sherry. (1979). *Psychoanalytic politics: Freud's French revolution*. London: Burnett.
Wexler, Philip. (1987). *Social analysis of education: Beyond the new sociology*. London: Routledge and Kegan Paul.
Winnicott, D. W. (1951). Transitional objects and transitional phenomena. In D. Winnicott, *Playing and reality* (pp. 1–25). Harmondsworth: Penguin.

Wright, Elizabeth. (1984). *Psychoanalytic criticism: Theory in practice*. London: Methuen.
Zizek, Slavoj. (1991a). Why should a dialectician learn to count to four? *Radical Philosophy, 58*, 3–9.
Zizek, Slavoj. (1991b). *Looking awry: An introduction to Jacques Lacan through popular culture*. Cambridge, Mass.: MIT Press.

2

Louis Althusser: Poststructural Materialist
J. M. Fritzman

> To change the world is not to explore the moon. It is to make the revolution and build socialism without regressing back to capitalism. The rest, including the moon, will be given to us in addition.
> — Althusser 1982: 186

As Althusser notes in his autobiography (Althusser, 1993), the future lasts a long time. The desire for social justice named Marx continues after the end of really existing socialism. Understanding the overdetermined nature of the ideological state apparatuses (ISA) not only shows how educational institutions — the primary ISA, according to Althusser — reproduce and reinforce the dominant ideology, it also reveals how educators can resist that ideology in their pedagogy and enable students to interrogate their circumstances.

SUCCESS AND FAILURE

> Sometimes a person has to go a very long distance out of his way to come back a short distance correctly.
> — Albee 1961: 21

The Right has gained sufficient hegemony to define the issues as well as the terrain upon which they are contested. Rather than distinguishing between the Left and the Right, the so-called political center now is located within the Right. When even liberalism is on the defensive, hope for any revolutionary project seems quixotic. The Left's attempts to articulate its positions are heard as utopian and irrelevant. No longer feared as subversive and dangerous, it is dismissed as silly and absurd. The result is melancholy and despair on the Left, accompanied by feelings of frivolity, foreboding, and boredom elsewhere. The only fitting response, it seems, is to have the courage — the courage of the work of mourning — to confess that the project of the Left always was hopeless and delusive, to embrace pessimism about fundamental change as realism, and to acknowledge that history has ended.

Those who heed such blandishments, as Zizek recognizes, succumb to the condition that Hegel diagnoses as the beautiful soul: "The falsity of the 'beautiful soul' lies not in its inactivity, in the fact that it only complains of a depravity without doing something to remedy it; it consists, on the contrary, in the very mode of activity implied by this position of inactivity — in the way the 'beautiful soul' structures the 'objective' social world in advance so that it is able to assume, to play in it the role of the fragile, innocent and passive victim" (Zizek, 1989: 216). Confessing that the Left is hopeless and delusive, pessimism is realism, and history is fulfilled always constitutes the world in such a way that this becomes a fitting response. The Left falls for this stratagem when it interprets its failure to achieve hegemony, not as a temporary situation to be overcome but as necessary outcome. One step forward, two steps back? Failure has occurred despite the best efforts of many, and that failure is experienced as trauma. To suggest that failure could become success merely by an act of reconstitution seems a relapse to idealism. What is to be done?

This discussion so far has accepted the Right's definitions of success and failure. The Left must not only seek to turn failure into success but also contest what counts as success and failure. In doing so, it will be seen that remembering what commonly is regarded as failure is a certain kind of success. It is necessary to follow Lacan in acknowledging — in addition to the ethics of perverted enjoyment, obsessional demand, and hysterical desire — the ethics of the drive. Zizek writes:

> It is not just that the subject must not "give way as to his drive"; *the status of the drive itself is inherently ethical.* We are at the exact opposite of vitalist biologism: the image that most appropriately exemplifies drive is not "blind animal thriving" but the ethical compulsion which compels us to mark repeatedly the memory of a lost Cause. The point is *not* to remember the past trauma as exactly as possible: such "documentation" is a priori false, it transforms the trauma into a neutral, objective fact, whereas the essence of the trauma is precisely that it is too horrible to be remembered, to be integrated into our symbolic universe. All we have to do is to mark repeatedly the trauma as such, in its very "impossibility," in its non-integrated horror, by means of some "empty" symbolic gesture. (Zizek, 1991: 272)

Far from success being a matter of overcoming past trauma and lost causes in favor of effective action, adopting such a course is to have failed already. Rather, the Left must remember its traumatic failures. Such a remembrance itself is a success of sorts. To cite Zizek one last time:

> This, then, is the point where the Left must not "give way": it must preserve the traces of all historical traumas, dreams and catastrophes which the ruling ideology of the "End of History" would prefer to obliterate — it must become itself their living monument, so that as long as the Left is here, these traumas will remain marked. Such an attitude, far from confining the Left within a nostalgic infatuation with the past, is the only possibility for attaining a distance on the present, a distance which will enable us to discern signs of the New. (Zizek, 1991: 273)

It is said that Marxism in general and Althusser's interventions on its behalf failed. Capitalism is said to have succeeded. The supposed triumph of the free market produces a situation in which the rich get richer and the poor get poorer and prison. If that is success, what would count as failure?

A BRIEF BIOGRAPHY

> I am one thing, my writings are another.
> — Nietzsche 1975: 69

A bibliography of works by and about Althusser is included at the end of this chapter. More complete bibliographies of Althusser's writings are in Elliott (1987), Miller (1981), and Nordquist (1986); a glossary may be found in Brewster (1986). The information on Althusser's life that follows is taken from Althusser (1993), Benton (1984), Elliott (1993), and Moulier Boutang (1992).

Louis Pierre Althusser was born in Birmandreis, Algeria, in October 1918. He attended schools in Algiers and Marseilles. From 1936 until 1939 he studied at the École Normale Supérieure in Paris, where he also became a member of the *Jeunesse étudiante chrétienne*, a Catholic student movement. In 1939, his studies were interrupted when he was conscripted into military service. Soon captured, from 1940 until 1945 he was a prisoner in a German concentration camp. During that time he lost his faith in Catholicism and began his life-long struggle with manic depression.

Althusser was first hospitalized in 1946. Subsequently, he was diagnosed as suffering from manic depression. He would be hospitalized many times during his life.

In 1948, he passed the *agrégation* — France's highest competitive examination for teachers — at the École Normale Supérieure with a thesis on

The Notion of Content in Hegel's Philosophy, supervised by Bachelard. In November of that same year, Althusser was appointed *caîman* — a teacher who prepares students for the *agrégation* — at the École Normale Supérieure and he also joined the French Communist Party.

The year 1965 saw the publication of the essays collected in *For Marx*, as well as the publication, with Balibar, of *Reading Capital*. Althusser published "Lenin and Philosophy" in 1968, "Ideology and Ideological State Apparatuses" in 1970, and *Essays in Self-Criticism* in 1972.

Having confessed to killing his wife Hélène during a manic-depressive episode, he was admitted to Saint Anne's Psychiatric Hospital in 1980. Althusser died in October 1990. His autobiography, *The Future Lasts a Long Time*, was published posthumously in 1992.

ALTHUSSER'S POSTSTRUCTURAL MATERIALISM

> Marx's repeated efforts to break down the objective limits of the existing Theoretical, in order to forge a way of thinking the question that his scientific discovery has posed philosophy, his failures and even his relapses are a part of the theoretical drama he lived, in absolute solitude, long ago, and we are only just beginning to suspect from the signs in our heavens that *his question is our question*, and will be for a long time, that it commands our whole future.
> — Althusser and Balibar, 1987: 193

Given the need for brevity, the propositions in this chapter will be didactic and dogmatic, the theses schematic and provisional. Althusser's poststructural materialism is an intervention in a specific conjuncture. Following Machiavelli and Lenin, Althusser believes that it is necessary to think in extremes and to bend the stick in the opposite direction:

If you want to change historically existing ideas, even in the apparently abstract domain called philosophy, you cannot content yourself with simply preaching the naked truth, and waiting for its anatomical obviousness to "enlighten" minds, as our eighteenth-century ancestors used to say: you are forced, since you want to force a change in ideas, to recognize the force which is keeping them bent, by applying a counterforce capable of destroying this power and bending the stick in the opposite direction so as to put the ideas right. (Althusser, 1990: 210)

The best way to explicate Althusser's interventions, then, is to contrast his positions with those he opposes: economism and humanism.

Economism claims that the economy is, if not the only, then the principle causal factor in society. This notion often is expressed by means of the metaphors of base and superstructure. Just as a building's foundation supports its upper stories, so it is claimed that economic relations of production support all other aspects of society, including the state and social consciousness. To this economism adds the metaphors of mirroring and reflecting. Here it is claimed that the superstructure simply mirrors the base; that is, the economy is the cause of all other contradictions — processes and events — in society. All contradictions in the superstructure are simultaneous reflections of their economic causes, and so all superstructural contradictions can be explained by reference to the present state of the economy. Frequently coupled with those metaphors is a belief in the necessary evolution to a communist society. Capitalism necessarily evolved from earlier economic structures; in turn, communism must develop from capitalism. On this model, the struggles of the working class against their exploitation may hasten this necessary evolution, but they cannot alter its course.

Because "in philosophy you can think only through metaphors" (Althusser, 1976: 140), Althusser proceeds by undermining economism's metaphors. In opposition to the evolutionary determinism of economism, Althusser maintains that there is an unevenness in the contradictions that constitute a social formation. Economism claims that the superstructure mirrors the base and that this mirroring occurs simultaneously with contradictions in the economy. Althusser argues that, even if the metaphor of mirroring is accepted provisionally, the superstructure need not be in synchronization with the base. The superstructure may reflect previous economic conditions that no longer exist. Indeed, some superstructural contradictions may anticipate contradictions in the so-called base, reflecting economic conditions that do not yet exist. Althusser insists that such contradictions may play a role in bringing about those conditions. Maintaining this, though, entails that the superstructure as well as the base has causal efficacy. At this point, the metaphors of mirror and reflection are subverted. Althusser further argues that neither the base nor superstructure is a monolithic entity and that there are contradictions within both. Also, there need not be any isomorphism between contradictions in the superstructure and those in the base. Whereas economism claims that the economy acts causally on the superstructure, Althusser urges that the superstructure also produces effects on the economy.

To further weaken the conceptual hold of the metaphors of base and superstructure, Althusser rejects both mechanistic causality and expressive causality, in which change is caused by an entity's progressive expression of its inner essence. Instead, he turns to Spinoza's theory of causality, where "the structure of the totality is *nothing other than* its effects, it is, in Spinoza's sense, a cause 'immanent in its effects' (just as, in Spinoza's philosophy, God is a cause immanent in His creation: God and Nature are identical)" (Benton, 1984: 64). To explicate this notion of structural causality, Althusser employs Freud's concept of overdetermination. Denying that contradictions are determined exclusively by the economy, overdetermination claims that any contradiction is caused by the conjuncture of all contradictions and that any contradiction produces effects in all contradictions. Put otherwise, "every event is overdetermined by all the aspects of the environment in which it occurs: all the cultural, natural, political and economic aspects" (Resnick and Wolff, 1992: 132). Rejecting the essentialism of economism, Althusser refers to this poststructural theory of causality as "aleatory materialism" (Navarro, 1988).

Although every contradiction is overdetermined — that is, caused by the conjuncture of all contradictions — some contradictions play a dominant role in a particular conjuncture, and so contradictions are not equally efficacious. Some contradictions have a preponderance of influence in affecting the relations within a given conjuncture. This idea can by expressed by Fish's distinction between two levels of analysis: "The first level is the level of a general truth: all activities in a society are interrelated in ways that render it impossible for the actions taken in any one to be without consequences for the shape of any other. But it is the second level, the level of the material, that largely determines the degree and immediacy of these consequences. That is to say, the present realization of the general truth will depend on the relays of power and influence that are currently in place" (1995: 57). Whereas economism claims that the economy determines all other aspects of society, Althusser maintains that the so-called superstructure may play the dominant role, and so it has a degree of autonomy from the economy. Nonetheless, the superstructure only has relative autonomy from the economy because the former is determined by the latter in the last instance.

The assertion that the economy is determinative in the last instance suggests that Althusser endorses, in however attenuated its form, economic determinism. Recognizing that "Althusser does reject the more vulgar base-superstructure arguments in refuting simplistic cause-and-effect models," Wood nevertheless mistakenly claims that "in the final analysis, an empiricist notion of economic determination dominates his work" (1982: 60). Immediately after asserting that the economy is determinative in the last instance, however, Althusser deconstructs it with the caveat that "from the first moment to the last, the lonely hour of the 'last instance' never comes" (1986: 113).

If the qualification that the last instance never arrives allows Althusser to escape the charge of economic determinism, it also points to a poststructural materialism, where everything causes everything. In turn, that materialism might seem to collapse into a causal indeterminacy, rendering futile all hope of specifying the cause of any particular contradiction. Althusser's position does not so collapse because the effects produced by different contradictions are not equal. Instead, some contradictions will be dominant in a given conjuncture and hence will produce more prominent effects than others. It is impossible to specify all of a contradiction's causes because there are an infinite number of them, but it is possible to identify significant ones. In addition, following Resnick and Wolff (1987, 1992, 1994) the notion of economic determination in the last instance may be refigured as an entry point — a "specifically focused theoretical intervention to bring a correspondingly specific kind of order to the infinity of complexly interacting processes comprising the totality of socionational life" (Resnick and Wolff, 1994: 46) — for Marxist social analysis. The caveat that the last instance never arrives should be read as a reminder that, although analysis must begin with an essentialist moment, there always exist an infinite number of causes, and so any analysis must be partial and an intervention.

Humanism sees humanity as the motor of history, as an agent that makes its own history. According to Althusser, humanism is the inverse of economism. Although economism says that history's motor is the economic relations of production, humanism claims that humanity is the motor. Both forget Marxism's central concept: class struggle. One of Marx's greatest accomplishments, thinks Althusser, is to have banished the notion of humanity as the motor of history. It is not generic humanity that makes history, it is the class struggle. If history has a motor, it is the struggle of dominated classes against their oppression. This undercuts every humanism, including that of the early Marx who places man at the center of history.

Although the early Marx is a humanist who accepts Feuerbach's anthropological philosophy and is innocent of any notion of class struggle, the Marx of *Capital* rejects humanism with its concomitant notion of man as the motor of history. Recognizing that reading itself is philosophically problematic, an insight he credits to Spinoza, Althusser provides a symptomatic reading that thematizes aspects of Marx's thought that remain implicit in his work. Although Marx provided no detailed discussion of his theory of dialectics, for example, that theory is operative in his writings and so can be made explicit. Reading Marx in this way, Althusser urges, shows a discontinuity between the early and later works. Althusser reads the later Marx as underscoring the centrality of class struggle. Disagreeing with humanists who assert that the writings of the later Marx are a development of the early Marx's philosophy, Althusser's reading leads him to posit a radical rupture in Marx's development.

Althusser divides the writings of Marx into four periods: the Early Works (1840–44) — this is subdivided into the Liberal-Rationalist (1840–42) and the Communalist-Rationalist Works (1842–45) — the Works of the Break (1845), the Transitional Works (1845–57), and the Mature Works (1857–83). The Early Works include Marx's doctoral dissertation, his articles for *Die Rheinische Zeitung*, the *Critique of Hegel's "Philosophy of Right,"* the *1844 Manuscripts*, and *The Holy Family*. The Works of the Break include the *Theses on Feuerbach* and *The German*

Ideology. The Transitional Works include Marx's first drafts of *Capital*, the *Communist Manifesto*, the *Poverty of Philosophy*, and *Wages, Price, and Profit*. The Mature Works, finally, include the *Grundrisse*, *Theories of Surplus Value*, and *Capital*.

This rupture was not accomplished in an instant. Even in the Mature Works, Marx may be found attempting to express new concepts in the language of an earlier philosophy, trying to pour new wine into old wineskins:

> Indispensable theoretical concepts do not magically construct themselves on command when they are needed. The whole history of the beginnings of sciences or of great philosophies shows, on the contrary, that the exact set of new concepts does not march out on parade in single file; on the contrary, some are long delayed, or march in borrowed clothes before acquiring their proper uniforms — for as long as history fails to provide the tailor and the cloth. In the meantime, the concept is certainly present in its works, but in a different form from that of a concept — in a form which is looking for itself inside a form *"borrowed"* from other custodians of formulated and disposable, or fascinating concepts. (Althusser and Balibar, 1987: 51)

Althusser refers to the rupture between the philosophies of the early and later Marx as an epistemological break. This epistemological break makes possible Marx's transition from ideology to science, the science of political economy.

Althusser initially relies on Bachelard for the concept of an epistemological break as well as the concepts of ideology and science (Bachelard, 1968, 1984, 1994). Bachelard identifies ideology as common-sense beliefs. Those beliefs, as well as the philosophies based on them, are erroneous. Science is possible only insofar as it breaks with ideology, thereby constituting a realm of knowledge. Bachelard's philosophy of science is conventionalist: scientific theories are correct inasmuch as they break with ideology, but they do not correspond to external reality.

The difference between ideology and science is not for Althusser, as it is for Bachelard, a difference between error and knowledge. For Althusser, ideology is the prereflective stance — the spontaneous or natural attitude — persons take to their world, a stance in which practice takes precedence. Science, in contrast, is that reflective attitude. Althusser denies that science wholly could supplant ideology. As Brewster notes:

> Ideology is the "lived" relation between men and their world, or a reflected form of this unconscious relation. . . . It is distinguished from a science not by its falsity, for it can be coherent and logical . . . but by the fact that the practico-social predominates in it over the theoretical, over knowledge. Historically, it precedes the science that is produced by making an epistemological break . . . with it, but it

survives alongside science as an essential element of every social formation . . . including a socialist and even a communist society. (Brewster, 1986: 252)

Science for Althusser, pace Bachelard, is knowledge of an external reality. Althusser also believes that the object of a science is brought into existence when that science is constituted. Put otherwise: "The vocabularies of disciplines are not external to their objects, but constitutive of them. Discard them in favour of the vocabulary of another discipline, and you will lose the object that only they call into being" (Fish, 1995: 58). Althusser claims, for example, that the subject matter of geometry was brought into existence with Euclid's founding the science of geometry, and not by the heuristic rules of Egyptian land surveyors.

It follows from Althusser's poststructural materialism that no social formation ever will be transparent to itself. There are two reasons for this. First, every contradiction is overdetermined, and so is caused by the conjuncture of all contradictions. Although it is possible to specify some of a contradiction's significant causes, there are an infinite number of them, and, hence, it is impossible to enumerate all of them. Second, ideology never can be transcended, and so there can be no perspective that sees things as they really are. That is, there is no vantage point wholly outside of ideology. Because no social formation is transparent, politics is inescapable and — while the stakes and sites may change — class struggle never ends.

In order to survive, every social formation must reproduce its conditions of production. Not only must such means of production as machines be reproduced but also the productive forces — primarily labor power — must be reproduced. Because the new labor power must be competent, "suitable to be set to work in the complex system of the process of production" (Althusser, 1971: 131), it must be diversely skilled. The reproduction of labor power formerly was achieved through apprenticeships, but now it is obtained by means of educational institutions. In addition to learning skills, students are taught rules of good behavior. The reproduction of labor power involves teaching skills and submission to the ideology of the established order.

Classical Marxism conceptualizes the state merely as a repressive state apparatus (RSA) — consisting of prisons, police, government, courts, and army — that compels individuals to submit. In so doing, classical Marxism is not wrong, it only is descriptive and so incomplete. Recognizing that force and its threat are only effective if most individuals already accept the state and its mandates as legitimate, Althusser argues that Marxism must recognize the role of ISAs in order to become a scientific theory. Religious, political, educational, cultural, and other institutions serve as ISAs that persuade individuals to submit to the dominant ideology.

The RSA differs from ISAs in three ways. First, there is only one RSA, but there is a plurality of ISAs. What unifies the diversity of the ISAs is that they function by the ideology of the ruling class, which itself is already unified. Second, the RSA exists in the public domain, while many ISAs belong to the private domain. Although every state apparatus functions by both violence and ideology, and although there is no such thing as an apparatus that is purely repressive or ideological, the third and decisive difference between the RSA and ISAs is that the former functions primarily by violence whereas the latter functions primarily by ideology.

There is a constant struggle between the dominant ideology of the ruling classes that must be imposed on the exploited classes and the dominated ideology that naturally expresses the lived relations of the exploited classes. "*No class can hold State power over a long period without at the same time exercising its hegemony over and in the State Ideological Apparatuses*" (Althusser, 1971: 146), and so classes struggle for hegemony. The ISAs themselves can become involved in these struggles, and, hence, "the Ideological State Apparatuses may be not only the *stake*, but also the *site* of class struggle" (Althusser, 1971: 147).

The dominant ideology employs every ISA function to reproduce capitalist conditions of production in an appropriate manner. This is as true for the educational ISA as for any other. One ISA always is dominant in every social formation, and the educational ISA has replaced the religious ISA as the dominant one. Althusser recognizes that educationalists may struggle against the dominant ideology, but he maintains that most are unaware of the extent to which they perpetuate capitalism:

I ask the pardon of those teachers who, in dreadful conditions, attempt to turn the few weapons they can find in the history and learning they "teach" against the ideology, the system and practices in which they are trapped. They are a kind of hero. But they are rare and how many (the majority) do not even begin to suspect the "work" the system (which is bigger than they are and crushes them) forces them to do, or worse, put all their heart and ingenuity into performing it with the most advanced awareness (the famous new methods!). So little do they suspect it that their own devotion contributes to the maintenance and nourishment of this ideological representation of the School, which makes the School today as "natural," indispensable-useful and even beneficial for our contemporaries as the Church was "natural," indispensable and generous for our ancestors a few centuries ago. (Althusser, 1971: 157)

Capitalism is resourceful and insidious. It is adept at exploiting the strategies employed against it. The skills of critical thinking can be used to interrogate the presumably natural imperatives of capitalism, for example, or to invent new ways to downsize — the recent cant now speaks of rightsizing — the work force. Nevertheless, it would be a mistake to read Althusser as supporting resignation and despair. Rather, the struggle against oppression must be persistent and continually must question its premises and methods.

Althusser's account of ISAs is not a species of functionalism, as Erben and Gleeson charge when they conclude that "Althusser has a functionalist tendency in his analysis of social order and adaptation" (Erben and Gleeson, 1977: 83). Functionalism maintains that all aspects of society harmoniously work together for a single purpose. The dominant ideology does attempt, frequently with success, to use the ISAs to reproduce its conditions of production. However, the ISAs can be sites of class struggle. Dominated ideologies can enlist the ISAs in their struggle against the dominant ideology. Such struggles would have no place in Althusser's analysis if he were guilty of a functionalist tendency. Contra functionalism, the dominant ideology itself is the result of a hegemony that has been imposed upon the contradictions within the dominant ideology; indeed, the dominant ideology is that hegemony. It is possible for some of those contradictions to be turned against the dominant ideology. The belief that all individuals should be treated equally, for example, generally reinforces the dominant ideology because it maintains that all individuals are treated equally. If dominated ideologies can demonstrate that many individuals are treated unequally and unjustly, and such a demonstration itself will be the result of a protracted struggle, then the dominant ideology's assertion that all individuals should be treated equally can be employed against it.

Although the content of particular ideologies differs because of their historical development, Althusser argues that the structure of ideology in general is constant, and thus *"ideology has no history"* (Althusser, 1971: 159). He refers to Freud in explicating this: "If eternal means, not transcendent of all (temporal) history, but omnipresent, trans-historical and therefore immutable in form throughout the extent of history, I shall adopt Freud's expression word for word, and write *ideology is eternal*, exactly like the unconscious" (Althusser, 1971: 161). Ideology is eternal because "ideology represents the imaginary relations of individuals to their real conditions of existence" (p. 162). Althusser rejects the suggestion that the dominant ideology is a false consciousness imposed on the exploited classes by a ruling class that sees through it; rather, the ruling class believes its own ideology. It is possible to thematize some of these imaginary relations and interrogate them — that is what science does — but this still must presuppose other imaginary relations: *"ideology has no outside* (for itself), but at the same time . . . *it is nothing but outside* (for science and reality)" (p. 175). Even a communist, classless society would exist in ideology.

Because "ideology has a material existence" (Althusser, 1971: 165), it is not merely subjective ideas. Ideology always exists in the ritual practices of an apparatus and such practices always are ideological. Ideology primarily is concerned with practices and not ideas, but both practices and ideas are material. "*All ideology hails or interpellates concrete individuals as concrete subjects,*" Althusser maintains, "by the functioning of the category of subject" (p. 173). Althusser's example of interpellation is hailing someone in the street. As Barrett observes, "in the moment of acknowledging a shout of 'hey, you there!,' of turning around to respond to the call, of confirmation that 'it really is he' who was hailed, the subject is both positioned in ideology and confirmed in his own recognition of himself" (Barrett, 1993: 174).

Ideology has interpellated an individual as a subject when that individual is identified as, for example, a teacher, spouse, sibling, parent, female, fan, employee, daughter, criminal, consumer, citizen, or believer. Put otherwise, that individual has been given roles with concomitant rules and expectations to which that individual will be subjected. Henceforth, those roles will shape that individual's values, self-understanding, beliefs, and behavior. Interpellation need not be, perhaps typically is not, pleasant. It is an illustration of Althusser's theory of interpellation, and not an objection to it, when Barrett notes that "many women might say that their experience of being hailed (especially by whistling!) on the street more often has the opposite effect of denying their individual identity and interpellating them in unnervingly generic terms" (Barrett, 1993: 174). Similarly, individuals are interpellated when they are subjected to racial or ethnic epithets.

Interpellation never is monolithic or unidirectional, an individual always is interpellated as a subject from many different sites. Further, there always is the possibility that the rules and expectations of various interpellations will conflict. A Catholic may consider a certain law so unjust that individuals of good will must disobey it, a police officer might be expected to enforce that same law, and the Catholic and the police officer could be the same individual. The forces of various interpellations are not equal. An individual interpellated as a conscript is subjected in a way quite different than someone interpellated as a motorcyclist.

An individual may resist interpellation. A conscientious objector inducted into the military may refuse to obey orders. Because ideology is eternal, however, "*individuals are always-already subjects*" (Althusser, 1971: 176) — indeed, the category of individual is itself an interpellation — and so whatever values or convictions allow an individual to resist interpellation are the result of other interpellations. An individual who resists the interpellations of soldier, patriot, and conscript, to return to the above example, already has been interpellated, perhaps as Quaker, pacifist, or conscientious objector.

APPLICATIONS TO EDUCATION

> One does not correct the texts of ideological struggle when conditions
> of the struggle change: one writes new ones.
> — Rancière, 1985: 136

It is not a matter of somehow applying Althusser's poststructural materialism either to education or to the present conjuncture. When circumstances change, as Rancière observes, so must the theory that was intended to alter them. Nonetheless, it is possible to suggest ways in which Althusser's interventions may be useful to educationalists.

Educationalists need to reflect on how individuals are interpellated as students. It is impossible for individuals not to be interpellated, individuals always are interpellated, and so interpellation as such cannot be avoided. What can be resisted, however, are particular instances of interpellation. What is at stake is not whether but how individuals will be interpellated. It is important, then, that teachers strive to interpellate their students in the dominated ideologies.

It was suggested that Althusser's assertion that the economy is determinative in the last instance be refigured as an entry point for analysis. Hence, educationalists can encourage their students to "follow the money." For example, students can learn to ask which corporations and individuals make substantial contributions to which politicians' campaigns. They can ask whether magazines have financial interests in products that are reviewed — perhaps a magazine is owned by the same corporation that manufactures the product or that makes a competing product. Again, when newspapers endorse candidates for public office, students can ask if there is a financial motivation for that endorsement.

Although Althusser asserts that the economy is determinative in the last instance, he also advances a theory of causation where events are overdetermined. That is, any contradiction is caused by the conjuncture of all contradictions in a social formation. Althusser further maintains that, in any particular conjuncture, one contradiction will be dominant and that the dominant contradiction need not be economic. In addition, he introduces the concept of a symptomatic reading, which thematizes what remains implicit in a text. Drawing on all of those emphases, students can perform symptomatic readings of cultural products. They could ask, for example, whether and why editorial opinions and commentary are surreptitiously presented as facts. They also could ask whether and why a news report has omitted information that would have been relevant. They could ask which events are discussed in the news media and which are ignored, as well as which significant questions are left unasked and so go unanswered. Students also could ask with which characters — and so with which values and practices — audiences are invited to identify by television, plays, movies, and novels. In the teaching of history, educators can stress what might be termed counter-history. In addition to learning the official history of the textbooks, students can be taught about the history of labor struggles, the displacement of indigenous peoples, the repression and exploitation of racial and ethnic groups, as well as alternative political and economic systems. Exposing students to this counter-history would provide them with an alternative perspective from which to interrogate the dominant ideology's version of history.

THE FUTURE

> It is never truth that determines the course of history, Alfred mused to himself — it was the *effect* of truth on those who acted and, in turn, they acted upon it.
> — Vachss, 1995: 76

It could be argued that Althusser's poststructural materialism supports Fish's contention that "a theory can only have the effects allowed to it by the very conditions it would alter" (Fish, 1995: 58). Nevertheless, in his interventions for Marx against humanism and economism, Althusser shows that the future cannot be prognosticated from any investigation, however exhaustive, of present or past tendencies and conditions. This means not only that the future is radically contingent but also that struggles against oppression and exploitation occur without any guarantees of success. To be sure, there are beautiful souls for whom that will serve as an excuse for inaction and despair. If there are no guarantees, however, there is the possibility of success. The future always is open, nothing ever is settled, and the desire for justice named Marx will continue. Revolutionary change is possible, although, in the last instance, it may not have been determined by human will, motivation, or intention. There also is the remembrance of traumatic failures as well as the drive to bear witness to the victims of injustice and martyrs for justice. This will have been enough. Far from being an occasion for pessimism, this conclusion will have been experienced as optimistic by those who recognize that liberatory struggles necessarily occur without guarantees.

REFERENCES

Albee, Edward. 1961. "The Zoo Story: A Play in One Scene." *The American Dream and The Zoo Story*. New York: Signet Books.

Althusser, Louis. 1993. *The Future Lasts a Long Time, and the Facts*. Edited by Olivier Corpet and Yann Moulier Boutang, translated by Richard Veasey. London: Chatto & Windus.

Althusser, Louis. 1990. *Philosophy and the Spontaneous Philosophy of the Scientists, and Other Essays*. Edited by Gregory Elliott. London: Verso.

Althusser, Louis. 1986. *For Marx*. Translated by Ben Brewster. London: Verso.

Althusser, Louis. 1982. *Montesquieu, Rousseau, Marx: Politics and History*. Translated by Ben Brewster. London: Verso.

Althusser, Louis. 1976. *Essays in Self-Criticism*. Translated by Grahame Lock. Atlantic Highlands, N.J.: Humanities Press.

Althusser, Louis. 1971. *Lenin and Philosophy, and Other Essays*. Translated by Ben Brewster. New York: Monthly Review Press.

Althusser, Louis, and Étienne Balibar. 1987. *Reading Capital*. Translated by Ben Brewster. London: Verso.

Bachelard, Gaston. 1994. *The Poetics of Space*. Translated by Maria Jolas. Boston, Mass.: Beacon Press.

Bachelard, Gaston. 1984. *The New Scientific Spirit*. Translated by Arthur Goldhammer. Boston, Mass.: Beacon Press.

Bachelard, Gaston. 1968. *The Philosophy of No: A Philosophy of the New Scientific Mind*. Translated by G. C. Waterston. New York: Orion Press.

Balibar, Étienne. 1978. "From Bachelard to Althusser: The Concept of 'Epistemological Break.'" *Economy and Society* 7(3): 207–237.

Barrett, Michèle. 1993. "Althusser's Marx, Althusser's Lacan." In *The Althusserian Legacy*, edited by E. A. Kaplan and M. Sprinker, pp. 169–182. London: Verso.

Benton, Ted. 1984. *The Rise and Fall of Structural Marxism: Althusser and his Influence*. New York: Saint Martin's Press.

Brewster, Ben. 1986. "Glossary." In Louis Althusser Louis. *For Marx*. Translated by Ben Brewster. London: Verso.

Elliott, Gregory. 1987. *Althusser: The Detour of Theory*. New York: Verso.

Elliott, Gregory. 1993. "The Lonely Hour of the Last Instance: Louis Pierre Althusser, 1918–1900." In *The Althusserian Legacy*, edited by E. A. Kaplan and M. Sprinker, pp. 233–239. London: Verso.

Erben, Michael, and Denis Gleeson. 1977. "Education as Reproduction: A Critical Examination of Some Aspects of the Work of Louis Althusser." In *Society, State and Schooling: Readings on the Possibilities of Radical Education*, edited by Michael Young and Geoff Whitty, pp. 73–92. Sussex: Falmer Press.

Fish, Stanley. 1995. *Professional Correctness: Literary Studies and Political Change*. Oxford: Oxford University Press.

Miller, Joan M. 1981. *French Structuralism: A Multidisciplinary Bibliography with a Checklist of Sources for Louis Althusser, Roland Barthes, Jacques Derrida, Michel Foucault, Lucien Goldmann, Jacques Lacan, and an Update of Works on Claude Levi-Strauss*. New York: Garland Pubications.

Moulier Boutang, Yann. 1992. *Louis Althusser: Une Biographie*. Vol. 1. *La Formation du Mythe (1918–1956)*. Paris: Bernard Grasset.

Navarro, Fernanda. 1988. *Filosofía y Marxismo: Entrevista a Louis Althusser*. Mexico City: Siglo Veintiuno Editores.

Nietzsche, Friedrich. 1975. *Ecce Homo: How One Becomes What One Is*. Harmondsworth: Penguin.

Nordquist, Joan. 1986. *Louis Althusser: a Bibliography*. Santa Cruz, Calif.: Reference and Research Services, Social Theory 3.

Rancière, Jacques. 1985. "On the Theory of Ideology — Althusser's Politics." In *Radical Philosophy Reader*, edited by Roy Edgley and Richard Osborne, pp. 101–136. London: Verso.

Resnick, Stephen A., and Richard D. Wolff. 1994. "Rethinking Complexity in

Economic Theory: The Challenge of Overdetermination." In *Evolutionary Concepts in Contemporary Economics*, edited by Richard W. England. Ann Chicago, Ill.: University of Chicago Press.

Resnick, Stephen A., and Richard D. Wolff. 1992. "Reply to Richard Peet." *Antipode* 24(2): 131–140.

Resnick, Stephen A., and Richard D. Wolff. 1987. *Knowledge and Class: A Marxian Critique of Political Economy*. Chicago, Ill.: University of Chicago Press.

Vachss, Andrew. 1995. *Batman: The Ultimate Evil*. New York: Warner Books.

Wood, George H. 1982. "Beyond Radical Educational Cynicism." *Educational Theory* 32(2): 55–71.

Zizek, Slavoj. 1991. *For They Know Not What They Do: Enjoyment as a Political Factor*. London: Verso.

Zizek, Slavoj. 1989. *The Sublime Object of Ideology*. London: Verso.

3

Michel Foucault: Philosophy, Education, and Freedom as an Exercise upon the Self

James Marshall

Michel Foucault is one of the more dazzling thinkers and writers to have launched himself on the intellectual scene in the last half of the twentieth century. His life, ideas, and works, however, are not without controversy. Nevertheless, he confronts Western intellectual thought, especially Anglo-American logo-centric thinking on such matters as rationality and the subject, with a series of daunting (and taunting) challenges.

His initial academic training was in philosophy, but he claimed to have exited philosophy. Nevertheless, in later life he came to talk more about philosophy as he turned to consider an ethics of the self and philosophy, not as the producer of grand ideas and totalizing general theories applicable to all human beings but, instead, as an exercise upon the self, and one that is committed to the pursuit of freedom. Conceived in this manner philosophy becomes more like an educational enterprise.

I will provide some biographical details on Foucault including some important influences upon him as a thinker. I will look at Foucault's position on the point of philosophy, before turning to consider how Foucault saw this view of philosophy as promoting freedom. Finally I will consider the educational implications of this position suggesting that, construed in this manner, philosophy becomes an educational enterprise.

Paul-Michel Foucault was born in Poitiers in 1926. At school he was known by either name, but he was later to drop the Paul, probably in opposition to his father and the notion of a hereditary family name (Eribon, 1991). He was raised in a middle-class bourgeois family — his father was a surgeon — and attended local schools. Of these he was to say:

> For someone like me, brought up as a provincial petty bourgeois, learning comes with your baby bottle before you even go to primary school. Knowledge was the rule of existence . . . [it was] the kind of learning that amounted to a prohibition against knowing certain things . . . [yet] learning is something erotic . . . [but] teachers manage to make learning unpleasant, depressing, grey, unerotic. We need to understand how that serves the needs of society . . . you have to make learning rebarbative if you want to restrict the number of people who have access to knowledge. (Foucault, 1974: 52)

Although he said little of his family (former school friends from Poitiers quoted in his obituary in *Libération*, 1984), he had fond memories of growing up and, with the exception of his father, was close to his family. He was to buy a house close to his mother, and she was to say: "he always gave me his August" (quoted in Eribon 1991: 14). His emotional memories seem to have been related to the political situation. He noted the influence of the impending war and the actual war upon himself and his contemporaries (Foucault, 1983a): "Our private life was really threatened," and; "boys and girls of this generation had their childhood formed by these great historical events."

He commenced his schooling at the local Lycée Henri IV but was moved to boarding at the college Saint Stanislas where, his parents thought, the local priests would discipline the rather corrosive aspects of Michel's character (*Libération* 1984). He hated those three years at Saint Stanislas and later was difficult in any form of institutionalized and communal living (Eribon, 1991). However, after his baccalauréat he was to return to a local lycée to prepare for the entrance exam to the prestigious L'École Normale Supérieure. He failed at his first attempt but, after further study in Paris at the prestigious Lycée Henri IV, he was accepted at the second attempt. At Henri IV he was taught by Jean Hyppolite (the translator and interpreter of Hegel) and Georges Canguilhem (the distinguished philosopher and historian of science) was on his oral panel for the L'École Normale Supérieure. He studied there and at the Sorbonne under such distinguished thinkers as Hyppolite, Canguilhem, Georges Dumezil (the historian of religion), and the Marxist structuralist Louis Althusser (who became both friend and colleague).

In 1948 he took his *licence de philosophie* but he was to abandon formal study of philosophy for psychology, completing his *licence de psychologie* in 1951. This was followed by a diploma in psychopathology and work in psychiatric institutions and prisons. His doctorate on the history of madness was undertaken while at the University of Uppsala and was completed in 1964. In this earlier work the influence of Canguilhem and

Bachelard is strong (Gutting, 1989). A pivotal influence here must have been Althusser's teaching of Bachelard while Foucault was at L'École Normale Supérieure.

Foucault came to Nietzsche through Blanchot, Bataille, and Heidegger. Reading Nietzsche in the early 1950s was not merely intellectually revealing for Foucault; it caused him to break with his life and work and to leave France in 1955. His overt homosexuality caused him psychological problems (Eribon, 1991) and this also may have influenced his decision to leave France; "when I left France, freedom for personal life was very sharply restricted" (Foucault, 1983a). He felt he had become a stranger, entrapped, and never again felt able to integrate fully into French social and intellectual life.

Foucault became a wanderer. For several years in the 1950s he taught and worked abroad, first at the University of Uppsala where he taught in the French department and later as Director of the French Institutes of Warsaw and Hamburg. On the surface, it may appear difficult to talk of him as emerging from Parisian intellectual, aesthetic, and political currents. Nevertheless, he should be understood in this way, but with emergence understood more as defining oneself in opposition to, or across, existing intellectual traditions or currents. He was a hybrid writer, outside of the customary genres, and therefore not constrained by any one disciplinary methodology. Here the early work on madness, on dreams in Binswanger, on Roussel, and the influences of Bataille, Bachelard, and Lacan on transgression, discontinuity, and defining the Other must be important.

Foucault was an albatross who was to return, taking a position at Clermont-Ferrand in 1962. In 1966, however, with the publication of *The Order of Things* by Gallimard, he went to Tunisia where he began to become politically engaged. The student revolution of 1968 saw Foucault returning to metropolitan France as Head of Philosophy at the experimental university at Vincennes. He attracted some excellent junior staff, including Alain Badiou, Etienne Balibar, Judith Miller (Lacan's daughter), Jacques Rancierre, and Michel Serres. This was to be a turbulent two years at Vincennes, which drained Foucault physically and emotionally. On the one hand, there were endless student protests, in which the philosophy department seemed to be in the vanguard, and, on the other hand, the continual attacks by the media upon the experiment at Vincennes. He also was heavily involved in a number of more public protests and causes (see the biographies: Eribon, 1991; Macey, 1993; Miller, 1993), with such people as Jean-Paul Sartre, Simone de Beauvoir, Jean Genet, François Mauriac, Simone Signoret, and Yves Montand.

Foucault was very active in the *Group d'Information sur les Prisons*, whose purpose was to provide means for prisoners to speak for themselves, thereby empowering prisoners to set up their own active organizations. His actions here were perfectly compatible with what he believed to be the proper role of intellectuals (Foucault, 1972). He also debated with the working class, reiterating these points on intellectuals (Foucault, 1973). Initially he provided support for Ayatollah Khomeini (Foucault, 1978a) but withdrew this support as the nature of the Islamic revolution unfolded. He was also a supporter of gay rights, although, as his later philosophical position was to require, he preferred terms, such as "homosexual," to be applied to acts and not to classify persons. If he never wished to be homosexual he was unable to hide it (Piel, 1986; *Libération*, 1984). In later life Foucault was to say of himself: "I don't feel that it is necessary to know exactly what I am. The main interest in life and work is to become someone else that you were not in the beginning. If you knew when you began a book what you would say at the end, do you think you would have the courage to write it? What is true for writing and for a love relationship is true also for life. The game is worthwhile insofar as we don't know where it will end" (1982: 9).

In relation to the notion of philosophy and education as involving work upon the self, Foucault's important works are his earlier works on psychology (Foucault, 1961), on epistemology in *The Order of Things* (1970), on governmentality in *Discipline and Punish* (1979a), and *Ideology and Consciousness* (1979b), on bio-power in *The History of Sexuality* (1978b), and on self-constitution in *The History of Sexuality* (1985, 1986). In relation to questions of modernity see Foucault (1984b). There are other ways to read Foucault, so this is offered only as a partial reading associated with the title theme.

Foucault wrote and said little explicitly on education. Until the publication of an edited collection on Foucault, Ball (1990), and Marshall (1996), there had been little written explicitly on Foucault and education. Foucault has been used very well by Walkerdine (1984), however, and there is a growing literature in the educational and philosophy of education journals and in collections on poststructuralism and postmodernism. Not all of these writers fully understand Foucault or recognize his originality, because they are guilty of tacking him on or attempting to marry him to other forms of critical theory.

THE POINT OF PHILOSOPHY

For Foucault the point of philosophy, insofar as he ever classified himself a philosopher, was that philosophy was concerned with the self; it involved working on the self. In a similar vein, teaching should allow "the individual to change at will" (1984a: 329). Philosophy is:

A way of reflecting, not so much on what is true and what is false, as on our relationship to truth? ... There is no sovereign philosophy, it's true, but a philosophy or rather philosophy in activity. The movement by which, not without effort and uncertainty, dreams and illusions, one detaches oneself from what is accepted as true and seeks other rules — that is philosophy. The displacement and transformation of frameworks of thinking, the changing of received values and all the work that has been done to think otherwise, to do something else, to become other than what one is — that, too, is philosophy ... it is a way of interrogating ourselves. (Foucault, 1984a: 329)

This is a quite different view of philosophy than that taught in Anglo-American undergraduate courses on philosophy. Philosophy there is often taught through its history: a history that starts with the Greeks — the pre-Socratics, Socrates, Plato, and Aristotle — and then moves (sometimes quickly) to the British empiricists and to Descartes and Kant. The emergence of the individual, and the political and epistemological importance to be granted to the individual, is to be found also in the writings of Locke and Descartes. Descartes opens the way for the subject to be epistemologically favored, to be seen as the endower of meaning, and for the individual to become identified with consciousness. Descartes also opens the way for man to be both subject and object of knowledge in the work of Kant. Descartes and Kant lay the epistemological bases for the very influential French existential humanism of de Beauvoir, Sartre, and Merleau-Ponty. Sartre's version was to become more closely aligned with Marxism. Foucault was to refer to this influence as the terrorism of *Les Temps Modernes*, the journal they published.

In Anglo-American teaching, philosophy tends to be taught through the history of its ideas, and done through some of those ideas, particularly those of logical argument, conceptual clarity through analysis of concepts, and the divulgence of assumptions. In some hands, for example, the logical positivist philosophy becomes more like a science (Ayer, 1935).

Teaching was different in France, for the philosophy curriculum in schools had scarcely changed between 1900 and 1968, and in the universities until 1968 it was little different. Foucault attempted to change the philosophy curricula in his contributions to the 1965 Implementation Committee for Fouchet's and the Fifth Republic's Reforms in Education (see Marshall, 1996).

In France the formal education of philosophers, including teachers of philosophy, had followed two broad, general curriculums. The first, which most followed, arose from the early teaching and translations by Kojève and Hyppolite, and was based on a revision of the philosophy of Descartes and Kant through the works of Hegel, Husserl, Marx, and Heidegger. This curriculum was about humanism and Marxism, in general, and existentialism and phenomenology, in particular. This was to be epitomized later in the writings of Sartre and the writings and teaching of

Merleau-Ponty (who also introduced students to de Saussure). Althusser's teaching of structuralist Marxism also attracted a large number of dedicated students (Poster, 1975: 359).

From an Anglo-American perspective, however, this curriculum also had a decidedly psychological-psychoanalytical perspective (especially with Freud and, later, Lacan), reeked of metaphysics, and lacked the logical foundations of a proper post-Kantian epistemology. Nevertheless, Descartes and Kant were there.

The second general, though less fashionable, strand in philosophy developed from Nietzsche's reading of Kant, through Heidegger and, in France, through Bataille, Blanchot, and Pierre Klossowski. This strand also built upon the ideas of philosophy of science, developed from Jean Cavailles (who was shot as a member of the resistance), and through the work of Gaston Bachelard, Georges Canguilhem, and Louis Althusser. This view of philosophy of science has considerable affinities to those of Thomas Kuhn in the Anglo-American tradition (Hacking, 1981). Foucault sites his own philosophical education firmly in this second strand.

Habermas, in ruing this path taken by Derrida, Deleuze, Baudrillard, Foucault, and Lacan (the young conservatives in his terminology), lays the blame upon Nietzsche and his reading of Kant, in particular. However, in the French scene it seems more plausible that it was Sartre's reading of Heidegger in *Existentialism is a Humanism* that set the problems for French intellectuals concerned by the broad humanist tradition.

Sartre had misread Heidegger on the issue of humanism, and Heidegger responded in his famous *Letter on Humanism* (1949), denying that he was ever an existentialist. Although *Being and Time* (Heidegger, 1962) provoked Sartre's existentialist reading of Heidegger and the adoption of the notion of a free consciousness, for Heidegger this later notion was not to be found either in that work or in his writing (Grene, 1957). Heidegger denied that he was either a humanist or an existentialist and criticized Sartre heavily. In so doing Heidegger provided a critique of humanism based on his pessimistic view of society, the history of mankind, and a rejection of the enlightenment message of the development and improvement of mankind. Heidegger argued (1949) that humanism was inadequate in an age of technology and impending nihilism and that the humanist search for an essence was mistaken because it made human being just another species of animal. As Miller puts it: "For him [Heidegger], as for Nietzsche and Spengler, modern history was nothing less than a calamity — not the happy emergence of the harmonious human freedom anticipated by Kant, Hegel and Marx" (Miller, 1993: 47). Heidegger's central point is that human being is in the world, deeply entangled in a world into which it has been cast, but this is a world that can be appropriated freely within the limits of facticity or contingency of that world. Heidegger first used the term "existentiality" for this notion but was later to use "transcendence."

It is this notion of transcendence that is important. It is not mere existence but an inner personal existence, an anticipation of its own possibilities, and of going beyond the given. Such transcendence can never exceed the boundaries of the givens. Transcendence is also subject to forfeiture, to being seduced, for we can forget our being because of other human beings and the distractions of everyday life. This is also an essential aspect of being, but an aspect to be overcome if freedom is to be attained: nihilism is the final outcome of forfeiture but can be avoided through transcendence. Heidegger then attempts to identify a notion of authentic being against the scattering of everyday life. Here are the bases of the critique of humanism and of Sartre. (The main teacher of Heidegger at L'École Normale Supérieure was Jean Beaufret, to whom Heidegger had written the *Letter on Humanism.*)

This was the Heidegger who excited Foucault and Derrida and was to provide opponents of humanism with the basis of an attack upon all versions of humanism. Foucault and Deleuze, among others, recognized the intellectual superiority of Nietzsche. Perhaps it was Nietzsche, as Habermas had claimed, who provided the post-Kantian path. It was mainly Deleuze who introduced Nietzsche to France, but Foucault began reading him because of Heidegger in 1953 (Eribon, 1991: 51).

The point of doing philosophy for Foucault was to work upon the self, to transcend the intellectual, social, and moral cages that the enlightenment notion of freedom and emancipation through knowledge mistakenly offers. Teaching was not to fit the individual into a certain aspect of society but to permit individuals to change, to transcend the normalizing classifications and objectifications that permitted them to be allotted into appropriate docile positions in society.

To do this the terrorism of *Les Temps Modernes* had to be overcome. It was partly the launching of structuralism into the cacophony of the philosophical marketplace (Poster, 1975: 307) that signaled the displacement of humanism, including existential Marxism. Lévi-Strauss attacked Sartre also, because in his view Sartre's account of language was inadequate. Sartre conceived language as involving struggles between thoughts and words that, in turn, caused gaps between what language permitted and what the author or speaker wished to say. From Lévi-Strauss's position this was an inadequate starting point for the study not only of language but also of society and culture. Marxism became gradually discredited as Stalinism's errors became more apparent. The failure of the *Parti Communiste Française* to support the workers and students in the revolution of May-June 1968 was a fatal error.

Foucault denied, sometimes quite vehemently, that he was ever a structuralist, but he also claimed that Nietzsche, Bataille, Blanchot, and

Klossowski "were ways of exiting from philosophy" (Foucault, 1975: 119). Nietzsche represented for Foucault the outer edge of philosophy, appearing to say, "What nonsense all of this is." Philosophy was not to be refined but to be avoided, or bypassed, or opposed by laughter (p. 119). Hence Foucault, in turning to discourses (including practices), turns to a certain form of historical investigation that he called genealogy, after Nietzsche. He does not directly engage with Sartre and the terrorism of *Les Temps Modernes* but avoids them, sometimes with astringent laughter, as when he referred to Sartre as a man of the nineteenth century trying to think in the twentieth century (Foucault, 1968: 40).

FREEDOM AS AN EXERCISE UPON THE SELF

Why must philosophy be an exercise upon the self? Foucault gives two main reasons, both associated with freedom and for freedom: the necessity of resistance to governmentality, and the more personal and ethical, but parallel aspect of work upon the self. Freedom in a positive sense is to be achieved through the latter course of action. But first we need to look at the notion of governmentality.

Foucault coined the term "governmentality" (Foucault, 1979b) to refer to a domain of research that might also be called "governmental rationality." By governmentality he meant something like a form of activity designed to guide, shape, affect, or change the conduct of some person or persons. Governmentality was to be understood both in a wide sense of the government of self and others and in a narrower sense of self government. The question for governments was how, since Machiavelli, to conduct their activity to ensure the security and perpetuity of the state. His research on this question and the research of others in this domain (see, for example, the edited collection by Burchell, et al., 1991), raises a number of issues and questions for the welfare state in general and for education in particular.

In 1976 Foucault said that in political analysis we have still not cut off the King's head. By this he meant that political language, analysis, and practice were mired in talk of such things as oppression, legitimation, rights, state, government, and authority. He was certainly not saying that it was futile to attempt to restrict the role of government in its ever-advancing claims to legitimize its exercises of authority. Rather, government is more than this; it is an art and activity that touches us all; it did not just fall from on high as a given but had to be invented or gradually constructed (Burchell et al., 1991: x). According to Foucault governmentality has touched us all, so that we are not the free, autonomous individuals and choosers of individual projects that the liberal framework (Nozick, 1974) and liberal education (Strike, 1982) would make us out to be.

Foucault advanced a thesis in *Discipline and Punish* (1979a) on the micropolitics of power as exemplified by the application of disciplinary techniques in various institutions, but particularly the prison. These are essentially concerned with how the self, or personal identity, is constituted by others, by official discourses, and by what Foucault calls "power/knowledge." This thesis is later amended and developed (Foucault 1983b). In *The History of Sexuality* (Vol. 1) and later writings, he looks at how we begin to do this to ourselves, so as to constitute our own identities. These techniques can be called, respectively, technologies of domination and technologies of the self. Technologies of domination are concerned with the way in which the human sciences, and professionals acting with the authority of the human sciences, have come to classify, objectify, and normalize us as persons who will lead useful, docile, and practical lives. Technologies of the self start from the incitement to talk about the self in confessional, remedial, or therapeutic consultations with professionals, who in turn change our talk about ourselves into the language of the human sciences and help us to constitute our selves through the therapeutic consultation. Eventually we learn how to do this to ourselves. Underlying these technologies are forms of power.

According to Foucault's strict nominalism, power only exists when power relationships come into play. His question on power is a how question, not a what question. Power is not something I can own or claim: from Foucault's how question (not meant to replace the other questions) power only exists as a relation when it is exercised or called into play. Power in this sense is distinguished from power/knowledge, which involves only certain relations of power and a certain kind of knowledge.

Power/knowledge involves a particular kind of truth for here knowledge is located within the deep regimes of discourse and practice. It is a knowledge that permits statements such as, "children with learning difficulties can be identified within the first year of formalised instruction," to emerge and be legitimized as truth. Hacking (1981) reads Foucault as asking Kantian-type questions about the conditions of knowledge in general, but Foucault's conditions are non-transcendental, and he locates them in sociohistorical contexts that he refers to as *epistémès*. According to Foucault this depth of knowledge cannot be dissociated from power and is designated therefore as power/knowledge.

Here we should return to the quotation on how to dissociate ourselves from these regimes of truth. If I read Foucault correctly the path to freedom requires us to detach ourselves from the regimes of truth associated with the human sciences, because these have become manipulative, if not dominating and enslaving. These power relations cause us to become subjects, that is, individuals with a certain identity and who, as subjects, can be subjected?

Foucault was fascinated by the desire in modern culture to tell the truth about one's self, saying often, "there has been a very strong incitement to speak of sexuality." Part of the cause of this incitement, he believed, was the negative power effects of various sexual prohibitions. If power is conceived as merely repressive, he argued, then to talk about sexuality would necessarily be a liberation. At the times in the nineteenth century when there were sexual prohibitions there was also a burgeoning discourse on sexuality caused, in part, by the need to create a scientific structure to explain sex and to train scientists. This structure and discourse meant that eventually the subject could no longer understand what was being said and, therefore, could no longer be the arbiter of the deepest truths. This role fell to the authority, the scientist, not only to incite the truth and to interpret these deep truths, but also to reconstruct the subject's experience of sexuality and discourse, thereby constituting and controlling the subject. In knowing one's true self one has not only to tell the truth in the confession but also to speak the truth in the concepts of the discourse on sexuality. In speaking this truth, in knowing one's true self one constructs the experience of sex and reconstructs one's self by adopting new descriptions and new practices. The performatory aspect of saying, makes it so (Austin, 1953; Searle, 1969). The therapy comes about from telling the truth, which can itself involve vicarious pleasurable and liberating effects; from thereby knowing one's self through speaking the truth and liberating one's self from the repressive aspects by the acts of speaking and reconstructing the self.

In speaking the truth one does not merely describe oneself but one makes it so because of the performatory function of language. Just as the judge makes the accused person guilty by a declarative performance of guilt, so, also, in speaking about ourselves in the new and refined concepts of the social sciences, do we construct ourselves, our very identities, in those acts of speech. Through the performatory function of speech we begin to construct ourselves (Foucault acknowledged similarities here with Searle's work on speech acts).

Foucault laments the shift in emphasis from "care of one's self" to "know thyself," because the self is now to be known through the human sciences. To care for one's self in the twentieth century has come to mean to fit oneself out (retail) with a set of truths that, by being learned, memorized, and progressively put into practice, constitute a subject with a certain mode of being and a certain visible manner of acting. Foucault believes that this modern self is not free because, insofar as it is the outcome of the human sciences, political control and not freedom has been the aim.

The constitution of identities, or subjects, is for Foucault a highly politicized set of acts. In *The History of Sexuality* (Vol. 1) he shows how we in part aid and abet these processes by constructing ourselves through the technologies of the self. In the latter work he introduced the term "bio-power" to show how the construction of the self through the concept of sexuality permitted the body to act as a point or locus of application for both the control of the individual and the control of populations.

If in the earlier work Foucault sounds fatalistic and deterministic, so that there is no room for meaningful human action directed toward the attainment of freedom, in his later work he corrects this almost nihilistic position to affirm the possibilities of freedom through resistance. He rejects the possibly deterministic framework in which his earlier accounts of power/knowledge had been couched. Instead, power can only exist where there is a possibility of resistance and, thereby, the attainment of freedom (Foucault, 1983b). Power is no longer an omnipresent and overarching presence but, rather, an open and strategic game. This freedom is not to be obtained because we are rationally autonomous beings. On the contrary, it is this very notion of being free through being rationally autonomous that has permitted us to become subjects through the effects of power/knowledge. Indeed, it is in part the post-Kantian notion of rational autonomy that has permitted us to become subjects according to Foucault. Insofar as the notion of the rationally autonomous person drives much of Western liberal education, this, too, is part of what he referred to as the post-Kantian slumbers (Foucault, 1984b).

Within the last decade a particular version of the autonomous person has emerged in neoliberal social and educational literature. This is the notion of the autonomous chooser. However, this does not involve the Foucauldean notion of bio-power, introduced above, because bio-power was directed at and through the body at the health and sexuality of the individual and through that at populations. With the constitution of the autonomous chooser a new form of power, what I call busno-power (Marshall, 1995), is directed at the subjectivity of the person not through the body but through the mind, through forms of educational practice and pedagogy that shape through choices in education the subjectivities of autonomous choosers. Education, embedded in the frameworks of busno-power and busnocratic rationality, is the first step in the individualizing and totalizing functions of busno-power (compare Illich's [1973] arguments that schools are the first step in the schooling mentality).

Busno-power is directed at constituting autonomous choosers for, in producing and reproducing the form of human nature — autonomous choosers — this busno-power also impinges upon the population as a whole, as individual consumer activity improves both society and the economy. Busno-power is directed at not only individuals, to turn them into autonomous choosers and consumers, but also the population as a whole, by a total immersion in the enterprise culture of the society, the economy, and the new rationality of state. In the exercise of busno-power there can be seen a merging of the economy, the society, and the activity of government.

Busno-power trades on the traditional notion of the autonomous person, but it takes a turn away with the constitution of the autonomous chooser. The normal notions of the personal autonomy needed to make choices in accordance with rational evaluations of such things as needs and interests, presuppose that such choices are the student's (or chooser's) own, that they are independent, and that needs and interests have not been manipulated or imposed in some way upon the chooser. It is not this normal notion of personal autonomy that underlies the educational reform literature but that of another that is covertly masked — the autonomous chooser.

The autonomous chooser of neoliberal theory might seem to be a logical outcome of the traditional liberal position. This is not so. Traditional liberal philosophy of education is well aware that talk of such things as needs and interests is ambiguous between what the child sees as its needs and interests, and what adults and educators see as the real needs and interests of the child. Needs and interests, after such fundamental notions as food and warmth, can reflect value positions, and while there is a sense in which we cannot avoid introducing our children to value positions in just living our everyday lives, these value positions are problematic. The busnocratic notion of the autonomous chooser collapses such a distinction and what the chooser chooses is the reality.

What is perceived as being worthwhile in education and as quality education are being imposed from outside the traditional educational institutions by consumers, especially the world of business. If the range of choices is determined by external, business-based definitions of quality, then the providers of education will become technicians imbued with these values, providing these quality offerings from which the autonomous chooser will choose.

The needs and interests of autonomous choosers are being shaped through ideologies, discourses, and multimedia presentations from governmental agencies that emphasize the need for skills. There is a continual need during a working lifetime to be reskilled and economic motivation for getting a quality education. The notion of autonomy becomes rather thin and that of choice somewhat thinner.

There is a certain form of human nature that seems to be encapsulated in the notion of the autonomous chooser. It is not the *homo economicus* of traditional liberal economic theory but an individual that does not merely act as an autonomous chooser, but acts because of its very nature. Busnocratic rationality legitimates, and busno-power actively encourages and promotes, this form of human being.

There is a fundamental human faculty of choice that is part of human nature and that humans need to exercise to be proper human beings. To put it another way, the autonomous chooser is not endowed with a will to truth or a will to power but a will to choose (Ford, 1995). The autonomy of the autonomous chooser is different from the autonomy of traditional liberal theory that could or could not be exercised. Now, it seems, choice cannot be resisted. It is not just that human beings are autonomous, or that their autonomy can be developed, or that it is a duty to exercise autonomy. Instead there seems to be a constituent faculty of choice that is necessarily continuously exercised on commodities, and that sweeps aside or overrides the traditional categories and frameworks of human nature and the human sciences.

Furthermore the autonomous chooser is seen as perpetually responsive to the environment. The autonomous chooser is capable of infinite manipulation by the structuring of the environment. The environment can structure the choices of the individual. Hence economic intervention in the society can manipulate the individual, thereby transgressing the fundamental rights of nonviolation of the individual and the individual's self-formulated purposes and projects of earlier liberal thought, encapsulated in the liberal view of personal autonomy as an aim of education.

The logical implication is that one's life becomes an enterprise — the enterprise of the autonomous chooser. However, it is not the self of classical liberal theory, in which the right to formulate one's own purposes and projects was seen as inviolate.

IMPLICATIONS FOR EDUCATION

How are we to dissociate ourselves from these regimes of truth? Do not expect to be given an answer or a theory by Foucault, as on his own terms that would be to commit the great indignity of speaking for others (Foucault, 1972). At another point he says use them as bombs! If we are not to do that literally then how are we to use his books, papers, interviews, and asides?

If we are not mere technicians or sociologists but instead philosophers, then we must be thrown back philosophically upon Foucault's view of philosophy as work upon the self. Even so, the metaphor of thrown back is inappropriate, for we must embrace this view of work upon the self, hold onto it, and use it for our own selves. In this sense philosophy becomes an educational enterprise. How are to proceed in this enterprise?

Foucault is adamant that education must be nonmanipulative and must permit us to change at will. To do that we must be able to dissociate ourselves from the regimes of truth that have classified, objectified, normalized, and constituted our identity as beings of a particular kind. The regimes of truth that contribute to and provoke these processes are, according to Foucault, the human sciences, or they derive from the human sciences. The way to dissociate ourselves from the tyranny of psychology, for example, is to show that its truths are not necessary, and the treatments associated with them avoidable, by undertaking some form of genealogical analysis.

Genealogy can be considered as a certain approach to history — an approach that is a history of the present. Foucault uses historical data in ways that make some historians shudder (for example, Stone, Megill), although not leading French historians such as Fernand Braudel, Phillipe Ariès, Georges Dumezil, and Paul Veyne. Given the present splintering of history and historical methodology, it is better to see Foucault as writing a different kind of history.

History has been conceived as narrative writing within the humanities, concerned with great events, great people, and the emergence of our constitutions and institutions. The emergence of social history has introduced not just a different set of topics such as the family, women, and classes, but also it has brought with it, from other social science disciplines, a bewildering number of social science methodologies that were used by historians. If philosophers had disputed historical methodology at the meta-level, this was a new conflict at the level of doing history.

Criticisms have been that Foucault's work is antihistorical (for example, Megill, 1985). These can be summarized as follows:

1. There is no complete history of the past, and no development or emergence of the present from earlier existing state of affairs. Instead, events disparate in time or involving procedures that are dramatically different, are juxtaposed.
2. Historical data from widely different sources are suddenly inserted into the history, but there is no apparent theory of selection as one moves from hospital to madhouse to schoolhouse and back again.
3. There are no notions of causality. Explanations of a why form are absent.
4. In *Discipline and Punish* (Foucault, 1979a) we are presented with a bewildering amount of data drawn from a number of widely differing sources. Details of the construction of hospitals, schools, military barracks, and the prison are run together when, at first sight, these appear to be different kinds of institutions constructed for different needs. Foucault shows through his notion of power/knowledge that there are relationships between these constructions.
5. Foucault gives us no teleological unfolding of reason. Indeed he argues convincingly that what appears as irrational to us in the twentieth century in the practice of torture is quite rational given certain assumptions of the time about guilt (here Charles Taylor [1986] says that he finds Foucault quite convincing). There is no Enlightenment future for mankind, according to Foucault, because reason is embedded in sociohistorical conditions and there is no rational unfolding of history in any developmental or improving sense. Neither reason nor history offers us liberation or indeed a return to the abyss (if his earlier writings up to *Discipline and Punish* are pessimistic his later writings are much more optimistic).

6. Foucault is not writing a history of ideas. The title of the chair he held at the College de France was "History of Systems of Thought." This title had been deliberately selected by Foucault to distinguish his methodology from the history of ideas. History of ideas tends to approach objects (as identified by concepts) as if there is a developmental emergence of these ideas in a more or less continuous and rational fashion. Against this view Foucault shows that the concept of punishment, among many examples that he uses, cannot be traced in any such manner. Instead there are ruptures and discontinuities that make the notion of punishment as a continuous object through time problematic and, hence, the physical and temporal juxtaposition in *Discipline and Punish* of disciplinary punishment and juridico-legal punishment.

Mark Poster, a historian generally sympathetic to Foucault, summarizes these problems well:

The flow of Foucault's texts, the way one thing is put after another, disturbs the expectations of the reader familiar with social history. There appear to be huge gaps in the narrative, silences that scream at the reader. Topics are annoyingly placed out of the normal order, disrupting one's sense of logical sequence. Levels of analysis are mixed together in irritating confusion: the difference between ideas and behaviour goes unrecognised and is violated. Simple questions of causality are ignored or appear in reverse order. The writing is thick and metaphoric and the point of view of the narrative line is often lost. The object of investigation is never quite clarified and appears to be neither individuals, nor groups, nor institutions. What is worse, things seem to shift in the course of the writing; at the beginning one issue is at stake, by the end we seem to be reading about something else. Worst of all, the author's attitude toward the topic of study never emerges clearly. He seems to take a perverse pleasure in shifting his stance, or simply in adopting provocatively an unorthodox attitude toward a topic. Finally, while much research has contributed to Foucault's studies, a great deal of material has not been looked at. The evidential basis of the texts is odd and incomplete. No wonder historians are sceptical about the value of his efforts. (1984: 72)

Poster sees Foucault as a philosopher of discontinuity, attempting to show how the past was strange and threatening and urging us to distance ourselves from the cozy relationships of continuity with the past. According to Poster his concern is not to support the present by tracing lines of inevitability from the past but to cut the past off, to show that it is foreign, and that it cannot be domesticated and put to use in the glory of the present. Foucault's concern, according to Poster, is that historical writing, whatever ideological position one is coming from, tends to erase differences and justify the present. History, Foucault reminds us, is a creation or a fiction and historians should not claim to have truths about the past that they represent in writing.

Foucault rejected this strong claim. Although acknowledging gaps or ruptures he disputed that his historical writing was founded upon discontinuity (Foucault, 1977: 111–113). What he did not deny was that genealogy was associated with work on the self:

If one is interested in doing historical work that has political meaning, utility and effectiveness, then this is possible only if one has some form of involvement with the struggles taking part in the area in question. I tried first to do a genealogy of psychiatry because I had a certain amount of practical experience in psychiatric hospitals and was aware of the combats, the lines of force, tensions and points of collision which existed there. My historical work was undertaken only as a function of those conflicts. (Foucault 1976: 64)

What cannot be attempted here is a full exposition of what is involved in genealogy, but for a discussion of how it works in practice and how the structure of *Discipline and Punish* reflects the notion of genealogy, see Marshall (1990, 1996).

If I am right that freedom is to be obtained through a personal philosophical and educational enterprise, Foucault has little in practice to say to curriculum planners or to pedagogy, particularly in pre-tertiary education. In his own practices he attempted to present his ideas and teaching as a model, which students could accept or reject. However, when we look at his pedagogical practices an interesting and contradictory picture emerges: that of a classical academic, concerned about the disciplines, truth, and teaching. In spite of his critiques of disciplinary blocks, some disparaging remarks about his own earlier education, and remarks on the need for reforms in education, his own practices were quite traditional. In commenting on Foucault's pedagogy, Miller quotes Foucault: "When I lecture dogmatically I tell myself: I am paid to bring to my students a certain form and content of knowledge; I must fashion my lecture or my course a little as one might make a shoe, no more and no less. I design an object. I try to make it as well as possible. I make a lot of trouble for myself (not always, perhaps, but often). I bring the object to the desk. I show it and then I leave it up to the audience to do with it what they want" (1993: 181). According to Miller, Foucault saw students as apprentices and himself as the master craftsman, even in those difficult times. Although he offered himself as an example he never saw himself as a guru with disciples. His teaching was compatible with his view of his works, of theory, and the general role of intellectuals in society. (For a detailed discussion of Foucault on education, see Marshall [1996].)

CONCLUSIONS

Foucault strenuously resisted labels such as structuralist, modern, or postmodern. What dissociating oneself from the terrorism of regimes of truth must imply is a multiplicity of truths, of ways of seeing and doing, and of discourses. The search for grand totalizing theory, or any search within subsets of the human sciences for overarching encompassing theories is, for Foucault, fundamentally mistaken in promoting freedom. Foucault, like Wittgenstein, is deeply suspicious of the human sciences and, like Heidegger, Nietzsche, and Wittgenstein, deeply suspicious of the messages of emancipation inherent in the Enlightenment message. The notion of emancipation through some form of empowering education, underlain by some version of critical theory is, for Foucault, anathema. As he once said: "If an honest man, today, has the impression of a barbarous culture this impression is due to a single fact: our system of education dates from the nineteenth century and there still reigns there the most insipid psychology, the most antiquated humanism... this is the fault of the organisation of education" (1966: 15).

It was not for Foucault a question of the reordering of education, its reconstruction, and attacks upon cultural, gender, or ethnic capital but, ultimately, a philosophical education that permitted the individual to change at will. This required a knowledge and understanding of the self that divorced itself from, rejected, and transgressed the accounts of human being given by the human sciences. The circle returns then through Bataille, Heidegger, Nietzsche, and Foucault's reading of Kant, to Kant.

REFERENCES

Ayer, A. J. (1935). *Language, truth and logic*. London: Gollancz.
Austin, J. L. (1953). *How to do things with words*. London: Oxford University Press.
Ball, S. (Ed.). (1990). *Foucault and education: Disciplines and knowledge*. London: Routledge.
Burchell, G., Gordon, C., & Miller, P. (Eds.). (1991). *The Foucault effect: Studies in governmentality*. Chicago, IL: University of Chicago Press.
Eribon, D. (1991). *Michel Foucault*. Cambridge, MA: Harvard University Press.
Ford, M. (1995). Willed to choose: Educational reform and busnopower. In A. Neiman (Ed.), *Philosophy of education 1995, Proceedings of the Philosophy of Education Society*. Urbana-Champaign, IL: Philosophy of Education Society.
Foucault, M. (1986). *The history of sexuality*. Vol. 3. *The care of self*, trans. R. Hurley. New York: Pantheon
Foucault, M. (1985). *The history of sexuality*. Vol. 2. *The uses of pleasure*, trans. R. Hurley. New York: Pantheon.
Foucault, M. (1984a). Polemics, politics and problematisation. In P. Rabinow (Ed.), *The Foucault reader* (pp. 381–393). New York: Southern.
Foucault, M. (1984b). What is enlightenment? In P. Rabinow (Ed.), *The Foucault reader* (pp. 32–50). New York: Pantheon.
Foucault, M. (1983a). The minimalist self. In L. J. Kritzman (Ed.), *Politics, philosophy, culture: Interviews and other writings, 1977–1984* (pp. 3–18). London: Routledge.

Foucault, M. (1983b). Afterword: The subject and power. In H. L. Dreyfus, and P. Rabinow (Eds.), *Michel Foucault: Beyond structuralism and hermeneutics* (pp. 208–226). Chicago, IL: University of Chicago Press.
Foucault, M. (1982). Truth, power, self. In L. H. Martin, H. Gutman, and P. H. Hutton (Eds.), *Technologies of the self: A seminar with Michel Foucault* (pp. 9–15). London: Tavistock
Foucault, M. (1979a). *Discipline and punish: The birth of the prison*. New York: Vintage Press.
Foucault, M. (1979b). On governmentality. *Ideology and Consciousness, 6,* 5–26.
Foucault, M. (1978a, October 8). A quoi revent les Iraniens. *Le Nouvel Observateur, 726,* 48–49.
Foucault, M. (1978b). *The history of sexuality*. Vol. 1. *An introduction*, trans. R. Hurley. New York: Pantheon.
Foucault, M. (1977). Truth and power. In C. Gordon (Ed.), *Power/knowledge: Selected interviews and other writings* (pp. 109–133). New York: Pantheon.
Foucault, M. (1976). Questions on geography. In C. Gordon (Ed.), *Power/knowledge: Selected interviews and other writings* (pp. 63–77). New York: Pantheon.
Foucault, M. (1975). On literature. In S. Lotvinger (Ed.) and J. Johnson (Trans.), *Foucault Live: Interviews 1966–1984*. New York: Semiotext(e).
Foucault, M. (1974). Michel Foucault: An interview. *Impulse,* pp. 50–55.
Foucault, M. (1973, May 26). L'intellectual sert a ressembler les idees, mais. . . . son savoir est partial par rapport au savoir ouvrier. *Libération, 16,* 2–3.
Foucault, M. (1972). Intellectuals and power. In D. Bouchard (Ed.), *Language, counter-memory, practice*. Ithaca, NY: Cornell University Press.
Foucault, M. (1970). *The order of things: An archaeology of the human sciences*, trans. A. M. Sheridan-Smith. London: Tavistock.
Foucault, M. (1968, March 1–15). Foucault répond à Sartre. *La Quinzaine Littéraire, 46,* 20–22.
Foucault, M. (1966, May 16). Entretien. *La Quinzaine Littéraire, 5,* 14–15.
Foucault, M. (1961). *Folie et Déraison: la histoire de la folie à l'àge classique*. Paris: Plon.
Grene, M. (1957). *Heidegger*. London: Bowes and Bowes.
Gutting, G. (1989). *Michel Foucault's archaeology of scientific reason*. Cambridge: Cambridge University Press.
Habermas, J. (1981, Winter). Modernity versus postmodernity. *New German Critique, 22,* 3–14.
Hacking, I. (1981). The archaeology of Michel Foucault. *New York Review of Books,* May 14, 32–37.
Heidegger, M. (1962). *Being and time*, trans. J. Macquarie. London: SCM Press.
Heidegger, M. (1949). *Letter on humanism*. Frankfurt am Main: Klosterman.
Illich, I. (1973). *Deschooling society*. Harmondsworth: Penguin.
Le canard et le renard ou la vie d'un philosophie. (1984). *Libération,* July 1, 16–19. [An obituary for Foucault]
Macey, D. (1993). *The lives of Michel Foucault*. London: Hutchinson.
Marshall, J. D. (1996). *Michel Foucault: Personal autonomy and education*. Dordrecht: Kluwer.
Marshall, J. D. (1995). Foucault and neo-liberalism: Biopower and busnopower. In A. Neiman (Ed.), *Philosophy of education 1995, Proceedings of the Philosophy of Education Society*. Urbana-Champaign, IL: Philosophy of Education Society.

Marshall, J. D. (1990). Foucault and educational research. In S. Ball (Ed.), *Foucault and education: Discipline and knowledge* (pp. 11–28). London: Routledge.

Megill, A. (1985). *Prophets of extremity: Nietzsche, Heidegger, Foucault, Derrida.* Berkeley: University of California Press.

Miller, J. (1993). *The passion of Michel Foucault.* New York: Simon & Schuster.

Nozick, R. (1974). *Anarchy, state, utopia.* Cambridge, MA: Harvard University Press.

Piel, J. (1986, August–September). Foucault à Uppsala. *Critique,* pp. 471–472.

Poster, M. (1984). *Foucault, Marxism and history: Mode of production versus mode of information.* Cambridge, MA: Polity Press.

Poster, M. (1975). *Existential Marxism in post-war France: From Sartre to Althusser.* Princeton, NJ: Princeton University Press.

Searle, J. (1969). *Speech acts: An essay in the philosophy of language.* London: Cambridge University Press.

Strike, K. (1982). *Educational policy and the just society.* Urbana: University of Illinois Press.

Taylor, C. W. (1986). Foucault on freedom and truth. In D. C. Hoy (Ed.), *Foucault: A critical reader* (pp. 69–102). Oxford: Blackwell.

Walkerdine, V. (1984). Developmental psychology and the child centered pedagogy. In J. Henriques, J. Holloway, C. Urwin, C. Venn, and V. Walkerdine. (Eds.), *Changing the subject* (pp. 157–174). London: Methuen.

4

Julia Kristeva: Intertextuality and Education
Lucy Holmes

In educational analysis issues of production and the associated problem of effecting social change have become part of the theoretical discourse. Recent theoretical work considering these issues criticizes the institution of education for founding its practices upon a concept of the individual as the "fount of all knowledge, signification and moral action."[1] These critics suggest that one way of thinking beyond that educational conception is to focus on production, "because education is concerned with understanding the principal socialising means in our society, and in particular, that of schooling. The school, along with the family as an institution, constructs us as 'individuals' through a network of educational practices."[2]

These are concerns similar to those addressed in Kristeva's essay on Barthes and his scientific theory of literature, "How Does One Speak to Literature?" which is a tribute to Barthes's contribution to the knowledge of how literature works and which has consequently enabled contemporary literary studies to focus "on the process of the meaning within language and ideology."[3] In this essay, Kristeva proposes that Barthes's knowledge of literary practice reveals the "missing link in the socio-communicative or subjective-transcendental fabric of the so-called human sciences."[4] The question of meaning, how it works, is the missing link in social science that had, as Kristeva perceived it in the 1960s, stumbled on how to connect the individual with structure. Educational theory that is concerned with the missing link has begun to analyze how the discourse[5] of educational philosophy makes the assumption that the subject is transcendental or exists outside and prior to the institution, rather than being constructed in and by the institution.

For Kristeva the missing link is literary or textual production as a practical knowledge of how the production of meaning plays a part in the constitution of a subject and in ideological traditions. Language is the link between a localized, specific subjectivity and a social, ideological practice; language, therefore, provides the condition for "objective understanding."[6] Recently educational sociology has been criticized for being "theoretically under-developed . . . [in] the area of the processes of identity-production and socialisation," and it has been proposed that "theories developed to deal with the production of meaning are of use" in the study of educational structures of production, distribution, and consumption.[7] Kristeva's theories, relevant as they are to the new impetus in educational analysis, can provide useful insights for expanding this field of meaning production and how it translates into subjective and social relations.

LIFE AND WORK: THE MATERIAL IN THEORY

A clear development in Kristeva's work has been her increasing involvement with psychoanalysis, first as a student with close intellectual and personal ties with Barthes and Lacan, next as a theorist who attributes the twentieth century with two great thinkers, Freud and Marx, and now as a practicing psychoanalyst since 1979. In an interview in 1990, Kristeva explains the stylistic development of her work in relation to her growing involvement with psychoanalysis:

We must make a distinction which is connected to my personal history and then to the nature of the theoretical discourse. I think there is a discourse of knowledge in the Occident which mobilises or disciplines stylistic experimentation. When one wishes to appropriate this discourse of knowledge, one imposes a certain asceticism on oneself at the level of style. From this perspective, when I began work, it seemed very important to me, as a person and as a woman, to show that I could take hold of that discourse. . . . This philosophical and theoretical discourse has become increasingly a very stylised, very fictional discourse. But I believe there is a defiance in it, a sort of critique with respect to certain restrictions on the discourse of knowledge and its pretensions to neutrality. As for myself, my pathway through psychoanalysis has perhaps reconciled me with my memory and my body and this has had a considerable importance for my change in style.[8]

The difference between Kristeva's earlier theoretical texts, such as the essays in *Desire in Language* or her doctoral thesis *Revolution in Poetic Language*, and the later texts, like *Powers of Horror* and *Tales of Love*, is a difference closely connected to her personal history. It seems that her early work as theoretical discourse was both an appropriation and an imposition: the theory was something outside of herself. As a reading of her texts, this does describe the emphasis in the earlier writings on the abstract, scientific, and mathematical, although the concepts are often passionately asserted. Kristeva characterizes her later work as a defiance of limitation and a reconciliation with her memory and body. In one obvious way her later works do exhibit this by the combination in the text of autobiography and theory. Because Kristeva maintains that there is a theoretical distinction in her work that is connected to her personal history, any analysis of the efficacy of her work needs to take account of that connection.

Until the publication of her first novel *The Samurai* in 1992 (1990 in France),[9] the main sources for Kristeva's defiance of neutrality have been in her theoretical writings from 1974. For example, the two books *About Chinese Women* and *Strangers to Ourselves* contain passages in which Kristeva writes about her own experiences as a foreigner, and in the essay "The Novel as Polylogue" Kristeva writes of the anguish of exile from her homeland and its language.[10] The essay "Stabat Mater" is partly an autobiographical text, in which Kristeva writes about her pregnancy and the birth of her son in 1976, and in the first chapter of the book *Tales of Love* Kristeva describes the emotion of love in a poetical and personal style.[11] Kristeva's novel *The Samurai* is clearly autobiographical while also being fictional, or, as she explains in an interview about the novel, "in fiction the actual facts may be distorted, but the intensity of subjective truth is restored."[12] The precedent to this autobiographical novel is an essay called "My Memory's Hyperbole,"[13] an essay Kristeva was asked to write on her "intellectual generation that would also record the individual experience of that generation."[14] Apart from these writings, Kristeva has also been candid about her personal history in an interview conducted just after the publication in France of her novel, *The Samurai*, in which she speaks about her family, childhood, and schooling in Bulgaria.[15]

In Kristeva's autobiographical writings, her intellectual career begins in 1965, when at the age of 25 she arrives in Paris from Bulgaria with a Franco-Bulgarian scholarship.[16] Kristeva was educated in Bulgaria as a linguist. She is fluent in Russian, which enabled her and a compatriot Tzvetan Todorov to introduce the work of the Russian formalists and Mikhail Bakhtin to the French intellectuals.[17] In Paris at the *École Pratique des Hautes Études* she first met Roland Barthes and Lucien Goldmann.[18] The latter directed her thesis, *Revolution in Poetic Language*, which was submitted in 1973 for the *doctorate d'etat* in Paris, and the former was the examiner.[19] In 1966 Kristeva joined the *Tel Quel* editorial board, an avant-garde review with political, artistic, and intellectual alliances that had, since 1964, included writers such as Derrida, Lacan, Barthes, Foucault, and Benveniste.[20] From 1966 on Kristeva was, like these writers, part of both the academic institution and the literary avant-garde.

Marxism and structuralism pervaded the intellectual climate in France at that time and the *Tel Quel* group was a major influence in this scene.[21] The uprisings in Paris in May 1968 by students and workers showed that the *Tel Quel* group did not promote a unified perspective of structuralism, nor were they in complete agreement with the French Communist Party.[22] Rather than being a force within the student rebellion, the group was aware of, as Kristeva says, "the limitations of structuralism."[23] The brilliance of Lacan's lectures at that time had again brought psychoanalysis into the circles of the avant-garde and instigated an inquiry into the subject of language, which it had been argued was missing in the social-based theories of structuralism and Marxism.[24] In her memoir, Kristeva explains that what was to be called poststructuralism was not antistructuralism but was instead a platform from which to consider notions largely indebted to Bakhtin and Freud.

For us structuralism ... was already accepted knowledge. To simplify, this meant that we should no longer lose sight of the real constraints, "material," as we used to say, of what had previously and trivially been viewed as "form." ... From the outset, however, our task was to take this acquired knowledge and immediately do something else ... it was essential to "dynamise" the structure by taking into consideration the speaking subject and its unconscious experience on the one hand, and on the other, the pressures of other social structures.... My conception of dialogism, of ambivalence, or what I call "intertextuality" — notions heavily indebted to Bakhtin and Freud — were to become gadgets that the American university is now in the process of discovering.[25]

I will return to the notions of dialogism and intertextuality later, but for my present purposes, Kristeva's account here of her relationship with structuralism indicates that this theoretical discourse was one that she had both appropriated and experimented with.

In the same year as the publication in France of her doctoral thesis, Kristeva and members of the *Tel Quel* group, now disillusioned with the French Communist Party for its choice of parliamentary politics instead of more unorthodox methods,[26] traveled to China to promote cultural research but also hoping to find in Maoism the antidote to partisan politics.[27] On this journey the group, which included Kristeva's husband, Philippe Sollers, whom she had married in 1967, realized that Maoism did not offer anything better than the already much-criticized Soviet model, and Kristeva returned to France no longer viewing politics as the only solution to social change.[28] In 1974 she began training as a psychoanalyst at one of the four major French psychoanalytic institutions of the time, the *Société psychanalytique de Paris*,[29] and in 1979 she started her own psychoanalytic practice.[30]

Since 1969 Kristeva has held an academic position at the University of Paris-VII in the Department of Texts and Documents, which was founded by Barthes. In 1974, at the age of 33, she obtained a professorship in the department.[31] Her work now involves, apart from her psychoanalytic practice and her writing, developing new research programs that function as interdisciplinary courses for doctors or teachers interested in psychopathology, psychiatry, and semiology.[32]

It is characteristic of Kristeva to employ a variety of writing styles in conjunction with the changes in her own theoretical investigations and in relation to the intellectual context in which her work has developed. In her words, these developments have moved from the imposition of theoretical discourse (one of which was structuralism) to a reconciliation involving her personal history and the specific interface of theory and practice in psychoanalysis. The development that she provides exists alongside work by other writers who have represented Kristeva's theories in relation to her personal history. A brief review of these texts adds to Kristeva's own interpretation of the connection between her personal history and theoretical discourse.

Possibly the most extensive works on Kristeva's personal and intellectual history are those by Elizabeth Roudinesco, *Jacques Lacan & Co: A History of Psychoanalysis in France 1925–1985* (1990), and Niilo Kauppi, *The Making of an Avant-Garde: Tel Quel* (1994). In comparison to scholarly writings that are more theoretically aligned, such as Kelly Oliver's excellent *Reading Kristeva: Unraveling the Double-bind* (1993), and John Lechte's *Julia Kristeva* (1990), whose book I will discuss soon. Roudinesco's and Kauppi's books are more historical than theoretical. The emphasis in these historical accounts is with the impact Kristeva had upon the French intellectual culture rather than on her theoretical innovations. By negation, the historical emphasis of these books exemplifies the very important need to recognize the developmental connections between personal history and theoretical discourse.

Roudinesco's book represents Kristeva's personal history as intrinsically linked to *Tel Quel* and the "intellectual terrorism" of Sollers, who was a founding member of the review.[33] For Roudinesco, *Tel Quel* was a mere "parody of surrealism"[34] because it failed to be the avant-garde journal it proposed to be at its inception in 1964 and similarly "never resulted in a literary or poetic creation."[35] Roudinesco's eclipse of Kristeva by the *Tel Quel* program is manifested in Roudinesco's interpretation of Kristeva's professional position: "For several years, it [*Tel Quel*] would thus *impose* a particular reading of structuralism, drawing along in its wake not only the theorists it had solicited but a number of university academics in search of a new "scientificity" in their approach to texts. After May, a university department in the sciences of texts and documents would be founded, in which Julia Kristeva would teach"[36] (emphasis added).

In Roudinesco's historical account, Kristeva's academic position is the culmination of the *Tel Quel* imposition of a certain reading of structuralism upon the French intellectual and academic scene. For Kristeva the theoretical discourse of structuralism that she encountered in France was a form of imposition, which she then appropriated and experimented with in order to dynamize structuralism. Roudinesco's book is concerned mainly with Lacan, although she does provide a great deal of information on many other psychoanalysts and theorists connected to Lacan as both his allies and critics. Yet Roudinesco's history of psychoanalysis in France is concerned with the history of Kristeva only until the theorist enters psychoanalytic training in 1974. Kristeva's many publications from the late 1970s to the mid-1980s, the period of Roudinesco's study, are where the theorist utilizes aspects of Lacanian theory (for example, the Imaginary, Symbolic, and Real) and revises them also (for example, the Imaginary becomes the semiotic *chora*). In representing Kristeva as the successful culmination of the *Tel Quel* program, Roudinesco is able to summarize Kristeva's post–*Tel Quel* work as "a return to official psychoanalysis,"[37] thus obscuring the importance of Kristeva's work in relation to Lacanian psychoanalysis, which is the subject of Roudinesco's book.

The historical subject of Kauppi's book is the review *Tel Quel* and the group of intellectuals and artists who contributed to it from 1960 to the early 1980s. Kauppi uses the same word as Roudinesco to describe the way that *Tel Quel*'s "intellectual practices were inseparable from power practices, struggles for the *imposition* of new criteria, and new means for symbolic domination"[38] (emphasis added). Kauppi further characterizes the discourse of the *Tel Quel* group as one where "obscurity and vagueness became the preferred means of domination."[39] For Kauppi, it is the theory of semanalysis that Kristeva invented by combining semiology and psychoanalysis that is a prime example of the *Tel Quel* discourse.[40]

This new literary science is discussed by Kauppi at some length: its proposed functions and aims and its criticisms by contemporary linguists. The efficacy for an intellectual endeavor of semanalysis is not discussed or referred to; instead Kristeva is represented as detaching herself "from the scientism of the production of the 1960s, as well as from *Tel Quel*."[41] This detachment by Kristeva from her earlier theories is defined in terms of the English translations of her work, which Kauppi presents as caused by the interpretive emphasis Anglophone readers have placed on her writing. In other words, unlike Roudinesco, Kauppi shows an awareness of the theoretical development in Kristeva's later, more psychoanalytical works, yet here, in Kauppi's book, this change is determined by the reception of the theories rather than any inherent difference in Kristeva's work over the years between 1965 and the 1980s. In this case, the outside world (the international readership) imposes a meaning on Kristeva's theories that enables her to be distinguished from the intellectual domination of

Tel Quel. Kauppi's representation of Kristeva's work is a curious anamorphosis of Kristeva's portrayal, in which her alliance with *Tel Quel* and its contributors enabled her to question "certain restrictions on the discourse of knowledge and its pretensions to neutrality."[42]

Kristeva's efforts to question the neutrality of theoretical discourse are precisely the reason she is so easily misunderstood by those who do not fully account for the intellectual and cultural context in which she works. This is the proposal of John Lechte, whose book *Julia Kristeva* begins by contextualizing the theorist not only through sociohistorical elements but also in regard to the philosophical background of French intellectual culture. Lechte explains the influence of Hegel, Marx, and phenomenology upon French structuralism, and specifies Kristeva's work as: "strongly marked by the influence of phenomenology and its theory of the subject. Rather than rid thought of the distinction between subject and object, Kristeva's Freudian approach leads to an investigation of the preconditions for the constitution of the subject-object division."[43]

In Lechte's assessment, the development in Kristeva's work is strongly grounded in the structuralist endeavor (Kristeva's appropriated theoretical discourse) in which the distinction between subject and object is emphasized through its study of language as determined by social difference.[44] To put it another way, language does not have some natural link with reality, the objective world, but rather it works in relation to the external world in a particular way so as to support a certain form of society. Structuralism then conceives of the subject as both constituted by language and, as a social being, contributive to the mediation of reality by language. This brief summary of structuralism could be analogous to the position Kristeva sees herself in with regard to the theoretical discourse she appropriated: to take hold of the discourse, as a person and as a woman, in order to criticize its pretensions to neutrality. For Lechte, this is exactly what Kristeva has done by analyzing language at the level of community and performance;[45] she has given emphasis to the material in language, that which Lechte calls "its scandalous and semiotic aspect."[46]

At this stage biography and theory become both distinct and connected, or nondisjunctive, that is, the two terms "personal history" and "theoretical discourse," which are usually divided from one another, are held in position where each becomes relevant to the other. For Kristeva, nondisjunction is a negative function[47] because it operates as both separation (disjunction) and "symmetrical reunion"[48] (nondisjunction), culminating in ambivalence, "without affirming their [the two terms'] identity."[49] Ambivalence, as in the novelistic discourse, is opposed by ideology, which Kristeva describes as "the form of utterances compositionally completed."[50] It is this performative dimension that Lechte finds in Kristeva's writing and as such he claims that those who do not recognize this dimension, "fail to have a real encounter" with it and those who use it.[51]

The literary style of the novel was and still is one of Kristeva's main interests, and, as Lechte explains in his book, is the means for Kristeva's own textual criticism of the neutrality of theoretical discourse.[52] The ambivalence that her writing generates can be summed up in these two disparate interpretations of Kristeva's theoretical style, the first from Kauppi's book, the second from a chapter by Hans-Peter Mai on Kristeva's theory of intertextuality:

According to Adriaens, a Dutch linguist, Kristeva's approach was due to two methodological faults: "First, there is the confusion between objective, purely formal description and (subjective) interpretation...." Her formalisation plan, or logicomathematical descriptive methods ... was considered by Adriaens "a pseudo-scientific cover for a purely interpretative procedure.[53]

Questions as to the scientific status of such an approach [Kristeva's] are somewhat misleading. They seem inappropriate, first of all, if one considers that Kristeva is trying to demonstrate that a "pure science" is an impossible notion in the semiotic sphere because there is no privileged meta-level from which we can ask/answer universal questions. But Kristeva also subverts scientific conventions: In her writing she blithely appropriates scientific terminology from diverse disciplines for her own purposes.[54]

The debate here is about the logical and mathematical concepts that Kristeva utilizes when formulating her theory of the material, rather than the represented meaning, of the text. Lechte's title for his section dealing with the theoretical debate over interpretation versus objectivity, or in his terms between the empiricist view of language and that of writing as an experience of limits, is "The missed (Anglo-Franco) encounter."[55]

I have reached the point where it is useful to give an explanation of intertextuality and by doing so propose a link between one specific structuralist-poststructuralist theory and the context of education. I have decided to look at the context of education because it is from where I write this, as a teacher and a student, and that the pretext for my positions in education is theory. First I will explain intertextuality through the mutations it undergoes in Kristeva's writing. Second, I will ask what intertextuality is in terms of educational practices. What might be an intertextual dimension between a social science such as education and Kristeva's human science of semanalysis?

INTERTEXTUALITY AND ITS VICISSITUDES

In 1960 the academic institution in Paris, the *École Pratique de Hautes Études*, opened its sixth section to semiology by creating a department that combined sociology, anthropology, and semiology, called the *Centre* d'Études Transdisciplinaires, for which one of the directors was Roland Barthes.[56] In 1966, Kristeva attended Barthes's seminar at the center where she presented the theories of the Soviet Russian scholar Mikhaïl Bakhtin, whose work had not been known in France. The presentation, in which Kristeva first used the term "intertextuality," was later published in French in 1967 and in English in 1980 as "Word, Dialogue and Novel."[57] The setting was a research program on structuralist semiotics in a department of sociology, attended by sociologists, psychoanalysts, and philosophers. In a broader sense, the seminar was part of the incorporation into the French universities of new disciplines, such as the so-called human sciences of structural linguistics, semiotics, and psychoanalysis, including a greater emphasis on Marxist political science spanning from Hegel to Althusser.[58]

Kristeva's approach was to take elements from these theoretical discourses in order to study the relationship between the linguistic and the social, positing from that study that there is a formal similarity between language and society in terms of the law (official practices) and its transgression. Because the society, its institutions, and productions support individual identity as much as language does, it follows, according to Kristeva's proposal, that identity is attained, maintained, and transformed by and through the stability or mutations of language. Intertextuality is the first critical practice that Kristeva develops for her theoretical procedure. It is described and exemplified in a number of essays from "Word, Dialogue and Novel" to her doctoral thesis in 1974.[59]

The word "challenge" resonates in the introduction of "Word, Dialogue and Novel." The challenge is on a number of levels that Kristeva will deal with throughout the essay in order to ground the theory of intertextuality. In one immediate sense, intertextuality is a challenge to all those concerned with the new disciplinary areas in the human sciences, that is, how to account for the place where society loses something of itself to enable it to move forward. Kristeva takes this idea of "negation as affirmation" from Bakhtin's notion of dialogism, which is in turn influenced by Hegel's philosophy in which a separating moment or junction precedes a transformation.[60]

The challenge here is to the structuralist division between synchronic structures or relations and diachronic linear history. The object of inquiry in this essay is poetic language to which the traditional approach has been diachronic, as in the study of literature through historical contextualization. Structuralism emphasizes the system or structure (of a language or a culture), and although the diachronic sequence is always present in structuralist studies such as those by de Saussure and Lévi-Strauss, it appears as an abstraction, external to the subject of language.

The human sciences have privileged scientific aims, which are logical and thus value communication as the object for linguistic inquiry, while the subjective realm of literary or artistic language has no relevance to this aim. The writer, though, has been able to incorporate historical configurations into the subjective activity of writing through language that is not necessarily, or even far from, logical. In this sense, poetic language collapses the diachronic into the synchronic;[61] the historical moments are conveyed within the existing terms of language, but only through the intersection of these relations is language both "subjectivity and communication."[62]

Rather than relegating poetic language to the margins of linguistic science, Kristeva recommends it be positioned "at the sensitive centre of contemporary 'human' sciences."[63] This center she identifies as the intersection where language, as social system and structure, meets with history and culture, that is, where meaning is generated. The questions here are: where is the subject in this intersection? and what is the nature of this intersection?

From Bakhtin's literary studies of the novels by Dostoevsky and Rabelais, Kristeva introduces the notions of ambivalence and dialogism to structuralist conceptions of the word, the minimal unit of signification. Structuralist linguistics had yet to move away from its conception of the word as "a point (a fixed meaning)"[64] and would benefit from Bakhtinian theory, which locates a movement toward another text within the text, conceived of "as a dialogue among several writings: that of the writer, the addressee (or the character) and the contemporary or earlier cultural context."

The dialogue of a text involves the writer endowing language (the synchronic structure) with experiences, whereby the character and context are situated in historical-diachronic relations. Added to this is ambivalence, in which the word or text of artistic language has always more than one meaning: "is read as at least double,"[65] the word referring to another word and another in varying degrees of significance. The dialogical element of the text, when combined with the ambivalent element, results in neither the fixed point of abstract meaning in structuralist theory nor a mere internal dialogue of subjective experience, but rather an intertextual operation "linking structural models to cultural (historical) environment, as well as . . . controlling mutations from diachrony to synchrony."[66]

Philosophy in the West has long been concerned with the question of subjective experience in relation to reality. In this opposition, art plays a mediating role by posing as a representation of reality that is valued for its degrees of subjectivity (for example, interior monologue, impressionism, surrealism) or objectivity (for example, realism, verisimilitude, the literal). Philosophically, the question might be posed as: what can we, as conscious beings, know about reality? Kristeva's theory of intertextuality reassesses this question — "situates philosophical problems within language"⁶⁷ — in terms of artistic language as a material, textual surface (in line with Barthes's notion of writerly and readerly texts⁶⁸) that is doubled (made ambivalent) in the text's spectacle of (a) reality.⁶⁹ Literary language is an example of how representation is a dynamic dimension of the structure (of language) made into spectacle, or as Kristeva puts it "realist representation."⁷⁰ In combination with the subjective, lived experience, the language of artistic practice exemplifies the place where the representation of reality meets with the processes of representation. In other words, by understanding the distinction between what is represented and how it is represented, it is possible to chart the changes in cultural representations of reality. The intertextual space of language is how Kristeva begins her theoretical conception of social stability, crisis, and change. The subject of language is integral to the notion of intertextuality in both a collective, synchronic way, as a participant in cultural representation, and diachronically, by endowing language with personal, historical experience.

By 1974, with the publication of her doctoral thesis *Revolution in Poetic Language*, the theory of intertextuality had expanded to incorporate the phenomenology of Husserl, Hjelmslev's structuralist linguistics, Freud's theory of the unconscious, and Lacan's notion of the mirror stage in the development of the subject. Michael Payne, in his book *Reading Theory: An Introduction to Lacan, Derrida and Kristeva*, provides an excellent interpretation of the way Kristeva, in formulating her concept of the semiotic in relation to intertextuality, demonstrates "the necessary interrelations among philosophy, psychoanalysis and linguistics."⁷¹ The English edition of *Revolution in Poetic Language* lacks the final third of the French edition; even so the English edition's concluding statements refer back to the theory of intertextuality in "Word, Dialogue and Novel," while summarizing the recent developments of that theory in the later work:

> The text, in its signifying disposition and its signification, is a practice assuming all positivity in order to negativise it and thereby make visible the process underlying it. It can thus be considered, precisely, as that which carries out the ethical imperative. . . . By stating scientific truths about the process of the subject (his discourse, his sexuality) and the tendencies of current historical processes, the text fulfils its ethical function only when it pluralises, pulverises, "musicates" these truths.⁷²

Added to the theory of intertextuality is an ethic that is embedded in the early theory in terms of the double of ambivalence and the dimensions of subject-addressee-context of dialogism. The ethical imperative in *Revolution in Poetic Language* is on one level about the unsettling of meaning and logic that underlies social institutions. The intertextual movement, or as Kristeva prefers in this later work,⁷³ the transposition from one sign system to another, is the ethical guarantee against a society or an area of knowledge that allows for no other meaning than its own dominant ideology, which Kristeva calls a "closed socio-symbolic order."[74] The closed system is characterized by permitting no question as to the relation between words (signifier) and thing (signified): "the social order [that] favours the order of knowledge, the signifieds Lévi-Strauss spoke of tend to encounter the floating signifier, and the bourgeois technocratic era imagines itself to be the one carrying out this reunion. In such an era, in any case, no sacrifice is available for presenting a signified . . . that has not yet met with its signifier but that remains nevertheless as the limit ensuring the functioning of the order."

In terms of intertextuality as a transposition of sign systems, the point here is that this type of society or intellectual inquiry, which requires the union of its representations with reality, has left out the ethics involved in the processes of representation. The ethics of the processes of signification (signifying practices[75]) are explained by Kristeva in the last sentences of the above paragraph, as: "poetic language [that] reminds us of its eternal function: to introduce through the symbolic that which works on, moves through, and threatens it. The theory of the unconscious seeks the very thing that poetic language practices within and against the social order: the ultimate means of its transformation or subversion, the precondition for its survival and revolution."[76]

At the heart of intertextuality is a practice of alteration and alterity, whereby the transposition of one meaning system to another, carrying with it the representational processes, constitutes a break between the subject and a posited object. For the subject to refind meaning in the passage between sign systems, identification with new signifying processes must follow the break with a former position. The unconscious processes, formulated by Freud as displacement and condensation, are further conceived by Kristeva as facilitating this break between one position of signification to another. The "thetic break," Kristeva's term for this unhinging,[77] reaffirms what was already established in social anthropology: that there is an "equivalence between the symbolic and the social when . . . society's various means of self-regulation . . . [are considered] as languages."[78]

Both Lechte and Payne in their books on Kristeva argue convincingly for her textual ethics as a means of social change. For Lechte, Kristeva "has been concerned to extend the limits of the signifiable, perhaps to the extent of relativising the role of the symbolic order."[79] Payne also asserts the importance of Kristeva's concept of the text as a revolutionary practice, that by "refusing to attach itself to established society, . . . promotes 'instinctual and linguistic change' in order to bring about new social relations and the 'subversion' of capitalism."[80] The question here is, in what sense does the theory of a transposition of sign systems, which is in no way a superficial "study of sources,"[81] have relevance to educational practice?

THEORY AND EDUCATIONAL PRACTICE

We could learn to take advantage of these microcognitive fluctuations, by letting go of our desire for total (rational) control over our mental processes and learning how to follow these microevents, drifting along with them while we explore a space of dynamic possibilities. If, as seems likely, our minds are partly symbolic, partly connectionist systems . . . , then tracking microfluctuations may involve giving more emphasis to our pattern-recognition capabilities than to our symbolic-reasoning ones.[82]

This passage from Manuel De Landa occurs in a paper about computer-created artificial worlds and the importance of insignificant diversification (bifurcation) in generating systems that are nonlinear and dynamic.[83] De Landa concludes the paper with the proposal that these artificial environments will one day provide a way to map both the stable and fluid nature of any biological information system, such as a language, an economic corporation, or an ecological environment.[84] That mapping allows an understanding of how a space of diversification can occur and then the possibility of taking advantage of this fluctuation. The paper advocates an educational principle (reminiscent of Donna Haraway's cyborg principle for life in the technosphere), where we "learn to become searching devices" moving between diversification and stability.[85]

De Landa's predictions have a strong similarity to elements of intertextuality, in that the concept in artificial life experiments of a space of diversification or a transition from one attractor to another[86] recalls Kristeva's "model for poetic language [as a] . . . space and infinity — concepts amenable to formalisation through set theory and the new mathematics."[87] Hans-George Ruprecht has already made this connection in a 1991 paper in which he describes a practice of intertextuality as a "dynamic non-equilibrium" between the polarity of a "stable attractor," and where bifurcation occurs, in at least one way, between author and critic.[88] As in De Landa, Ruprecht proposes that the practice of intertextuality be based on "a search . . . focused on the catastrophic theoretic implications of the critic's intertextual readings."[89] In both papers, the process of diversification depends upon a searching device, that of the artificial or natural memory, that in De Landa's synthetic experiment results in properties emerging that were "unimagined by the designer."[90]

Instability can be placed at the key moment in an intertextual transposition, that which Kristeva has described as a "redistribution of several different sign systems"[91]; which in education can be understood as the merging of disciplines in which one or more disciplinary discourses are placed within the boundaries of another discipline. According to the theory of intertextuality as a trans-linguistic process that conceives of the text as a social practice,[92] disciplinary crossovers would involve both teachers and students in a process in which signification is exchanged and each discipline is permutated with the other.

My own teaching experience in art schools from a previous training in literary scholarship can supply one way to begin an inquiry into the possible place for intertextuality as an educational theory. Rather than use a research methodology based on given aims and objects, my approach is drawn from Kristeva's early essay on semiotics and science. Here she argues that ideology exists in all scientific research, and that the semiotic approach of questioning its own models and theories promotes movement between theory and model and an openness to contemporary practice, as opposed to a closed scientific-philosophical system.[93] The ideological elements of a closed system can be renewed by the "introduction of a new terminology and the subversion of the existing terminology,"[94] such as the incorporation of one or more disciplines into another in education. In other words, an intertextual approach is one in which "in the space of a given text, several utterances, taken from other texts, intersect and neutralise one another."[95] With this in mind, I am interested in educational research that evades systematization and that instead "is a place of dispute and self-questioning,"[96] an imperfect and emerging design.[97]

The main signifying systems here are education, literary theory, and the visual arts. The institution of education in New Zealand accepts the inclusion of contemporary literary theory into its pedagogical areas of fine arts and design. Literary theory, as it is called in English departments, loses its name when it is incorporated into art departments, and instead becomes just theory, art theory, or contextual studies in course abstracts. What is called philosophy in France, or at least the work of intellectuals, turns into another discipline as it travels through the United States and England on the way to the South Pacific. Philosophy is clearly marked off from theory in New Zealand, and the more fictional realm of literature (the revolutionary text for Kristeva and others) is left largely to undervalued literary departments to study the works of Derrida and company. Over the last two or three years, art and design schools have shown a sometimes guarded, sometimes enthusiastic interest in the new theories. Much of this development can be attributed to the influence of sociology, education, feminism, and film studies, which have taken up poststructuralism following similar patterns in France, England, and the United States.

In working as a teacher in an art school, situating a new terminology or terminologies within another, the epistemological break can be conceived as an issue of language. The question and problem that always present themselves are how to explain a particular theory in terms of artistic practice. The outcome of these concerns leads not only to an intervention of textual concepts and literary theory into the visual disciplines, but in the reverse, by which a theory of language will at times intersect with an artistic practice, and relativize or even neutralize that practice.

Students in a class I taught for a year requested more visuals in lectures to help explain, describe, or exemplify the theoretical topics. By incorporating visual art works, such as film or slides, into my lectures when the topic was Marx's theory of commodity fetishism or Lacan's realms of the Imaginary, Symbolic, and Real, the images could be used to contradict Barthes's notion that the technique of linguistic message is to fix the floating signifieds of an image.[98] In using an image, such as a photograph by Joel Peter Witkin in relation to Kristeva's notion of abjection, the image works to fix, even momentarily, the theoretical concept, making it material and of subjective relevance within the educational practice. The visual, in this case, becomes a model for the theory, which allows a questioning to move between the discourses of theory and art.

Properties that emerge from an encounter between literary-philosophical theories and art education can occur when teacher and student are able to make connections and associations, not just to other art works, but also to their own work. By doing so, a connection is made between the theory, art, and the searching subject. Ideologies existing in both disciplines come under question, such as the traditional opposition between the visual and the textual. Those involved often question the privileging of language as constitutive of the subject, while others investigate the convergences of text and visual. These inquiries are developing from a recent intertextual practice in New Zealand art education that has so far affected art practice and disciplinary boundaries. Its diversification is as yet unknown.

NOTES

1. Peters, M. & Marshall, J. (1993). Beyond the philosophy of the subject: Liberalism, education and the critique of individualism. *Educational Philosophy and Theory*, 25, p. 20.
2. Ibid., p. 26.
3. Kristeva, J. (1980). How does one speak to literature? *Desire in language*, T. Gora, A. Jardine, & L. S. Rondiez (Trans.) (p. 98). New York: Columbia University Press. [Original essay published 1971]
4. Ibid.
5. Here I am defining discourse in line with Benveniste and Kristeva, as language appropriated by the individual as practice. This definition refers to how discourse functions in sociocommunicative structures, in this case education. See Kristeva, J. (1986). Word, dialogue and novel. In T. Moi (Ed.), *The Kristeva reader*, T. Gora, A. Jardine, & L. S. Rondiez (Trans.) (p. 37). Oxford: Basil Blackwell.

6. Kristeva, J. How does one speak to literature? p. 98.
7. Appel, S. (1992). *Psychoanalysis and "new" sociology of education: Positioning subjects* (pp. 54–55). Unpublished doctoral dissertation, University of Rochester.
8. Clark, S. & Hulley, K. (1990). An interview with Julia Kristeva: Cultural strangeness and the subject in crisis. *Discourse, 13*(1), 159, 178.
9. All publication dates for works by Kristeva are to the English translations except when specified.
10. Kristeva, J. (1980). The novel as polylogue. In *Desire in language* (p. 161). New York: Columbia University Press; Kristeva, J. (1986). *About Chinese women*, A. Barrows (Trans.) (pp. 12, 157–160). New York: Marion Boyars; Kristeva, J. (1991). *Strangers to ourselves*, L. S. Rondiez (Trans.) (pp. 15, 21). New York: Columbia University Press.
11. Kristeva, J. (1987). *Stabat mater*. In *Tales of love*, L. S. Rondiez (Trans.) (pp. 246–247). New York: Columbia University Press; Kristeva, *Tales of love*, pp. 1–6.
12. Savigneau, J. (1990, May 13). New novelist pitches fiction and fact into the melting pot. *Guardian Weekly*, p. 16.
13. Kristeva, J. (1984). My memory's hyperbole, A. Viscusi (Trans.). *New York Literary Forum, 12–13,* 261–276.
14. Savigneau, New novelist pitches fiction and fact into the melting pot, p. 16.
15. Clark & Hulley. An interview with Julia Kristeva, pp. 171–172.
16. Kristeva, My memory's hyperbole, p. 263; Kristeva, J. (1992). *The samurai* (pp. 7–9). New York: Columbia University Press.
17. Kristeva, *The samurai*, pp. 20–22; Payne, M. (1993). *Reading theory, An introduction to Lacan, Derrida and Kristeva* (p. 205 n5). Oxford: Basil Blackwell.
18. Kristeva, My memory's hyperbole, p. 265.
19. Payne, *Reading theory*, p. 205 n5.
20. Roudinesco, E. (1990). *Lacan & Co. A history of psychoanalysis in France 1925–1985*, J. Mehlman (Trans.) (pp. 526–527). London: Free Association Books.
21. Clark & Hulley, An interview with Julia Kristeva, pp. 172–173; Roudinesco, *Lacan & Co.*, p. 528.
22. Kristeva, My memory's hyperbole, pp. 270–274; Roudinesco, *Lacan & Co.*, p. 535.
23. Clark & Hulley, An interview with Julia Kristeva, pp. 152, 172.
24. Kristeva, J. (1980). The ethics of linguistics. In *Desire in language* (p. 24). New York: Columbia University Press; Kristeva, J. (1984). *Revolution in poetic language*, M. Waller (Trans.) (p. 202). New York: Columbia University Press.
25. Kristeva, My memory's hyperbole, pp. 266–267.
26. Moi, T. (Ed.). (1986). *The Kristeva reader* (pp. 4–5). Oxford: Basil Blackwell.
27. Kristeva, My memory's hyperbole, pp. 273–274.
28. Ibid., p. 275.
29. Roudinesco, *Lacan & Co.*, p. 545.
30. Moi, *The Kristeva reader*, p. 7.
31. Kauppi, N. (1994). *The making of an avant-garde: Tel Quel* (pp. 122, 133). Berlin: Mouton de Gruyter.
32. Clark & Hulley, An interview with Julia Kristeva, p. 162.
33. Roudinesco, *Lacan & Co.*, p. 528.

34. Ibid., p. 530.
35. Ibid., p. 529.
36. Ibid.
37. Ibid, p. 545.
38. Kauppi, *The making of an avant-garde*, p. 107.
39. Ibid., p. 178.
40. Ibid., pp. 247–260.
41. Ibid., p. 364.
42. Clark & Hulley, An interview with Julia Kristeva, p. 178.
43. Lechte, J. (1990). *Julia Kristeva* (p. 17). New York: Routledge.
44. Ibid.
45. Ibid., pp. 24–25.
46. Ibid., p. 28.
47. Kristeva, J. (1980). The bounded text. In *Desire in language* (p. 47). New York: Columbia University Press.
48. Ibid.
49. Ibid.
50. Ibid., p. 55.
51. Lechte, *Julia Kristeva*, p. 25.
52. Ibid., p. 22.
53. Kauppi, *The making of an avant-garde*, p. 259; Adriaens, M. (1981). Ideology and literary production: Kristeva's poetics. In P. V. Zima (Ed.), *Semiotics and dialectics: Ideology in the text* (p. 195). Amsterdam: Johns Benjamins.
54. Mai, H.-P. (1991). Bypassing intertextuality. Hermeneutics, textual practice, hypertext. In H. F. Plett (Ed.), *Intertextuality* (p. 41). Berlin: Walter de Gruyter.
55. Lechte, *Julia Kristeva*, pp. 24, 25.
56. Kauppi, *The making of an avant-garde*, p. 118.
57. Kristeva, J. (1967). Le Mot, le dialogue et le roman. *Critique 239*, pp. 438–465, reprinted as Word, dialogue and novel. In *The Kristeva reader*, pp. 34–61.
58. Kauppi, *The making of an avant-garde*, pp. 118, 127.
59. Those most relevant are: Word, dialogue and novel; Semiotics: A critical science and/or a critique of science. In *The Kristeva reader* (pp. 74–88) [Original work published 1968]; The bounded text (pp. 36–63) [Original work published 1969]; How does one speak to literature? In *Desire in language* (pp. 92–123) [Original work published 1971]; The system and the speaking subject. In *The Kristeva reader* (pp. 24–33) [Original work published 1973]. The ruin of poetics. In S. Bann & J. Bowlt (Eds.). *Russian formalism*, V. Mylne (Trans.) (pp. 102–119). Edinburgh: Scottish Academic Press.
60. Kristeva, Word, dialogue and novel, pp. 40, 58.
61. Ibid., p. 36.
62. Ibid., p. 39.
63. Ibid., p. 36.
64. Ibid.
65. Ibid., p. 37.
66. Ibid.
67. Ibid., p. 58.
68. See Lechte, *Julia Kristeva*, pp. 23–224.
69. Kristeva, Word, dialogue and novel, p. 58.

70. Ibid.
71. Payne, *Reading theory*, p. 174.
72. Kristeva, *Revolution in poetic language*, p. 233.
73. Ibid., pp. 59–60.
74. Ibid., p. 81.
75. Ibid., p. 214.
76. Ibid., p. 81.
77. Ibid., pp. 43–45, 58–60.
78. Ibid., p. 72.
79. Lechte, *Julia Kristeva*, p. 56.
80. Payne, *Reading theory*, p. 180. Citations to Kristeva, *Revolution in poetic language*, p. 105.
81. Kristeva, *Revolution in poetic language*, p. 60.
82. De Landa, M. (1993). Virtual environments and the emergence of synthetic reason. *South Atlantic Quarterly*, 92 (4), 813.
83. Ibid., pp. 811, 813.
84. Ibid., pp. 805, 807–808.
85. Ibid., p. 814.
86. Ibid., p. 798.
87. Kristeva, Word, dialogue and novel, p. 58.
88. Ruprecht, H-G. (1991). The reconstruction of intertextuality. In H. F. Plett (Ed.). *Intertextuality* (p. 68). Berlin: Walter de Gruyter.
89. Ibid.
90. De Landa, Virtual environments and the emergence of synthetic reason, p. 800.
91. Kristeva, *Revolution in poetic language*, p. 59.
92. Kristeva, The bounded text, p. 36; Kristeva, J. Semiotics: A critical science and/or a critique of science, p. 87.
93. Kristeva, Semiotics: A critical science and/or a critique of science, pp. 79–80.
94. Ibid., p. 79.
95. Kristeva, The bounded text, p. 36.
96. Kristeva, Semiotics: A critical science and/or a critique of science, p. 78.
97. De Landa, Virtual environments and the emergence of synthetic reason, p. 800.
98. Barthes, R. (1977). Rhetoric of the image. *Image, music, text*, S. Heath (Trans.) (p. 39). New York: Hill & Wang.

5

Jacques Derrida: The Ends of Pedagogy — From the Dialectic of Memory to the Deconstruction of the Institution

Peter Trifonas

> Our age, whether through logic or epistemology, whether through Marx or through Nietzsche, is attempting to flee Hegel.
> — Foucault, 1972: 235[1]

Let us take to heart Foucault's near-closing remarks made during the inaugural lecture commemorating the auspicious occasion of his election to a place among the elite intelligentsia of the *Collège de France* as the self-titled professor of history and systems of thought. Considering the anti-Hegelian backlash of the postmodern evolution of French thought spanning the ideology-based vicissitudes of Continental philosophy over the past 25 years, it is perhaps not so difficult a task.[2] These intra- and transnational sites of contestation that have emerged to engage the epistemological forcefulness of speculative idealism encompass the interdisiciplinary junctures of a hermeneutic terrain permeated, more often than not, by a critical radicality defined in direct relation to deconstruction, a philosophical endeavor of a decisively nondialectical fervor.[3] What the designation of this era as poststructuralism clearly attests to is the grand scale of its impact both within and without academia; this breadth of its manifestations underscored an unprecedented capacity to alter the reproducible stability of knowledge configurations. At the same time, because of this or perhaps, to a notable degree, in spite of it, the rapid rise of deconstruction to an enviable position of prominence at the higher echelons of the pedagogical institution has not been without controversy. Its unique provocations to the long-standing codes of the universities as a theoretical phenomenon transgressive of normal contingencies of value has fascinated, engaged, and, in some cases, even enraged intellectuals — either of the Left or of the Right[4] — reacting to the mutability of its many forms incurred among the human sciences, including the areas of educational studies.[5] The last stages of a transitional passage from the endings of a modern age pedagogy well-versed in the cogitative techniques of the dialectical Hegel and expanded upon from early Greek thinking[6] to the beginnings of an other age are exemplified by the unique challenges the teachings of Derrida pose to the metaphysical pediments of Western philosophy. As the legacy of a pedagogical tradition preserved through the mode of argumentation constructing the logicality of Plato's dialogues, the Hegelian conception of dialectic fervently guards the spirit of an ancient body of knowledge once believed to be wholly educative, in every sense of the word, but most certainly experiencing successive phases of decline well into the latter half of the twentieth century.[7] Inevitably, it is speculative idealism, the absolute reason of the dialectic, as a teaching-learning strategy that carries the critical burden of an incalculable risk to the integrity of Hegelianism when the honor of its philosophical memory is violated by unforeseen transgressions into the uncharted territories of fundamental epistemic and pedagogical change.

The pedagogical path of deconstruction Derrida has initiated and has chosen to pursue both in France and abroad cannot, however, be arbitrarily reduced to the singular purpose of simply enabling a revolutionary defiance to the authority of the teachings of a Hegel. Such an uninformed caricature is primarily the facile result of a distortion or ignorance of textual sources.[8] Tempting as this stereotypical tract might be, it places unmanageable limits upon the scope, if not the intention, of a philosophical deconstruction to fulfill nothing beyond a fatalistic rejection of the orthodox prophetics of modernity.[9] The charge of paving the way for advancing a pandemic nihilism — the discord of an apocalyptic tone[10] — usually accompanies the rationalization of this accusation when and where it has been leveled against Derrida. The demonstrated potential of deconstruction to address the discourse ethics of the self-reasoning institutions of teaching-learning subsequently inaugurated from the thought of Hegel is dismissed outright.[11] Rather, given the developmental course of postmetaphysical thinking since the first serious challenges Friedrich Nietzsche issued to the monography of Occidental reason, I would argue, it would be fairer and considerably more accurate to view the guiding role for the future of deconstruction more or less imposed upon Derrida by those who read his texts or extol his thoughts in quite another light: that is, as the inescapable summons to responsibility demanded of an intellectual undertaking thoroughly inscribed by the conditional effects of a gradual, though steady, intensification of the ethico-political maturation of the states of theory.[12]

Derrida, for his part, has clearly acknowledged, "What we call deconstruction in its academic or in its editorial form is also a symptom of a deconstruction at work elsewhere in society and the world."[13] The importance of this symptomatic aspect of deconstruction is often overlooked. Its case of interceding to disrupt the calculability of the interchange between the subjective topographies of mind and body traversing discourse and life unquestionably complicates the idea of a theory-praxis dualism. A separation of the interiority of thought from the exteriority of action — inasmuch as it grounds the criteriological basis of consequences ostensibly in the real — only succeeds to close off the social dimension of the institutional sphere to the ethics of implications accompanying any act of interpretation, whether formalized creatively through the pragmatic signs of language as reading or writing. The following passage from Derrida (1992) is worth quoting here at length to illustrate how the heteronomous situation of deconstruction happens:[14]

If, then, it lays claim to any consequence, what is hastily called deconstruction *as such* is never a technical set of discursive procedures, still less a new hermeneutic method operating on archives or utterances in the shelter of a given and stable institution; it is also, and at the least, the taking of a position, in work itself, toward the politico-institutional structures that constitute and regulate our practice, our competences, and our performances. Precisely because deconstruction has never been concerned with the contents alone of meaning, it must not be separable from this politico-institutional problematic, and has to require a new questioning about responsibility, an inquiry that should no longer necessarily rely on codes inherited from politics or ethics. Which is why, though too political in the eyes of some, deconstruction can seem demobilizing in the eyes of those who recognize the political only with the help of prewar road signs. Deconstruction is limited neither to a methodological reform that would reassure the given organization, nor, inversely, to a parade of irresponsible or irresponsibilizing destruction, whose surest effect would be to leave the everything as is, consolidating the most immobile forces of the university.[15]

What today Derrida recognizes to be the richness of an unceasing profusion of deconstructions concedes the multiplicity of conceptual dislocations readily achievable from the seeds of his own texts. Yet this particularization of theoretical practice that is required to address the contextual aporias of performing analytic gestures suitable to a critical task still comes to be motivated by the antinomic vocation of finding ways to extinguish the mastery of the pedagogical icons of the ages before.[16] For Derrida, as is reaffirmed more and more by his recent writings, the situation of deconstruction is, was, and should be the result of the conscious subjectification of a desire to enact "a positive response to an alterity,"[17] regardless of the mainstream opinions or beliefs its working out may alienate along the way. Targeting the institutional ground that constructs the distinguishing of pure difference as the judgemental basis upon which to entrench a viable and tangible separation of essentialized subjectivities — for example, the same from the Other[18] — could lead in turn to a dissolution of the interpretative foundations for arbitrary inclusions and exclusions. Deconstruction presupposes an affirmative answering of the call of the Other that, above all else, emphatically strives to hasten the concrete possibilities of ushering forth a more equitable new world picture. The ethical-political aftermath of its aggressively interventional questioning of the limits of normativeness allows for a qualitative expansion of the existential borders of selfhood (being and Being) beyond the narrowly regulated structures of institutionalized authority framing the material horizons of realities we inhabit.

Whether it be incorporated within the manifold guises of post-Marxisms, post-feminisms, post-colonialisms, or any other post-critical discourses promoting the emancipatory need for protecting the agency of the subject against the ideological tamperings of cultural institutions, the ground-breaking work of Derrida has influenced recent theoretical reevaluations of how to go about this common political and altruistic intent.[19] Deconstruction has breathed life into a host of current modifications of stale methodological lenses through which to identify and to reapproach the ethical dilemma of social inequalities. In short, the thought of Derrida has availed us the opportunity for an original recasting of the complicitous grounds of our own academic responsibility.[20]

Given that the problem of the institutionalization of education is posed "at the [epistemological and performative] root of philosophy as teaching,"[21] the theorized status of the applied site of pedagogy has been of sustained interest for Derrida. He has painstakingly reiterated this point many times before, for example, as in *Où Comment et Comment Finit un Corps Enseignant*, to clarify the depth of its parameters for the sake of protecting the right to philosophy education: "Deconstruction — or at least that which I proposed under this name that is as good as another, but not more — has therefore always had bearing in principle on the apparatus and the function of teaching in general."[22] The initiative Derrida has taken to expose the umbrage in the decidable ethics of right and wrong active below the surface structures of the educational institution is counterpoised in accordance with the responsibility of a political obligation "to interrogate, to exhibit, to criticize [the conceptual cadre framing its characteristic features] systematically — with an eye toward transformation."[23] By unearthing the systemic indications of coersive elements in the actual machinery of schooling that have the potential to shape the trajectory of knowledge presentations or creations as the curricular products of a normative projection of a unified code of subjectivity, the concealed biases of pedagogical goals or aims are laid bare. It cannot be denied that in minimizing the gap or delay of a conceptual dichotomy separating theory from praxis the general principles of Derridean deconstruction have sharpened the analytic wherewithal for the recrafting of critical tools with which to reveal the covert interests that infuse the actual conditions of teaching and learning.[24] This focus alone has helped educational theorists or critics of diverse ideological bents to politicize the ethology of the cultural situatedness of pedagogy once and for all with a view to the righting of wrongs. Deconstruction has heretofore set apart, among others, those who would scrutinize the power/knowledge nexus at work for the pedagogical canonization of texts such as Hegel's, from those who would uphold the sanctity of a system of educational institutions engendered from the heritage of their philosophical lessons. Born "of an other logic"[25] — outside but within the enclosure — of the conceptual oppositions of Western rationality, the intrepidity of its inferences has done that much to change the usually unexamined notions of polity assumed for the transmission of given or common understandings.

Despite the recurrent tendency of many proponents of educational reform associated with the aforementioned movements to overzealously use Derridean tenets for the expressed purpose of institutional inquiry or cultural critique (for example, difference, *différance*, trace, inversion-displacement, binarity, [phal]logocentrism, metaphysics of presence, supplementarity, dissemination), the ethical and political efficacy of deconstruction continues to be vehemently argued.[26] In a cross-disciplinary and cross-cultural study of the reception of French and German theory by academia, Robert C. Holub correctly notes that the ongoing "attempt to politicize deconstruction [especially after the 'Yale school' brand of rhetorical poststructuralism], of course, can more properly be considered a repoliticization of deconstruction for [North] American criticism, since the affinity with radical and Marxist thought had existed in France from its very inception."[27] The matter-of-course underestimation or outright dismissal of the potential, if not the substantive value, of deconstruction for reconceptualizing the ethical questions of political issues such as those associated with pedagogy of interest for us is most curious. Nevertheless, it may be due to a lack of critical attention to a considerable part of Derrida's writings: the texts deliberating the institutional plight of philosophy, the serious problem of maintaining the teaching-learning of its curriculum, indigenous to the ideological fluctuations of the educational climate in France.

Primacy having been allocated to the so-called philosophical or argumentative texts, the remaining writings have been unduly marginalized from the main work on the basis of rhetorical or stylistic considerations.[28] A large portion of what has been forged together at the periphery to form a significantly less-recognized subcanon that has been short-shrifted, if addressed at all, is explicitly oriented to examining the politics of the institutionalization of philosophy; the pedagogical insolvency of its ethical underpinnings, as it were. The majority of these texts (essays, lectures, interviews, letters, etc.) were written in the 1970s up to the mid-1980s, at what was the height of Derrida's involvement with the *Groupe de Recherches sur l'Enseignement Philosophique* (GREPH), a collective of professional philosophers, teachers, students, and others devoted to protecting the discipline of philosophy against the educational mandates of a French state threatening its eradication. Considering the speed and the diligence with which Derrida's more recent writing has been translated, the fact that a good deal of these minor texts have not been available for the perusal of non-French-reading scholars reflects a certain downgrading of their critical weight.[29] This omission concerning the most overtly ethical and political phases of his philosophical labor notwithstanding, there remains quite a healthy trend to quasimethodologize well-known elements of the proclaimed canon by reappropriating their theoretical precepts under the all-too-generic label of an applied deconstruction, supposedly modified and thus more amenable to facilitating the study of real-world phenomena than the authentic thing, whatever that may be.[30]

I will not go over the minutia of these well-worn contentions to support or to refute them per se. Yet, its sightlines do more than merely map over the vast plane of what has been written in or against the name of deconstruction. Converging on what pertains to educational theory and philosophy, the specificity of detail to be found here seeks, at the very least, to fill some of the lacunae these recurrent phases of critical conjuncture have left open to date. Specifically, I will try to illustrate how the text-based machinations of a Derridean instance of deconstruction itself can offer a resistance to the instruments of domination embedded within the praxeology of teaching-learning. Further, I address how it can provide a manner for undoing the ethical substrata reinforcing the politics of educational policy, theory, and practice that suffuse the discursive gradients of concepts such as freedom, truth, reason, or humanity with ideological significance. What better place to begin to open to scrutiny the accepted codes or institutional codability of schooling than from a marginalized text of Derrida, "The Age of Hegel"?

To do this, I offer a reading of Derrida's deconstructive rereading of a special report about the cultural predicament of philosophical pedagogy in the Prussian educational system, a document that Hegel was requested to prepare for submission to the Ministry of Public Instruction in 1822. The main body of this chapter is divided into three sections. The first section commences by reinvoking the ethical and political circumstances of the text-context relation Derrida elucidates to situate the report Hegel signs within the conditions of its necessity and the fate of its reception. With constant reference to deconstruction, the analysis explores how the state of affairs that spawned the ideology of the report for the purpose of actualizing educational policy can be reread through a gauging of the speculative presuppositions of the pedagogical memory of childhood Hegel reveals, as is found in the dialectical laws of the philosopher's own texts (for example, the *Philosophy of Right* and the *Phenomenology of Spirit*). This section is followed by a technical analysis of the autobiographical moment of the philosophical age of Hegel. I consider the reflexive instant of ideality — when the subjective identity of being is concreted through a self-referential writing posed against the reality of itself as an auto-affective recapitulation of the thought of memory — stemming from the Hegelian rejuvenation of a Platonistic rewriting of anamnesis without the creative intuition of signs. The question here is: How does the signature of the proper name as a life-writing of the self stabilize the pedagogical truth of a childhood memory from the past to sanction the institutionalization of a speculative modality for the teaching and learning of philosophy? The third section moves the deconstructive protocol of reading away from the contradictions of the representation of subjective identity that penetrate the ideology of the report Hegel signs into the actual ethics and politics of the scene of teaching. It ends with a discussion of some of the recommendations Derrida makes to the GREPH for achieving a rewarding critique of the pedagogical institution of philosophy and expands upon their implications.

THE TEXT-CONTEXT–CONTEXT-TEXT *DIALANGUE*: BREAKING DOWN THE PHILOSOPHICAL BARRIERS BETWEEN THE SUBJECT, THE STATE, AND THE PEDAGOGICAL INSTITUTION

> And if I may be permitted to evoke my own experience . . . I remember having learned, in my twelfth year — destined as I was to enter the theological seminary of my country — Wolf[f]'s definitions of the so-called idea clara and that, in my fourteenth year, I had assimilated all the figures and rules of syllogism. And I still know them.
> — Hegel, 1822[31]

To begin with then, a rememoration of, and for, a curriculum. The autobiographical portrayal of a pedagogical moment from childhood is ascribable to the experience of the German philosopher identified by the proper name of Hegel (Georg Wilhelm Friedrich), for his signature sanctions its reiteration a posteriori of the labor of its extraction, from the nadir of another time and space that is memory, into writing. Citation to the pastness of this event evokes the historicity of the selfsame subjectivity marked from the autoappellative force of the signature of the proper name operating as a closing salutation to an official correspondence. In actuality, the anecdote is not part of a letter at all, but of an official study commissioned from Hegel, Derrida reminds us, "by a [Prussian] State bureaucracy in the process of organizing the nationalization of the structures of philosophical education by extracting it, based on historical compromise, from clerical jurisdiction."[32] This seemingly wandering digression of subjective thought rethinking itself in the spontaneous flashing of an interiorizing reflection — the example of a memory of adolescence that interrupts the illustrative contents of the report for argument's sake — is anything other than accidental *retors*, a slip of the pen.

What happens within the textual confines of this report follows closely on the enforcement of mandatory schooling during the reformation of the pedagogical institution in early nineteenth-century Germany, having been "recently adopted for academic freedom, and the defence of the university against feudal powers."[33] Altenstein, minister of public instruction since 1817 — and Hegel's benefactor — proves to be a devoted advocate to the State cause of seeing through the initiation of a public schooling.[34] The position he occupies as a career bureaucrat in the dawning of the "age of European civil service"[35] is "sensitive, precarious, vulnerable."[36] It is soon evident to the parties concerned that the struggle against the more resolute among the proponents of feudalism must be waged with "suppleness, negotiation, and compromise"[37] to ensure a complete victory. Hegel — the apologist for the rationality of the State (expounded in the three revisions of the *Philosophy of Right* [1822][38] that had, in his own words, "thoroughly scandalized the demagogues")[39] — is desperately needed to assist the "budding bureaucracy"[40] with the major task of enacting the cultural instauration of educational policy. Expediently summoned to Berlin by Altenstein himself, he is unceremoniously offered Johann Gottlieb Fichte's chair and appointed to the university's faculty as professor of philosophy.

For Hegel, the intricate subtleties of networking to secure faithful alliances of patronage from within the bureaucratic ranks of the state's government is at the personal jeopardy of losing non-political liasons. That is, the cost to be paid for the stakes, both private and professional, is high, the risks to be taken immense. An unstable, albeit promising, locality of fortuitous transpositions that creates this sudden opening, it leaves Hegel "caught between the 'feudalists' and the 'demagogues,' giving signs of allegiance to the 'right' when the situation or the relation of forces seems to require that he do so, [while] secretly protecting his persecuted friends on the 'left,'"[41] as Derrida has cause to note of the philosopher's double bind. The bureaucratic desire to quell the irrepressible tensions enveloping the contextual field of intersecting though discrete interests is all-pervasive (for example, "this skein where 'private interests' and the interests of historical reason, special interests and the interests of the State, the interests of the particular state and the universal historical rationality of the State are so conveniently intertwined"[42]). The growing urgency of the situation, now ripe for intervention, underwrites the axiology of the ethico-political premises required to secure the countersigning of yet-unspoken-of contracts enjoining philosopher and State in the hard-to-be-fought mission of pedagogical restoration. The institutional and monetary terms of reciprocation — those tangible advantages Hegel explicitly wants and most assuredly will receive after the fierce lobbying of "the same ministerial sponsor"[43] fighting for the privilege of genius — are to be exchanged by the bureaucratic fraternity Altenstein speaks for in return for the philosopher's unwavering public support of the State's educational policy mandates. The details of the agreement are scrupulously stipulated in the Hegel-Altenstein correspondences before and after the appearance of the report.[44]

The pact, once made in principle, is contingent on the immanent eminence of the proper name of Hegel; a value measurable by the extent of its ability to exert influence on the discourse or the actions of others for the benefit of the State technocracy. Altenstein requires the veneration inspired from the straightforward utterance or rewriting of the sign of Hegel to empower the visionary spirit of his project of educational reform. The legitimating authority of the proper name is adjudicated as the metalinguistic expansion of its potential to affect reality by superceding the semiological restrictions of representational forms available for signifying identity. For Derrida, the laws of proper name operating here to the obvious advantage of both parties are commensurable with a logocentric aspiration to bridge the pneumatic abyss between writing and difference.[45] Altenstein counts heavily on the symbolic propriety to be derived from the deictic stimulus of onomasia that the signature of Hegel must consistently and irrefutibly validate in spite of the mediacy of language. This totalizing movement from ideality to identity hopes to preserve the continuity of subjectivity and world through the erasure or the absence of the subject in writing. I will return to this later. For now, let us concentrate on analyzing how the ideological pretext of the anecdote abides with the stringent pressures the situation places Hegel under to act without haste. Let us see how, in Derrida's judgement, a remembrance of childhood as the memory of memory itself "is intended to carry a conviction and pave the way for political decisions"[46] by lending the credibility of intellectual support to a thesis referring to the proper age for philosophy education.

The strategic reserve of this "techno-bureaucratic region of Hegelian confiding"[47] permeates the unsolicited memory of childhood that the signature of the philosopher ratifies. It works, most conveniently, to counterbalance, on the one hand, the politico-economic site of its engendering with, on the other hand, the philosophico-ethical reasons of the arbitration for the attainment of pedagogical ends. Derrida elucidates the extent to which the implicit goals of the philosopher and the explicit objectives of the State are aligned for the eventual attainment of a speculative knowledge on which to ground the development of learning:

> By addressing his report to Altenstein, he [Hegel] is not simply acting as a "realistic" philosopher, compelled to reason with the powers that be, with the contradictions inherent in these powers, and with his interlocutor's strategy within these contradictions. It is not the powers-that-be (*Le pouvoir*) — considered as a monolithic whole — which are compelled to reckon with the Hegelian system; and indeed, Hegel will say nothing in his pedagogical-philosophical propositions that is not in keeping with this system, a system which, admittedly, can fold and turn in on itself without breaking. Only a *fraction* of the forces in power is represented in the summons to Hegel. At any rate, the space for the intricate negotiations between the forces in power (however contradictory they may be and however determined may be a particular stasis of contradiction) and Hegel's philosophical strategy must be open, possible, already practicable. Without this, no compromise, no implicit contract would even have been sketched. This space, like the topic upon which it depends, can construe itself neither within Hegel's *oeuvre* — as if something of the sort existed in a pure state — nor in what we could regard as the non-philosophical realm exterior to it. Neither the "internal necessities of the system" alone nor the generally accepted opposition between "system" and "method" can account for the complexity of these contracts or compromises.[48]

Altenstein reinforces "the locus of the exchange and of the contract, the insurance of the one and the assurance of the other"[49] by defending the decision to honor the request Hegel makes (to him) for extra dispensations in consideration for the loyalty of previous services freely rendered unto the State. The minister brings to the attention of the bureaucratic elite, not only the scholarly solidity of speculative idealism — the deftness of its demonstrated capacity to repulse the "pernicious infiltration of a philosophy without depth"[50] — but also the admirable skillfulness with which its philosopher "has dashed the presumptions of young minds."[51] Derrida does not fail to tell us how in the report surrendered to Altenstein, Hegel admits he is acutely aware of the State resolve: to prevent "philosophical teaching in the Gymnasium [high school] from losing itself in a babble of hollow formulas (*sich in ein holhes Formelwesen verliere*) or from transgressing the limits of school-teaching."[52] There must be the figment of a negative educational correlate to speculative philosophy, one whose postulates are supposedly relentless in their unmitigating hostility to the future attainment of a correctively prescriptive reason within the populace of the State.

This refined universal logic of communitarianism is the philosophical bedrock for the State's purpose of working toward the reinscription of the same through the education of the subject. It solicits the motivational basis entreated to sustain the minister's claim for arbitrarily securing the implementation of one curriculum at the expense of another. The political urgency of implementing new educational policy is ideologically structured as the impetus of a perceived need that both philosopher and State commend: first and foremost, to censor the distractions lesser philosophical discourse imposes on the indiscriminate tastes of young (and rebellious) minds. Realizing political support to bolster the forcefulness of this educational policy decision Altenstein urges his colleagues to make necessitates the citational authority of the formal recommendations for a propaedeutic Hegel had elaborated in the letter to the Prussian Ministry of Education only months before. Its attainment involves the minister's predicting the answers to the following kinds of questions Derrida would ask about the latent ideology of the presuppositions the philosopher carefully put forward in the concrete form of a teachable curriculum: "What is the hollowness of formulas? What is babble? Who is to define it? From what point of view? According to what philosophy and whose politics? Does not every new or subversive discourse always constitute itself through rhetorical effects that are necessarily identified as gaps in the prevailing discourse, with the inevitable phenomena of discursive degradation, mechanisms, mimetisms, etc.?"[53] So, for the essential purpose of politically justifying the ethics of the curricular choice Altenstein is seen to have given way to — the higher reasons to exclude metaphysics proper from the gymnasium — Hegel cannot avoid presenting a precise content and methodology of philosophy instruction. He believes it is one that "does not exceed the intellectual capacities (*Fassungskraft*) of Gymnasium students"[54] and would therefore be remediating in its response to the undisciplined transitoriness of juvenile memory.

The apparent complicity of the pedagogical proposal the philosopher endorses with the expressed urgency of the ministerial request can be of no great surprise to Derrida: "[I]n this case [it is] the dialectic of speculative idealism — as a general criteriology that distinguishes between empty and full language in education. And which also determines the limit between schoolteaching and that which lies outside its domain."[55] As we have seen, Hegel's most difficult decisions very naturally display the tendency to predicate the agendas of the major actors — those subjects in power — driving the crucial outcomes of this complex situation. Derrida's rhetorical questions punctuate the sharp irony of the alliance when he pointedly asks, "Can we not say that the basis of the negotiation with the ministerial request was extraordinarily narrow? Does this not explain why the Altenstein-Hegel episode was without issue (*sans lendemain*)?"[56]

Let us return momentarily to the autobiographical anecdote of the report. Taking the stylistic form of an aside, almost an afterthought or a flashback of memory, the portrait of childhood self that Hegel puts forward supplies the minister with the good reasons for navigating the fine line drawn between the competing discourses of oppositional forces in the political arena. An ethic of commitment to the educational priorities of these good reasons is above the need to be explained or even broached, modeled as it is after the philosophical conviction of a naturally progressive capacity for conceiving the system of the absolute idea in the university after the formative years of early schooling. The image of quiet genius Hegel discreetly lays out "justifies itself, thereby effacing its anecdotal singularity by invoking an older common experience (*die algemeine ältere Erfahrung*)."[57] The ideology of its design is intended to bolster political support for a non-speculative propaedeutic the philosopher seeks to promote by a restructuring of core areas of the existing philosophy curriculum around the faculty of *Gedächtnis* (flatly translatable as "memory," but a more apt meaning here because of the pedagogical thrust of expediating the natural gifts of the faculty is the classical routine of "rote-memorization" or "learning-by-heart"). The faint aura of a semidetached humility consolidating the appeal of the representation licenses the implementation of a philosophical curriculum of unproductive memorization. Derrida very succinctly underlines the theoretical importance of a developmental theory of mnemonics to speculative idealism to evoke the well-known recitations of Hegelian philosophy:

For Hegel, memory was both a beginning and an end; he remembers (his twelfth year) and remembers that he began by remembering that which he first learned by heart. But at the same time, this homology of the system (the dialectical concept of *Gedächtnis*) and of the autobiographical situation that gave Hegel the inducement and freedom to think, this homology is to be enriched again by its pedagogical version: by beginning with teaching the content of knowledge, before even thinking it, we are assured of a highly determined prephilosophical inculcation which paves the way for good philosophy (*la bonne philosophie*).[58]

The curricular system outlined in the report to Altenstein is most remarkable. It sketches a method for how the teaching-learning of philosophy should be initiated at an early age with the administering of a highly formalized method of instruction that is intended to facilitate the conscientious transference of ideas from teacher to student, from writing to mind, and so forth, via the memorization of preselected kernels of knowledge. Insofar as Hegel attempts to react favorably to the professional requirements of the episode in its singularity, there is a betrayal of the logic of noncontradiction between his thought and actions, to which Derrida draws attention:

This capacity, to which the little, eleven-year-old Hegel bears witness, is *not yet* a philosophical capacity as such (that is a speculative capacity, but rather, a memory of certain lifeless contents, contents of understanding (*entendement*), contents that are forms (definitions, rules, and figures of syllogisms). And this not-yet propogates its effects throughout the letter, permeates the entire pedagogical machinery that Hegel proposes to the Minister. This *not-yet* of the *already* . . . interdicts precisely that which it would seem to promote, namely, the teaching of philosophy in the Gymnasium.

When Hegel says that he still remembers the *idea clara* and the syllogistics, we note a mixture of coyness (refinement and play, the put-on puerility of the great mathematician who feigns astonishment that he still remembers his multiplication tables), a certain affected tenderness for the remnants of the child in himself; most of all, a portion of irony in his challenge to pedagogic modernity, "a challenge directed at current prejudices against autonomous thought, productive activity." And what is more current (even today, for the age of Hegel will have lasted that long) than the monotonous pedagogic modernity that takes issue with mechanical memorization, mnemotechnics, in the name of *productive* spontaneity, of initiative; of independent, *living* self-discovery, etc.? But Hegel's irony is double: He knows that he has, elsewhere, objected to mnemotechnic formalism and learning "by heart." We cannot, therefore, suspect him, of being simply and *generally* a partisan of such techniques. It is a question, precisely of age, of the order and teleology of acquisition, of *progress*.[59]

With the appearance of the *Philosophische Propädeutik* in 1808, a good while before the problematic occlusion of the anecdote related to Altenstein, these public resolutions on the subject of philosophical pedagogy are well documented.[60] Hegel, in fact, had resisted the nostalgia of recapitulating the connivance of teaching matter without meaning by speaking derisively at this time of the dangers of a memorization devoid of materiality, of a de-accented learning without the in-signing of images.

TEXTUALITY, HISTORY, INSTITUTION

Deconstructing the Ideology of Educational Policy Reform: Autobiographical Memories of a Philosophical Child of State Reason

To query the validity of this recollection of childhood that reinforces a pedagogy of memory, Derrida problematizes the generalizability of what is foregrounded in the textual staging of this personal retrospection outlined in the report the philosopher freely signs, for "to render apparent the essence of a [curricular] possibility: every normal healthy child could be Hegel. At the moment when the old Hegel remembers the child Hegel, but also thinks him and conceives him in his truth, this child Hegel plays, no doubt, like all children, but plays here the role of a figure or of a moment in the pedagogy of the mind."[61] The double reading of the memory episode attended to in "The Age of Hegel" tests the value of its certainty by clarifying the intertext of philosophical arguments germane to working toward a fuller understanding of the ideology of the report proper, for example, the desire of what is left unsaid, held in reserve, or closely in check as insufficient explanation. It does so by locating the authority of the signature of the life-writing of Hegel at the ethico-political parameters of a discursivized field enframing the tensions of competing socio-economic and epistemological-historical forces vying for sovereignty over the pedagogical institution. It also allows for the allusion to what might be called a vulgar chronology evident in the memory Hegel signs for to be played-off homonymically against itself, in light of the dialectical precepts of speculative philosophy, by a more eclectic recourse to,

> The basic interpretation of the philosophical "age" as *epochality* (that is, a Heideggerian interpretation that designates the Cartesian event as one of certitude, as a reassuring foundation of subjectivity that becomes the basis of all post-Cartesian metaphysics until and including Hegel). This *epochal* interpretation, with all its machinery, could be connected (either as proof or as derivation) to the Hegelian, onto-teleological interpretation of the philosophical "age" as moment, form, or figure, totality or *pars totalis*, in the history of reason. We could then pose the question whether, in this form or in ancillary ones, such a debate could dominate, indeed could shed light on, the problematic of the structures of teaching . . . — whether that which we first recognize in terms of its regional determinants — psycho-physiological, technical, political, ideological, (etc.) — could be rendered comprehensible by such a debate, or whether it would, instead, force us to revise our premises.[62]

The confluence of this replacement of the epistemic contents of the report to which the signature of the philosopher gives value within the juridical scope of the issues apropos the pedagogical institution and philosophy education illustrates the importance of the ethical obligation to solve the dilemma that brings together the State and Hegel. This tactic enables Derrida to undertake an interpretative modulation in the reading of the letter temporarily away from the problem of memory to stress the central question of developmental age. More precisely, he addresses the nebulousness of this question of the age (both as epochality and as chronology) deemed most suitable for the teaching-learning of philosophy.

The warring factors bringing the issue of pedagogy to an apex in the early years of nineteenth-century Prussia are, Derrida contends, "neither simply *within* nor simply *external* to philosophy."[63] Their cumulative effects span the breadth of sociocultural and ethicopolitical forces lurking beneath an irreducible aggregate of discourses that imbue the spectrum of ideologies specific to the historical site of the struggle for control over the institution of education and reach far beyond the immediate distance of its horizons. Although conflicting perspectives about outcomes proliferating from the rich signifying frame of such a heterogeneous textuality are often irreconcilable in the end, Derrida lists primary sources to which an interpretation of the age of Hegel must refer "for a minimal intelligibility of the Letter":⁶⁴

Hegel's place [in the context of the situation and the role of the "letter" in the complexity of it] can really not be determined without the simultaneous and structural cognizance of an entire general textuality, consisting (at least) of: (1) his "great" philosophical works, the most obvious being the entire *Philosophy of Right*, which is to say . . . the "three" philosophies of right; (2) his other writings, that is, *at least* all his letters, even the secret ones, those which he hid from the police as an act of solidarity with certain victims of persecution; (3) his actual practice in all the complexity that has always been more or less evident, but which, as we know, cannot be reduced (far from it) during the Berlin period to that of an official and respectful (indeed, obsequious) philosopher of the State.⁶⁵

The hermeneutic stance suggested does not harbor aspirations of accessing complete understandings of past actions or events that coordinate the educational problematic of the age of Hegel. "Certain of the sharper features of this episode [that is isolated] indeed remain without issue,"⁶⁶ the contextualization of the curricular battle revolving around the principal efforts made to resolve "a situation whose political interpretation is immediately and necessarily relevant to the fundamental stakes of all the political struggles in Europe during the 19th and 20th centuries."⁶⁷ Derrida goes on to explain:

Rather than constituting a philosophical, political, or pedagogical revolution, it developed (like Hegelian philosophy) and accumulated a past; and to a large extent it has survived. . . . Which is neither to allege that Hegel responded so admirably and in such detail (art or chance?) to a demand formulated *elsewhere*, in the empirical field of historical politics; nor vice versa. But a possibility had been opened to this common language, to all its secondary variations (for Hegel was not the only philosopher to propose his pedagogy, and the entire systematic range of these variations remains to be studied), to its *translatability*. This common possibility is legible *and* transformable neither simply within the philosophical system [of Hegel], if such a thing existed in a pure state, nor in a domain foreign to any sort of philosophy.
  Taken in its greatest singularity, the Altenstein-Hegel endeavor was undoubtedly a failure; but the general structure that opened it and that Hegel tried to keep open is where we find ourselves today, and it does not cease to modify its modalities. This what [sic] I call the age of Hegel.⁶⁸

The interpretative thrust of the retranslation of philosophy to pedagogy, of text to context impels the deconstructive rereading and hence rewriting of the archive situating Hegel's age, the contextuality adumbrating the nuances of the report. The retranscription of the operative expansiveness of this "decelebration of a great philosopher"⁶⁹ and "his great philosophemes in their most forceful internal arrangement"⁷⁰ expunges the reductionist predilection of arbitrarily historicizing the intellect. Moving diacritically across the rebus of the past from the textual demesne of ideas and philosophy to the actual world of pedagogy and politics and then back again abates the dangers of arbitrarily externalizing the expressivist complexions of the human mind by merely contextualizing thought vis-à-vis the cultural materiality of writing. To assess the magnitude of Hegel's text it becomes unavoidable for Derrida to furnish an account of, and to account for, a deconstructive tract that would interpellate for the dynamism of a life-work matrix enjoining reality and thought, being and consciousness, history and language.[71] Again, the interpretative purport is not aimed at reconstituting the *Zeitgeist* of a metaphysical logos that can be attributed ex post facto to the textualized products of culture: to render their contents immanently legible as the self-directed projections of a truthfulness of spirit symbolic of the times.[72] The original or intentional meanings of a writing may not be made concrete from the de-reading of an opaque textuality readily poised to inhere within the facticity of its discursive and narrative structures the obtainable conditions of its inception within a transparent history.

An exegesis of the significance of context to the production and consumption of the report Hegel writes for Altenstein entails that the axioms of the interpretative focus be induced from the culpability of reading the interstices or interspaces of text-context relations. Entering into a cross-textual dialogue pitting the diachrony of textuality and culture against the synchrony of writing and subjectivity, the rereading of the letter Derrida presents summarily converges on the discursive ruptures in the conceptual structuring of the argument the philosopher weaves, the framework of an interlocking core of concepts (for example, philosophy, justice, rationality, and teaching) that inscribe the operating space of ideology in the unifying logic of the ideas about education.[73] Analyzing the *philosophemes* permeating the premises of Hegel's report — for example, those controlling concepts of speculative dialectics that function in the ideational structuring of the argument to help guide Altenstein and State in defending the actualization of such specifically reproductive pedagogical or curricular practices — is tied to penetrating the interactions between a symbol system governing stylistic considerations of morphology for encoding the representation of ideas in the form of signs and a social system facilitating a semantic code for the goal of decoding the signs to make them meaningful at some level of abstraction beyond sheer referential analogy. What this semio-deconstructive approach to reading the ideology of the report incurs in "The Age of Hegel" is the obligation of supplying the historiographic means for exploring the cultural politics of textuality. This approach incurs the critical liability for a surveying of the rational bases of sign-referent–signifier-signified associations punctuating the conjunctions and disjunctions of the conceptual veneer of language as an interpolation of reality.

Although referring to the curricular pragmatics of teaching-learning that Hegel's report condones, Derrida indicates precisely such an analytic shifting of emphasis to a semiotic textuality of communication "to move beyond a prestatist problematics of education and of philosophical education."[74] A linking of the semantic consequences of signification to the sociopolitical and historico-cultural dimensions constituting the discursive field of sense automatically problematizes the articulation and dissemination of meaning as it relates to the controversy over the issue of schooling. The ideology of the textuality spun around the concept of philosophy education comes to be defined from the uncovering of residual excrescenses of value stemming from the exhibited self-interest of the parties involved. In "The Age of Hegel," Derrida shows how the ineffable of language belies what are believed to be the natural correspondences of sign-referent–signifier-signified relations within the variable structures of this text-context *dialangue*. Instead of the truth of the signs of writing or of discourse, what deconstruction teaches us to read literally of the report is the meaning of its meaning; or, more generally, how the affectivity of what is negotiated through the retranslation of concepts, turns of mind, progression of thought, values and ideals of individuals, groups, or societies embodied in various textualized forms across the cultural milieux of an epoch comes to be enunciated as the sayable and the unsayable.[75] A semiotic rethinking of text-context distinctions — that Derrida identifies in "The Age of Hegel" with "the original irreducible configuration in which our questions [about education] are asked"[76] — makes it feasible to disrupt the relative autonomy once granted ideology to ensure the total reproducibility of meaning-constructions in the subject as the order of the conceptual sense of signification propagated through the media of an inflected discourse. The linguistic turn of a deconstructive reading of the report can then illustrate how the written text itself contains self-rationalizing aspects working to normalize the matter of a conceptual content while reinforcing the prefigured meanings of a collection of ideas indicative of truth. By keeping the semantic network in tune with the ideological alterations of the interpretation, the ethical-political idiom of the discourse Hegel unfolds seeks "to pass itself off as universal or absolute"[77] in an effort to expedite the future institutionalization of speculative idealism as a State pedagogy in the age of the concept.

Derrida confronts the problem of the ideological in "The Age of Hegel" by superimposing an array of epistemology oriented questions on the historico-cultural scene of the letter to connect the content of the text with its intraphilosophical context relative to the political conditions that produced the discourse on the role of the State in public education:

Interpreting the age of Hegel involves keeping in mind this boundless textuality, in an effort to determine the specific configuration that interests us here: the moment at which systematic philosophy — in the process of becoming philosophy of the State, of Reason as the State — begins to entail, more or less obviously, but essentially, indispensably, a pedagogical systematics governed by the necessity of entrusting the teaching of philosophy to state structures and civil servants. The business most certainly began before Hegel. . . . But can we not date from the age of Hegel the most powerful discursive machine of this problematic? Is this not indicated by the fact that the Marxist, Nietzschean, and Nietzscheo-Heideggerian problematics that now dominate all questions concerning the relations of education and the State must still come to grips with Hegelian discourse?[78]

The discourse of a radical resistance to the institution — reflective of an unfettered will-to-action à la Nietzsche, Marx, or Heidegger — is elided with a transformational rereading of the metaphysical infrastructure supporting the political use of ideology prevalent in Hegelian pedagogical architectonics, remediated as it is by the ethical theory of the State. For Derrida, this slipping of Hegelianism or speculative dialectics into a fusion of philosophy and history in the form of non-universalizable rules for educational praxis implodes the usual text-context distinctions. As Michael Ryan has correctly observed of demystifying the "applied ethics" of hegemonies after deconstruction, "Ideology is the political use of metaphysics in the domain of practice."[79] Derrida, from this perspective, is left to push the sociocultural exigencies of this post-Hegelian, post-speculative ground even further to dissolve the epistemological possibula of an extradiscursive or linguistically unmediated point of departure from which to study the report without neglecting the philosophical intricacies of the concept of age or the politicization of what now are well-known reconfigurations of pedagogical issues surrounding the ethical problem(s) of the state of education and the education of the State that are rehearsed in the letter (for example, What content should be taught? Who should define it? How should it be defined? How should it be taught? How should it be implemented in the curriculm?). The text-context rapprochement on which to query the ideological basis of the philosophical propaedeutic Hegel outlines in the report to Altenstein is the space identified by Derrida to be "between the Idea of the State defined in the third part of *The Philosophy of Right* (reality as an act of substantial will, as a goal in itself, absolute, immobile, knowing what it wants in its universality, etc.) and personal subjectivity or particularity, whose most extreme forms the modern State has the power to perfect."[80]

Hegel's *Philosophy of Right*:
The Right of Hegel's Philosophy

Hegel did indeed anticipate (philosophically, if not practicably), in *The Philosophy of Right* — the theoretically overdetermined idea or concept of the modern State central to his political thought and on which his conception of education interdepends — the fundamental decree of his commitment, that is, "making teaching — particularly philosophical teaching — into a structure of the State."[81] For Hegel, the education of subjectivity constitutes the subordination of individual freedom(s) to an overarching principle of undeniable universality or reason apprehended from within the Spirit or Mind and actualized through its progressive becoming as the essence of Being. The mediacy of a willful determination of human consciousness culminates vicariously in the formation of the State: a "hieroglyph of reason"[82] supplying the uncontestable grounds for existence relative to the sociopolitical and juridico-ethical constructions of an autotelic nomothetic order (for example, institutions of civil society, state bureaucracies, military apparatus) constituted from the indissoluble linkage of inner and outer senses of reality moving toward the attainment of absolute knowledge.[83] Filling the void of immanence in its passing to transcendence, this self-determinateness of being as the logic of Being signals the emergence of objective spirit from subjective spirit and finally to absolute spirit and takes the shape of a tripartite dialectical division encompassing the totality of thought or the finitude of Mind, understanding (*Verstehen*):

I. Logic: the science of the Idea in and for itself.
II. Philosophy of Nature: the science of the Idea in its otherness.
III. Philosophy of Spirit: the science of the Idea come back to itself out of that otherness.[84]

Affective influences on the distillation of individual identity outside of the rational technologies of self are not quickly discounted but placed in auxiliary importance to the intersubjective nature of a communal development that codifies the nexus of Being from the symbolic products of a shared cultural capital or from the results of conscious *energeia* for engendering the memory[85] of the Spirit or Mind and of its reasoned development throughout the enactment of history. What is crucial to the Hegelian systematic exposition of categories — as an infinitesimal extension of the Kantian imperative toward the apprehension of reality in Spirit or Mind — is the continuity of memory (*Gedächtnis*) and the anamnesic interiorization (*Erinerrung*) of empirical knowledge for the procreative unfolding of human self-consciousness. Following the dialectical metaphysics of the speculative stratagem to its logical closure, there is a limitation to thought (*Gedanke*) that is bound to the certainty of sensory sources of empirical reality, the perceptual fulfillment of which springs forth a transcendentalized meaning tempered from the *apocalypsis* of Spirit or Mind as a "self-producing, self-justifying and self-correcting system, an eternal activity of self-alienation, self-discovery and self-union."[86] Spirit or Mind therefore reveals itself in the pronounced ideality of its own structures and is verified in the transiting of subjective and objective states of consciousness to absolute knowing. It bears out its right from the detailed logic of a systematic grammar of the conditions of thought, the knowledge that we already possess: for what is not interiorized and subjected to the living memory of itself cannot be known in totality. But what of the valuation of memory in this pedagogical quest for pinpointing the age of philosophical identity Hegel pursues in the report?

The Limits of Signing and the Dialectic of Pedagogical Identity: The Undecidability of Anamnesis and the Life-Writing of the Self

The idealization of memory in the example of impressionable youth that Hegel evinces is permitted by an a priori notion of subjectivity. The unitariness of an autoreflexive reconciliation of consciousness to self-consciousness unwaveringly succors the decidability of the mnemotechnically engineered pedagogical identity that is demarcated to moderate for the truth of a memory of unphilosophical age. Hegel can attest to the efficacy of this educational methodology as a surviving model of the discernable ends of a schooling nearly identical to what is described in the letter written to Altenstein. The apologetic form of the example adjudicates the start of subjective identity, the life-writing of which is authorized by the indelibility of the signature functioning as the mark of the truth of memory to the self. The "Age of Hegel" asks (among other things) whether what Hegel is doing with (and to) the anecdote in the report by staking the claim of being able to determine with undaunted precision and absolute singularity the major source of pedagogical influence on the realization of "philosophical selfhood" is even plausible; whether the story of origins, itself suspect, is a clever invention for the institutional sake of speculative philosophy; "if he plays with the example the way, elsewhere [in the *Phenomenology of Spirit*], he teaches the *Beispiel* [example]."[87]

Paralleling the Nietzschean preoccupation for exploring "how one becomes what one is," Derrida interrogates the autobiographical limits constitutive of subjective identity through a life-writing-of-the-self to undermine the sense-certainty of the unsolicited retrospection Hegel freely gives testimony to by ever-so-humbly signing for it. There is a strong deconstructive rationale for sustaining the autobiographical reading of the report that concentrates, more or less, on the signing of memory veiled under the guiles of the proper name, while addressing the ethical-political aspects of key curricular questions regarding the institutionalization of philosophical pedagogies of ages past and present: the contradiction or "incompatibility between the teaching and the signature, a schoolmaster and a signifier . . . even when they let themselves be thought and signed, these two operations cannot overlap each other (*se recouper*)."[88] The pedagogical ramifications of this double metaphorical writing of the signature of the proper name of Hegel as a sign of the truth of the philosophical memory of speculative dialectics have been dealt with extensively by Derrida:

Hegel presents himself as a philosopher or a thinker, someone who constantly tells you that his empirical signature — the signature of the individual named Hegel — is secondary. His signature, that is, pales in the face of the truth, which speaks through his mouth, which is produced in his text, which constructs the system it constructs. This system is the teleological outcome of all Western experience, so that in the end Hegel, the individual, is nothing but an empirical shell which can fall away without subtracting from the truth or from the history of meaning. As a philosopher and as a teacher, he seems to be saying that not only is it possible for his signature and his proper name to disappear without a loss, to fall outside of the system, but that this is even necessary in his own system because it will prove the truth and autonomy of that system. . . . It appears, then, that Hegel did not sign. . . . Yet, in fact, Hegel signs. . . . One could show, as I have tried elsewhere,[[89]] in what way it was difficult to dispose with the name of Hegel in his work, to withold its inscription — call it personal or biographical from his work. It implies a reelaboration of the whole biographical within philosophy.[90]

The idea that one can write the self from the archtext of memory, and by so doing, extract from the terms of representation an intersubjective code of meaning-making pregnant in its pedagogical implications for the other, is linked to a dialectics of the signature, or the sign-function of identity, as recuperative of the built-in differentiality of subjectivity. By reconceptualizing subjectivity and its exteriorizable corollary of identity as consolidated in the guises of the signature of the proper name, Derrida can deconstruct the pedagogical formulations of the report to reveal what is concealed in the ideological subtext of the speculative logic informing the ethics and politics of the life-writing of the memory.

The empirical act of signing Hegel performs is a cathexis of the example. Moving beyond the form of representation to real life, it names and appropriates for the disunity of subjectivity in the very materiality of its significatory content. It replaces and supplements the semblances of an originary difference of self-identity that this instance of life-writing from memory would otherwise unveil in the transl(iter)ation from sign to eidos, from text to context, from writing to life itself: "Memory and truth cannot be separated. The movement of aletheia is a deployment of mnèmè through and through. A deployment of living memory, of memory as psychic life in its self-presentation to itself."[91] Endorsing the pedagogical authenticity of such an attempt at utter and unmitigated self-representation are the borders of a negative space stipulating the affirmation of selfhood or identity to be delineated from the conscious ascription of difference to an other. The signature of Hegel itself notarizes the autonomy of this inwardly projecting totalization of subjectivity by containing the implication of a consolidation of origins, wherein the nominative capacity of the form of the proper name that is excerpted in writing is granted the right to self-sign or to sign-self from the continuity of the living-memory trace.[92] The signature comes to personify the visible difference of identity: a conflation of the subject Hegel with the sign of the proper name of Hegel. From the arbitrariness of a self-referential sign-grouping, the heterogeneity of subjectivity is expunged under the dominant modes of graphematic articulation available for the concatenation of the proper name.

Hegel signs for the memory of childhood. The signing of the proper name that Hegel reenacts to justify the curricular schema is (and also must be) the synoptic periphrasis of a surfeit of textuality concentrated within the structures of the signature; it maintains the illusion of not exceeding the strictures of its formal features, but does just so, given the teleological systematicity of the epistemological presuppositions on which it rests. Because the signature is a politico-juridical fetishization of writing gathered under what Martin Jay calls the normative ethics of a "phallogocularcentric"[93] non-supplementarity of the graphical form, it substitutes the resemblance of the sign of identity for the truth of identity. That is so the sign of Hegel can be made to stand in ideal or unequivocal relation to the non-arbitrariness of itself as a semaphorical retypification testifying to the truthfulness of its referent, the philosopher Hegel. More importantly for Altenstein's political purposes, what the inscription of the empirical signature of Hegel at the conclusion of the letter ensures is: the availability of a mechanism for a retransposition of the real-world estimation (for example, societal, economic, cultural, and academic) deemed the human signified that the signature refers to, to the content of thought the philosopher espouses in the text about philosophical education on behalf of the State. The signature discharges unto the subject-philosopher Hegel what is the equivalent of an undiminishing and after-the-fact responsibility for the pronouncements of memory and for the memory of self expounded in the report. The act of signing carries over to join the anteriority of the past to the posterity of the future. Its effects are perceived much later. This juridical-ethical power of the signature Hegel appends to this letter is duly conferred by the oath Hegel took as a citizen of the State to uphold a bureaucratic code of decorum that decrees the officiousness of bearing witness to the truth of signing one's own name. The proper name of the philosopher countersigns the legalistic jurisdiction of its own symbolic authority to intercede in the intense politics of the debate over education: to attempt to affect those conditions by a defense of speculative idealism and of the State, for the rights of which Hegel has signed before and often enough, throughout the corpus of his philosophical texts, lectures, correspondences, and so on. Derrida "do[es] no more than name, with a proper name as one of the guiding threads, the necessity of a deconstruction"[94] of the memory of the sign of self.

Déjà-Pas-Encore: The *Already-Not-Yet* of a Post-Cartesian Subjectivity

The exemplar of unschooled youth that Hegel imparts is a reminiscence depicting the quality of a not-as-yet philosophical subjectivity, or what was, once upon a time, the childhood experience of his own developing pedagogical identity. An attempt to reify a past subjective identity from the life-writing of an ideal reflexivity — to make the truth of memory speak the self-consciousness of itself, as it were — entails the eradication of the undecidability already immanent to the personal conception of what one is. There is too much interfering with the ego's reception of perceptual sense-data coloring the way it sees itself as subject that Hegel chooses to disregard or to explain away. The signing of the life-writing of memory in this retrograde vision revolves around the recognizable presence of a self-presence that is present to itself and signs for the Being of itself as being. It is a projection of an autogenetic subjectivity or an effortless reflexivity amalgamating the diversity of the realms of consciousness combining the simultaneity of self, as both same and other, in its returning to itself through the spectacle of introspection.[95] The teleologicality of the reminiscence is adducible only by positing prior to the instance of the ego's self-remembering a timeless state of Being charged fully as the enunciation of unchanging presence.[96] The continual suppression of the absence of presence that hypostatizes (fixes, enframes, parodies) subjectivity makes it capturable in the still of life and perpetuates the idealistic premises igniting the memory of non-philosophical identity Hegel puts forward. Pretending to look back in time and space at the source of the present-day self through the inverted lens reflecting a mirror-like past, Hegel has immediately interceded to predict for any retranslation of the pedagogical significance of the living memory trace the episode highlights. By defining the terms of a subjective writing of identity from the consistency of a negatively-defined logic designed to fulfill the speculative ends of dialectical philosophy, the "teleological gesture of return inquiry"[97] establishes an ideal frame of reference crucial to the engendering of the ego's absolute knowledge of itself. The subjective vision could then be generalized (by Altenstein or Hegel) to serve as the fountainhead of universalizable curricular or pedagogical truths.

The "entire 'system' of speculative dialectics organizes this childhood anamnesis to suit the ministerial project"[98] for a concrete icon of the imaginable outcome of a speculative pedagogy that could be Hegel and more than Hegel. The first two modalities denoting the performance of memory are essential to the representational politics of a general economy of the signature Hegel supplies (for example, the signer actively engaged in authenticating the impression of self-identity, either by conscious intent or by accident, resulting in the leaving of a set of idiomatic marks to fulfill the stylistic demands of the genre of transmission).[99] The signature enables the life-writing of memory to allude to two chronological ages, for example, the spatio-temporal figurativeness of dissonant modes of subjectivity that exhibit divergent stages of mental development relative to states of being — the wisdom of Hegel, the elder philosopher versus the folly of Hegel, the untutored child. The dialectical synthesis of identity from the interiorizing effects of memory overcomes the symmetrization of the self and anti-self as the false identities of opposites. By resolving this binary structuration of subjectivity that Hegel presents as a thesis versus antithesis construction to the prospect of a third term, the speculative result of what is subsumed within the force-gesture of a sublation (*Aufhebung*), that "raises, denies, suspends, and preserves the first."[100] The penultimate movement is suspended indefinitely, held in reserve, for reasons that are revealed by Derrida to be not altogether altruistic or ethical, but immanently self-serving and selfishly motivated by the narrow interests of the time. The reader is left to ponder over it, to decide what it all means. What can we make of the autobiographical reliability of the life-writing of memory that Hegel signs for, to preserve a philosophical pedagogy?

The representation of pedagogical experience Hegel yields to, incumbently for reasons of argument, is not and could not ever be identical to the conceptual tenor of the ideas evoked. Even though a life-writing-of-the-self must be responsive to a subjective transcendence of the memory trace, it is still supplementary to thought itself — a sign of a sign — and not analogous, correlational, motivational, or iconic of the eidetic workings of the human psyche.[101] The conceptual limits of the exposition (*Darstellung*) Hegel proffers to Altenstein are exceeded by the undecidability of an already-not-yet (*déja-pas-encore*) reconfiguration of philosophical subjective identity that Derrida introduces to displace, to dislocate, and to disfigure (*Enstellung*) the self-confident prosopopoeia of the portrayal.[102] The enjambed logic of the structure of this neologism connotes the philosophical selfhood of the subject Hegel to be a veritable conundrum of multiply-suspended educational beginnings, rather than the assertion of a teleologicality of Being that is re-presented as the likelihood of the first steps to a speculative pedagogy. The destructuration of the ideal route to a regaining of identity stultifies the absolute certainty of a subjective self-representation the life-writing of memory is wont to warrant. Derrida explains the deconstructive complication:

At the age of fifty-two, he [Hegel] speaks of his twelfth year. He was already a philosopher. But just like everyone else is, right? That is, not yet a philosopher since, in view of the corpus of the complete works of his maturity, this *already* will have been a *not yet*.

If we don't think through this conceptual, dialectical, speculative structure of this *already-not yet*, we will not have understood anything (in its essentials, as he would say) about the *age* (for example, that of Hegel). Or about any age whatsoever, but especially, and *par excellance* that *of* philosophy or *for* philosophy. . . . Under the cover of the *already-not-yet*, autobiographical confiding enlists the anecdote in a demonstration, treating the issue of (the) age as a figure in the phenomenology of the mind, as a moment in the logic.[103]

It is not a matter of who the real Hegel is or was. Such understanding could never be realized *in toto*: the rhizome of actions and events of discourse carried-out by or enacted-upon a subject do not and cannot concede such accuity of insight. For Derrida, the pedagogical purposiveness of the life-writing of memory Hegel surrenders to is an extant indicator of an intransitory subjectivity, a coming-into-being-of-the-self that the signature of the proper name authorizes and is authorized by, to dissimulate identity as a presence feigning absence behind the masks of confiding.[104]

The predisposition of this writing of the identity of self from the ruins of life's memories assures that Hegel will speak only of the deaths of unnamed and expropriated younger selves. What is excluded from the representation of being is an intrinsic forgetfulness of Being that Derrida acknowledges. It is a prosopopoeia that spans the dark chasm of a space-time continuum to veritably undo the mimetic impulse of the life-writing of anamnesis by keeping its structures open to the machinations of difference, wherein meaning reconstruction is deferred from the traces of differential movements of the signification process away from an intangible source. Derrida explains: "The powers of *lèthè* simultaneously increase the domains of death, of non-truth, of non-knowledge. This is why writing, at least insofar as it sows 'forgetfulness of the soul,' turns us toward the inanimate and toward non-knowledge. But it cannot be said that its essence simply and *presently* confounds it with death or non-truth. For writing *has* no essence or value of its own, whether positive or negative. It plays within the simulacrum. It is in its type the mime of memory, of knowledge, of truth, etc."[105] Hegel's depiction of this pedagogical moment from the pasts of childhood must inevitably surrender the living presence of life-writing itself to the contaminating effects of a first outside

— the monumental (*hypomnèmatic*) supplementarity of a form — that is the absence (or death) of essence within the economy of memory that incurs a loss of profit(s) (the up side of its meaning potential) because of the very materiality of its production.[106] It is in this sense that what is included under the authority of the sign of Hegel are the fragments of a thanatographical discourse that looks forward in time to the end beyond the impending death of the philosopher and of his philosophical pedagogy, although also insures for or against it; because what is signed remembers the self to the other, yet also remembers the death of the self to the other and to the self.

DELIMITING THE TEACHINGS OF METAPHYSICS

The Pedagogical Institution and the Perils of Philosophy: Deconstruction and the GREPH in the Postmodern Age of Hegel

To further the discussion of the nature of educational presentation adequate to philosophy education, Derrida turns loose the specters of the Hegelian legacy on the "analogous and contiguous"[107] context of post-revolutionary France. Twenty-two years after the self-portrait Hegel sketched-out, the again very public confidence of a progeny of Hegelianism, Victor Cousin, is added to the file. A disciple and friend of the German philosopher (whose release from prison Hegel had secured after six months of incarceration for participation in demonstrations occuring during the period of social unrest involving the university student fraternities of Bavaria [1824]),[108] Cousin expostulated an eloquent argument to oppose the threatened eradication of philosophy from the colleges by the powers-that-be in a discourse presented before the House of Peers. Derrida summarizes it as follows:

The jist [sic] of Cousin's reply: Definitely not [in regard to the abolition of metaphysics from the *lycée* curriculum]; since philosophy teaches natural certitudes (for example, the existence of God, the freedom or immortality of the soul), in principle, it can never be too early to begin. In other words, as long as the contents of instruction reinforce, as it were, the predominant forces, it is best to begin as early as possible. And the contradictory unity that reconciles the predominant force with itself and constitutes the basis of historical compromise is a mutually desired contract between secular State and Religion.[109]

On the one hand, by insisting on the "reciprocal independence of philosophy and theology"[110] Cousin attenuates the liberal and neutralist scope of pedagogy to take on the epistemological demeanor of a national French character in that of a Cartesian rationalist dreamscape. His mentor

Hegel, we must remember, had originally attempted to introduce the German context to the recapitulation of these equivocal motifs, because what "extends the domain of 'general culture'"[111] within curriculum is what "always remains highly determined in the contents it inculcates."[112] Cousin is in some ways more precocious. He promises to instill at the beginnings of the philosophy curriculum a program of study concentrating on a dualist metaphysics of knowing derivative of a provisional and methodic doubt, whereby the "naturality of truth" tracks a transcendental route as proceeding from the self-evident resolution of the reflexive sensibilities of Mind realized through the activation of epistemological subjectivity (the *cogito*) to a perfect certainty of Spirit. The affirmation of the rational soul of the self in Cousin's pedagogical revising of Cartesian epistemology verifies the existence of God to unite religion with philosophy for the eradication of skepticism and for the betterment of the State. On the other hand, Hegel denies the gymnasium (the primary grades) entrance to the "Pantheon of Western Metaphysics"[113] by invoking the "limits of schoolteaching"[114] to safeguard against the pedagogical short-sightedness of allowing the material components of instruction — its curriculum — to surpass the mental capabilities of these students.

Regulating the implementation of a prephilosophical (read non-metaphysical) content core that Derrida objects to, the Hegelian curriculum is made up of "the humanities (the Ancients, the great artistic and historical ideas of individuals and peoples, their ethics and their religiosity)"[115] as well as other areas (for example, empirical psychology and logic). The pedagogical aim Hegel pursues here is to cultivate seamlessly a natural progressivity of learning to be inaugurated from the first non-contemplative steps of interiorizing memorization (*Erinerrung*)[116] to an outwardly speculative rationality of thought "for, [as he insists in the report] in order to possess knowledge of any kind — even the highest sort — one must have memorized it (*im Gedächtnisse haben*); regardless of whether this is to be a beginning *or* an end in itself."[117] In "The Age of Hegel," the theo-philosophico-rationalist conceptualization of intellectual maturity Cousin advances for nurturing the mental capacities of the average student to apprehend the natural truths of Spirit-Mind is juxtaposed against the organicist archetype of the mnèmè of Spirit-Mind Hegel entreats to assert a hierarchy of instructional contents excluding metaphysics. The approach permits Derrida to lay bare the great extent to which both discourses harbor deep-seated ideological compulsions aspiring to pedagogically replicate nationalistic or State-sponsored assumptions indicative of a general culture from which the suitability of subject matter and the appropriateness of instructional maneuvers for the teaching-learning of philosophy are determined. The undertexts of both discourses condone the educational institutionalization of a philosophical knowing that ensures and is ensured by the reproducibility of dominant modes of cultural (re)transmission for the perpetuation of the ontotheology of Western metaphysics.

The yielding of contrasting positions with respect to the correct age for the teaching-learning of first philosophy is not coincidental; the higher reasons of religion, for Cousin (for example, to placate the skepticism of the church), and the good reasons of State, for Hegel (for example, to appease the power of a government bureaucracy) encroach on the pedagogical methodologizing of epistemology in their search for the most appropriate means to acceptable ends. From this quasi-eschatological viewpoint, a cross-organizational harmonizing of the structures of the educational organum with those sociocultural institutions that it must, sooner or later, answer to is metaphorically subsumed in an overcoded symbol of teleology, the "onto-encyclopaedic system of the *Universitas*"[118] as the microcosmic counterpart of the totality of the real world:

There is a Hegelian hierarchization [Derrida is referring to the assignment of the "letter" as a minor pedagogical moment in the philosophical canon of Hegel] but it is circular, and the minor is always carried, sublated *(relevé)* beyond the opposition, beyond the limit of inside and ouside in(to) the major. And inversely. The potency of this age without age derives from this great empirico-philosophical cycle. Hegel does not conceive of the school as a consequence or the image of the system, indeed, as its *pars totalis*: the system itself is an immense school, the thoroughgoing auto-encyclopaedia of the absolute spirit in absolute knowledge. And it is the school we never leave, hence, an obligatory instruction, which obliges (by) itself, since the necessity can no longer come from without.[119]

Neither Cousin nor Hegel ignores the conservativism of the type Derrida abstracts above from the speculative system of dialectics. We are again reminded that the defence of the right to philosophy teaching-learning in the public (dis)course of education must project an ethico-political accountability for the concept of the pedagogical institution and for the lasting results of its curricular ordinances. Unsurprisingly enough, this sense of responsibility to the power of external forces contained within the internal bounds of the disciplinary infrastructure of the educational system reinforces the "distinction between metaphysics and dogmatic theology"[120] for Cousin and Hegel. The partitionary function of the historical paradigm of the faculties for separating epistemology from religion in both situations allows them to gloss over the prejudices of the curricular prerequisites unique to each context for inculcating the experience of a civic sense of duty in students through the procedures of schooling. The overwhelming irony, however, is that this common goal is also the *stigme* of their departure in judgement when both philosophers are pushed to the limit by the requirement of recommending solutions to the problem of the age befitting the teaching-learning of pure philosophy.

Of common and singular importance to the strategies of Cousin and Hegel is to keep the philosophical formulations on which their pedagogical propositions depend manifestly pliable or ostensibly open so as to make the substance of their ideas appear favorable to the prevailing doctrines of the day. The political overtones of the criteria they both employ for the setting out of what are oppositional curricula are temporarily defused by a restatement of their respective pedagogical visions in the metaphysical surety of a post-Cartesian meditation. More than likely, the rationalist mannerisms of the style would be perceived to be nonthreatening to the ideological predilections of the nineteenth-century State bureaucracies they were presenting them to: either because of the distinctive penchant for perpetuating an effigy of epistemological nationalism by transmuting it into the flexible stock of cultural capital or because of the favorable predisposition of an educational methodology toward a benign controllability of the natural faculties of thought.[121] Feigning a rational disinterestedness for setting the parameters of what can be thought and of how thought is to be expressed, Cousin and Hegel sufficiently neutralize the political upshot of what could be construed to be, on the one side, reactionary or, on the other, biased in the meticulous rhetoric of their speculative musings on education.

Derrida reads the ethical coherence of this ideologico-philosophical hedging as a verbal alibi for reinstating many of the well-known naturalist motifs of a pedagogical humanism considered potentially less dangerous to the stability of the status quo. Redirecting the critical emphasis to the material conditions of the educational institution inherited from these major dialecticians by contemporary makers of curriculum or educational policy (for example, bureaucrats, public servants), "The Age of Hegel" directly engages (but has it ever really left?) the postmodern sphere of partisan politics engulfing France during the mid-1970s. Derrida consciously puts foremost the relevance of the historical context to tamper with the two complementary poles of nationalism and universalism that Cousin and Hegel eulogize, "not [wanting] to abandon the field to empiricism and thereby to whatever forces are at hand":[122]

It is always by insisting upon the "natural," by naturalizing the content or the forms of instruction, that one "inculcates" precisely what one wishes to exempt from criticism. GREPH must be particularly careful in this respect, since its tactics could expose it to this risk of naturalist mystification; by demanding that the age at which a young person begins the study of philosophy be lowered, and that the scope of instruction be extended, there is a risk of being understood (without intending it; but the adversary will do his best to further this impression) as suggesting that once prejudices and "ideologies" have been erased, what will be revealed is the bare truth of an "infant" always already ready to philosophize and *naturally* capable of doing so. Those modes of discourse that are currently held to be the most "subversive" are never entirely free of this naturalism. They always appeal to some sort of return to primitive desire, to the simple lifting of repression, to the unbinding of energy, or to the primary process.... The natural truths taught by metaphysics proceed from divine writings and will have engraved in the soul of the disciple that which the teacher of philosophy can only reveal through self-effacement: an invisible writing that he causes to appear on the body of the pupil. Are the discourses of the GREPH always free of this schematization? Does it not return, necessarily, in a more or less disguised form?[123]

"The Age of Hegel" localized the precipitous complexity of the pedagogical ideal of progressivity in respect to the metaphysical genealogy of the Western institution of pedagogy. It facilitated the point of entry for a radical broaching (*l'entame*) into the heterogeneity of the intense deliberation over State educational policy reform that was needed at the time the text was written and first appeared in *Qui a Peur de la Philosophie?*[124] a research manifesto into philosophy teaching-learning published under the aggregate authorship of the GREPH. Derrida addresses the historicity of these pressing issues very plainly to accent the alacrity of how the historico-political circumstances preceding the situational considerations of the philosophical age Cousin presided over while a member of parliament and in which Hegel "found himself implicated, advancing or floundering,"[125] are akin to the social climate initiating the pedagogical reform movements of post-1968 France that culminated with the issuance of the Haby Reform (1975).

A State proposal for drastic educational restructuring named after the then newly-appointed minister of education, René Haby (who served in the Gaullist [right-wing] government of Giscard d'Estaing), the Haby Reform promised to reduce the number of classroom hours available for philosophy instruction in the *lycée*. Moreover, the imperatives of the Giscard-Haby plan very much threatened the future of the discipline in the university. The consternation that the severity of its edicts bred about the overarching or longer-ranging ramifications of this preemptive intervention on the part of the State into teaching-learning was one of the factors that eventually led to the official mobilization of the GREPH against the Haby Reform in January 1975.[126]

Derrida, a founding member and a major force, wished to help move forward the group's avowedly activist involvement in the public debate over philosophy. In speaking to the GREPH, "The Age of Hegel" provides only one illustration of how to interrogate the ethico-political decipherability of the Haby Reform through these metastatic fluctuations of the juridical aegis of epistemology before and since Hegel. That the example — the exemplarity of the example — is itself deconstructive is incidental (one might also say idiosyncratic) to Derrida's own intricate style of reading and writing. The mission of the GREPH had "defined itself [from the outset] as a locus of work and debate, and not as a center for the broadcasting of slogans or doctrinaire messages"[127] without the benefit of intense research, both empirical and theoretical.[128] To stimulate dialogue that could prove useful for negotiating a consensus within the diversified interests of the group, Derrida did, in fact, formalize the "Preliminary Proposal for the Constitution of a Research Group on Philosophical Education" (the *Avant-Projet*)[129] by synthesizing ideas from notes taken at their meetings. He was not adamant about, or interested in, transforming the GREPH into a *"deconstructive machine,"*[130] if this were even possible.[131] Derrida has preferred instead — as he has done in "The Age of Hegel" and afterwards — to warn of the likely dangers of confronting the State and its management of the pedagogical institution head-on through a leveling of injunctions that are intended to bring down the structures of the oppressive edifice itself, once and for all. Such a teleologico-eschatological zeal to dismantle a system of education with a view to setting up its replacement anew could only serve to prohibit the advent of appreciable change within the general composition of the whole.

In referring to the archetype of the university as the "onto- and auto-encyclopaedic circle of the State,"[132] Derrida counsels that "the deconstruction of its concepts, of its instruments, of its practices cannot proceed by attacking it *immediately* and attempting to do away with it without risking the *immediate* return of other forces equally capable of adapting to it. *Immediately* to retreat and make way for the 'other' of the *Universitas* might represent a welcome invitation to those very determinate and very determined forces, ready and waiting, close by, to take over the State and the University."[133] The aftermath of this wasted labor would undoubtedly be to reaffirm the doxies of precisely those institutional conventions in question. The casualness of its all-or-nothing mandate will inadvertently fail: given that the totalizing force of the ideal must reproduce the generic organization of standardized forms or models (for example, utopic, metaphysical, anarchic) whose limits take shape between the dyad of opposing argumentative guardrails marking out the space amid the less-than-agreeable chimeras of nihilism and despair. For example, one can either, on the one side, protect against the fearful responsibility of misdoing by fostering inaction or, on the other side, provoke irresponsible decision-making leading to reckless action.

Where the premise is to alter appreciably the formal boundaries of the educational system, to make its performative structures more responsive to the alterior qualities of subjective differences, Derrida is most exact about what kind of resistive activity is called for: "In consequence: battling as alway on two fronts, on two scenes and according to two ways, a rigorous and efficient deconstruction must at the same time develop the critique (practice) of the current philosophic institution [from within the enactment of its aberrations] and to engage in a positive transformation, rather affirmative, audacious, extensive and intensive, of the teaching called 'philosophic.'"[134] It is the aporia of the educational system itself — an institutionalized interiority of *pouvoir/savoir* without pure exteriority — that licenses the agonistics of a double science Derrida has culled, always taking great care to remind us that the field of oppositions deconstruction criticizes "is also a field of non-discursive forces."[135] The pragmatic territoriality of this space, once cleaved open from the intertwining and doubly invaginated folds of its inside and its outside margins, reveals a deterritorialized nonspace where the counterhegemonic locality and illocality of deconstruction can bring to light the heteronomous autonomy of the excluded at the peripheries of the institutionalized center.

Of course, the juridico-political stakes of the ethical struggle for equality of educational opportunities that the GREPH has pledged to carry on are an important denouement of this redressing of the performative relation of philosophy and pedagogy, formalized as it is in the praxiological cybernetics of the educational institution.[136] For Derrida, aspiring to rectify the catachresis of past injustices requires exposing the hidden fallibility and innate fragility of comforting centers of established order that permitted them in the first place. Showing the unpredictability of play within the seemingly fixed hierarchical structures of a dominating logics breaks the coherence of its autarchic control.[137] "The Age of Hegel" skillfully orchestrates the schematics of this well-known deconstructive compulsion that imminently enables work against the concrete abuses of institutionalized systems of cruel authority or repressive power.[138] By way of reference to the legitimation of the notorious letter Altenstein received, Derrida advocates an audacious transformation of the normative structures of culture that justify and ascribe the privilege of worth to a subject or object.

What is to be done with this Letter of Hegel's? Where is it to be situated? Where does it take (its) place? Evaluation is inevitable: is it a "major" text or a "minor" one? Is it a "philosophical" text? What status, as they say, do we grant it? What title? One of the tasks of the GREPH could be a critique (not only formal, but effective and concrete) of all existing hierarachies.... Without such a reelaboration, no profound transformation will be possible. The force that dominates the process of classification and the institution of hierarchies allows us to read whatever it is interested in having us read (which it then labels major texts, or texts of "great import"); and it renders inaccessible whatever it is interested in underestimating, and which in general it *cannot read* (describing such texts as minor or marginal). And this holds true for the discourse of the educator and for all his evaluatory procedures (grading; juries for examinations, competitions, theses; so-called supervisory committees; etc.); it is the evaluative standard determining all discourse: from that of the critic and the upholder of tradition to that determining editorial policy, the commercialization of texts, etc. And once again, it is not simply a matter of texts in print or on blackboards, but rather of a general textuality without which there is no understanding and no action.[139]

Beginning with the preliminary phases of "a general reelaboration of the entire problematic of hierarchies,"[140] deconstruction unbalances the deliberate equation of language and meaning as the only authentic reading and writing of the concept of the truth of education. It challenges and disrupts the historical continuity of the institution's capability to reproduce its logic through the nurturing of a "pure[ly] egological subject"[141] that has its codic source for truth in the systematic stratification of the meaning of signification and the fixed rules of its evaluation or rendering. Unlike more conventional forms of ideology critique, deconstruction denies recourse to any intuition or conception of reality unmediated by language from which to glean a glimmer of the falsity of consiousness."*Il n' y a pas de hors-texte*"" (There is no outside-text; there is nothing outside of the [con-]text),[142] Derrida will insist. That is the marching order of deconstruction.

Derrida therefore also places the premises of the GREPH at risk in "The Age of Hegel" through a careful expansion of the unavoidable pitfalls of a critique of normativity without the cautious reflectivity of an autocritique of the desire of the self and of the same:

Reread the Preliminary Project of the GREPH: every sentence demands that the censured or devaluaed [sic] be displayed, that the vast holdings of a more-or-less forbidden library be exhumed from the cellars. And that there be a lack of respect for prevailing evaluations: not only to indulge certain perverse bibliographic pleasures (on the other hand, why not?); nor even in order to better understand what links philosophy to its institution, to its institutional underside and recesses (*dessous et envers*); but rather to transform the very conditions of our effective intervention in them. *Underside* or *recesses*, because it is not a matter of discovering today, belatedly, what has been known all along: that there is such a thing as a philosophical institution. Indeed, "Philosophy" ("*la* " *philosophie*) has always had a dominant concept to take this into account, and *institution* is at bottom the name it has reserved for this task. Underside and recesses, because we are not satisfied with what the institution reveals about itself: neither with what we can perceive empirically, nor with what we can conceive according to the law of the philosophical concept. Underside and recesses would no longer have a signification dominated by the philosophical opposition that continues to order discourse in terms of a concealed substance or essence of the institution, hidden beneath its accidents, circumstances, phenomena, or superstructures. Underside and recesses would designate, rather, that which, while still being situated within this venerable (conceptual metaphoric) topos, might begin to extricate itself from this opposition and to constitute it in a new manner.[143]

At the bordercrossings of the transhistorical strife over the praxiological intelligibility of the signifier philosophy enacted as pedagogy is the discourse of the educational institution, the eternal gatekeeper of the sense of reason ordering and translating for the curricular substance of the discipline. Positing an unassailable *oikos* of language as the order of the "house of Being" has safeguarded the particular directions adopted in the West for the instruction of the subject.[144] And what Derrida calls the cure and poison of this discursive/non-discursive circularity construes the *pharmakon* of a teaching-learning that one can never escape. Language is the symbolic violence that informs the conceptual-metaphorical schemata of the psyche for dealing with everyday reality.[145] It is within the mastery of the rhetoricized heart of the institution's disciplinarity that the ingrained *habitus* of one's own subjectivity is subject to and a subject of the flux of language expended upon the ideology of a free-will.[146] Derrida is succinct: "There is no neutral or natural place in education (*l'enseignement*). Here, for example, is not an indifferent place."[147]

To be sure, the institutionalization of knowledge consolidating the philosophical lessons of Western epistemology bears the transcription of a logoarchy that intertwines the ontotheological foundations of a metaphysical language with the intellectual backdrop of a pedagogical history inseparable from the truth of its object.[148] The semiotic effectivity of this operative modeling of learning upon a knowledge-centered teaching of closed values is described by Derrida as follows: "Teaching delivers signs, the teaching body produces (shows and puts forth) proofs (*enseignes*), more precisely signifiers supposing knowledge of a previous signified. Referred to this knowledge, the signifier is structurally second. Every university [or general system of education] puts language in this position of delay or derivation in relation to meaning or truth."[149] A pedagogical method patterned after the instrumentality of a Platonic-Hegelian mimetologism of the eidos cannot be anything but a laconic dictation of self-obscuring memory. Such an invasive instruction cast of a mechanical repetition that has as its *techne* a retrospective rather than a prospective function is more apt to valorize the reproduction of knowledge than to create the conditions for discovering or inventing it[150]:

Along the stages that are always idiomatic, we are always guided back to the most durable tradition of the philosophical concept of teaching: revelation, unveiling, the discovered truth of the "already-there" (*déjà là*) according to the mode of "not-yet" (*pas encore*), a Socrato-Platonic anamnesis sometimes taken up by the philosophy of psychoanalysis. Throughout these specific determinations may be found, time and time again, the same scheme, the same concept of truth, of a truth linked to the same pedagogical structure. But the interpretation of these specificities must not succumb to this determination, as though one had to settle for the discovery of the same beneath all variations. One should never settle for this but also never forget to take its power into account . . . the question at issue is always, as it was for Plato, one of a double metaphoric of inscription: a bad writing (*une mauvaise écriture*), secondary, artificial, cryptic or hieroglyphic, voiceless, intervenes to obscure good writing (*la bonne écriture*); it overdetermines, occults, complicates, perverts, makes a travesty of the natural inscription of the truth of the soul. By effacing himself, the teacher (*maître*) is also promoting the unlearning of bad writing. But if this motif retains a certain "Platonic" allure, the specificity of its "age" marks itself by a profound "Cartesian" reference.[151]

The "teaching body"[152] Derrida refers to has a regenerative role in the educational institution fundamental to an ancillary fulfillment of the dominant pedagogical theme of Western philosophy, the "metaphysics of presence" or "logocentrism."[153] Where teaching characterized by the mere delivery and reception of signs "has its ideal, with exhaustive translatability, the effacement of language (*la langue*),"[154] learning is and can be — no more, no less — equivalent in difficulty to the cognitive capabilities of a minimal technical competence required for the error-free exchange of transmitted concepts. It presumes, and Derrida is clear on this, that the living spirit of a writing enfleshed of preestablished empirical proofs can be actively etched into the conscious corps of a passified student body. This positive value of signifier-signified/sign-referent relations that is exhibited and perpetuated as the traditional discourse of a teaching-learning practice (for example, a positivistic didactics of total cognition) connects thought to expression to bring about the essential possibility of faultlessly duplicating the content of signification in the contours of the mind. Its transcendental inspiration of a "transportable univocality or of formulizable polysemia"[155] propagates the illusion of a correspondence theory of pedagogical truths. When the presuppositions of the well-known teaching-learning model that Derrida describes above are combined with the absolute idealism of speculative dialectics Hegel supplies for supporting the case of a curriculum driven by the fruits of Mnemosyne, two things are foreshadowed: the end of pedagogy and the end of philosophy. Nothing remains untheorized outside the oppositional complementarity of this metaphysical system that could counter the dialectic of its glorious memory, essentially because the conceptualization of meaning, truth, and reality is sequestered in the liminal scope of the singular, the finite, and the totalizing.

It will follow that the scene of teaching alluded to by Derrida via "The Age of Hegel" comprises the student, the teacher, and the institution defined not only in and of themselves, with respect to their rights, obligations, freedoms, duties, and so forth, as the entities of a tripartite division of the educational space.[156] Each body is more (and conceivably less) than the sum of its accumulative parts as the grounding for the synchrony and diachrony of interrelations between the principal actors of the topos oscillates. Moreover, these educational entities are subjectively prone to the ideological effects of internally- and externally-motivated influences upon the situated formations of the scene of teaching that create a specific sociocultural and ethico-political niche for the possibility of pedagogy. Support for the material conditions of the system's structure so crucial to its living on is maintained by the hegemonic entrenchment of legitimating metanarratives justifying, and justified by, an ethos of praxis.[157] The applicability of the general principles of deconstruction to the historical contextuality of the pedagogical institution is because the educational bodies comprising the material scene of teaching are themselves mediated by the constructions of discourse or of a pervading textuality effectively determinant, as such, of the subjectivation of experience. The discourse infusing the (inter)disciplinarity of this educational site is a fertile ethical and political ground for deconstruction because the actual circumstances of a particular pedagogy (for example, a philosophical one) imply the institutional privileging of a set of ideological assumptions toward teaching and learning, the logic of which underlies and guides the prescriptive implementation of a hierarchical framework of knowledge in the concrete form of a curriculum. On this point, Derrida is concise: "The university [as both *Umwelt* and schooling organization], is philosophy, a university is always the construction of a philosophy."[158]

To destabilize the centrality of a dominant conception of philosophy to the existing disciplinary structure and valuations of the pedagogical institution, one that has done much to annex its position, charges neither a destruction of the old system nor a flat denial of the conventionality of epistémè inherited from the ages before and after Hegel. Deconstruction concedes not to the naïve enlightenment of an either/or, neither/nor proposition simply to be on the other side of reason in all situations despite the circumstances.[159] It obliges a patient and unrelenting resistance from within the system that challenges the arbitrary working-out of its practices through the magnified inconsistencies in the logic of its discourse:

Following the consistency of its logic, it [deconstruction] attacks not only the internal edifice, both semantic and formal, of philosophemes, but also what one would be wrong to assign to it as its external housing, its extrinsive conditions of practice: the historical forms of its pedagogy, the social, economic or political structures of this pedagogical institution. It is because deconstruction interferes with solid structures, "material" institutions, and not only with discourses or signifying representations, that it is always distinct from analysis or "critique." And in order to be pertinent, deconstruction works as strictly as possible in that place where the supposedly "internal" order of the philosophical is articulated by (internal *and* external) necessity with the institutional conditions and forms of teaching. To the point where the concept of the institution itself would be subjected to the same deconstructive treatment.[160]

As Derrida's deconstruction of the Foucauldian archeology of madness has demonstrated, "all history [of the system of the institution, pedagogy included] can only be in the last analysis, the history of meaning, that is of Reason in general."[161] And if reason and history are the only conceivable ends of the institutional structure of pedagogy as an objectification of philosophy, there is a double bind, or a bidirectional fold in the laws of the system and of its philosophical analysis, impinging upon the GREPH's project — as it did upon Foucault's — that makes it difficult, if no precautions are taken, to avoid the dual traps of either reinstating the heterology of another monolith while opposing the privilege of an epistemological reduction of meanings or to escape imposing a willful silence upon the languages of the self while assenting to the fittingness of a theoretical posture.

The recommendations Derrida makes to the GREPH regarding a political resistance to the Haby Reform incorporate these deconstructive principles in an effort to regulate the "preconditions of a political practice that seeks to be as coherent as possible in its successive steps, in the strategy of its alliances and in its discourse."[162] What justifies deconstruction to move through the arena of discourse to the empirical conditions of real-world injustices forged by the pedagogical institution is the ethical nature of sociopolitical effects following any act of criticism. More notably, a deconstructive rereading of the discursive archive of pedagogy to locate its institutional inclusions and exclusions, its orderings and disorderings, its valuations and devaluations, and so on, must precede the reconstructive phase(s) of a rewriting of the existing subdivisions configuring the disciplinarity of epistemological foundations, because a "critical reelaboration of this hierarchy and of this problematics of hierarchy must not be restricted to new 'theorems' in the same language (*langage*)."[163] It requires the heteroglossary of a fresh writing that inscribes and is inscribed by the rules of an unborrowed code following "an other logic,"[164] one that can self-consciously evade the conceits of the metaphysical arrangements it is reacting to or may use in the performance of critique. This would presuppose, first, the inversion of the argumentative logics, the hierarchy of which privileges a normative arrangement of concepts from a binarization of terms (for example, good-bad, right-wrong, and so forth) and, second, a displacement of the epistemological groundwork coordinating the ethical acceptance of the formal structuring of its concepts that organize the essential possibilities of thought itself.

Conclusion for an Ending:
A Monstrosity for which There Is No End

Deconstruction is wary of origins. It does not account for them because it does not believe in reinstating them or in reinforcing their legitimizing value to celebrate their privileging of an immutable foundation. Yet deconstruction derives its critical force from the differential markings of the chains of signification that emanate from the search for a definitive finality; that last link, always so near, but forever out of sight, that only a Hegel could foresee in the absolute knowledge of a dialectical *u-topos* as the end of meaning and of history, the end of philosophy and of pedagogy. If there can be no end to the situation of deconstruction, it is surely appropriate to ask whether the strategies discussed in this chapter are simply promoting a futile and self-defeating task, especially for pedagogical issues that often beg some sort of resolution. Absolute finality is nonidentity signifying the death of being: the death of the subject and the death of meaning, not to mention history. To say that something like a pedagogical issue ends, that it exists no more, is absurd, because then there would be no remainder, only the space of silence and the silence of space. There would be nothing left to say that would not already be known. Discourse will probably never cease to exist until the demise of the last of humanity, but until then we almost certainly will have deconstruction with us, for the expression of ideas initiates responses that seek to understand the complexity of a plethora of motivational factors looming below the surface of any subject position. Identifying what is right and wrong also goes along with discovering how these values are constructed and sometimes, perhaps why. Deconstruction can certainly help us with that. Minimizing the dangers of forgetting the past would inevitably dull the passion of memory and of the soul's desire for fulfilling a meaningful regeneration of the human spirit or mind, if not the credibility of exercising the freedom of a nascent will as a spur from catalyzing thought to emancipatory action. This glimmer of an Archimedean point that is always already unreachable is what pedagogy should aim for to extend teaching-learning beyond the tendency to merely imitate a brief scholastic adventurousness as one would watch the cascading flicker of a fading memory casting empty shadows on a cave wall.

NOTES

The research for this essay was made possible by a Social Sciences and Humanities Research Council of Canada Postdoctoral Fellowship. I also thank John Willinsky, Nicholas Burbules, Carl Leggo, Richard Cavell, and Elefteria Balomenos for their helpful and generous insights.

1. Michel Foucault, *The Archeology of Knowledge and the Discourse on Language*, trans. A. M. Sheridan Smith (New York: Pantheon, 1972), p. 235.
2. For a most comprehensive discussion and documentation of this phenomenon of anti-Hegelianism, see Vincent Descombes, *Modern French Philosophy*, trans. L. Fox-Scott and J. Harding (Cambridge: Cambridge University Press, 1980).
3. See Michael Ryan, *Marxism and Deconstruction: A Critical Articulation* (Baltimore, Md.: Johns Hopkins University Press, 1982). Here Ryan develops a very thorough comparative analysis of deconstruction and speculative idealism

while addressing the central question of his book: the potential of deconstruction for a rearticulation of orthodox Marxism and dialectical materialism.

4. Jürgen Habermas, *The Philosophical Discourse of Modernity: Twelve Lectures*, trans. Frank Lawrence (Cambridge, Mass.: MIT Press, 1985); Gerald Graff, *Literature Against Itself* (Chicago, Ill.: University of Chicago Press, 1979) are examples of the rank and file of this division on opposite sides of the political fence of theory or criticism.

5. For example, Barabara Johnson, *The Wake of Deconstruction* (Oxford: Blackwell, 1994); Jeffrey T. Nealon, *Double Reading: Postmodernism after Deconstruction* (Ithaca, N.Y.: Cornell University Press, 1993) are two recent books that present an even-handed outline of the trials and tribulations of the splintering of deconstruction in the North American academy.

6. See Roy Bhaskar, *Plato Etc.: The Problems of Philosophy and Their Resolution* (London: Verso, 1994).

7. In Gregory L. Ulmer, *Applied Grammatology: Post(e)-Pedagogy from Jacques Derrida to Joseph Beuys* (Baltimore, Md.: Johns Hopkins University Press, 1985), the metaphysical standards of a Hegelian pedagogy are outlined according to the demands of the dialectic and its protection of memorization for what is an enlightened learning.

8. See Jacques Derrida, "Afterword: Toward an Ethic of Discussion" in *Limited Inc.,* ed. Gerald Graff, trans. Samuel Weber and Jeffrey Mehlman, (Evanston, Ill.: Northwestern University Press, 1988). The retort to his critics Derrida provides here (in the form of written answers to the questions of Graff) does much to dispel the myth that deconstruction is apolitical and that its textualization of human experience does not take ethics into account. William B. Stanley in *Curriculum for Utopia: Social Reconstructionism and Critical Pedagogy in the Postmodern Era* (Albany: State University of New York Press, 1992) presents an excellent overview of the discussion along with some insight into the curricular implications of the ethics of deconstruction.

9. This is the basis of the critique of Derrida and deconstruction in Habermas, *The Philosophical Discourse of Modernity*.

10. The (non)relation of deconstruction with apophatic thought (for example, negative theology) is discussed in Jacques Derrida, "Of an Apocalyptic Tone Recently Adopted in Philosophy," trans. John P. Leavy, Jr., *Oxford Literary Review* 6(2) (1984): 3–37.

11. Compare Gayatri Chakravorty Spivak, *Outside in the Teaching Machine* (New York: Routledge, 1993); Rodolphe Gasché, *Inventions of Difference: On Jacques Derrida* (Cambridge, Mass.: Harvard University Press, 1994).

12. Although many have hailed the most politicized statement of deconstruction to be Jacques Derrida, *Specters of Marx: The State of the Debt, the Work of Mourning, & the New International*, trans. Peggy Kamuf (New York: Routledge, 1994), the continuation of an elaboration on general themes taken up in this text around the problems of ethics, democracy, ideology, and history has been addressed in earlier texts. See, for example, Jacques Derrida, "Force of Law: The 'Mystical Foundation of Authority,'" trans. Mary Quaintance, *Cordozo Law Review* 11(5–6) (1990): 919–1045; Jacques Derrida, *Du Droit à la Philosophie* (Paris: Galilée, 1990), a collection of previously published texts (from 1975 to 1990) on the ethico-juridical and sociopolitical sphere of the institution of philosophy education in

France; and more recently, Jacques Derrida, *Politiques de l'Amitié* (Paris: Galilée, 1994).

13. Jacques Derrida, "On Colleges and Philosophy," in *Postmodernism: ICA Documents,* ed. Lisa Appignanesi (London: Free Association Books, 1989), 22.

14. See the interview with Jacques Derrida entitled "Deconstruction and the Other," in *Dialogues with Contemporary Continental Thinkers,* ed. Richard Kearney (Manchester: Manchester University Press, 1984), pp. 105–126, for a lucid explanation of this symptomatic appearance of deconstruction and its concern with the repressed other of desire that demands recognition.

15. Jacques Derrida, "Mochlos; or The Conflict of the Faculties," trans. Richard Rand and Amy Wygant, in *Logomachia: The Conflict of the Faculties,* ed. Richard Rand (Lincoln: University of Nebraska Press, 1992), 22–23.

16. See Jacques Derrida, "Some Statements and Truisms about Neo-Logisms, Newisms, Postisms, Parasitisms, and other Small Seismisms," trans. Anne Tomiche, in *States of Theory: History, Art, and Critical Discourse,* ed. David Carrol (New York: Columbia University Press, 1990), 63–95, for Derrida's contribution to the polylogue and polyglot of "isms" currently bandied about in academia and for a clarification of some of the ethical-political value that is misread out of deconstruction.

17. Derrida, "Deconstruction and the Other," p. 118.

18. This antiphenomenological theme (for example, the dissimulation of autoaffection) goes back to an early text, Jacques Derrida, *Speech and Phenomena: And Other Essays on Husserl's Theory of Signs,* trans. David B. Allison (Evanston, Ill.: Northwestern University Press) in which the identity of representation and the trace of the other are major preoccupations as regards reflexion. See also Rodolphe Gasché, *The Tain of the Mirror: Derrida and the Philosophy of Reflection* (Cambridge, Mass.: Harvard University Press, 1986).

19. For an example of incorporating deconstruction in post-Marxist social theory, see Ernesto Laclau and Chantal Mouffe, *Hegemony and Socialist Strategy: Towards a Radical Democratic Politics* (London: Verso, 1986); for a feminist knod to deconstruction — albeit a reductive one because the point is to discuss postmodernism — as related to research and education, see Patti Lather, *Getting Smart: Feminist Research and Pedagogy with/in the Postmodern* (New York: Routledge, 1991); for smatterings of a postcolonial rendering of deconstruction see Homi K. Bhabha, *The Location of Culture* (New York: Routledge, 1994).

20. See Denise Egéa-Kuehne, "Deconstruction Revisited and Derrida's Call for Academic Responsibility," *Educational Theory* 45(3) (1995): 293–309.

21. Jacques Derrida, "Où Commence et Comment Finit un Corps Enseignant" in *Du Droit à la Philosophie* (Paris: Galilée, 1990), p. 119. (All translations from this text are my own.).

22. Ibid., pp. 118–119.

23. Ibid., p. 115.

24. Some representative examples include: Cleo Cherryholmes, *Power and Criticism: Poststructural Investigations in Education* (New York: Teachers College Press, 1988); William F. Pinar and William M. Reynolds, eds., *Understanding Curriculum as Phenomenological and Deconstructed Text* (New York: Teachers College Press, 1992); Donald Morton and Mas'ud Zavarzadeh, eds. *Theory/Pedagogy/Politics: Texts for Change* (Urbana: University of Illinois Press, 1991).

25. Derrida, "Où Commence et Comment Finit un Corps Enseignant," p. 121.

26. See Paul Jay, "Bridging the Gap: The Position of Politics in Deconstuction," *Cultural Critique* 22 (Fall 1992): 47–73; Gregory S. Jay, *America the Scrivener: Deconstruction and the Subject of Literary History* (Ithaca, N.Y.: Cornell University Press, 1990); John D. Caputo, *Against Ethics: Contributions to a Poetics of Obligation with Constant Reference to Deconstruction* (Bloomington: Indiana University Press, 1993).

27. Robert C. Holub, *Border Crossings: Reception Theory, Poststructuralism, Deconstruction* (Madison: University of Wisconsin Press, 1992), p. 112.

28. See Richard Rorty, "Is Derrida a Transcendental Philosopher?" in *Derrida: A Critical Reader*, ed. David Wood (Oxford: Blackwell, 1992), pp. 235–246.

29. Many of these institutional or pedagogical texts are collected in Derrida, *Du Droit à la Philosophie*. A voluminous book (663 pages in all) that is edited for a decidedly French audience, it assuredly would be familiar with the institutional plight of philosophical pedagogies. All of the book's contents seriously engage some fundamental educational problems at the cutting edge of debate today in many disciplines. Some of the chapters in the compendium have been translated into English as separate texts (for example, "Mochlos: or, the Conflict of the Faculties," "The Age of Hegel," "The Principle of Reason: The University in the Eyes of its Pupils"), but have been acknowledged by only a handful of critics referring primarily to poststructural-postmodern transformations of literary studies and even less by the more radical schools of educational theory that need to address the real effects of power-knowledge distributions in pedagogy directly. This neglect on behalf of both groups, although more conspicuously of the second, may account to some extent for the fact that the ethics and politics of deconstruction have remained in a constant state of questioning, even by those who nevertheless cite its proper name to derive an avant-garde or postmodern authority without applying its general principles to the search for various methods of cultural criticism. To illustrate, a recent book states (rather baldly, I might add): "In writing about Derrida and education we are faced with the problem that he appears to have *nothing directly to say about education* [emphasis added]." If this were not enough of a gross error, the authors continue, "Thus to read Derrida from the standpoint of an educator, with an educational perspective and with a view to gaining educational 'pay-offs' from one's reading, must inevitably force us beyond our immediate standpoint into foregrounding, sooner or later, the general question of how a writer is to be read, of how a writer 'speaks' to us." I submit that this is precisely the uninformed opinion that has passed for expert commentary on Derrida when the point is more to rehash a conservative reading of deconstruction without sufficient depth for the expedient purpose of convenient generalizations or harried co-optation. Both quotations were taken from Robin Usher and Richard Edwards, *Postmodernism and Education* (New York: Routledge, 1994), p. 119.

30. This is because of the now quite fashionable trend of appealing to or for a radical authority or poststructural respectability by attaching the label of deconstruction to a particular approach, to a critico-theoretical cause, or to a research project to sanction the semblance of such a methodological validity in terms of periodization or timeliness. This is the theoretical "double speak" of feigning an

obedience to the aura of these so-called deconstructive precepts while adapting the core concepts of something else more methodologically stable or palatable for the purposes of passing it off as new.

31. Citation in Jacques Derrida, "The Age of Hegel," trans. Susan Winnet in *Demarcating the Disciplines: Philosophy, Literature, Art*, ed. Samuel Weber (Minneapolis: University of Minnesota Press, 1986), p. 3.

32. Ibid., p. 4.

33. Ibid., p. 23.

34. See Shlomo Avineri, *Hegel's Theory of the Modern State* (Cambridge: Cambridge University Press, 1972).

35. Derrida, "The Age of Hegel," p. 11.

36. Ibid., p. 23.

37. Ibid.

38. G.W.F. Hegel, *Elements of the Philosophy of Right*, ed. Allen W. Wood, trans. H. B. Nisbet (Cambridge: Cambridge University Press, 1991).

39. Hegel's letter to Duboc, July 30, 1822, cited in Derrida, "The Age of Hegel," p. 15.

40. Derrida, "The Age of Hegel," p. 23.

41. Ibid., pp. 23–24; see also the account of this complex situation in Avineri, *Hegel's Theory of the Modern State*.

42. Derrida, "The Age of Hegel," p. 15.

43. Ibid., p. 12.

44. Derrida cites extracts from Hegel's correspondence on the subjects of Bavarian lottery tickets and the matter of contributions to the General Fund for Widows, a form of institutional life insurance for professors.

45. See Jacques Derrida, *Writing and Difference*, trans. Alan Bass (Chicago, Ill.: University of Chicago Press, 1978); Jacques Derrida, *On the Name*, ed. Thomas Dutoit, trans. David Wood, John P. Leavey, Jr., and Ian McLeod (Stanford, Calif.: Stanford University Press, 1995).

46. Derrida, "The Age of Hegel," p. 17.

47. Ibid., p. 4.

48. Ibid., p. 24.

49. Ibid., p. 15.

50. Altenstein's letter of June 6, 1822, cited in Derrida, "The Age of Hegel," p. 15.

51. Ibid.

52. Derrida, "The Age of Hegel," p. 25.

53. Ibid.

54. From the letter of G.W.F. Hegel "To the Royal Ministry of Spiritual, Academic, and Medical Affairs" (April 16, 1822) appended to Derrida, "The Age of Hegel,"p. 40.

55. Derrida, "The Age of Hegel," p. 25.

56. Ibid., p. 28.

57. Ibid., p. 17.

58. Ibid., p. 26.

59. Ibid., pp. 17–18.

60. See David Farrell Krell, *Of Memory, Reminiscence, and Writing: On the Verge* (Bloomington: Indiana University Press, 1990), especially Chapter 5; Jacques

Derrida, *Margins of Philsophy*, trans. Alan Bass (Chicago, Ill: University of Chicago Press, 1982).

61. Derrida, "The Age of Hegel," p. 17.
62. Ibid., pp. 8–9.
63. Ibid., p. 24.
64. Ibid., p. 34n1. More thorough discussions on the problem of rethinking the concept of ideology in terms of the linguistic turn of intellectual history after poststructuralism and specifically deconstruction that are beyond the scope of analysis here are to be found in Dominic LaCapra, *Rethinking Intellectual History: Texts, Contexts, Language* (Ithaca, N.Y.: Cornell University Press, 1983); George Attridge, Geoffrey Bennington, and Robert Young, eds., *Poststructuralism and the Question of History* (Cambridge: Cambridge University Press, 1987); Hayden White, *The Content of the Form: Narrative Discourse and Historical Representation* (Baltimore, Md.: Johns Hopkins University Press, 1987).
65. Derrida, "The Age of Hegel," p. 22.
66. Ibid.
67. Ibid.
68. Ibid., p. 28.
69. Jacques Derrida, "Between Brackets I," trans. P. Kamuf, in *Points . . . Interviews, 1974–1994,* ed. Elizabeth Weber (Stanford, Calif.: Stanford University Press), p. 26.
70. Ibid.
71. In Jacques Derrida, *The Ear of the Other: Otobiography, Transference, Translation,* ed. Christie McDonald, trans. Peggy Kamuf and Avital Ronell (Lincoln: University of Nebraska Press, 1988), the question of autobiography and otobiography is interrelated to the problem of the proper name and the signature. Derrida confronts the academic freedom of Nietzsche's pedagogy and its reception, interpetation, and so forth, through a discussion of how one becomes what one is, one of the central themes underlying "The Age of Hegel."
72. Michel de Certeau, *The Writing of History,* trans. Tom Conley (New York: Columbia University Press, 1988). De Certeau has some interesting insights into the limitations of the Hegelian *Geistesgeschichte* (a cultural form of intellectual history) for capturing the ideal of the spirit of the times, but goes further to set down a theory of the writing of history that incorporates many Derridean features (for example, writing and death, difference and trace).
73. See David Ingram, *Reason, History, and Politics: The Communitarian Grounds of Legitimation in the Modern Age* (New York: State University of New York Press, 1995).
74. Derrida, "The Age of Hegel," p. 23.
75. See Hayden White, *The Content of the Form*.
76. Derrida, "The Age of Hegel," p. 23.
77. Descombes, *Modern French Philosophy*, p. 137.
78. Derrida, "The Age of Hegel," pp. 22–23.
79. Ryan, *Marxism and Deconstruction*, p. 118.
80. Ibid., p. 25.
81. Ibid., p. 24.
82. Hegel, *Elements of the Philosophy of Right*, p. 321.

83. See also G.W.F. Hegel, *Phenomenology of Spirit*, trans. A. V. Miller (Oxford: Clarendon Press, 1977).
84. Cited in Jacques Derrida, "The Pit and the Pyramid: Introduction to Hegel's Semiology," trans. Alan Bass, in *Margins of Philosophy* (Chicago, Ill.: University of Chicago Press), p. 73.
85. See Martin Heidegger, *Questions Concerning Technology and Other Essays*, trans. William Lovitt (New York: Harper and Row, 1977).
86. Andrew Vincent, *Theories of the State* (Oxford: Basil Blackwell, 1987), p. 125.
87. Derrida, "The Age of Hegel," p. 17.
88. Jacques Derrida, *Glas*, trans. John P. Leavey, Jr. and Richard Rand (Lincoln: University of Nebraska Press, 1986), p. 1.
89. Ibid.
90. Derrida, *The Ear of the Other*, p. 56.
91. Jacques Derrida, *Dissemination*, trans. Barabara Johnson (Chicago, Ill.: University of Chicago Press, 1981), p. 105.
92. See Derrida, *The Ear of the Other*.
93. Martin Jay, *Downcast Eyes: The Denigration of Vision in Twentieth-Century French Thought* (Berkeley: University of California Press, 1993). This is an unusual twisting of the Derridean neologism phallogocentric because of the antiphenomenological inferences pointed to by the visual focus of the word "ocular."
94. Jacques Derrida, *The Truth in Painting*, trans. Geoff Bennington and Ian McLeod (Chicago, Ill.: University of Chicago Press), p. 19.
95. See Manfred Frank, "Is Self-Consiousness a Case of Présence a Soi? Towards a Meta-Critique of the Recent French Critique of Metaphysics," in *Derrida: A Critical Reader*, ed. David Wood (Cambridge: Blackwell, 1992), pp. 218–234.
96. In Jacques Derrida, *Memoires for Paul de Man*, trans. Cecilia Lindsay, Jonathan Culler, and Eduardo Cadava (New York: Columbia University Press, 1986), the experience of memory, subjectivity, and intersubjectivity is probed as the de-facement of *autos* or *prosopopoeia*.
97. Derrida, *Dissemination*, p. 27.
98. Derrida, "The Age of Hegel," p. 18.
99. See Jacques Derrida, *Signéponge/Signsponge*, trans. Richard Rand (New York: Columbia University Press, 1984).
100. Gayatri Chakravorty Spivak, "Speculations on Reading Marx: After Reading Derrida," in *Poststructuralism and the Question of History*, ed. George Attridge, Geoffrey Bennington, and Robert Young (Cambridge: Cambridge University Press, 1987), p. 43.
101. See Umberto Eco, *The Role of the Reader: Explorations in the Semiotics of Text* (Bloomington: University of Indiana Press, 1979); Jacques Derrida, *Of Grammatology*, trans. Gayatri Chakravorty Spivak (Baltimore, Md.: Johns Hopkins University Press, 1976).
102. See Fedric Jameson, *The Political Unconscious: Narrative as a Socially Symbolic Act* (New York: Cornell University Press, 1981); Samuel Weber, *Institutions and Interpretation* (Minneapolis: University of Minnesota Press, 1987).
103. Derrida, "The Age of Hegel," pp. 3–4.
104. See Jean Baudrillard, *Simulacres et Simulation* (Paris: Galilée, 1981).

105. Derrida, *Dissemination*, p. 105.
106. Ibid.
107. Derrida, "The Age of Hegel," p. 5.
108. Avineri, *Hegel's Theory of the Modern State*.
109. Derrida, "The Age of Hegel," p. 5.
110. Cousin cited in Derrida, "The Age of Hegel," p. 9.
111. Derrida, "The Age of Hegel," p. 29.
112. Ibid.
113. Ibid., p. 22.
114. Hegel cited in Derrida, "The Age of Hegel," p. 26.
115. Ibid.
116. See Derrida, "The Pit and the Pyramid."
117. Hegel cited in Derrida, "The Age of Hegel," p. 26.
118. Ibid., p. 11.
119. Ibid., p. 33.
120. Ibid., p. 6.
121. See Jacques Derrida, "Languages and Institutions of Philosophy," trans. Sylvia Söderlind, Rebecca Comay, Barbara Havercroft, and Joseph Adamson, *Recherches Semiotique/Semiotic Inquiry* 4(2) (1984): 91–154.
122. Derrida, "The Age of Hegel," p. 33.
123. Ibid., pp. 6–7.
124. GREPH, *Qui a Peur de la Philosophie?* (Paris: Aubier-Flammarion, 1977).
125. Derrida, "The Age of Hegel," p. 5.
126. The GREPH originally banded together in 1974. See Derrida, *Du Droit à la Philosophie*.
127. Derrida, "The Age of Hegel," p. 19.
128. See GREPH, *Qui a Peur de la Philosophie?*
129. In Derrida, "Où Commence et Comment Finit un Corps Enseignant."
130. Personal conversation with Jacques Derrida, Paris, July 1994.
131. See also Jacques Derrida, "The Time of a Thesis," trans. Kathleen McLaughlin, in *Philosophy in France Today*, ed. Alan Montefiore (Cambridge: Cambridge University Press, 1983), pp. 34–50.
132. Derrida, "The Age of Hegel," p. 33.
133. Ibid.
134. Derrida, "Où Commence et Comment Finit un Corps Enseignant," pp. 120–121. Compare Derrida, *Dissemination*.
135. Derrida, *Margins of Philosophy*, p. 329.
136. Opening the philosophical door to a possible alliance of the GREPH with Marxist politics, Derrida writes in "The Age of Hegel": "If the current French State is afraid of philosophy, it is because its teaching contributes to the progress of two types of threatening forces: those wanting to change the State (those, let's say, belonging to the left-wing of Hegel) and to wrest it from the control of those forces currently in power, and those which, on the other hand or simultaneously, allied or not with the fore-going, tend toward the destruction of the State. These two forces cannot be classified according to the prevailing divisions. They seem to me, for example, to cohabitate today within the theoretical and practical field known as 'Marxism.'" (pp. 33–34)
137. See Jacques Derrida, "Structure, Sign, and Play in the Discourse of the

Human Sciences" in *Writing and Difference*, trans. Alan Bass (Chicago, Ill.: University of Chicago Press, 1978).

138. See, for example, Thomas E. Wartenberg, ed., *Rethinking Power* (Albany: State University of New York Press, 1992).

139. Derrida, "The Age of Hegel," pp. 19–20.

140. Ibid., p. 19.

141. Derrida, "Mochlos: or, The Conflict of the Faculties," p. 11.

142. Derrida, *Of Grammatology*, p. 158. (The form of the quotation has been modified.)

143. Derrida, "The Age of Hegel," p. 20.

144. Gilles Deleuze and Felix Guattari, *A Thousand Plateaus: Capitalism and Schizophrenia*, trans. Brian Massumi (Minneapolis: University of Minnesota Press, 1987).

145. See Pierre Bourdieu and Jean-Claude Passeron, *Reproduction in Education, Society and Culture*, trans. Richard Nice (London: Sage Publications, 1977). The violence of writing as the letter of the law of exclusion is the focus of the second half of Derrida's *Of Grammatology*.

146. See Pierre Bourdieu, *Language and Symbolic Power*, trans. Gino Raymond and Matthew Adamson (Cambridge: Polity Press, 1991).

147. Derrida, "Où Commence et Comment Finit un Corps Enseignant," p. 114.

148. This is the motivating premise of Derrida's, *Of Grammatology*.

149. Derrida, "Où Commence et Comment Finit un Corps Enseignant," p. 130.

150. Bourdieu and Passeron, *Reproduction in Education, Society and Culture*.

151. Derrida, "The Age of Hegel," pp. 7–8.

152. See Derrida, "Où Commence et Comment Finit un Corps Enseignant" for further elaboration on the role of the teaching body in the forms of reproduction that saturate and amplify the contradictions of the scene of teaching, its field.

153. See Derrida, *Of Grammatology*.

154. Jacques Derrida, "Living On: Border Lines," trans. James Hulbert, in *Deconstruction and Criticism*, ed. Harold Bloom, Paul de Man, Jacques Derrida, Geoffrey Hartman, J. Hillis Miller (New York: Continuum, 1979), pp. 93–94.

155. Ibid., p. 93.

156. See Ulmer, *Applied Grammatology*.

157. See Jean-Francois Lyotard, *The Postmodern Condition: A Report on Knowledge*, trans. Geoffrey Bennington and Bernard Massumi (Minneapolis: University of Minnesota Press, 1991).

158. Derrida, "Où Commence et Comment Finit un Corps Enseignant," p. 119.

159. See Derrida, "On Colleges and Philosophy."

160. Derrida, *The Truth in Painting*, pp. 19–20.

161. Derrida, *Writing and Difference*, p. 308.

162. Derrida, "The Age of Hegel," p. 30.

163. Ibid., p. 20.

164. Derrida, "Où Commence et Comment Finit un Corps Enseignant," p. 121.

6

Gilles Deleuze: Practicing Education through Flight and Gossip
Mary Leach and Megan Boler

> From an always nomadic and anarchical difference to the unavoidably excessive and displaced sign of recurrence, a lightning storm was produced which will, one day, be given the name Deleuze: new thought is possible.
>
> — Foucault, 1994: 1[1]

Continental poststructuralism represents one of the intellectual and political innovations of the twentieth century that has profoundly shifted the terms of our struggles for justice, disrupted our boundaries, and ruptured master narratives of Western thought. The serious challenges to traditional Anglo-American studies of philosophy, literary theory, and the so-called sciences of man are in no small measure the work of poststructuralists and, equally we would say, of feminist and post-colonial theorists and the political interventions of a range of radical social movements. For poststructuralists, these myriad disruptions might be summarized as a call for thinking differently. Problematizing the very foundations of philosophical and political thought, thinking differently has infected Anglo-American debates between modernists and postmodernists, between communitarians and liberals.[2]

Typically, however, much of this new work is ahead of the academic disciplines and teaching institutions that have obvious reasons of their own for preserving the status quo. Although within the last decade, the debate over the meaning and purpose of education has occupied much of the political and social life in such countries as the United States and New

Zealand, the center of these debates has ordinarily focused on renewed and increased imperatives to organize both public schooling and higher education around the related practices of reprivatization, standardization, and individualism with revived emphasis on the traditional disciplinary structures and on individual achievement as the primary unit of value.[3]

While public polemical battles debate whether the modern nation-states should reproduce the academic culture and public schooling of the past half century or revert to an even older one, scholars using the emerging discourses of feminism, postcolonialism, and cultural and literary studies are rethinking fundamental relationships between language and experience, pedagogy and human agency, and ethics and social responsibility as part of a larger project for promoting democratic schooling in a social-cultural-educational world of human making.[4]

How might Gilles Deleuze's work, often ignored by poststructural advocates and feminists, be understood in relation to educational debates? It is the basic aim of this chapter to explore the work of French poststructuralist Deleuze in an effort to examine the radical potential of thinking differently with respect to the public and current scholarly debates around educational theory and practice.

Probably the most popularized poststructuralist thinker is Michel Foucault. Deleuze himself described Foucault as "the greatest thinker of our time." Foucault and Deleuze were mutual admirers: Foucault wrote a number of articles about Deleuze, and Deleuze wrote often on Foucault including "A Portrait of Foucault" following Foucault's death. They met in 1962 and were active together after May 1968. Although not apparently close friends, they were certainly in contact in the next decade although not toward the end of Foucault's life.

Foucault's greater popularity may have to do with his being the "greatest thinker of our time," but more likely has to do with the readability of Foucault across disciplines (history, sociology, philosophy) and the way his words can be malleably interpreted to fit diverse social perspectives of a generation yearning for precise yet open-ended political critique. In addition, Foucault toured numerous countries with lectures while Deleuze remained for the most part fixed in France. Ironically, the philosophy of Deleuze (and Deleuze and Felix Guattari) without doubt provides the more strictly philosophical foundations of poststructuralism and in some senses may more thoroughly rethink the terms of Western thought than does Foucault's work. In particular, Deleuze not only analyzes existing forces of power and subjectification, but also offers new directions for epistemologies, metaphysics, and ethics. Deleuze's work is philosophically systematic in a way Foucault does not attempt. Deleuze lends himself less easily to budding sociologists and historians, and Deleuzian concepts do not dash off the pen the way that any scholar can write "As

Foucault says" and interpret a pithy sentence or two to justify an argument on popular authority.

Foucault's preface to *Anti-Oedipus* completes a portrait of the mutual Deleuze-Foucault fan club and illustrates the differences in their contributions and styles within poststructuralism. The preface is both accessible and readable. Foucault warns the reader against seeing *Anti-Oedipus* as a new totalizing theory; the reader must not seek a philosophy that stands in as the new flashy Hegel. Rather he sees the text as erotic art. "Informed by the seemingly abstract notions of multiplicities, flows, arrangements, and connections, the analysis of the relationship of desire to reality and to the capitalist 'machine' yields answers to concrete questions."[5] Asking the forgiveness of the authors, Foucault refers to the text as a book of ethics. In characterizing *Anti-Oedipus*, Foucault offers two lists — first, "the three adversaries confronted by *Anti-Oedipus*." Then Foucault describes *Anti-Oedipus* as an "Introduction to the Non-Fascist Life," and proceeds in typically Foucauldian fashion to summarize the essential principles "if I were to make this great book into a manual or guide to everyday life."[6]

The extent to which Deleuze and Foucault each saw the other as advocating thinking differently is clear, and each saw thinking differently as a material and dangerous undertaking. In an interview Deleuze remarks on the passion and danger of Foucault's work:

People will readily agree that intense physical pursuits are dangerous, but thought too is an intense and wayward pursuit. Once you start thinking, you're bound to enter a line of thought where life and death, reason and madness, are at stake, and the line draws you on. You can think only on this witches' line, assuming you're not bound to lose, not bound to end up mad or dead. That's something that's always fascinated Foucault, the switching, the constant juggling of what's close and distant in death or madness.[7]

Deleuze's portrait of Foucault's pioneering work names several of the themes we pursue in this introduction to Deleuze. In this chapter we outline possibilities of thinking differently through two of Deleuze's concepts: rhizomes, and lines to name the multiple at work in the classroom through educators' and students' bodies. Deleuze's notion of rhizomes and his language of the lines that constitute us offer philosophical and metaphoric systems useful in considering how the dynamic processes of identity and knowledge construction can be challenged in the process of education.

The quotation above illustrates some of Deleuze's promise for feminism and some of its limits. Deleuze injects all of his work with assiduous attention to desire and to effect. This we see as part of the promising danger of thinking differently: as he says, "Once you start thinking, you're bound to enter a line of thought where life and death, reason and madness, are at stake.... You can think only on the witches' line." What is the witches' line? It is a line of thought not assimilated to binaries or to the master narratives of what counts as truth or real. Yet Deleuze's fascination with death and tendency to romanticize madness offer a glimpse of the deeply gendered limits of poststructuralism.

We use the concepts of rhizomes and lines here to illustrate women's practices and interventions within the traditional institutions of education and knowledge. Such an examination is appropriate considering that Deleuze held the model of becoming woman as exemplary for all. We preface these analyses of alternative figurations of thought — rhizomes and lines — with a brief overview of the Deleuzian project, which locates his interventions within the philosophical tradition. Toward the end of the chapter, we query Deleuze's warning that the most transgressive line risks a flirtation with death and we ask about the gendered nature of this death fear.

Of course our scope provides only a first step; the projects of Deleuze and Deleuze and Guattari are huge, and the feminist response increasingly is undertaken in provocative ways. In reading poststructural work in general — Irigaray and Cixous provide fine examples — our task has been to come to a particular respect for each text: the need to immerse, to allow certain kinds of demands to evaporate, to immerse oneself in the text with the body, as it were, in order to understand. This is perhaps why, in secondary writings on Deleuze, he is not extensively quoted. Rather, writings on Deleuze have often been infected: a mimesis has occurred, there is a poetic grasp of meaning that extends through the writer's pen into new resonances of intensities and understandings. To say, "Go and read it" makes good sense, and one will have to keep returning to the texts, until — as with most philosophy — the concepts take on that new plateau of bodily intellectual sense so that certain doubts and fears of understanding allow new sense of movement with text: an erotic reading to be sure. At those moments of achieved reading we become aware that, however much Deleuze draws on Spinoza and Nietzsche, we are in another world, like a science fiction novel. It is a spatio-temporal world where we need to suspend our disbelief, a world of desiring machines, territories, and lines of flight. Sometimes these descriptions have an eerie quality of premonition: he may be describing the subjects we are now, in this era of post-identity politics, post-morality, an era of globalized culture — but he may also be describing some of what has yet to come.

To accomplish this reading we have taken the view that the importance of poststructural work is not captured by posing a new series of oppositions but by recognizing the alternatives it proposes within modernity, within the philosophical tradition, within the contemporary field of social practices. Poststructuralism is not oriented toward the negation of theoretical foundations, but rather toward the exploration of new grounds for philosophical and political inquiry; it is involved in the articulation and affirmation of alternative lineages that arise within the tradition itself. From this point of view, the work of Deleuze is exemplary of the entire generation of poststructural thinkers. His work, as the work of others such as Irigaray, Foucault, Kristeva, and Derrida, lends credence to the notion that the history of metaphysics is not dead, that it contains powerful and radical alternatives still vitally alive in the contemporary problems we face.[8]

The focus of Deleuze's work is very much on the present and more especially of the difficulty of and the necessity for thinking the present. In his own effort to move beyond the dogmatic image of thought embedded in the canonized, institutionalized tradition of the history of philosophy toward an intensive practice of philosophy, Deleuze stresses the need for new images as ways to make meaning differently. This results in the elaboration of a unique philosophical style that aims at expressing new, postmetaphysical figurations of the subject. The following is a brief exposition of his general project, if such a task can be said to be accomplished for a scholar who demonstrates in his writing both the process of thinking and the thinking subject differently. As Judith Butler articulates his approach: "It seems clear that these deconstructions are not destructions but rather a kind of historical affirmation that not only resists the rancor of failed historical ideals but works that site of failure to resignify the very terms that, having become unmoored from their ground, are at once the tenants of that loss and the resources from which to articulate the future."[9] The subversive persuasion of Deleuze exemplifies a humorous yet radically serious rethinking of the unmoored terms of Western philosophy.

THE DELEUZIAN PROJECT

> What I have detested more than anything was the Hegelianism and the Dialectic.
> — Deleuze, 1977: 12[10]

The roots of French poststructuralism and its unifying basis lie, in large part, in its quarrel with the Hegelian tradition. How to evade the ubiquitous Hegel and the order and authority of his legacy to the continental tradition as the ineluctable centerpiece of philosophical speculation, social theory, and political practice is a central concern.[11] "Hegel determined a horizon, a language, a code that we are still at the very heart of today. Hegel, by this fact, is our Plato: the one who delimits — ideologically or scientifically, positively or negatively — the theoretical possibilities of theory."[12] In Deleuze's early works he enlists Bergson, Nietzsche, and Spinoza to mount a total critique and a rejection of the negative dialectical framework so as to achieve a theoretical separation from the entire Hegelian problematic.[13] This proved most difficult to do, however. Not only does Hegel address the problems central to Deleuze's interests — the determination of being, the unity of the one and the multiple — but "references to a 'break' with Hegel are almost impossible, if only because Hegel has made the very notion of 'breaking with' into a central tenet of his dialectic."[14]

To achieve his goals, Deleuze pursued the construction of an alternative terrain for thought — one that recognizes nondialectical difference, that is, negation, in its actuality (its lack of positivity or creation and its concrete destructive tendency), as an element in our world — but seeks, through different registers and on different planes of thought, to achieve a constitutive theory of practice.[15] His speculative ontology, limited to a strictly immanent and materialist discourse, denies any preconstituted structure of being, any teleological order of existence — any deep or hidden foundation of being, in favor of a constitutive conception of practice as a foundation of ontology — a nature produced in practice.[16] To the negative movement of determination he offers the positive movement of differentiation, the irreducible multiplicity of becoming.[17] Although Bergson's critique of negative ontology provides for Deleuze an absolutely positive movement of differentiation, Nietzsche's analysis of power provides the theoretical passage to an ethic of active expression. Spinoza's work contributes for him the affirmation of practice or joy at the center of ontology.[18]

Broadly speaking, Deleuze's philosophy supplants the thought of the same and representation with the play of difference and repetition.[19] Difference and repetition are, in effect, indices of a move toward nonrepresentational and radically horizontal thought. The structure of his corpus, perhaps paradoxically, leads away from an order of sameness (everyone on the same level) to the instability of differences.[20] The horizontal axis does not entail the firming of boundaries and barriers — bypassing the vertical thought of everyday, bureaucratic hierarchy, the thought that entails the consolidation of identities as is the case with representational thought — but leads to the quasi-order of radical difference, to the permeability of all boundaries and barriers.[21] Horizontality, inaugurated in the modern era by Nietzsche, opens the way to thought as creative, a form of art or poetry. In the excess of their style, which characterizes both Nietzsche and Deleuze, their practice of philosophy confirms that there is no transcendental, philosopher-subject over and above the products of her philosophy. Viewing subjects (actors) as entrenched or relatively unchanging thus gives way to the notion that there is no actor separate from her acts or any cause separate from its effects. The actor is constituted of desire and desire is always in movement, always made up of different elements depending on the situation; it is machine-like, rather than an Oedipal theatre of representation.[22] The phrases "desiring machines" and "body without organs" reinforce the theory's horizontality.[23] Desire is not based on lack or want, which are negative, but is always reforming itself: it is an affirmative process of flows and lines of flight. In their critique of Freud and psychoanalysis, Deleuze and his colleague Guattari reject the concept of repression in the process of the child's separation from the mother and its entry (as Lacan sees it) into the symbolic order.[24] For them there is no distinction between the individual and the collective — defined by the name-of-the-father and the order of the law; rather there is only social desire. The "body without organs" (the term borrowed from Antonin Artaud) is predictably, not at all an organic body, the "body of Oedipal reproduction," but a body like the body politic, produced in a connective synthesis: rhizomatic, not engendered or tree-like.[25]

Although Deleuze writes in fact from the position of someone who is steeped in the history of continental philosophy, his work has struck a democratic chord in many English-speaking countries.[26] Few contemporary thinkers have become more important to the prospects for post-Marxist thought.[27] Deleuze and Guattari's minimalist ideal for social organization (improvisational in a Spinozian sense) situates the struggle of freedom within and as part of the development of nature, rather than its conquest and mastery: "Liberation is not a manipulation of reality by a subject who would situate himself somehow outside of the arrangement he imposes on it; [liberation] is the expression, the exertion of the ontological force that constitutes the subject himself, not as an independent individual, but as the [most] versatile element of the collective system within whose network of interrelations his action is inscribed."[28]

Theory for Deleuze and Guattari is practice. Their writing possesses an engaging intensity and lively, baroque humor, a refreshing absence of rancor and resentment, a generous spirit of affirmation in their treatment of others, such that their own joy becomes apparent; no small contribution to philosophy or educational theory. Studying Deleuze provides us the possibility of immersion in a system of thought that not only represents a radical break but also systematically develops and extends in a thoroughgoing manner conceptualizations that are in a sense only hinted at in other literatures. Deleuze should have appeal both to philosophers and to those interested in literally radical epistemologies and politics.

ALTERNATIVE FIGURATIONS FOR THOUGHT

Deleuze's philosophical urgencies have resulted in elaborations of alternative accounts of the processes constitutive of subjectivity as well as urgencies to think differently about the subject and thought — to invent new frameworks, new images, and new modes of thought. Labeling the representational mode of thought that has characterized Western metaphysics since Plato as the philosophy of the state, he describes it as reposing on a double identity: of the thinking subject and of the concepts it creates and to which it lends its own presumed attributes of sameness and constancy.[29] Representational thinking is analogical; its concern is to establish a correspondence between the symmetrically structured domains of the subject, its concepts, and the objects of the world to which the concepts are applied — the "arborescent model of thought," fueled by an abstract machine of language that is fixed, linear, and based on dualities.[30]

Deleuze displaces this old, sedentary image of thought with a description of a dynamic process, making thinking an activity of flux, intensities, movement, and tensions.[31] He reiterates this thinking as an engagement of concept, percept, and effect characterized by energies vibrating and resonating along nomadic itineraries that cause those who travel to become other than themselves. How different this is from sedentariness with its rules of identity, resemblance of the self-identical form, and characterized by the predicative "is."

In *The Logic of Sense*, his extended meditation on the separation-connection of being (states of things, thoughts, and language), Deleuze repeatedly expresses the autonomy of these parallelisms and their simultaneous imbrication. Things, thought, and language are distinct but in reciprocal presupposition, they are overlapping moments of becoming that can be placed either in continuity or disjunction. Meaning is the articulation of their difference.[32]

Language in this view sets limits but also can go beyond limits. It can be active, transformational; its actions straddle many different levels; it is linear. However, language may also and most often does convey codes in the form of identity categories or general ideas. To the extent that it does, it can be said to function ideologically (language as a vehicle for good or common sense). For Deleuze, such codings of language existing in a classical style reflecting the oldest, "weariest kind of thought" and abstracted into a static phonetic system function to discipline language in an attempt to rein in its range of variation. Such codings are never neutral or objective and are in service of the institution of a standard language masking the domination of a transmission or communicative model of language.[33]

To counteract that model he employs the figuration of a style of thought that evokes or expresses a way out, the rhizome.[34] One of his (and Guattari's) ultimate goals is to break into the existing order, the system of molarity itself in order to dismantle it and free human bodies to reclaim fully their potential, that is, to self-destruct, de-form themselves by dissociating their bodies and desires from the apparatus of overcoding that has up to now defined them, and forced complementary definitions on others in their name. To accomplish this goal, they present to us an alternative image of nature. Their aim is to bypass the fundamental image of classical reflection, the root-tree.[35] As they say; "Nature doesn't work that way: in nature, roots are taproots with a more multiple, lateral, and circular system of ramification, rather than a dichotomous one. . . . The tree or root as an image, endlessly develops the law of the One that becomes two, then the two that becomes four. . . . Binary logic is natural reality and the spiritual reality of the root-tree."[36]

The binary logic of dichotomy as a system of thought has never reached an understanding of multiplicity and their claim is that this binary logic and its multivocal relationships still dominate the theories of psychoanalysis, linguistics, structuralism, and information science. To that list we would add the discourses of education. Even when a "multiplicity is taken up in a structure, its growth is offset by a reduction in its laws of combination," producing in the last instance a circular or cyclic unity that does not really "break with dualism, with the complementarity between a subject and an object, a natural reality and a spiritual reality."[37]

With the pragmatic realization that the multiple must be made with the dimensions already available, Deleuze and Guattari focus on the alternative figuration produced by a root that grows underground, sideways; functioning as a relay, connecting, circulating, moving on. A system of this kind they call a rhizome. "A rhizome as a subterranean stem is absolutely different from roots and radicles. Bulbs and tubers are rhizomes . . . some animals in their pack form, rats (for example) are rhizomes."[38] Crabgrass and cockroaches are rhizomes.[39] Their characteristics can be enumerated: the principles of connection and heterogeneity, multiplicity, rupture, the principles of cartography and decalcomania, and antigeneology operating by variation, expansion, conquest, capture, offshoots composed not of units but of dimensions, or rather "directions in motion."[40]

Drawing on the work of Irigaray, Deleuze, and Foucault, we offer as an example the activity of women's talk in the form of serious gossip as a practice close to rhizomatics in the sense described. Serious gossip, as distinguished from the trivial or malicious conversations often attributed to the term, is a practice that eludes the molarized discursive system that relies on the transmission model of communicating and learning, the model embedded within state philosophy and typically embraced in educational settings as constitutive of the discursive practice of dialogue. In an attempt to displace the opposition between meaningful, everyday talk on the one hand, and on the other authentic discourse (read as the important, educational expressions of an ideal point of view, the true grounds of being), we call attention to a common women's practice: gossip. Although gossip ordinarily endures a terrible reputation, we argue that gossip enacts the complex principles Deleuze characterizes as rhizomatic: connection and heterogeneity, various, expansionist, and multidimensional. In an analysis of the subversive possibilities of serious gossip, what is revealed are the following: gossip's investment in the participants' corporeal field, its polymorphous network of discursive production, its disruptive mix of the private and public, and its incalculable scope. We can never know quite where it goes, whom it reaches, how it changes, or how and by whom it is understood. Its nomadic quality can be translated into a feminist problematic in philosophy that helps us address fundamental traits of the patriarchal theoretical system: its chronic inability to recognize states of flow, fluidity, incompleteness, inconclusiveness, and the relational import of intense engagement — the becoming that emerges in the personal transaction of talking.

Gossip is certainly not one of the columns upon which the hegemonic political and theoretical order rests. Indeed, its value to subversive groups has been noted. Because gossip is hard to repress it supplies a weapon for outsiders: it often reflects moral assumptions different from those of the dominant culture and it provides language and knowledge potentially disruptive to the state order but vital to individual and community life of subordinated classes. In these aspects it provides oral histories for groups of people or nations who have been colonized by oppressors. Loose talk has been recognized as dangerous by the absolute state. Those oppressed by the state can and do use it to challenge the discourse of sovereign judgment, of stable subjectivity legislated by so-called good sense, of universal truths and (white male) justice. In enactment, gossip is often about the importance of not taking everything at face value, the need to inquire, to learn from other's experiences: it is about the desire for the sort of knowledge that goes against the grain of official interpretations of people or events. It frequently leads us to go beneath the surface of what is said and done, to try to account for conflicting appearances of official institutional stories, and then to test these contradictions, to evaluate them with others in conversations. This is not so different from some current recommendations for critical pedagogical excellence.

Gossiping can be understood as a relatively freeing activity standing quite consciously outside ordinary social inhibitions and established rules for discourse. As such, talkers often engage in a non-sense performance, exhibiting energy-filled manifestations of a sense of fun in an atmosphere of play and laughter. Indeed, one can wonder if our critics' admonitions stem from their realization of the intensity, unselfconscious impulses, creative imagination, and genuine satisfaction derived from this kind of interaction as opposed to the more heroically profound they have deemed essentially educational or important.

The often joyous and playful aspects of gossiping suggest compelling motives for friendly relations that incorporate a libidinal economy quite different from orgasmic orientation. In gossiping there is no pretense to finality. Mind, effect, and body become defined uniquely in a circulation of states, a play of differences that produces meanings, although of course there is no guarantee of the same (or right) kind. The latitude of free play in which parties engage can release the passionate substructures of thought and feeling in a space safe to wonder about or speculate on diverse forms of evidence about ourselves' or others' humanness. At times we try on different emotions, attitudes, attributes, or personas to feel how they fit or see what reactions they may elicit. To do this we dredge up our personal myths where pain and hilarity blur, where anguish coexists with joy, and sanity flirts with its opposite — a schizoanalytic practice.

These conversations become the treasures we remember. In them we find the setting up of relations that precede the specific predicates others come to attribute to the substance they see as our self. As a practice, gossiping shows us an alternative space in which to find the actual conditions of possibility for both the creation and examination of difference, in this case a difference in a dynamic Bergson might call indetermination. Importantly we also observe the aim of a practice that is to help unburden: not to load life with the weight of higher values, but to create new values that are those of life, that make life light and active. Although (or perhaps because) gossip inhabits the borderlands of socially sanctioned oral discourse, it expresses the minutiae of relations that create the texture of life, the small truths like the small talk that infuse the details of living with meaning. As such it is much like the example of music Deleuze and Guattari refer to in *A Thousand Plateaus*. Contrasted to the organization and interpersonal dynamics of a symphony, we have improvisational jazz. Contrasted to the authoritative, didactic efforts of dialogic teaching in which we try to instill the idea that meaning inheres in concepts, propositions that are transparent, we have the rhizomatic practice of gossip.

USING LINES TO GET THINGS ROLLING

The Deleuzian project of rhizomatics (which Deleuze uses interchangeably with schizoanalysis and cartography) is distinct from other poststructuralist descriptions by virtue of the insistence on desire and affect as part of every desiring machine or assemblage. As Braidotti summarizes, "The embodied subject is a term in a process of intersecting forces (affects) and spatiotemporal variables (connections)."[41] Thinking differently, then, includes affect and desire; and spatiotemporal variables describe the preferred Deleuzian metaphoric system. It is crucial to understand that these notions for Deleuze, while requiring an individual, take on a life of their own (almost reminiscent of Plato's forms, but "affect" for example remains, as with all of Deleuze's metaphysics, immanent and material). In part, this speaks to the inseparability of the individual and the social for Deleuze. As we saw, the rhizomatic practices of gossip are potent both because of the spatial trajectories and multiple directionality of gossip and because of the subtexts of affect and desire that drive the desiring machine of gossip as a transgressive practice.

In *A Thousand Plateaus*, Deleuze and Guattari discuss lines in terms of micropolitics and segmentarity. Micropolitics refers in part to the affective, conversational, and molecular dimension of the social and political world we inhabit and create. Deleuze and Guattari use molar and molecular to characterize the different potentials of lines that constitute us. To simplify, (molar/segmented) lines help explain how we become fixed; (molecular) lines of flight how we can interrupt the trajectories of molar lines.[42]

Lines are one part of the vast visual metaphor that is constantly being built through Deleuze's philosophizing. The geometrical image of lines leads to planes, each of which helps constitute the assemblage of the desiring machine. The concept of desiring machines serves Deleuze's commitment to functionalism and materialism. Desiring machine also provides an alternative to subjectivity and to the frustrating dualism of the individual and social. The desiring machine enables us to think differently, to allow differently for the intensities, flux, and movement of thinking. It also allows an increased imagination of the ways in which there is no inside or outside for the individual: the simultaneous constitution of subject and social, popularized through Foucault's emphasis on discourses, finds itself put into motion by desiring machines. Within this depiction of the assemblage it is not possible to separate the individual from the social: for example, the line of revolution is already part of the generalized desire to revolt. The lines that partially compose the desiring machine are not only my lines: they may be yours, they may be a generalized line (such as the desire to revolt, woman, or teacher). Contrast, for example, the kinds of static images invoked by identity or identity politics: the concept of any other, which must always be set against the dominant culture, is like a fixed photograph rather than a movement in process. In part, lines offer a metaphor for thinking about the articulations of power and bodies.

In "Many Politics" in *Dialogues* and in "Micropolitics and Segmentarity," three kinds of lines are discussed as the object of study common to rhizomatics, schizoanalysis, and cartography.[43] At first glance line seems an unattractive word with implications of linearity now associated with modernism's faith in progress; line of flight becomes increasingly intriguing. In fact, Deleuze and Guattari comment on the question of the suitability of line: "Perhaps, then, the words 'line' and 'segment' should be reserved for molar organisation, and other, more suitable, words should be sought for molecular composition. And in fact, whenever we can identify a well-defined segmented line, we notice that it continues in another form, as a quantum flow."[44] Yet we come to understand that lines describe routes or paths and that lines only indicate a beginning or end point (as in modernist visions) when cut or segmented. Molar lines are rigid and limiting in part because of these cuts and segmentation. For Deleuze, identity politics stems from the rigid molar lines, hearkening back to Nietzsche's critique of *ressentiment*. In these ways lines appear to serve Deleuze's interests in describing the processes of becoming.

The first are the most stultifying lines, rigid segmentarity that we know as "family, profession, job, holiday . . . to retirement." These lines are "clearly defined segments, in all kinds of directions, which cut us up in all senses, packets of segmentarized lines."[45] Binary oppositions play a central role in segmentation. "Segments depend on binary machines which can be very varied if need be."[46] He gives the example that if one is neither black nor white, a third term of the dualisms is nonetheless produced to contain — that is, half-breed. In this sense, it is possible to see that familiar forms of resistance to dominant culture also can function as rigid segments. Identity politics and feminism both represent for Deleuze examples of molar thought, likened to Nietzsche's "slave-morality."[47]

The second type of line can refer to the same line of rigid segmentation, but describes with more dimension what goes on: a "profession is a rigid segment, but also what happens beneath it, the connections, the attractions and repulsions, which do not coincide with the segments, the forms of madness which are secret but which nevertheless relate to the public authorities."[48] The second kind of line is not molar, but rather is more "supple, as it were more molecular — molecular fluxes with thresholds of quanta. . . . Many things happen on this second kind of line — becomings, micro-becomings, which don't even have the same rhythm as our 'history.'"[49]

The third sort of line is "even more strange: as if something carried us away, across our segments, but also across our thresholds, towards a destination which is unknown, not foreseeable, not preexistent. This line is simple, abstract, and yet the most complex of all, the most tortuous: it is the line of gravity or velocity, the line of flight . . . 'nothing other than the progression of the soul not the dancer.'"[50] Another way of describing the energy of a line of flight might be as a pull or draw: we can feel pulled or drawn toward or away from; we can also pull or draw things toward us.

The multiplicity and inseparability of lines are crucial features to understand. Deleuze and Guattari assert that molar and molecular describe "every society and every individual." We can associate molar with macropolitics, or, for example, with fixed ways of identifying ourselves as father or mother, man or woman; while molecular can be associated with micropolitics. It would be tempting to think of molar lines as the rigid segmentations of state power; while molecular seems to resonate with Foucault's idea of power productive through the subject. Deleuze refuses to let us think in terms of these two lines as a dualism: dualisms are not constituted by the "number of terms."[51] "You only escape dualisms effectively by shifting them like a load, and when you find between the terms, whether they are two or more, a narrow gorge like a border or frontier which will turn the set into a multiplicity."[52] Their characterization of dualisms is refreshing: dualisms cannot simply be evaded, but necessarily constitute us; yet, dualisms cannot be conceived to exist simply in terms of binary pairs. Rather, we can think of dualisms as one effect of certain effects of the lines that constitute us. Likewise, we can immediately consider the third kind of lines that immediately create multiplicity and movement away from segmentation.

The third type of line, or a line of flight, is not a synthesis but "always comes from elsewhere and disturbs the binarity of the two. . . . It is not a matter of adding a new segment on to the preceding segments . . . but of tracing another line in the middle of the segmentary line, in the middle of the segments, which carries them off according to the variable speeds and slownesses in a movement of flight or of flux."[53] They suggest the example of the powerful geography of West to East and the conflicts between the powers of these two oppositions. It is the cracks and ruptures introduced by the line from the south that destabilizes the East-West binary opposition: "everyone has his south. . . . Nations, classes, sexes have their south."[54] The south represents the line of imperceptible ruptures.

To escape dualisms is to trace another road, to create a multiplicity also known as an assemblage. "Any assemblage necessarily includes lines of rigid and binary segmentarity, no less than molecular lines, or lines of border, or flight or slope."[55] Here we begin to see both the significance of desiring machines as a way of indicating multiplicity and the constitutive place of lines in composing the desiring machine.

The tangled lines evidence one example of how Deleuze's metaphors make complex some of Foucault's popularized conceptions. Foucault's oft-cited analysis of panopticon as the symbol of the centralized state resonates with the concept of the molecular line: each individual is singularly aware of being watched and therefore self-governs out of fear. Within the panopticon the directions of power are fixed; the governing sight of the tower is a god's-eye view; the subjects cannot reciprocate the gaze but internalize the sense of being surveyed and through this one-way surveillance enact the sense of right discipline. At first glance the self-governing individual seems to resonate with the molecular line. The molecular can replay the molar segments "without necessarily being centralized in a particular apparatus of the State. We have left behind the shores of rigid segmentarity, but we have entered a regime which is no less organized where each embeds himself in his own black hole . . . with a self-assurance about his own case, his role and his mission, which is even more disturbing than the certainties of the first line . . . microfascisms."[56] In other words, as with the panopticon the molecular is inscribed with the discourses of the surveying power. The lines and assemblage of the desiring machine need not rely on a centralized state apparatus.

These concepts of lines help address the question: how is it that the subject complies with her own subjugation? It is not simply a matter of being forced by ideology; and it is not simply being duped by false consciousness and perpetuating the abuse done unto me onto the next victim. Nor have we simply entered a regime with no possible exit. Molar and molecular can be distinguished, but do not exist in isolation from one another. They are, indeed, a tangled web, tracing no beginnings or predictable intersections.

USING DELEUZE FOR THE TEACHING OF HISTORY AND LITERATURE

How do rhizomatics and lines help us to think about what happens in educational environments? For some of us who do radical education, there is a call to reflect on how our ostensibly radical approaches may in fact reflect rigid segmentations. We are thinking in particular of our own lessons in coming to recognize the extent to which even radical approaches are thoroughly defined in Western terms. "Leftist organisations will not be the last to secrete microfascisms. It's too easy to be antifascist on the molar level, and not even see the fascist inside you, the fascist you yourself sustain and nourish and cherish with molecules both personal and collective."[57] Although microfascism may seem too strong a word to describe the hesitation we feel now about teaching certain skills of critical reading or means of reading history that insist on frameworks of contesting narratives — in the context of a colonized nation, and as Americans-cum-imperialists, steeped in Western conceptions, it is easy to see that one's sense of values can function as apparently radical molecules but rigidly molar as they ignore the worlds that contest our own.

It is desire that makes us want to think.[59] How might we conceive of lines of flight as they are indicated by assemblages of desire? What accounts for attesting to the desires? Recently two women historians were invited to speak about their work to a course taught by one of us on history of education. Desire infused their words, and could be heard and seen in their bodies as they spoke. Each of their stories seems to express what Deleuze describes as the third kind of line, the line of flight. "It is as if a line of flight, perhaps only a tiny trickle to begin with, leaked between the segments, escaping their centralization, eluding their totalization. The profound movements stirring in a society present themselves in this fashion, even if they are necessarily 'represented' as a confrontation between molar segments."[59] In other words, a line of flight will often be represented as the rigid opposition to a molar line in order to contain its ability to thwart and break through those molar rigidities. What was striking about these women's testimonies was the ways in which they had struggled against molar lines and in which each embodied the potency of feeling and passion for what they do as historians struggling against the rigid segmentation. As the women described the voice of the molar line of their discipline, "You are a historian and that means you study history as it has been defined during the past two hundred years." Yet somehow, Linda Smith[60] had managed to find a line of flight from medieval European history, where neither she nor any of her people was ever mentioned, to a space in which she could pioneer histories of colonization in Aotearoa or New Zealand. At the same time, she redefined the form of those histories quite in line with molecular intervention: "I want to ask, when colonisation occurs and people are relocated, where do they go? What happens to the people? What happens to the children?" This emphasizes an aspect of the molecular. She began by telling the class of 80 students: there is no necessary connection between history and justice. To illustrate, she spoke of how the Maori people[61] have been in the process of testifying about the injustices of history of colonization to the tribunal, and how the judges listen impassively to accounts that are painful, brutal, and difficult to speak. She spoke of how one would think, "Isn't this enough? Don't you get it?" However, it is not enough; for history (in the popular or academic sense) to have a bearing on justice will indeed require lines of flight.

The next historian's testimony was equally passionate, and she was able to attest to a line of flight that brought history to bear on justice. Kay Morris-Matthews[62] recounted how the one female historian, with whom she worked in her entire schooling career, said to her, "Don't accept what you're reading! Ask other questions, look for other histories." She also told the story of collaborating with Kuni Jenkins on a book about Hukarere Girls School, a secondary school for Maori girls, which had been closed while the boys' schools remained open. In the process of their research, they studied the archived books and accounts of the school and discovered an untold bit of history. The boys' school had run into financial debt, while Hukarere was operating well. However, it was Hukarere, not St. Joseph's, that was closed. Because of their work, Jenkins returned to Hukarere (from which she had graduated) and helped to reopen the school to young Maori women. These two pioneering — and, within the molar and rigid disciplines of the institutions of higher education, relatively isolated feminist and post-colonial — historians[63] were able to transfigure the molar lines of the institution that condoned their work, to affect the lives and possibilities of others beyond that institution. The powerful message issued by both women was that their historical work opened up lines of flight for others.

We can also think of many instances in which language and perceptions depicted in literature exemplify the radical potential of lines. Virginia Woolf's modernist genre represents the gendered characterizations of thinking differently. Two passages from her novel *To the Lighthouse* illustrate woman's relationship to molar and molecular lines. Each distinct visual image portrays space and time quite differently. In the first passage Mrs. Ramsey is referring to the (molar) knowledge discussed by her husband and sons:

What did it all mean? To this day she had no notion. A square root? What was that? Her sons knew. She leant on them; on cubes and square roots; that was what they were talking about now; on Voltaire and Madame de Stael; on the character of Napoleon; on the French system of land tenure. . . . She let it uphold her and sustain her, this admirable fabric of the masculine intelligence, which ran up and down, crossed this way and that, like iron girders spanning the swaying fabric, upholding the world.[64]

As Deleuze consistently argues, the lines are inseparable; a person may make use of only one, or all, but their inseparability allows us to understand that although Mrs. Ramsey recognizes these rigid iron girders as not hers she gains sustenance nonetheless. Mrs. Ramsey, so much part of the upper-middle class, is also alienated from its iron girders. Woolf uses another molar line — the alphabet — to depict the husband's philosophizing. Mr. Ramsey's fear of death and desire for immortality come through in another of Woolf's amusing portraits of man's relationship to the segmented line of the alphabet. Mr. Ramsey is consumed with his own self-importance and wants to believe that as a thinker he is extending thought measurably beyond its earlier thinkers. At these moments Mr. Ramsey's desire is represented with the alphabet; in a very humorous portrait of his frustration, he cannot seem to get past "r."

Throughout the novel, Woolf depicts through Mrs. Ramsey the supple line of the molecular (which we hesitate to call a line of flight, as one can debate whether, within the novel, Mrs. Ramsey flees, although the character Lily Briscoe might be said to flee). Nonetheless, Woolf's description here seems uncannily to portray the masculine knowledge as molar, and then powerfully juxtaposes her own molecular perception against these molar lines.[65] Here Mrs. Ramsey sits at her own dinner party, which she has orchestrated expertly from beginning to end.

They were off again. Now she need not listen. It could not last, she knew, but at the moment her eyes were so clear that they seemed to go round the table unveiling each of these people, and their thoughts and their feelings, without effort like a light stealing under water so that its ripples and the reeds in it and the minnows balancing themselves, and the sudden silent trout are all lit up hanging, trembling. So she saw them; she heard them; but whatever they said also had this quality, as if what they said was like the movement of a trout when, at the same time, one can see the ripple and the gravel, something to the right, something to the left; and the whole is held together; for whereas in active life she would be netting and separating one thing from another.

The two passages contrast in descriptive content the kind of spatio-temporal relationships constructed in the molar and molecular moments. The rhythm of the prose also adds a dimension to the notion of molar and molecular. The first passage demonstrates a certain rigid segmentarity: it contains short, isolated phrases; the voice is marked with tentative question marks, a choppy list separated by semicolons. This voice appears to represent a more faithful description of the segmented reality in which she finds herself. On the other hand, her perception of the room and its dynamics, her insight and multiple-awareness is expressed through Woolf's hallmark. This voice moves without stumbling; it captures and releases as it moves like a waterflow over the rocks of real objects against which consciousness lights and grates. "So she saw them; she heard them" — here we feel the rockiness; "but whatever they said also had this quality, as if what they said was like the movement of a trout when, at the same time, one can see the ripple and the gravel. "

In this last line Mrs. Ramsey reflects on the difference between these two modes of perception: regarding molecular perception, "as if what they said was like the movement of a trout when, at the same time, one can see the ripple and the gravel, something to the right, something to the left; and the whole is held together" — what could better describe poststructuralism's emphasis on process, motion, flux? Mrs. Ramsey notes to herself that, on the other hand, with respect to molar lines, "in active life she would be netting and separating one thing from another." Woolf's choice of words — that in real life one would be netting and separating — indicates separation, in the binary segmentarity of the molar, and netting in relation to the trout infers death. We come to query: is it not possible that woman's relationship to death is so regularly experienced within the molar lines, that to fear "a passion for abolition"[66] as the risk of the line of flight seems a fear imposed and transplanted from the realm of the molar?

FEMINIST CAUTIONS

The concepts of process rather than destination, means rather than end, change rather than static identity summarize one aspect of poststructuralist thought.[67] As Rosi Braidotti characterizes the notion of becoming, developed by Deleuze and Irigaray, "one has to assimilate the dead to produce the new living order: the apocalypse is from now on. Once this process is triggered, there is little knowing where it will end, but all that matters is the process, the act of going, not the destination."[68] We can map only where we have been, and not where we are or where we are going. This implies a constant shedding of identity and rather a continual becoming, which entails a mourning, a loss built into the process of what we call life.

What are the risks we encounter in this promising line? I share with Deleuze and Guattari the desire to avoid romanticizing the lines of flight. "We may well have presented these lines as a sort of mutation or creation drawn not only in the imagination but also in the very fabric of social reality; we may well have attributed to them the movement of the arrow and the speed of an absolute — but it would be oversimplifying to believe that the only risk they fear and confront is allowing themselves to be recaptured in the end. . . . They themselves emanate a strange despair, like an odor of death and immolation, a state of war from which one returns broken."[69] Here is where Deleuze and Guattari spin off into discussion of death and fear that seems a highly gendered fear, if we may be so bold and invoke a molar pair, less applicable to women than to men. Like many discussions one reads of the body, the ways in which men and women express their relation to the body and its potentials and threats are significantly gendered. The fears that Deleuze and Guattari claim as universal to lines of flight are gendered. Perhaps it is only the examples they have chosen — as is common in their writings, examples of men in literature or men on the battlefield. Although Deleuze of course denies this fear as anything to do with a death drive, we are left to wonder if these articulations of fear of death pose a different threat to (becoming) man than to (becoming) woman. At the very least we think there are many questions to be examined regarding women's relationship to death, which would take into account the extensive work of such philosophers as Irigaray and Kristeva. Women's daily contact with fears that have to do with the omnipresence of physical threat, violence, death, or even childbirth or menstruation — would these not shape one's fear of death? What of the desire for immortality? This fear or desire is also gendered, for in a sense man's vulnerability is great: one's namesake may well not be of one, or as so often, this representation of one's immortality will remain the responsibility of woman.

Deleuze and Irigaray both insist that the subjectivities they describe are historically determined. In that case, it makes sense to attend to the different kinds of molar and molecular lines that one lives out. For example, the first line of rigid segmentation may be experienced as a more singular and continuous line by women than by men. In many cases, the line she experiences growing up as daughter will extend without great resegmentation into her life as wife and mother. She will not experience "now you are in school," "now you are in the army," "now you are retired." To be sure, others' experiences of these lines will affect her: if her husband dies in the army, loses his job, retires — these resegmentations will affect her lines — but as

Braidotti and Irigaray argue, the repetitions of the second temporal zone in a sense describe another dimension of her molar lines. This describes well Deleuze's idea that a line can belong to me as well as to another and a line can be rigid and supple at the same time. For example, with respect to the second type of line, women may have overall greater access to the less visible supple segmentarities of micropolitics. Women's gossip, for example, is an example of the circulating repetition of power that remains less visible to certain public spheres of civil life. Her becoming through the more supple possibilities of the second line is in part by virtue of her being less segmented by the first kind of line. Her position is not necessarily more molecular, but circulates in different directions than a man's, demonstrating less overt modes of power and resistance. Perhaps Deleuze advocated becoming woman for all, because the typos woman is more likely to perceive molecular paths of resistance. We might ask, is woman a member of a molecular class, well-poised for lines of flight?

CONCLUSIONS

Taking Deleuze seriously is no small project. For those concerned to understand difference and its implications for educational projects, for those concerned with the promises of radical epistemologies, Deleuze's work is promising, and contemporary theorists have only just begun to introduce his thinking into wider circles of analysis.

Here are a few questions we might want to ask if we are sincere about wanting difference to be as valued as commonality and as useful to us in our school tasks, policy-making tasks, and teaching, as well as in our whole lives — and if we are to take Deleuze at his word. How do we, as intellectual workers in a posthumanist moment, learn to do research differently, without security? How do we reconceptualize teaching as nonlinear, neither unidirectional nor representing unambiguous progress? How do we foster an understanding by researchers on teaching that some paradoxes, contradictions, and uncertainties cannot and should not be eliminated? How do we learn with joy as opposed to dread and fear of failure in this postcapitalist reign? Practicing Deleuze involves opening multiple lines of exploration for our own work as well as for our students. Naming the multiple at work in education is put in motion by engaging rhizomatic practices whose effects and outcomes may be (one hopes) far beyond our control.

NOTES

1. Michel Foucault, *Language, Counter-Memory, Practice*, ed. and trans. Donald F. Bouchard (Ithaca, N.Y.: Cornell University Press, 1977). Cited in Constantin V. Boundas and Dorothea Olkowski, eds., *Gilles Deleuze and the Theatre*

of Philosophy (New York: Routledge, 1994), p. 1.

2. This debate ranges over a number of discipline fields and lines of thought. For an introduction see Madan Sarup, *Poststructuralism and Postmodernism* (Athens: University of Georgia Press, 1993).

3. See for example Stanley Aronowitz and Henry Giroux, *Postmodern Education* (Minneapolis: University of Minnesota Press, 1991).

4. See for example Diane Elam, *Feminism and Deconstruction* (New York: Routledge, 1994); Patrick McGee, *Telling the Other* (Ithaca, N.Y.: Cornell University Press, 1992).

5. Gilles Deleuze and Felix Guattari, *Anti-Oedipus: Capitalism and Schizophrenia*, trans. Robert Hurley, Mark Seem, and Helen R. Lane (Minneapolis: University of Minnesota Press, 1983), p. xii.

6. Ibid., p. xiii

7. Gilles Deleuze, *Negotiations 1972–1990*, trans. Martin Joughin (New York: Columbia University Press, 1995), pp. 103–104.

8. For a guide to his works and how his ideas are productive readings of others, see especially Ronald Bogue, *Deleuze and Guattari* (New York: Routledge, 1989).

9. Judith Butler, "Contingent Foundations: Feminism and the Question of Postmodernism," Judith Butler and Joan Scott, eds. *Feminists Theorize the Political* (New York: Routledge, 1992), p. 7.

10. Gilles Deleuze, "Anti-Oedipus," trans. Janis Forman. *Semistext(e)* 2(3) (1977): 12.

11. See Bogue, *Deleuze and Guattari*.

12. Francois Châtelet, *Hegel* (Paris: Seul, 1968). Quoted in Michael Hardt, *Gilles Deleuze* (Minneapolis: University of Minnesota Press, 1993).

13. Judith Butler, *Subjects of Desire* (New York: Columbia University Press, 1987), pp. 183–184.

14. See especially Gilles Deleuze and Felix Guattari, *A Thousand Plateaus*, ed. and trans. Brian Massumi (Minneapolis: University of Minnesota Press, 1987), pp. 232–309.

15. Ibid.

16. See Gilles Deleuze, *Nietzsche and Philosophy*, trans. Hugh Tomlinson (New York: Columbia University Press, 1983), pp. 2–38; Deleuze and Guattari, *A Thousand Plateaus*, pp. 232–309.

17. Deleuze and Guattari, *A Thousand Plateaus*, pp. 310–350.

18. Ibid., pp. 351–423.

19. Ibid.

20. Ibid., pp. 149–168.

21. See Deleuze and Guattari, *Anti-Oedipus*, esp. Part I; Constantin V. Boundas, *The Deleuze Reader* (New York: Columbia University Press, 1993), Part III.

22. Deleuze and Guattari, *A Thousand Plateaus*, pp. 149–166.

23. See Paul Patton, "Conceptual Politics and the War Machine in Mille Plateaux, *Substance* 44(5) (1984): 61–80; A. Collier, "The Inorganic Body and the Ambiguity of Freedom," *Radical Philosophy* 57(4) (1991): 3–9; Regis Debray, *Critique of Political Reason* (London: Verso, 1983); Peter Macherey, *A Theory of Literary Production* (London: Routledge, 1978).

24. Peter Macherey, "On a Meditation of the Constitution," *Cahiers Spinoza* 4 (1982–83): 9–37.
25. See Boundas, *The Deleuze Reader*, pp. 27–36.
26. Ibid., p. 34.
27. Ibid., p. 28. See also Deleuze and Guattari, *A Thousand Plateaus*, pp. 39–110.
28. Deleuze and Guattari, *A Thousand Plateaus*, pp. 232–309.
29. Ibid., pp. 75–110.
30. See Boundas, *The Deleuze Reader*, pp. 27–36.
31. Ibid., p. 27.
32. Ibid.
33. Ibid., p.28.
34. Ibid., p. 29.
35. Ibid. See also Mary Leach, "Trespassing 'State' Political Philosophy: Giving S/way to a Cockroach Theory," unpublished paper, 1996.
36. Boundas, *The Deleuze Reader*, p. 9.
37. See Mary Leach "Researching Dewey for Feminist Imaginaries: Linguistic Continuity, Discourse, and Gossip," James Garrison, ed., *The New Scholarship on Dewey* (Boston: Kluwer Academic, 1995), pp. 123–138.
38. Ibid.
39. See Deleuze and Guattari, *Anti-Oedipus*.
40. See Hardt, *Gilles Deleuze*, pp. 1–25.
41. As Rosi Braidotti describes in "Of Bugs and Women: Irigaray and Deleuze on the Becoming-Woman," (in Carolyn Burke, Naomi Schor, and Margaret Whitford, eds., *Engaging with Irigaray*. [New York: Columbia University Press, 1994]), radical epistemology conceptualizes thinking as an active process, in which affect offers impetus and affect is released in the process. *Anti-Oedipus* is one place to begin researching how Deleuze and Guattari reconceptualize subjectivity. In a sense, they plant Freud's feet in the material world of Marxism; refuse Oedipalization as a domestic theatre for neurotics, and thus extend Freud's questions far beyond the nuclear family; and analyze the schizophrenic for a breath of fresh air as reprieve from a theory almost entirely founded on the neurotic experience. In Gilles Deleuze and Felx Guattari, *What is Philosophy?* trans. Hugh Tomlinson and Graham Burchill (London: Verso, 1994), the authors systematically set out the interrelationship of affect, concept, and percept. In rethinking the body, Deleuze's works are frequently cited. For example, a recent collection, Juliet Flower MacCannell and Laura Zakarin, eds., *Thinking Bodies* (Stanford, Calif.: Stanford University Press, 1994), represents contemporary fascination with reintroducing the body into epistemology. The sites of this Kantian reversal stem predominantly from literature, critiques of ideology, and psychoanalysis.
42. It is interesting to note that molar is an anagram for moral, and in a sense morality appropriately references the fixity of molar lines.
43. Our discussion of lines is informed by Deleuze and Guattari, *A Thousand Plateaus*; Deleuze, *Negotiations 1972–1990*; Gilles Deleuze and Clair Parnet, *Dialogues*, trans. Hugh Tomlinson and Barbara Habberjam (New York: Columbia University Press, 1977); Braidotti, "Of Bugs and Women"; Rosi Braidotti, "Towards a New Nomadism: Feminist Deleuzian Tracks; or Metaphysics and Metabolism," in Michael Hardt, *Gilles Deleuze* (Minneapolis: University of

Minnesota Press, 1993); Elizabeth Grosz, "A Thousand Tiny Sexes: Feminism and Rhizomatics," in Michael Hardt, *Gilles Deleuze* (Minneapolis: University of Minnesota Press, 1993); and Alphonso Lingis, "The Society of Dismembered Body Parts," in Michael Hardt, *Gilles Deleuze* (Minneapolis: University of Minnesota Press, 1993).

44. Deleuze and Guattari, *A Thousand Plateaus*, p. 217

45. Deleuze and Parnet, *Dialogues*, p. 124. See also Gilles Deleuze and Felix Guattari, "Micropolitics and Segmentarity" in *A Thousand Plateaus*, in which the authors apply the question of molar and molecular lines in an extremely provocative analysis of how we can think of fascism, totalitarianism, democracy, masses, and classes in terms of how molar and molecular describe the interrelationship of devices of power, the overcoding machines, and the state apparatus — all of which together is a machine in its own. However, here we will limit the discussion to a clarification of lines as they relate to becoming, and will then concentrate on the promising third line, the line of flight, and ask how this can inform our educational endeavors. We hope our discussion signals how lines of flight may be conceived in relation to these related questions of class, mass, and power.
   There are three aspects to be distinguished in thinking about the network of power relations that help constitute this first line, the line of rigid segments. "Segments also imply *devices of power* . . . *the apparatus of the State* is a concrete assemblage which realizes the machine of overcoding of a society. This machine in its turn is thus not the State itself, it is the abstract machine which organises the dominant utterances and the established order of a society, the dominant languages and knowledge, conformist actions and feelings, the segments which prevail over the others. *The abstract machine of overcoding* ensures the homogenisation of different segments, their convertibility, their translatability"(Deleuze and Guattari, *A Thousand Plateaus*, p. 129). One can see that this description of the abstract machine of overcoding, and the devices of power, are closely aligned with Foucault's refiguring of how we conceive of the power of the State and the law. This description seems particularly appropriate to a discussion of education: clearly, the university and school are sites of operation for the abstract machine of overcoding. Further, the concept of consciousness-raising might be precisely about learning to identify how these devices of power are at work and how we are engaged with them, for example, engaged with conformist actions and feelings.

46. Ibid., p. 128.
47. Braidotti, "Of Bugs and Women," p. 117
48. Deleuze and Parnet, *Dialogues*, p. 125
49. Ibid., p. 124.
50. Ibid., p. 125.
51. Ibid., p. 132.
52. Ibid.
53. Ibid., p. 131.
54. Ibid., p. 132.
55. Ibid.
56. Ibid., pp. 138–139.
57. Deleuze and Guattari, *A Thousand Plateaus*, p. 215.
58. See Deleuze and Guattari, *What is Philosophy?* esp. pp. 1–34, 163–199.
59. Ibid., p. 216.

60. Linda Smith is the head of the Department of Maori Education, University of Auckland. For an example of her work, see "Maori Women: Discourses, Projects, and Maori Wahine," in Sue Middleton and Alison Jones, eds., *Women and Education in Aotearoa* (Wellington: Bridget Williams Ltd, 1992).

61. In Aotearoa (New Zealand), Maori are the indigenous people who have lived on the island since approximately 950 A.D.. In 1835, some Maori signed a document titled the Treaty of Waitangi, witnessed by the British Crown. The treaty stipulated the conditions of agreement by which Europeans (*Pakeha*) were permitted to live in Aotearoa. In the history of colonization that has ensued, the treaty remains as a document against which claims regarding land, resources, and rights are made by the Maori. The Maori Sovereignity Movement continues to make its case effectively, and to work toward sovereignity, or *Tinorangatiratanga*, as specified in the treaty, in progressive steps of social, political, and legal change.

62. Kay Morris-Matthews, until recently, taught in the Department of Cultural and Policy Studies in Education and Kuni Jenkins teaches in the Department of Maori Education, School of Education, University of Auckland. They are coauthors of *Hukarere: the Politics of Maori Girls Schooling 1875–1995* (Palmerston North: Dunmore Press, 1995).

63. This isolation reflects only one view: in fact, because of the way Maori work collectively within the institution, my perception of isolation may be an academic point.

64. Virginia Woolf, *To the Lighthouse* (London: Penguin, 1992), p. 159.

65. This perceptive-field is reminiscent of strands of phenomenology such as Edmund Husserl's notion of horizon, developed in educational work such as William Pinar, *Understanding Curriculum as Phenomenological and Deconstructed Text* (New York: Teachers College Press, 1992); Madeleine Grumet, *Bitter Milk: Women and Teaching* (Amherst: University of Massachusetts Press, 1988).

66. Deleuze, "Semistext(e) Anti-Oedipus," p. 140.

67. It is important in the same breath to recognize that poststructuralist thought did not introduce these ideas. Perhaps it is fair to say that Deleuze has followed through to its extreme the implications of becoming as an alternative to Heideggerian being, for example, and this persisting movement toward new ways of thinking. Poststructuralism's version of challenging notions of fixed and static identity should be understood specifically as emerging in a French context, dated to May 1968 for Deleuze.

68. Braidotti, "Of Bugs and Women," p. 134.

69. Deleuze and Guattari, *A Thousand Plateaus*, p. 229.

7

Jean-François Lyotard: Education for Imaginative Knowledge

A. T. Nuyen

It is axiomatic that to educate is to educate for knowledge. To say the same thing differently, knowledge is the *sine qua non* of education. It follows that the structure of education is determined by the structure of knowledge, or at least it should be. It also follows that changes and innovations in education must follow from a different understanding of the structure of knowledge or the discovery of hitherto unnoticed aspects of knowledge. The fact that the latter is rare probably explains why nothing much seems to be happening in education in terms of the fundamentals of pedagogy. Activities seem to be taking place at the periphery where there are increasingly new things to know — new problems, new relationships, new ways of doing things. This is not to say that developments in these areas are not important or exciting. However, in the enthusiasm and exuberance generated by such developments, it is easy to forget to ask ourselves whether any rethinking about the very structure of education is warranted. In this chapter I discuss a possible addition to the structure of knowledge as traditionally understood, and explore the educational implications of this adjustment to our understanding of knowledge.

Traditionally, knowledge is understood as divided into three kinds: knowing-by-acquaintance, knowing-that, and knowing-how. The first kind of knowledge consists of our actual experience of the world. To teach this kind of knowledge is to allow the learner to experience the world directly, such as in field trips, study excursions, and so forth. (Naturally, the experience would be enhanced if it is guided by a certain amount of knowing-that and knowing-how.) The second kind of knowledge consists of all the information one possesses expressed in terms of propositional knowledge. Much of that derives from actual experience, but a great deal comes from secondary sources such as books and other media. The traditional way of acquiring this knowledge is book-learning, but interacting with the electronic sources is increasingly crucial. The third kind of knowledge can be divided further into: knowing-how-to-do and knowing-how-to-think. The former consists of technical skill and the latter of analytical skill. Technical training is the traditional method of imparting technical knowledge. Analytical skill is either acquired in the process of acquiring other kinds of knowledge or generally in learning critical reasoning.

What is missing in the above classification is knowing-how-to-imagine. This is a kind of knowing-how the end product of which is what I call imaginative knowledge. If I am right in thinking that this is a legitimate aspect of knowledge then it has to form part of the structure of knowledge. Any change or addition to the structure of knowledge will have educational implications. My task now is to justify this addition and to discuss its implications.

The domain of imagination is not the actual world but possible worlds. To acquire imaginative knowledge is to acquire the capacity to transcend the actual world and to enter the realm of possibilities. However, the point of imaginative knowledge is not to escape reality. It is not to dream up something totally remote from reality either for entertainment or to serve some non-cognitive pursuit. There is a close connection between reality and imaginative knowledge. To begin with, the point of departure for imaginative knowledge is reality itself, and it is reality to which one eventually returns. Indeed, it may be said that in this form of knowledge, we try to imagine reality itself differently. Thus, it is in no sense an escape from reality. On the contrary, as I shall argue below, the point of imaginative knowledge is to help the learner see what is possible and thus be in the position to actualize the most desirable possibility. In this way, imaginative knowledge helps bring about a better reality, a better actual world.

It is usual to explain first what exactly it is that one proposes and then explain why one proposes it. Although I have already said something about the nature of imaginative knowledge, I have by no means explained what exactly it is. However, instead of completing the task of explaining what it is, I turn now to the question of why knowledge of the general sort described above is called for. The reason for reversing the usual procedure is that imaginative knowledge, being a kind of know-how, serves a particular need, and so it will be useful first to examine that need. Indeed, the details of what will best serve the need can only be filled out after we know what the need is. In the case of imaginative knowledge, we have to find out first why it is that we need something like it. After answering the why question, I shall return to the what question before examining the how question, that is, the educational implications.

The need for something like imaginative knowledge arises from what the French postmodernist Jean-François Lyotard calls the "postmodern condition."[1] Many commentators have drawn implications for education from Lyotard's account of the postmodern condition.[2] The one aspect of Lyotard's work that receives the most attention from commentators is what Lyotard calls the "legitimation crisis."[3] However, there is another aspect of Lyotard's postmodernism, prominent in his more recent publications, that deserves close scrutiny. I refer to a phenomenon that Lyotard calls the *différend* and the related phenomenon of the *unpresentable*.[4]

Lyotard defines the *différend* as "a case of conflict, between (at least) two parties, that cannot be equitably resolved for lack of a rule of judgment applicable to both arguments" (Lyotard, 1988: xi). Conflicts can arise when people are engaged in discourses that are incommensurable. Because there are no rules that apply across discourses, the conflicts become *différends*. To enforce a rule in a *différend* is to enforce the rule of one discourse or the other, resulting in a wrong suffered by the party whose rule of discourse is ignored. Furthermore, the wronged party cannot appeal against the wrong because the rules of its own discourse are not recognized and because to appeal in terms of the rules of the other discourse is already to have given up. One of Lyotard's own examples of *différends* is the following argument by the revisionist historian Robert Faurisson: "In order for a place to be identified as a gas chamber, the only eye witness I will accept would be a victim of this gas chamber; now, according to my opponent, there is no victim that is not dead; otherwise, this gas chamber would not be what he or she claims it to be. There is, therefore, no gas chamber" (Lyotard, 1988: 3–4).

In this case, the victims of gas chambers have been wronged. They are unable to prove their case in terms of the rules of Faurisson's historical discourse. Should this become the dominant discourse, their case would be totally unpresentable. According to Lyotard, in addition to the legitimation crisis, another aspect of the postmodern condition is the prevalence of *différends*. This is so because in the postmodern condition there is a plurality of discourses, or what Lyotard calls *petits récits* (little narratives). As such, *différends* are inevitable, and wrongs are likely to be suffered.

To bear with the postmodern condition, to cope with it, there is a need to limit the amount and extent of wrongs. To satisfy this need is to ensure that the unpresentable is somehow presented. Thus, the ethical problem for postmodernity is to present the unpresentable, or as Lyotard puts it, to "bear witness to differends" (1988: 13). According to Lyotard, we have to face this ethical problem with the utmost urgency because what is at stake is life and death itself. What happened to the Jews can happen again: "the question `Auschwitz'? is also the question `after Auschwitz'?" (p. 101). Indeed, we know that it did happen again under Stalin; we know that after the "extermination (Auschwitz) . . . [was] . . . a sacrificial `beautiful death' (Stalingrad)" (p. 106). Toward the end of the essay "Answering the Question: What Is Postmodernism?" Lyotard warns us that "we can hear the mutterings of the desire for a return of terror," and urges that we must be "witnesses to the unpresentable."[5] In a recent book, *The Inhuman*, Lyotard declares that the question of presenting the unpresentable is "the only one worthy of what is at stake in life and thought in the coming century."[6]

Just how does one present the unpresentable? In *The Postmodern Condition*, Lyotard advocates learning from literary geniuses. For instance, the "work of Proust and that of Joyce both allude to something which does not allow itself to be made present" (Lyotard, 1984: 80). What we have to do is to search "for new presentations, not in order to enjoy them but to impart a stronger sense of the unpresentable" (p. 81). He goes on to say that "it is our business not to supply reality but to invent allusions to the conceivable which cannot be presented." Because literary geniuses are the experts in the art of allusion, we have a great deal to learn from them. In *The Inhuman*, Lyotard suggests that we can also learn from another group of artistic geniuses, the avant-garde artists. What these and the literary artists have in common is their power of imagination. With imagination, we can invent allusions to the conceivable, or invent possibilities. With these possibilities, we can get a sense of, or a feeling for, what is not presented in our discourse. With imagination, we have a hope of presenting the unpresentable, thus minimizing the wrongs of *différends*, minimizing the possibility of the return of terror.

We have seen through the works of Lyotard the need for imaginative knowledge, for the category of knowing-how-to-imagine. I return now to the what question to consider the kind of imagination we need to develop in order to bear witness to *différends*. The answer to this question can be found in Kant's aesthetics. Lyotard himself has turned to Kant, particularly to Kant's account of the sublime. In his *Lessons on the Analytic of the Sublime*,[7] Lyotard gives a patient reading of that account. In summary form, that account is as follows. Kant locates the feeling of the sublime in the interplay between the mind's faculties of reason and imagination. As is well known, reason is an intellectual faculty that produces rational concepts in the same way as the understanding produces categories. In addition to the intellectual faculties, the mind also possesses what Kant calls the faculties of sense, namely sensibility and imagination. The role of sensibility is to collect raw sensuous data and that of the imagination is to organize them into sensuous intuitions. In the case of empirical knowledge, the imagination synthesizes and schematizes sensuous data into manifolds of intuitions that, when meshed with the categories, become empirical knowledge. What is of interest is the role of the imagination with respect to the faculty of reason.

Unlike concepts of the understanding, concepts of reason, such as God, freedom, and so on, are not applicable to sensuous objects. They do have objects (they would be empty otherwise) but their objects are not to be found in the world of sense. They are, as Kant puts it, supersensible. We cannot demonstrate concepts of reason with anything sensuous. In *Critique of Judgement*, Kant refers to them as indemonstrable.[8] However, it is important to show that at least certain concepts of reason are not remote to sensibility, particularly those concepts that determine moral precepts. In both *Groundwork* and the second *Critique*, Kant stresses the need to gain a favorable hearing for the moral law. One way of doing so is to bring the determining rational concepts "closer to intuition," as he puts it in *Groundwork*,[9] or to set them *in concreto* as he puts it in the second *Critique*.[10] Because the imagination mediates between the intellect and sensibility to bring concepts of reason closer to sensibility, the mind naturally makes use of the imagination. As Kant explains in *Critique of Judgement*, the imagination is called upon to provide sensuous images, not to demonstrate concepts of reason — they are indemonstrable — but to symbolize them. For the understanding the imagination supplies schemata, whereas for reason it supplies symbols. However, in addition to the logical difference between a schema and a symbol, there is also a big difference between the work that the imagination does for the understanding and what it does for reason. For the former, the imagination simply follows certain rules, operating mechanically as it were in synthesizing and schematizing sensuous data. By contrast, as we shall see, what the imagination does for reason is truly creative. Simply put, what I am proposing is that knowing how to imagine is knowing how to harness this creativity.

The creative power of the imagination can be illustrated best with one of Kant's own examples. Consider the "sublimity and majesty of heaven" as an idea of reason, and consider further that this sublimity and this majesty are represented in the idea of "the mighty king of heaven," a supersensible object (Kant, 1952: 177). Now, we can bring this idea of reason closer to intuition, giving it some reality, by calling on the imagination to supply a sensuous image to symbolize "the mighty king of heaven." For this purpose, the imagination might come up with something like "Jupiter's eagle, with the lightning in its claws" (p. 177). In this way, the imagination has given "the mighty king of heaven" a sensuous attribute. With this symbol as the base, the imagination can call to mind further images through association and other mechanisms, thus giving rise to a collection of sensuous attributes. In this way we get a feeling for, or a real sense of, the idea of the sublimity and majesty of creation. To be sure, these sensuous attributes "do not, like *logical attribute(s)*, represent what lies in our concepts of the sublimity and majesty of creation, but rather something else — something that gives the imagination an incentive to spread its flight over a whole host of kindred representations" (p. 177). Kant calls these sensuous attributes aesthetic attributes, and the collection of such attributes that symbolizes an idea of reason an aesthetic idea.

The creative power of the imagination can be seen in the example above. Thus, what the imagination has done is to take from its storehouse of images of actual objects, such as the eagle and the lightning, to create a possible object, namely, "Jupiter's eagle with the lightning in its claws." In the same way, the mind can create possible objects such as the unicorn, the centaur, the chimæra, and so on. In all these cases, familiar animals and body parts have been put together differently. Thus, the imagination is "a powerful agent for creating, as it were, a second nature out of the material supplied to it by nature" (Kant, 1952: 176). The material "borrowed ... from nature" can be "worked up ... into something else — namely, what surpasses nature" (p. 176). From the actual, the imagination can create what is possible and produce what is conceivable. To be sure, the whole creative process has to be "in accordance with [the] law [of association]" (p. 176). This means not just that impossible objects are ruled out, but also that certain objects will serve no useful purpose. As Kant puts it, "in lawless freedom imagination, with all its wealth, produces nothing but nonsense" (p. 183). The laws that govern the work of the imagination turn out to be the laws of the understanding, that is, laws that are determined by the categories. Thus, the possibilities or the conceivables created by the imagination have to be understandable, or "consonant with the understanding" (p. 183).

How does knowing-how-to-imagine respond to the need, identified by Lyotard, to present the unpresentable? There are two ways in which the possibilities created by the imagination can be said to serve that need. The sensuous images supplied by the imagination merely symbolize rational concepts and are in no way adequate to those concepts. Rational concepts are for Kant indemonstrable. Indeed, the inadequacy of the imagination to the demand of reason lies at the heart of Kant's account of the sublime. The sublime is the idea of the absolutely great. The imagination has to supply sensuous objects to represent this idea, but it can only come up with images of objects in nature that are vast in scale and suggestive of great force, such as tall mountains, stormy seas, and raging torrents. Because such objects are inadequate to the idea of the absolutely great, the mind feels a pleasure in realizing that nothing in nature can compare with the ideas of its reason. However, this pleasure is mediated by a displeasure at the inadequacy of the imagination to represent the ideas of reason. Kant refers to this mixture of pleasure and displeasure as the feeling of the sublime, defining it as "a feeling of displeasure, arising from the inadequacy of the imagination in the aesthetic estimation of magnitude to attain to its estimation by reason, and a simultaneously awakened pleasure, arising from this very judgement of the inadequacy of the greatest faculty of sense being in accord with ideas of reason" (1952: 106). It is in the dynamics between reason and the imagination characteristic of the sublime that we can locate the idea that the imagination can present the unpresentable. Whenever the feeling of the sublime arises, we get a sense of something unpresentable, or indemonstrable in Kant's terminology, namely, a certain idea of reason, struggling to be represented by certain images of the imagination. It is in this way that the imagination serves the need to present the unpresentable.

There is another way in which images of the imagination may be said to serve that need. Aesthetic ideas, the creations of the imaginations, are sensuous images of the possible, or the conceivable. They themselves, unlike actual objects and experiences, do not fit into concepts. We cannot conceptually represent them adequately. Aesthetic ideas invoke a host of kindred representations that can be extensive, depending on how rich the aesthetic ideas are. This sensuous mixture of imagery cannot be adequately expressed in words. Aesthetic ideas are those "with which... such a multiplicity of partial representations are bound up, that no expression indicating a definite concept can be found for [them]" (Kant, 1952: 179). They are, as Kant puts it, "inexponible" (p. 210). The inexponible is the other side of the indemonstrable. The latter refers to a concept (of reason) that cannot be shown adequately in terms of sensuous objects, the former to sensuous images that cannot be captured adequately in concepts. Being inexponible in the Kantian sense, aesthetic ideas are unpresentable in concepts. Thus, to have aesthetic ideas is to have a sense of the unpresentable, a sense of something there that needs to be expressed, to be put in words. It is in this way that the imagination, the faculty that produces aesthetic ideas, responds to the postmodern challenge posed by the *différends*.

My excursion into Kant provides the answer to the question concerning what kind of imagination is meant in imaginative knowledge. I come now to the question concerning the educational implications of Lyotard and Kant. In a sense, this question has to do with education for imaginative knowledge, but given the nature of the knowledge in question, there are no actual procedures to follow in teaching or learning how-to-imagine. Kant regards the art of producing aesthetic ideas as well as expressing them either in words or in other artistic forms to be unteachable. He refers to the ability in question as aesthetic genius, and as such it cannot be taught. By this he means there are no steps to follow, no rules to observe, no procedures to adopt. If there were, the imagination would not be what it is, namely a truly creative faculty. If there were, the imagination, in following the rules, and so forth, could not be said to create but rather copy or imitate. As Kant puts it, imaginative genius "cannot be brought about by any observance of rules, whether of science or mechanical imitation, but can only be produced by the nature of the individual" (1952: 181). However, Kant makes it quite clear that although aesthetic genius cannot be taught and learned, it can be developed. Furthermore, there is a sense in which one can learn from geniuses, although not in the sense of copying or imitating them. One can learn from them in the sense of allowing oneself to be influenced by them, allowing the work of a genius to arouse in oneself "a sense of his own originality" (p. 181). Interestingly, arousing the learner is precisely what Richard Rorty believes to be the role of the postmodern teacher. Thus, he claims that what teachers have to do is to "make students thrill to the same things they themselves thrill."[11] Even more interestingly, Rorty believes that good teachers should themselves be highly imaginative, constantly inventing new alternatives, displacing an intellectual world by considering a new one, transfiguring tradition with original and utopian fantasies, like those of Plato and St. Paul.[12]

Although there are no specific steps to take, no definite rules to follow, certain broad educational strategies suggest themselves given Kant's account of the imagination. Beginning with reality itself, the learner can be encouraged to break it down into component parts and recombine the parts in different ways. From component parts, we can move to objects and their properties, taking the properties thought to belong uniquely to certain objects and attributing them to other objects not known to have such properties. In this way, human beings can fly, animals can talk, fish can walk on dry land. Fortunately, children already engage in imaginative game playing in which possible objects and scenarios are imagined. Given the importance of imaginative knowledge in the postmodern condition, this should be regarded as a solid foundation to build on rather than treated as mere child's play, to be overtaken by serious learning, or worse still to be displaced by a heavy dose of harsh reality. What needs to be done is to make the process of imaginative pretending already there in the games children play more sophisticated and the task for imagination more challenging. As a final ingredient, purpose can be added, such as solving a particular problem, resolving a particular conflict, or improving on a certain way of doing things.

In the broad strategy described above, the imagination is pushed along on the ground of actual reality. Given Kant's account of the imagination as serving the function of exhibiting rational concepts, we can adopt a strategy in which the imagination is pulled up from above as it were. As we have seen from Kant, the imagination goes to work to satisfy the demand of reason. It is reasonable to suggest that the greater that demand, the harder it has to work. Thus, abstract concepts can be introduced and the learner encouraged to exhibit them concretely, to find imaginative symbols for them. With some rudimentary understanding of concepts such as justice, equality, motherhood, democracy, and so forth, the learner can be encouraged to come up with imaginative sensuous images to represent them. Perhaps we can do better than Kant in coming up with something more imaginative than "Jupiter's eagle, with the lightning in its claws," as the symbol for "the sublimity and majesty of heaven."

Given the dynamics between reason and the imagination, another broad strategy suggests itself, combining both the strategy of pushing the imagination along and also that of pulling it up from the conceptual high ground. In this strategy the imagination can be alternately pushed and pulled. From a given piece of reality, the learner can first be encouraged to imagine what is possible or conceivable to build up certain aesthetic ideas. As Kant puts it, those aesthetic ideas are inexponible, meaning that they cannot be contained in any definite concept. Nevertheless, the learner can be encouraged to think up concepts that might contain those aesthetic ideas. With such concepts, the imagination can in turn be pulled up from above. For instance, the learner can be encouraged to imagine that non-human animals feel pain and suffer in the same way as humans do (if the learner does not already know this to be a fact). From this starting point, the learner can be encouraged to think of a concept that fits this imaginative scenario (which happens to be true), for instance the concept of animal right. The learner can be encouraged to exhibit that concept, to symbolize it in imaginative sensuous images. Perhaps animals can think and reason as we do. From the images of thinking and reasoning animals, the learner can be encouraged to move to the concept of animal morality, of animals as moral agents, and from there to sensuous images representing that concept, and so on.

The strategies discussed above by no means exhaust all possibilities. However, it is beyond the scope of this chapter to explore further.[13] My aim has been simply to argue for the legitimacy of knowing-how-to-imagine or imaginative knowledge. If I am right in my reading of Lyotard, there is an urgent need for such knowledge, or for the development of it if it already exists in some form. With it, we have some hope of presenting the unpresentable. Without it, we risk oppression, violence, and terror. It is perhaps appropriate to conclude with Lyotard's own words. In the foreword to a volume on education and the postmodern condition, Lyotard speaks of a child fortunate enough to have been asked, as homework, to build on Erhardt Dietl's imaginative flight to a distant planet in a spaceship. He writes: "When are we educated? When we know more or less which is the far-off planet that we desire, and when we do all that we can to set off for it. If adults are often tough and sad, it is because they are disappointed. They do not listen well enough to the invitation to grace which is in them. They let the spaceship rust.[14]

NOTES

1. See Jean-François Lyotard, *The Postmodern Condition: A Report on Knowledge*, trans. Geoff Bennington and Brian Massumi (Minneapolis: University of Minnesota Press, 1984).

2. See for instance Michael Peters, ed., *Education and the Postmodern Condition* (Westport, Conn.: Bergin & Garvey, 1995).

3. For a discussion of this, see A. T. Nuyen, "Lyotard on the Death of the Professor," *Educational Theory*, 42 (1992): 25–37.

4. See for instance Jean-François Lyotard, *The Différend*, trans. Georges Van Den Abbeele (Minneapolis: University of Minnesota Press, 1988).

5. Jean-François Lyotard, "Answering the Question: What Is Postmodernism?" trans. Régis Durand, in *The Postmodern Condition*, p. 82.

6. Jean-François Lyotard, *The Inhuman*, trans. Geoffrey Bennington and Rachel Bowlby (Stanford, Calif.: Stanford University Press, 1991), p. 127.

7. Jean-François Lyotard, *Lessons on the Analytic of the Sublime*, trans. Elizabeth Rottenberg (Stanford, Calif.: Stanford University Press, 1994).

8. Emmanuel Kant, *Critique of Judgement*, trans. James Creed Meredith (Oxford: Clarendon, 1952).

9. Emmanuel Kant, *Foundations of the Metaphysics of Morals*, trans. Lewis White Beck (Indianapolis, Ind.: Bobbs-Merrill, 1959), p. 55.

10. Emmanuel Kant, *Critique of Practical Reason*, trans. Lewis White Beck (Indianapolis, Ind.: Bobbs-Merrill, 1956), p. 70.

11. Richard Rorty, "The Dangers of Over-Philosophication: Reply to Arcilla and Nicholson," *Educational Theory*, 40 (1990): 42.

12. Richard Rorty, "Is Derrida a Transcendental Philosopher?" in *Essays on Heidegger and Others* (Cambridge: Cambridge University Press, 1991), pp. 121, 126.

13. In Maxine Greene, *Releasing the Imagination: Essays on Education, the Arts and Social Change* (San Francisco, Calif.: Jossey-Bass, 1995), Greene advocates incorporating the arts into school curricula, arguing that "encounters with the arts have a unique power to release imagination" (p. 27). Although she claims to be "deeply dissatisfied with . . . postmodern thinkers" (p. 2), she at times comes close to Lyotard in her justification of the imagination and in her claims concerning its power. For instance, she speaks of the "alienated or marginalized [who] are made to feel distrustful of their own voices, their own ways of making sense, yet they are not provided alternatives that allow them to tell their stories or stage their narratives" (pp. 110–111). Like Lyotard, she argues that the imagination allows us to hear their voices, to see their ways, to understand their narratives, because it "requires reflectiveness on our part to acknowledge the existence of those unexpected and unpredictable vistas and perspectives in our experiences" (p. 125).

14. Jean-François Lyotard, "Foreword: Spaceship," in Michael Peters, ed., *Education and the Postmodern Condition* (Westport, Conn.: Bergin & Garvey, 1995).

8

Luce Irigaray: One Subject Is Not Enough — Irigaray and Levinas Face-to-Face with Education

Betsan Martin

> As long as I do not exist face to face with you, you will always be falling into the impersonality of the 'one'. You are undermined in your own being by the fact that I belong to your world without ever appearing in it.
>
> — Irigaray, 1992: 48

There is only one subject of Western philosophy, of Western history, of psychoanalysis — the universal rational male subject. Luce Irigaray, philosopher, psychoanalyst, and linguist has written of this privileged subjectivity as being accomplished through the sacrifice of women and of nature, an immolation that constitutes an unrecognized debt to the feminine and an erasure of genealogy of women.[1] Irigaray scrutinizes the multifaceted ways in which women are made absent in Western culture and in particular from philosophy. There has been no time for or of woman in philosophy. A place for women as subjects in philosophy will bring a new place for women and a new time in philosophy.

Philosophy has presumed universality in what it means to be and what existence is about; it has been concerned with the ontological subject whom Heidegger in particular interpreted as existing in the finite time between being and nothingness, as Being. Time is therefore interpreted as essential to Being. Time, characterized by past, present, and future, is a linear and chronological measurement of Being that provides an integrating thread for the disparities of the subject that has been conceived as both unitary and universal.[2] Irigaray's analysis of universality and of neutrality (which can be equated with the universal) has shown these to be masculine.[3] If linear time is equated with masculine identity, then time must be a focus in a feminist project of repositioning women as subjects, rather than objects or other, in philosophy. Irigaray's ethic is toward the production of representations of women as subjects rather than objects, and toward relations between women and men that preserve the subjectivity of both. In the Western philosophical and logocentric tradition the subject-object, same-other binaries are mirrored in the sexual division between maleness and femaleness in an oppositional economy in which the feminine is devalued. The revaluation of women in Irigaray's schema is a project of cultural representation of women and respect for sexual difference. For these developments to become realities a new dynamic will have to be in play, a new mediation of love that can respect difference rather than repress it.

Irigaray leaves no stone in the Western cultural edifice unturned in seeking a new philosophy, a new future that is engendered through women and men in ethical relationships. Rather than challenge the notion of subjectivity per se as a means to dissolving the subject-object dichotomy of binary opposition, Irigaray elucidates the importance of women-becoming-subjects. This is a task, she says, that involves the necessity of rethinking time and space, those being the philosophical conditions of the subject and of being. Irigaray introduces this seemingly abstract challenge with her well-known piece on sexual difference, "Sexual difference is one of the major philosophical issues, if not the issue, of our age. According to Heidegger, each age has one issue to think through, and one only. Sexual difference is probably the issue in our time which could be our 'salvation' if we thought it through." (Irigaray 1993a: 5). She continues:

> In order to make it possible to think through, and live, this difference, we must reconsider the whole problematic of *space* and *time*.
> In the beginning there was space and the creation of space, as is said in all theogonies. The gods, God, first create space. And time is there, more or less in the service of space. On the first day, God makes a world by separating the elements. This world is then peopled. . . . God would be time itself, lavishing or exteriorizing itself in its action in space, in places.
> Philosophy then confirms the genealogy of the task of the gods or God. Time becomes the interiority of the subject itself, and space, its *exteriority*. . . . The subject, the master of time, becomes the axis of the world's ordering, with its something beyond the moment and eternity: God. He effects the passage between time and space.
> Which would be inverted in sexual difference? Where the feminine is experienced as space, but often with the connotations of the abyss and night (God being space and light?), while the masculine is experienced as time.

> The transition to a new age requires a change in perception and conception of *space-time*, the *inhabiting of places* . . . or *envelopes of identity*. It assumes and entails an evolution or transformation of forms, of the relations between *matter* and *form* and of the interval *between*. (1993a: 7)

Irigaray associates time with the mastery of the male subject and space with the domesticated female role of accomodation (of men) in patriarchal social arrangements. The new age that Irigaray hopes for is a time and a space for ethical relations between the sexes — a new configuration brought about by "a change in the economy of desire" (1993a: 8). Desire is the attraction between the sexes but it is based on women learning to be objects of attraction. This makes her available to be given away. She does not have her own place, or space; she provides or is space for him; for there is one genealogy in patriarchy: his. She must have her own place in which to do the work of her own genealogy — a condition of feminine subjectivity that may be found in the time of intimacy and connection, rhythmical repetitive time, sometimes referred to as dailiness of female time.

Woman in Western culture is represented as the object of male desire. She has not yet done the work of self-representation for she is not represented in a genealogy of her own and therefore has no source of her own identity. The bonds of the mother-daughter relation are cut so that women can take up their place in patriarchy. The possibility of women achieving symbolic and representational status depends on the recovery of her own genealogy, the recognition of her own body, the creation of language that speaks and writes women's sociality and spirituality, that shapes economic exchange and recognizes the differences between women.

This chapter will focus on the challenge to the universal subject of philosophy in some of Irigaray's texts and proposals for the achievment of feminine specificity as subjects. For women to become subjects and for the possibility of subject-to-subject relations between the sexes, Irigaray has to find a means to argue for a new formulation of subjectivity, a reallocation of the subject-object dialectic to a nonobjectifying means to subjectivity. Irigaray uses the work of Emmanuel Levinas as a significant theoretical resource for subjectivity that is formed through ethical regard for the other.

Levinas, also a French philosopher, provides a different challenge to the philosophical subject. He also refutes the neutrality of the universal in philosophy[4] — not, like Irigaray, on the basis of sexual difference, but because neutrality has no face. It is nonspecific and therefore does not generate the desire that is necessary to relationality. He identifies Being as being-for-one's self; an undesirable relation. In contrast, he articulates a philosophy of being-for-an-other; relationality that he calls ethics and that he describes as the face-to-face relation.

Being-for-the-other introduces a primacy of responsibility for the other as the basis of ethical philosophy. Levinas seeks to replace the preeminence of being with ethical subjectivity, which he conceives in terms of absolute alterity. In philosophy the universal has been a basis for ethics, of relationships of respect, and struggles for human dignity through the capacity of one to identify with another on the basis of common humanity. The universal has been the basis for most struggles for human rights that have been based largely on equality. To think absolute alterity, to think an other with whom I cannot identify is an incredible shift in philosophy.[5]

Irigaray finds in Levinas's notion of absolute alterity a philosophical means to think sexual difference, although she is vigorously critical of his inability or refusal to think sexual difference. Levinas has not responded to Irigaray's questions to him on this matter of the feminine in his work.[6] He retains the primacy of his sexually neutral ethical difference,[7] which Irigaray's critique of his work exposes as having the effect of retaining the subordination of the feminine to the masculine. His silence, however, is not empty — it resonates with an ethic that transcends sexual difference because it is premised on responsibility for the other. In claiming this ideal he misses the necessary step of women-becoming subjects. Her responsibility for the other has been her role and her dereliction; her responsibility for caring has been her sacrifice, a deprivation of subjectivity and thus her cultural devaluation. Unless women do the work of subjectivity and self-representation women's devaluation is likely to be reinscribed by Levinas's ethics.

Levinas's focus is not on feminism but on ethics, which I think he would say transcends sexual difference. Like Irigaray he is charged with the imperative to confront violence, of which his primary experience is racism. Levinas's philosophy is driven by the urgency of finding a means to relations that are not determined by the threat of the other. Writing after the Holocaust, Levinas (Lithuanian-born and Jewish) dedicated *Otherwise than Being or Beyond Essence* to the "memory of those closest among six million assassinated by the National Socialists, and of the millions on millions of all confessions and all nations, victims of the same hatred of the other man, the same anti-semitism" (Levinas, 1981: i).

He achieves this by engaging the relational source of subjectivity. To recognize subjectivity not as me an individual, but as dependent on relationship is to beam the light of subjectivity on the Other who comes face-to-face with me and to whom I have the opportunity and responsibility to respond with hospitality. This is being-for-the-Other. To respond to the Other with hospitality and obligation might cause destructive violence to wither; because Levinas's face-to-face relation is peaceful: it is an approach of welcome rather than threat, hospitality not hostility is the means by which it is mediated.

Levinas's notion of alterity that undergirds the ethics of the face-to-face relation provides the theoretical resource for intersubjectivity in Irigaray's ethics of sexual difference. It opens a theoretical space for her to argue for women becoming subjects. Levinas's weakness is in his use (in his earlier work) of maternity as a figure of alterity; it is inadequate to meet the requirements of woman-as-subject in Irigaray's ethics. With reference to Irigaray's two essays on Levinas and her recently translated work I will discuss her introduction of multiple subjectivity into philosophy — a time for the multiple of two sexes as subjects and a time governed by a process of becoming rather than the mastery of being. Ethical relations require ethical subjects. In Irigaray's methodology these are becoming subjects, infinitely open to regenerative exchange across difference.

Both Irigaray and Levinas are working from within the ontological structure that governs philosophy. Irigaray claims there is no outside of patriarchy,[8] and Levinas claims to be working within metaphysics although he reclaims the meaning of metaphysics.[9] Their ethics are referenced to philosophy. Levinas's meticulous methodological approach enables him to discover new openings within it. He brings his religious and philosophical imagination into these new spaces to articulate a new ethic although he claims that the face-to-face relation is not new; it has been unrecognized in philosophy.

Levinas often refers to the ethical relation as a teaching relation, so there are immediate extrapolations from his work to be made for education. The richness of Irigaray's ethics provides important intellectual resources for contemporary educational theory. The Milan Women's Bookstore Collective and Diotima (in Verona) are groups of Italian feminist philosophers who have worked in collaboration with Irigaray for several years. They offer reflection for different pedagogical theories and educational practices that have found inspiration in her philosophy of sexual difference.

LEVINAS'S CONSTRUCTION OF ETHICAL SUBJECTIVITY: ALTERITY AND THE FACE-TO-FACE RELATION

Levinas conceives of ethical subjectivity as time for the Other.[10] This temporality is not the finite time of Being (for oneself). Responsibility for the Other is infinite; there is no limit to the call of the other that materializes in the face-to-face relation. The time, therefore, that governs ethical subjectivity is infinity; it is a relation of a future proposed against the subject of ontology, which is enclosed in the time of the present. Levinas confronts the singularity of the subject in philosophy by recognizing that the subjectivity is conditional upon a preceeding relation. The Levinasian subject is not singular, it is not one but two because it is formed as subjection to the Other. The Other for Levinas is conceived not as the other in me or the other of the same. The other for Levinas becomes absolutely Other, quite discrete. He describes this Otherness as alterity or absolute alterity.

Philosophy has been premised on the knowing subject (the same) who achieves knowing consciousness and identity by objectifying the Other. Levinas recognizes here the existence of relationship prior to the constitution of this subject. He focuses on the existent,[11] the other, prior to objectification, whom he brings foward as the stranger to whom I have absolute responsibility. This Other is privileged as transcendent and not reducible to enclosure in the totalizing structure of the same. This is a new relationship in philosophy — a relationship with another who is recognized as excessive of my capacity to know or understand; who is more than my need of her or him. This is alterity: that which is beyond the comprehension of the knowing subject. It is respect for alterity that constitutes an ethical relation. The capacity to relate to absolute alterity requires a restructuring of subjectivity.

In *Totality and Infinity* Levinas argues for the capacity for alterity to derive from a separation within subjectivity; separation between need and desire. The separation in the existent is a separation between egotistical need and transcendent desire. The necessity of satisfying human needs corresponds to the value of freedom. Freedom is the condition that enables people to meet their needs. Levinas's effort to rethink subjectivity is addressed to the individual ontological subject as the subject premised on freedom (from responsibility for the other), whom Levinas refers to as the same. In encountering the Other the same either reduces the other to the same, that is, to its own understanding, which gives rise to the claims of universal, or commonality; or excludes that which is excess of its own comprehension. The subject of freedom is the knowing subject of philosophy with its "comprehensive claims to mastery" (Critchley, 1992: 8). This freedom is necessary to the fulfillment of needs — material, bodily, and human needs. Refreshingly, Levinas brings the body into philosophy by honoring and celebrating the pleasures and satisfactions of materiality.

Desire for Levinas is quite different. It does not proceed from a lack, as need does, but from relationship with another in their exteriority, who is a face. It is the mode by which subjectivity is shaped in ethical responsibility to the stranger, one that I cannot presume to know, who is absolutely other and cannot be reduced to an object of my consciousness. To respond to another ethically takes a person beyond Being, because Being is being for oneself. To become ethical is therefore to become otherwise than Being. The face-to-face relation is ethical, is otherwise than being, because it means respons(e)-ibility to respond to the other as absolutely

Other, rather than respond by objectifying the other. The meaning that Levinas gives to desire is willingness to respond to the other, who as absolutely other, transcends my capacity for knowing and escapes the possibility of being mastered. Ethics, which proceeds from desire, is willingness to respect the alterity of an Other. The stranger, the neighbor, interrupts and interpolates the subject in his freedom and in doing so, in this moment presents the opportunity for an ethical response.

Ethical subjectivity dispenses with the idealizing subjectivity of ontology, which reduces everything to itself. The ethical "I" is subjectivity precisely insofar as it kneels before the other, sacrificing its own liberty to the more primordial call of the other. For me the freedom of the subject is not the highest or primary value. The heteronomy of our response to the human other, or to God as the absolutely other, precedes the autonomy of our subjective freedom. As soon as I acknowledge that it is "I" who am responsible, I accept that my freedom is anteceded by an obligation to the other. (Levinas, 1986a: 27).

Against individualistic subjectivity Levinas proposes an ethics in which the other must be rethought as a priority, as incomprehensible as absolutely other, and therefore strange — acknowledged as different — the stranger for whom I have absolute responsibility.

In my reading of Levinas, alterity is to be regarded as multiple — as internal, an aspect of the separation within the subject, and external: as the one who comes and interrupts my freedom, the stranger or neighbor who is Other and who "[puts into question my] spontaneity by the presence of the Other" (Levinas, 1969: 43).

Notice how this language is intentionally in the first person. It is intended to challenge abstraction so characteristic of philosophy for it refers to the specific Other, whom Levinas calls the stranger, the neighbor, the widow, the orphan — those whose need evokes in me a response, invites me to respond with welcome and hospitality. The me or my spontaneity is intended in the personal sense — it challenges generalization and abstraction and engages responsibility that is embodied, material, and personal. The Other is the face who appears and to whom I, particularly I, have responsibility to respond. As a relation with one who is not my equal, it is an asymmetrical relation.[12] It is not equal because the Other is given priority to the extent of "taking the bread from my own mouth" for him or her. It is a relation with one who is near with the proximity of calling me to respond; and far away, respected in his or her alterity, not grasped or possessed, so in that sense exterior. The exteriority of the Other constitutes transcendence in that it escapes the totalizing categorization of being. The temporality of this transcendence Levinas finds to be infinity. He draws on Descartes's deduction that because the I is capable of thinking beyond its own capacity, this is evidence for the idea of infinity. Infinity here refers to that which is beyond the comprehension of the subject and eludes enclosure in the structure of totality. Levinas interprets the transcendence of this Other who appears and whose alterity I do not reduce to the same to be the manifestation of desire. Desire is unfulfillable. Desire " desires beyond anything that can simply complete it. It is like goodness — the Desired does not fulfill it, but deepens it" (Levinas, 1969: 34).

In naming the relation with alterity the face-to-face, Levinas introduces the sensible into philosophy. The face is the site of human encounter in which all the senses are employed. It is the site of language and communication. Teaching is the communicative mode of the ethical relation because the Other is not reduced to the same, assumed to be knowable. Alterity can only be taught because alterity is in excess of what can be apprehended by the knowing subject.

Of course, I may still treat him [the stranger] as a different version of myself, or if I have power, place him under my categories and use him for my purposes. But this means reducing him to what he is not. How can I co-exist with him and still leave his otherness intact? According to Levinas, there is only one way, by language. . . . The questioning glance of the other is seeking for a meaningful response. Of course I may give him only a casual word, and go on my way with indifference, passing the other by. But if communication and community is to be achieved, a real response, a responsible answer must be given. This means I must be ready to put my world into words, and to offer it to the other. There can be no free interchange without something to give (Wild, 1969: 13–14).

Language and communication are the modes also of Irigaray's ethics as well as a primary means to the accomplishment of women-as-subjects. The face-to-face relation as a notion of subjectivity is not proposed as an alternative to the ontological subject but an ethical choice within subjectivity. It is a possibility within a deconstructive project that disturbs the foundation of philosophy as the knowing subject.

Responsibility for the Other, who is my neighbor, means elevating the Other beyond objectification, beyond the confines of the consciousness of the knowing subject. In Levinas's words, a person who engages a relation of absolute alterity is otherwise than being. "The absolutely other is not the *other of* a same, *its* other, in the heart of that supreme sameness that is being; it is *other than* being" (Levinas, 1986b: 119). Alterity is important because it enables the possibility of difference, of absolute discreteness. It provides for subject-to-subject relations rather than the exclusive subject-object paradigm. The universal can allow only for otherness that can be explained in terms of sameness.

Alterity provides Irigaray with the theoretical resource from which to construct subject-to-subject relations as a foundation for an ethic of sexual difference. Irigaray is not the only philosopher to find that Levinas's work on alterity and the face-to-face relation leads to the alterity of woman. Jacques Derrida, in an intricate reading of Levinas in "At this Very Moment in this Work Here I Am"[13] wants to know who is the Other of Levinas's own texts. Derrida's deconstructive reading of Levinas identifies the metaphysical subordination of women, and therefore finds that the stranger to whom hospitality must be given, who must be given precedence, is woman. To give women ethical precedence, Irigaray says that women must position themselves as subjects if an ethical economy between the sexes is to be achieved.

Before pursuing sexual difference as an Irigarayan theme, I wish to signal the importance of Hebraic theology and to indicate a theme of cultural difference in Levinas's writing, although Levinas himself does not make the latter explicit. He maintains a universalism in his work, an ethical universality of relationship and retheorized subjectivity that is intended to transcend the specificities of structural injustices such as racism and sexism, despite Irigaray's critique of this as masculinist and the outcome of Derrida's examination of who constitutes the Levinasian Other.

Although his work is against individualism it is also not about collectivity. His way between these two historical Western polarities is his articulation of a relation of two — the face-to-face. Interestingly, John Wild, in his introduction to *Totality and Infinity* reads this as a third way between individualism and collectivism, between anarchy and tyranny.[14]

Levinas's exposition of the responsibility of the face-to-face relation as prior to and necessary to the development of the subject is Levinas's response to the suffering and murderous violence borne out of metaphysical repression of the other. Levinas refers to Auschwitz as:

The catastrophe of the human and the Divine. This pain in its undiluted malignity, suffering for nothing. It renders impossible and odious every proposal and every thought which would explain it by the sins of those who have suffered or are dead. But does not this end of theodicy, which obtrudes itself in the face of this century's inordinate distress, at the same time in a more general way reveal the unjustifiable suffering in the other person? The scandal that would occur by my justifying my neighbour's suffering? (Levinas, 1986a: 163).

This piece indicates how philosophy and theology-divinity are interwoven by Levinas, a characteristic also of Irigaray. As the above quotation affirms, the Holocaust cannot be adequately responded to only from philosophy. Theology is of course deeply implicated, for the Holocaust is not only a crime against humanity, it confronts us with the question of what it means to be human. Levinas's attention cannot be limited to philosophy in the face of the inescapable religious implications of the Holocaust. Therefore the Greek tradition of philosophy must be drawn into an encounter with the Hebraic religious and theological traditions, an encounter that gives Levinas theological resources for ethical subjectivity. Levinas's ethics are imbued with theology as Irigaray's proposals for feminine subjectivity are imbued with spirituality. Her notion of woman's divinity conceptualized as a sensible transcendental derived undoubtedly from Levinas's very material ethical relation.

The inordinate political, racial, and religious horror of the Holocaust is the stage set for Levinas's post-war writing. The personal experience of persecution fires his challenge to the totalizing philosophy of identity. Robert Bernasconi (1994)[15] points out that Levinas's specific reference to the Holocaust brings into philosophy cultural pluralism, and therefore, cultural difference. Philosophy has hitherto not been located in experience — experience such as the Holocaust. Philosophy has found its orientation in what I have referred to as the universal subject of being. In claiming the experience of the Holocaust as unavoidable for philosophy, Levinas redefines philosophy not only as ethical responsibility, which he prioritizes over subjective being; but by grafting this cultural (and theological) cataclysm into philosophy, Bernasconi recognizes in Levinas a new pluralism in philosophy — that of cultural difference.

AN ETHICS OF SEXUAL DIFFERENCE.

Irigaray's two pieces, "The Fecundity of the Caress" (1993a) and "Questions to Emmanuel Levinas — On the Divinity of Love" (in Whitford, 1991) are directly addressed to Levinas's work, but his influence on her work is much deeper. His face-to-face relation provides her with a theory and a method for thinking sexual difference in terms of absolute alterity. Her critique and her new proposals are given through brilliant, written enactments of the face-to-face relation with philosophy and philosophers. Carolyn Burke (1989) refers to these exchanges as "romancing the philosophers."[16] Irigaray's titles alone convey her strategy and her ethic of love: *Marine Lover of Friedrich Nietzsche*, "The Fecundity of the Caress," and "Questions to Emmanuel Levinas: On the Divinity of Love" (essays in response to Levinas), *L'Oubli de l'air chez Martin Heidegger*, and *I Love to You* (a reading of and writing with Marx and Hegel). Chapter 1 of the latter is titled "Introducing: Love Between Us":

> Marx defined the origin of man's exploitation of man as man's exploitation of woman and asserted that the most basic human exploitation lies in the division of labour between man and woman. Why didn't he devote his life to solving the problem of this exploitation?. . . The reason lies to some extent in Hegel's writings, especially in those sections where he deals with love, Hegel being the only Western philosopher to have approached the question of love as labour.
> It is therefore entirely appropriate for a woman philosopher to start speaking of love. (Irigaray, 1996: 19)

Irigaray's problematic lies in the oppressiveness of ontological assumptions that view the other as a potential rival and therefore to be mastered. This is a relationship premised on opposition. Levinas's awareness of this is revealed in his frequent references to the Mosaic law "thou shalt not kill." The necessity of such a law betrays the dynamic at work. For the ethical relation to be possible those with power have to take the risk of relinquishing dominating power, the control that is implicit in being able to guarantee the consequences of one's actions; a power that is in control of time. This control is close to Irigaray's challenge to the necessity of sacrifice; extradition should not be necessary to the formation of the social body, nor to the formation of subjectivity. "So is it a matter of killing? That is not the goal. To reveal that murder has been committed means not killing but putting an end to the hidden crime, aggression, sacrifice. This forces the group or groups, and the individual to find a new balance. To tell someone that he is a criminal, even against his will, is not a punitive act but rather a way to make him conscious of the self and allow the other to be" (Irigaray, 1993c: 87).

Irigaray and Levinas both open pathways to peaceful revolution. For Irigaray this necessitates women becoming reconstituted as subjects. The corollory of this is the reconstituted subjectivity of men, which Levinas offers as subjectivity to the other. The mastery of the male subject is modified in the ethical subject. What he does not himself recognize is the sexual particularity of his work, for it is premised on the universal subject. A feminist analysis must recognize this to be a masculine subject.

In privileging ethics over sexual difference Levinas falls into the danger of offering a way to bridge cultural and ethnic difference that leaves sexual oppression intact. Ethics must involve a choreography of cultural and sexual difference. The historicity of the positioning of women is as compelling as that of racism, the latter of which informs every sinew of Levinas's writing. Specific histories must be faces in any ethical education.

SEXUAL DIFFERENCE: ESSENTIALISM OR IRIGARAY'S CHALLENGE TO THE UNIVERSAL?

Irigaray's proposals for sexual difference and feminine specificity have led to many charges of essentialism. Without dismissing the importance of the discourses on essentialism, not least for the need to reject fundamentalism, suffice it to say that a degree of essentialism is necessary to feminism. Feminism, in its multiple expressions and agendas, is a politics and practice that is specifically for and about women.[17]

Essentialism refers to women's confinement within given configurations and structures and material practices through embodied limitations (such as the confinement of women to the private place of domesticity because of their maternal functions) that position them in society as (devalued) objects. Moves toward women becoming subjects cannot be conceived in essentialist terms because they entail recategorization from object to subject, a move that involves a reconfigured notion of subjectivity — ethical subjectivity — that might mean the assimilation of aggression within the consciousness of the subject (as suggested in the previous quote) rather than the projection from the subject to the object as in objectifying practices.

What Irigaray is above all concerned to work out is the conditions of women's subjectivity — how women can assume the "I" of discourse in their own right and not as a derivative of the male "I". This discourse presupposes of course that what it is to be male and female is available to change, since they are possibilities provided by the symbolic order. Speaking (as) a woman is not only a psycholinguistic description, it is also the name for something which does not yet exist, the position of the female subject in the symbolic order. (Whitford, 1991a: 42).

Opening this space for women has been hitherto unthought. Although it depends on identity, it is not the unitary identity of the ontological subject.

Irigaray is clear. Not only is woman-as-subject never prescribed, she also is considered as multiple and plural. "The geography of her pleasure is far more diversified, more multiple in its differences, more complex, more subtle, than is commonly imagined — in an imaginary rather too commonly focussed on sameness" (Irigaray, 1993b: 29). Difference itself is a multiple concept. Feminist theory includes the description of an essential difference. This difference is not a difference based on gender, but, rather, and more fundamentally, it is a difference in outlook, philosophy, style, and attitude that resides with feminism. Feminism is not one. Not only is feminism marked by differences between women;[18] cultural differences also provide significantly different reference points for women's struggles.

Naomi Schor says that the hue and cry about essentialism in Irigaray misses her most important point, which is not her proposals for women becoming subjects, but the challenge to universalism. In the context of recognizing the common purpose of the liberationist goals of Beauvoir and the woman-as-subject goal of Irigaray, Schor argues:

For women to accede to subjectivity clearly means becoming speaking subjects in their own right. It is precisely at this juncture that the major difference between Beauvoir and Irigaray begins to assert itself . . . : whereas for Beauvoir the goal is for women to share in the privileges of the transcendent subject, for Irigaray the goal is for women to achieve subjectivity without merging tracelessly into the putative indifference of the shifter. What is at stake in these two equally powerful and problematic feminist discourses is not the status of difference, rather that of the universal, and universalism may well be one of the most divisive and least discussed issues in feminism today. When Irigaray projects women as speaking a sexually marked language, a "parler femme," she is, I believe ultimately less concerned with theorizing feminine specificity than debunking the oppressive fiction of the universal subject. To speak woman is above all *not* to speak "universal." (Schor and Weed, 1994: 47)

Irigaray sees the male universal to be the most significant focus for deconstruction, not the question of feminine essence. In the ontological structure of Western metaphysics, the masculine subject represents all that is valued and the feminine is the negative Other. In structural terms the feminine provides the ground from which male identity is achieved. The privileged place of male identity is born out in material terms — in the economy; language; psychoanalysis, religion, and mythology; political economy; law; and the family — all of which are subjected to Irigaray's scrutiny throughout her texts. Many of these bring a critique to feminist aspirations to equality with the recognition that to be equal to men does not constitute a challenge to the male economy, it is wanting to be on the privileged side of the binary opposition. A much more profound and fundamental challenge lies in dislodging the structure that requires an other.

Irigaray herself does not make defenses against essentialism or the perceived universalizing of women in her work, nor does she have much regard for criticisms that take inadequate account of the political significance of woman as a category and the strategic importance of identity. She does not try to topple the notion of a universal; it is what comprises the universal that interests her. She is unwavering in her conviction about the cultural significance of sexual difference: "The fact remains that we are men and women. And that this constitutes a living universal. It is a universal related to our real person, to his or her needs, abilities and desires. The particularity of this universal is that it is divided into two.... If man and woman respect each other as those two halves of the universe that they represent, then by recognising the other they overcome their immediate instincts and drives" (Irigaray, 1996: 51).

This passage is worth further comment. The ontological economy is characterized in Levinas's terms by "the grasp."[19] The grasp signifies the movement of the subject to possess, absorb, or annihilate that which is other to it as the subject's means of attaining selfconsciousness and identity. The sexual expression of this is murderous to women, because they are situated in this economy as the property of men. Women, consequently, are deprived of their subjectivity. Women's repression and confinement to the private space of domesticity produce social imbalance that deprives society of the political participation of women contributing in their full capacity. There are no public provisions for accountability to women. In the above passage it is not so much the necessity of universals that is being questioned as what constitutes the universal. Elsewhere she argues that money has become a universal. Money mediates capitalist property ownership vested in individuals and distributed through competition. It reflects the system of which it is the means of exchange in reproducing hierarchies of wealth between persons and countries. This systematic maldistribution into extremes of wealth and poverty means that many cannot meet their basic needs, denying, in effect, the right to life for those who are poor. The distribution of money is equated with differences in power and different allocation of rights.

Irigaray believes that the right to life must take precedence over the right to property. Instead of the limit of subjectivity being acquired through an endlessly expanding horizon of possession through "man's technological domination of nature" (1996: 13) — a negative constituted by exploitation — she envisages subjectivities that are limited through their respect for, rather than possession of, the other.

The universal that Irigaray considers will produce conditions that could regenerate life as sexual difference. "Sexual difference is, as it were, the most powerful motor of a dialectic without masters or slaves. . . . It necessitates a law of persons appropriate to their natural reality, that is, to their sexed identity" (Irigaray, 1985: 51). The debate about essentialism is a distraction from the challenge to do the work of women's subjectivity, sexual difference, and an ethics of sexual difference. Irigaray herself says, "Philosophers take a keen interest in the destruction of ontology, in the ante- and the post-, but little interest in the constitution of a new, rationally founded identity" (Irigaray, 1994: 32).

To be prescriptive about women-as-subjects is likely to divert attention from the strategic importance of this challenge. It is similarly likely to miss the political significance of the challenge to the male universal. Identity, strategy, political necessity, and historical universalism are multiple foci that are woven into Irigaray's texts with such complexity that it is difficult to separate one strand from another. Her purpose is always multiple: critique and construct.

The reality and importance of sexual difference can be argued without dispute on the basis of women's absence from history, philosophy, economic recognition, and independence. The currency of this argument can be readily obscured in the late twentieth century when political equality can be used to mask economic (and other) inequalities between the sexes. What is not well recognized is that liberalism has contradictory historical strands. One of these, an economic strand, relates to the construction of individualized competitors on the market (from which women were excluded historically). Another is the democratic struggle for political equality. These two are too readily conflated. Political equality is often translated to equate with equality of economic opportunity, hiding the structural feminization of poverty that is characteristic of global capitalism. In terms of the economy of the capitalist market, women are differentiated from men.[20]

WOMEN BECOMING SUBJECTS

History is integral to any consideration of subjectivity. It is easy to fall into the binary of modernist-postmodernist in political and philosophical considerations of feminism and be caught in an opposition between the necessity of identity and the becoming woman[21] associated with poststructural subjectivity. In a careful analysis of Deleuze's suggestions for becoming as a means to move beyond gender dualisms, Braidotti is wary of being drawn by the "process of decolonising the thinking subject from this dualistic grip of [Western dualism, which] requires as its starting point the dissolution of all sexed identities based on the gendered opposition" (Braidotti, 1994: 116). This entails women relinquishing the status of subject before coming into a position that enables the cultural contribution for which historically, subjectivity has been necessary. Irigaray refers to becoming-woman in terms of freedom and ethics. To refer to Levinas again for a moment, and to use the separation within the subject metaphorically, ontological freedom and the ethics of otherwise than being both constitute becoming woman in Irigaray's complex notion of subjectivity. This requires bridging the past and the future, the past of history and the future of becoming. "In order to *become*, we need some shadowy perception of achievement; not a fixed objective . . . rather a cohesion and a horizon that assures us the passage between past and future, the bridge of a present *that remembers*" (Irigaray, 1993c: 69). Becoming, for Irigaray, is "the goal that is most valuable . . . to go on becoming infinitely. . . . To become means fulfilling the wholeness of what we are capable of being" (Irigaray, 1993c: 61).

Irigaray is opening up space for differently conceived subjectivity that allows for differences of culture and language. Whether there will become a more dispersed notion of sexualities beyond the time of two sexed subjectivities is a question for that time. In the meantime, I suspect from the depth of Irigaray's conviction and from areas of women's work outside philosophy, particularly in therapy and spirituality, that there is evidence of sexually specific energies. Braidotti comes close to this in her essay, in the end section where she relates the story of Clarice Lispector, as a story of a woman's becoming into subjectivity by passing through a series of thresholds. This leads her to a sexually specific recognition of interconnection with others — indeed with all of life and with all living matter — a connectedness that dislodges women from the system in which they must be other. Instead she becomes a subject able to receive, to respect another in its alterity.[22] This subjectivity cannot be articulated in the traditional language of philosophy, because it is sourced outside the logos. This is the tenor of Irigaray's writing in parts of *I Love to You*.

> I give you a silence in which your future — and perhaps my own, but *with* you and not as you and without you — may emerge and lay its foundation.
>
> This is not a hostile or restrictive silence.... This silence is space-time offered to you with no a priori, no pre-established truth or ritual. To you it constitutes an overture, to the other who is not and never will be mine. It is a silence made possible by the fact that neither you nor I are everything.... This silence is the condition for the possible respect for myself and for the other within our respective limits.... If I am to be quiet and listen ... — the world must not be sealed already, it must still be open, the future not determined by the past. (Irigaray, 1996: 117)

Identity for Irigaray is multiple. She is not prescriptive about identity. Her arguments for identity are not based on confining women to an identity imposed because of her maternal functions or definitions derivative of her position within patriarchy. Nor does she concur with some postmodern feminist positions that argue against sexual identity (identified with modernist agency and rationality) and in favor of varying subject positions dispersed across the sexes. A complexity in her work needs to be recognized here. Although she retains the notion of identity for women as a means to arguing for the possibility of women becoming subjects she is not arguing for the same (masculine) notion of subjectivity. Nor is she suggesting that that subjectivity will be expressed in a unitary way: rather the subjectivity of more than one of feminine sexuality, which she introduces in "This Sex Which is Not One." Feminine sexuality does not have to be configured through the satisfaction of male desire. Female sexuality may be refigured by reference to the female body, not in essentialist terms but as a body culturally and historically constituted. Within these conditions, the female body cannot be essentialized or universalized as it is variously or multiply produced. Furthermore, the sexuality of women may be quite differently configured from the genital location of desire and pleasure in the penis, a configuration that translates into the active and passive opposition representing the male-female binary. "In these terms, women's erogenous zones never amount to anything but a clitoris-sex that is not comparable to the noble phallic organ, or a hole-envelope that serves to sheathe and massage the penis in intercourse" (Irigaray, 1993b: 23). It is in this essay that Irigaray makes her well-known claim for the representation of women as two lips — a remarkable representational ploy that carries the risk of a definitive proposal. However, this is far more than a simple attempt to represent women in a symbolic economy that has excluded women from representation. The two sets of lips signify two major necessities to women becoming subjects: language and genealogy.

According to Irigaray women have been excluded from the symbolic — language is the vehicle for the articulation of the male subject, and conversely the vehicle whereby women have been objectified. It is therefore necessary for women to have language that constitutes women-as-subjects. "It would be better if women, without ceasing to put sexual difference into words, were more able to situate themselves as I, I-she / they (je-elle[s]), to represent themselves as subjects, and to talk to other women. That requires a development in subjectivity and a transformation in the rules of language" (Irigaray, 1994: 34).

She warns though, "To prove that discourse has a sex amounts to a show of force, and its outcome is challenged even when the most rigorous and scientific standards of proof are followed . . . the stakes are so high that everything is subject to denial, incomprehension, blindness, rejection. Inquiries into the sexuation of language are treated with vague suspicion. . . . Is this a reversal, a 'return of the repressed' of the mastery over language exercized by one sex?" (Irigaray, 1993a: 133–134).

Language is a primary vehicle of subjectivity, and much of Irigaray's research is given to demonstrating that the symbolic of language is structured on male privilege. Language, therefore, must be a primary means through which women accede to subjectivity. Language has been the means of conveying women as lacking subjectivity; language has created her as the m-other. "Your nature has always been defined by men, and men alone. Your eternal instructors, in social science, religion or sex. Your moral or immoral teachers. They are the ones who taught you your needs and desires. You haven't had a word to say on the subject" (Irigaray, 1985: 203).

The subtlety of Irigaray's thinking is that she does not reject the role of mother or the ascription of the body to women. The cultural ascription of body to woman has constructed the male as free from the responsibilities of caring for materiality (free, we might say, to exploit materiality, that is, the female body and the earth-nature), free to be transcendent. Subjectivity does not preclude the responsibility and pleasure of materiality. For both men and women it needs to be included in a new balance, a new rhythm, a new time of ethical relations between the sexes, who both have their own languages of subjectivity with which to speak to each other.

Historically we are guardians of the flesh. We should not give up that role, but identify it as our own, by inviting men not to make us into a body for their benefit, not to make us into guarantees that their body exists. All too often the male libido needs some women (wife-mother) to guard the male body. This is why men need a wife in the home, even when they have a mistress elsewhere. . . . Thus it is desirable that we should speak as we are making love. We should also speak as we feed a baby so that the child does not feel that the milk is being stuffed down his or her throat, in a kind of rape. It is equally important that we should speak as we caress another body. . . . Let us not become the guardians of dumb silence. (Irigaray, 1993c: 19)

Irigaray's definition of patriarchy is "an exclusive respect for the genealogy of sons and fathers, and the competition between brothers" (Whitford, 1991a: 174). It is genealogy that constitutes the cultural space of men.[23] Against this, genealogy for women assumes great significance; genealogy is cultural space in which women can gain representational significance.

In very simple terms, there are two parents involved in reproduction. There should be two sexes involved in the construction of the social order. Reproduction does not have to be confined to the birth of children; it can be extended to the regenerative creativity of the subjects of each sex. For women this subjectivity will free them to be mothers and women. "A woman's subjectivity must accommodate the dimensions of mother and lover as well as the union between the two" (Irigaray 1993c: 63).

Genealogy for women incorporates many aspects of representational status and a means for the resolution of identity. A genealogy of women brings forward a woman-to-woman sociality and, therefore, language between women, language that symbolizes feminine specificity in material, historic, economic, philosophical, and spiritual terms. Western male genealogy incorporates God the father as the transcendent signifier. Such a metaphor means that male subjectivity is premised upon the attributes of God — a dangerous model of subjectivity in the view of some feminist theologians, for the characteristics of God become incorporated into the ideals of male subjectivity, that is, omnipotence, creativity (by the word) transcendence.[24] For Irigaray, women need a notion of feminine divinity as an ideal necessary to their autonomy, their sexually specific subjectivity. The mother-daughter relation is a divine relation for women.

We women, sexed according to our gender, lack a God to share, a word to share and to become. Defined as the often dark, even occult mother-substance of the word of men, we are in need of our subject, our substantive, our word, our predicates: our elementary sentence, our basic rhythm, our morphological identity, our generic incarnation, our genealogy.

It is essential that we be God for ourselves. . . . It is equally essential that we should be daughter-gods in the relationship with our mothers, and that we cease to hate our mothers in order to enter into submissiveness to the father-husband. We cannot love if we have no memory of a native passiveness in relation to our mothers, of our primitive attachment to her and hers to us.

Does respect for God made flesh not imply that we should incarnate God within us and in our sex: daughter-woman-mother?

And yet, without the possibility that God might be made flesh as a woman, through the mother and the daughter, and in their relationships, no real constructive help can be offered to women.

The God we know, the gods we have known for centuries, are men; they show and hide the different aspects of man. He(they) do(es) not represent the qualities or predicates of the female made God. (Irigaray, 1993c: 72)

Furthermore: "When women get bogged down in their search for freedom, for liberation, there seem to be many themes: the absence of a God of their own and inadequate management of the symbolic. The two things are linked and necessary to the constitution of an identity and a community" (Irigaray, 1993c: 72).

The only place of genealogical belonging and intergenerational continuity is through alignment with the male line — entailing having a husband and a son. Woman is thus valued only for her maternal function. Bereft of her own genealogy and source of identification with her own kind, she is derelict, unrepresented, and without access to identity. This positions women in an ambivalent relation to their own sex, a relation of love and hate. She must identify with the mother whom she is like, yet there is no means for her to separate satisfactorally to become a woman in her own right, a woman who is not a mother. Woman-as-subject must be repressed in this economy. She is tied to singular identification with the mother. She must become a mother to have a place in patriarchy. A genealogy of the mother-daughter relation would provide the possibility of an identity for women that is freed from the necessity to be a mother — although that identity may include motherhood. This is part of the symbolic redistribution that Whitford clarifies as a reallocation of the sensible and transcendental functions that has been divided between women and men, to become incorporated by both women and men.[25] "Our urgent task is not to submit to the desubjectivised social role, the role of the mother, which is dictated by an order subject to the division of labour — he produces, she reproduces — that walls up in the ghetto of a single function. When did society ever ask fathers to choose between men and citizens? We don't have to give up being women to be mothers" (Irigaray, 1993c: 18).

The infinity of the genealogical relation between mother and daughter brings women into relation with their own past as well as providing them with an infinite future. Let us not confine this relation to infinity as one that necessitates blood ties. Although Irigaray insists on the importance of representing the mother-daughter relation, she problematizes motherhood as the only valid role available to women in patriarchy and calls out creativity that goes far beyond the confines of reproduction. In fact, Irigaray specifically problematizes the mother-daughter relation as it is presently configured. Although the mother provides all needed nourishment it may also be a suffocating nourishment, because the daughter is inaugurated as an object in the patriarchal arrangements. In the opening lines of "One Does Not Stir without the Other": "With your milk Mother, you also fed me ice" (Irigaray, 1981: 1) — what chilling evocation of the life-giving fluidity that Irigaray says represents the feminine and thus the mobility, and lubricative qualities necessary for change, for the becoming process, and what contrast with the solidity of ice — that indicated the cold inertia of bounded meanings of the metaphysical structure that is self-perpetuating and repetitive of the subject-object, same-other relations and the violence and destructiveness that ensue from that.

Her greatest interest is in cultural regeneration and for this the revolution that is needed for women to assume the aspirations and responsibility for creating women-as-subjects, for regenerating society through this new ethics. Genealogy for women has much more to do with cultural regeneration. The mothers of the past with whom women can establish relations are the writers, those who have struggled in social movements. They are to be found in the memories and inheritance that have given women in the West the freedom that now brings the challenge of the future.

Genealogy through the mother is not a history that forgets matter or nature.

If we are not to be accomplices in the murder of the mother we also need to assert that there is a genealogy of women. Each of us has a female family tree: we have a mother, maternal grandmother and great-grandmothers, we have daughters. Because we have been exiled into the house of our husbands, it is easy to forget the special quality of female genealogy; we might come to deny it. Let us try to situate ourselves within that female genealogy so that we can win and hold onto our identity. Let us not forget that we already have a history, that certain women, despite all the cultural obstacles, have made their mark on history and all too often have been forgotten by us. (Irigaray, 1993c: 19)

Bearing in mind the educational focus of this book it is almost impossible to discontinue this theme of genealogy in Irigaray's work on feminine subjectivity and mimesis as a strategy in achieving this, because it offers infinitely rich resources for education and is so integral to the development of sexually specific language that is necessary to feminine specificity. Language is an essential medium in education, so the gendering of language must be a claim in further developments of education for girls and women. This offers the material for curriculum texts for education in sexual difference.

Irigaray is never far from the difficulties of women's self-representation in a culture of the universal because this culture only provides her with the resources of the universal. She only has the tools of the system that has enclosed women in the phallocentric notion of woman. Embedded in Irigaray's work is the question: how to speak and write woman — women-becoming-subjects — when we only have the language of patriarchy with which to do it?

Irigaray's response to this exclusion of the feminine from the economy of representation is effectively to say, Fine, I don't want to be in your economy anyway, and I'll show you what this intelligible receptacle can do to your system; I will not be a poor copy in your system, but I will resemble you nevertheless by miming the textual passages through which you construct your system and showing that what cannot enter it is already inside it (as its necessary outside), and I will mime and repeat the gestures of your operation until this emergence of the outside within the system calls into question its systematic closure and its pretension of self-grounding. (Butler, 1994: 157)

Levinas has a similar question. Totality and infinity are explications of the meaning of the ethical relation. Otherwise than Being is Levinas's development of this as the textual event of the face-to-face relation — his work to convey the ethical relation in non-totalizing language. He refers to saying as the language of ethics; the said as the language of totality. Saying is the language that speaks alterity. This is his expression in linguistic terms of distinguishing between the said as the language of the same and the saying as the language of the Other. He finds the space to do this in openings in the enclosure of totality. The said is the language of ontology, of Being. It is the language of assertion and proposition that rests on the assumption that truth (or falsity) can be ascertained. The said rests on the assumption of the identifiable meaning of words. One might say that this is the language of the philosophical logos and of orthodoxy, which Levinas defines as "the alchemy whereby alterity is transmuted into sameness by means of the philosopher's stone of the knowing ego" (Levinas, 1994: 6).

The saying is the language of the self in relation to the Other; it is not the language of self presence but the language of "performative stating, proposing, or expressive position of myself facing the Other" (Critchley, 1992: 7). This is the ethical relation, a doing whose meaning cannot be confined to an essence. Considering Levinas's definition of ethics as "the relation that I have with the Other and . . . the unique demand that is placed on me by him or her" (Critchley, 1992: 17), the saying is the taking cognizance that speech is an action of relationship; the words are addressed to another, an interlocuter.

These arguments lead into Levinas's central philosophical problem. If the text, that is, the book, represents the language of the said, how may it be possible to represent the saying, to represent a philosophy of ethical alterity, when the only tool, the only method, is that of ontology? How might the saying be expressed in the language of the said without betraying the saying? A reading that engages openings in the text suggests that it is possible to have both. It is not feasible to articulate the saying without the said, just as it is not possible to conceive of an outside or exterior without an inside.[26]

The richness and depth of these notions cannot be given justice in this chapter. What I hope to do is substantiate Irigaray's multifaceted strategy of introducing the female as subject into philosophy. Irigaray's purpose is not that of replacing one sexual economy for another, but in "conceptualising a double syntax" (Whitford 1991a: 181) and a relationship between the two. It is in this context that she speaks of love — love as a necessary intermediary between two autonomous and specific subjectivities; (although it must be said that these are not prescribed subjectivies — moreover they are reconfigured subjectivities, in which aggression and the death drives are not exported onto the Other, but are incorporated into consciousness.

When faced by questions such as these, many men and women start talking about love. But love is only possible when there are two parties and in a relationship that is not submissive to one gender, not subject to reproduction. It requires that the rights of both male and female be written into a legal code. If the rights of the couple were indeed written into the legal code, this would serve to convert individual morality into collective ethics, to transform the relations of the genders within the family or its substitutes into rights and duties that involve the culture as a whole. Religion can then rediscover how each gender interprets its relation to the divine — a religion freed from its role of guardian of a single gender and financial trustee for the property of one gender more than another. Hardly a godly role! (Irigaray, 1993c: 4–5)

The love between two, precisely because it is not a cover for an economy of displacement of the negative, the repression of the other, is an "ethical mode of being" (Whitford, 1991a: 165), which is a requirement for a relation. It is a relation that requires mediation — a bridge so that the place, the boundaries that frame the subjectivities of each sex are not transgressed. Irigaray conceptualizes mediation in a number of ways using the morphology of the female body as her source of representations. Mucosity conveys the fluidity with which she often characterizes female specificity and is a metaphor for the proposed movement out of the totalizing structure of ontological philosophy. Mucosity is necessary to loving encounters. Fluidity/mobility is also enhancing to amorous exchange. And from a number of further interpretations that mucosity lends itself to, not least is that it is necessary to speech and to sexuality (Whitford, 1991a: 163). The placenta is another suggestion as a representation of mediation, by means of which the necessities for sustaining life pass from mother to child, yet in which the distinctiveness of each is preserved. Perhaps Irigaray is suggesting love as a space between, the intermediary between the two subjectivities, and the means by which the subjectivities would be preserved. "The mediator, the bridge, must either pass through generation (two sexes) or through God . . . , in order to ensure a reciprocal limitation of container, so that one is not swallowed up forever in the other" (Whitford, 1991: 165).

One of the difficulties in selecting themes in Irigaray's writing is that her resources and her tasks are multiple, for hers is a cultural critique. As will be recognizable from the quotations, psychoanalysis and philosophy interweave, subjectivity and relationships are inseparable, and ethics are theorized and practiced as her process of engaging with philosophers — for critique, interrogation, and reworking the future of philosophy.

FACE TO FACE WITH EDUCATION

> For little girls, education, the social world of men-amongst-themselves and the patriarchal culture function as Hades did for Kore/Persephone.
> — Irigaray, 1994: 111

What does Irigaray's thesis on the cultural and revolutionary importance of sexual difference mean for education, and how might Levinas's preeminence of ethics be translated into educational practice?

Education is the social and institutional expression of cultural value and cultural reproduction, that is, reproduction of the universal. Irigaray supposes this when she says that education functions for girls to separate the daughter (Kore/Persephone) from her mother.[27] It is the virginity of daughters that is made a commodity, and that in an exchange between men functions to separate her from her mother. Western cultural mythology offers explanation of these arrangements.

How can Irigaray's seemingly outrageous idea of women becoming virgin contribute to a culture of two sexes? Becoming virgin is to do with refusal of patriarchal definition and women's selfconscious rebuilding of female genealogy. For women to become virgin is Irigaray's symbolic representation of retaining the fertility of the mother-daughter relation and the fecundity of language between them to maintain female genealogy.

The universal functions in two ways in education; the reproduction of a system that is constructed on one sex and the reproduction of individual competitors for a capitalist economy. Girls' and women's participation, therefore, depends on their alienation from their sexed, embodied identities and being produced as free, rational, knowing subjects. Bill Readings eloquently exposes the operation of institutional education as fundamentally reproductive of the capitalist system, under the guise of the system producing so-called free, independent individuals. In Levinas's terms, these are individuals whose subjectivity is premised on freedom; not on responsibility for the Other; they are, therefore, not ethical subjects. Education that produced ethical subjectivity would produce a major cultural shift of the revolutionary order that Irigaray has claimed to be necessary. It would require the presence of two sexes in education; the production of ethical subjectivity and the production of knowledge that represents two sexes and does not veil masculine sex in universality.

I recall Levinas's attention to subjectivity, in which he demonstrates the ontological subject as one who assimilates or negates otherness in order to retain the freedom required for autonomy and competitiveness, which he characterizes by the metaphor of the grasp. If nonviolence and peace are to be serious goals then consideration must be given to the education of ethical subjectivity that is capable of thinking of the other absolutely — of thinking the Other is welcome. Levinas says that the ethical relation is necessarily a teaching relation because knowledge of the Other cannot be presumed. The asymmetry that characterizes this relation is present in the teaching relation, but not as the asymmetry of the teacher as master of knowledge. The asymmetry lies in the teacher as the receiver of the Other, the teacher is not merely an intellect in pursuit of the mastery of reason because Levinas says that reason is not mastery it is receptivity, the welcome of the new.

He challenges the Socratic method of teaching, in which the teacher elicits knowledge or understanding from the child (or learner) as if it was already within the child. Levinas's description of this is maieutic, drawing on the figure of the midwife. "Teaching does not simply transmit an abstract and general content already common to me and the Other" (Levinas, 1969: 98). Levinas claims for teaching the experience of exteriority, the "more than I can contain" (Levinas, 1969: 51). Teaching is the responsibility to bring the student to what he does not yet know. Otherwise there is no pathway toward the production of new knowledge or ways of being. The teacher-student relation cannot be collapsed into equality or be obscured in "intersubjective communication" (Readings, 1995: 202), because this would amount to a fusion that would preclude the dynamics of learning and teaching. Heteronomy is at the heart of this relation as a recognition of the asymmetry of the learner's relation to knowledge. Furthermore, the learner is one who cannot be seen as merely a recipient of knowledge; she or he is the absolutely Other.

Levinas says that this relation is characterized by conversation or by saying, to use his words from *Otherwise than Being*: "To approach the Other in conversation is to welcome his expression, in which at each instant he overflows the idea a thought would carry away from it. It is therefore to receive the Other beyond the capacity of the I, which means exactly: to have the idea of infinity. . . . But this also means to be taught. The relation with the Other, or Conversation, is a non-allergic relation, an ethical relation; but in-as-much as it is welcomed this conversation is a teaching" (Levinas, 1981: 51).

It is very close to Irigaray's respect for alterity that must be mediated in a way that preserves the integrity of each of the terms. In "Wonder: A Reading of Descartes," Irirgary (1993a) writes of wonder as a passion that has the quality of alterity. In the following passage silence is her mediating term.

I am listening to you, as to another who transcends me, requires a transition to a new dimension. I am listening to you: I perceive what you are saying, I am attentive to it, I am attempting to understand and hear your intention. Which does not mean I comprehend you, I know you, so I do not need to listen to you and I can even plan future for you. No, I am listening to you as someone and something I do not know yet on the basis of freedom and an openness put aside for this moment. I am listening to you: I encourage something unexpected to emerge, some becoming, some growth, some new dawn, perhaps. I am listening to you prepare the way for the not-yet-coded, for silence, for a space for existence, free intentionality, and support for your becoming. . . . This silence is space-time offered to you with no a priori, no pre-established truth or ritual. To you it constitutes an overture, to the other who is not and never will be mine. It is a silence that is made possible by the fact that neither *I* nor *you* are everything, that each of us is limited, marked by the negative, non-hierarchically different. (Irigaray, 1996: 116–117)

I will move from Irigaray's and Levinas's profound theorizing of alterity, the possibility of difference that is not premised on sameness, to her critique of equality in education. For Irigary, equality supposes sameness. This means that girls' participation on the basis of equality is to leave the universal intact as sexually indifferent. Irigaray scrutinizes equality for its basis in the universal, which is masculine. She does not deny the importance of equality but is eloquent about its inadequacy. Equality for Irigaray means the right to status within the structure of the single universal. She elucidates:

To demand equality as women is, it seems to me a mistaken expression of the real objective. The demand to be equal presupposes a point of comparison. To whom or to what do women want to be equalised? To men? To a salary? To a public office? To what standard? Why not to themselves?

Women's exploitation is based on sexual difference; its solution will only come through sexual difference. Certain modern tendencies, certain feminists of our time, make strident demands for sex to be neutralised. This neutralisation, if it were possible would mean the end of the human species. What is important, on the other hand is to define the values of belonging to a gender, valid for the two genders. (Irigaray, 1994: 12)

She is adamant about the need to replace equality with rights to sexual difference. The supposed neutrality of the universal is untenable.

Irigaray's research on language, which is the symbolic articulation of cultural values and the structuring of sexuality, shows that there is no neutrality in language:[28]

Sexual difference cannot therefore be reduced to a simple extralinguistic fact of nature. It conditions language and is conditioned by it. . . . This accounts for the fact that women find it so difficult to speak and be heard as women. They are excluded and denied by the patriarchal linguistic order. . . . It is this untenable position in relation to discourse that causes most women who wish to have a say in culture to fall back on what they believe to be a neutral position. Yet this position is impossible in our languages. A woman denies her sex and gender in doing this. (Irigaray, 1994: 21)

Language is a key to repositioning women in culture. Again the implications for education are profound as the socializing institution that might enhance the autonomy and sexual specificity of girls and women.

Irigaray's analysis brings disturbing scrutiny to women in education — as teachers and as students who are surpassing the achievements of males. In her view, these achievements must be on male terms through the denial of women's sexed subjectivity. Education is an institution of the male symbolic order, so girls' achievement must be constituted on male authority, and "forced entry into the male order and the male genealogy, [resulting in] a gap between being a body and being a mind" (Puissi 1990: 83).

The consequences of these two political and theoretical perspectives are well known to us, because we have had to deal with them in our personal lives and professional practice. On the one hand, implicit but nevertheless real in the perspective of emancipation, there was homologation to the masculine, which was taken to be the universal value, and thus normative also for women — whose female experience was consequently erased. On the other hand, there was the social marginality and the symbolic non-existence of a separate female universe which was characterised by egalitarianism, lack of differentiation, and fusion in relationships between women — all of which impeded the recognition of authoritative female figures as possible sources of value and magisterial authority for young women. (Puissi 1990: 82)

Irigaray has worked with Italian feminists who have for many years undertaken practices of sexual difference and sought ways to institute a female symbolic. This has been written about by the Milan Women's Bookstore Collective, by Mirna Cicioni, Theresa de Lauretis, and members of Diotima, another group of feminist philosophers in Verona, of which Puissi is a member. Irigaray's papers and addresses from her work with them are published as *Je, Tu, Nous* and *Thinking the Difference for a Peaceful Revolution*. These Italian women began a practice of *affidamento*, one-to-one relations of entrustment or, borrowing from Levinas, face-to-face relations among themselves. They began with expectations of equality and egalitarianism, a common goal of feminism, constructed as a political strategy against the hierarchies that are supposed to characterize systems of male privilege. These women found that, in fact, their relationships were marked by asymmetry and by differences among the women (age, experience, competence). Instead of interpreting these as a failure of equality, the asymmetry was interpreted as symbolically representative of the mother-daughter relation. Positioning women as authoritative effectively positioned them as mediators of a female symbolic, an enabling power mobilizing women to go ahead with the challenge to follow aspirations specific to each woman and take the risk of becoming female subjects. This symbolic reconstitution of female genealogy (on a vertical axis, as Puissi refers to it) allows women "to create symbolic and social orders (ethics, law, education, knowledge, etc.) that correspond to their female way of being" (Puissi 1990: 86).

One of the outcomes of the *affidamento* practices of these communities has been to apply these to educational practice. Puissi and others established *affidamento* relations between teaching colleagues, between mothers and teachers, and between teachers and students.

The effect of making these relationships intentional in education is that visibility and significance are given to women becoming subjects. The solidarity of this gave the women the possibility of assuming responsibility for decisions or new ideas without isolation.

The among-women culture in education will not only constitute subjectivity for women. It will constitute a production of new knowledge. Puissi recognizes that:

> This subjectivity requires new ways of knowing: holistic and relational thought, the knowledge which retains the wisdom of the fertile body. The value and the sense of ease that women can experience by constituting themselves as subjects in the processes of production and teaching/learning knowledge, avoiding confinement to the margins of culture (as is often the case of Women's Studies where the female gender is only the object of inquiry — women's history, female psychology, etc. — while the logical structure of the analysis remains male. (Puissi, 1990: 88)

Puissi is quite unapologetic about educational practices of bias toward responsibility for girls' education and the ethical demand from these commitments to challenge young women to take responsibility for their education and their sex. The occasional division of classes by sex goes alongside the practice of partiality in mixed-sex classrooms through which boys must also develop an analysis of the culture of the male sex. It is not only educational relationships that can produce female sexual symbolism. The educational content would include teaching history from women's perspective — not from the weak position of oppression, but building girls' "awareness of estrangement from the male culture (which in us ripened so slowly) right from the beginning, from the strong position of freedom guaranteed by female authorities" (Puissi, 1990: 87). Study of women writers and artists and leaders gives power to the symbolic representation of women, which deepens the cultural genealogical resources for women. The possibilities of critical studies are boundless, and social analysis with the resources of mythology, religion, linguistics, languages, and economics are available for interpretative dialogue with these disciplines. Most Western countries are implicated in colonization one way or another, so imperialism and racism need to be part of cultural studies so that ethnicity is not overlooked in the production of female symbolism. Irigaray gives sexual difference a primacy that obscures the question of cultural difference. Writing, as I do, in Aotearoa–New Zealand as a Pacific nation, cultural difference and anti-colonialism cannot be neatly separated from issues of sexual difference. Besides, I am surrounded by cultures that retain the genealogy of women and men. Sexual difference is practiced in Polynesian cultures in subjectivities that are already poststructural.

The ethical subject and the ethical relation therefore have to be theorized for educational practice if the cultural paucity of a universal male ontological subject is going to be replenished with two ethical sexes. The pedagogy that ethical and two-sexed subjectivity invites is an educative relationship that emanates from the teacher in the welcome of the student as sexed and cultured.

The above critique of the universal has to be brought to bear on institutional education, whether in separate education for girls (and boys) or education in coeducational settings. Irigaray never separates education from the sex of language because language produces sex(es). Irigaray repeatedly refers to the subjectivity of women becoming constituted in the sociality of women speaking to each other. So she argues:

In verbal exchanges, create sentences in which I-woman (je-femme) talks to you-woman (tu-femme) particularly of yourself or of a third woman. The fact that this sort of language barely exists greatly restricts women's space for subjective freedom. It's possible to start to create it with everyday language. Mothers and daughters could do it in affective and educational games. In concrete terms that means that the mother-woman could speak to the daughter-woman, use feminine grammatical forms, talk about the things that concern the two of them, talk about herself and ask her daughter to do the same, bringing up her genealogy . . . , tell her daughter about women currently involved in public life, or Historical or mythological women, ... When girls start school, the discourse they learn is that of he/they (il(s)), or the between-men-culture (l'entre-il(s)). Even if coeducational schools do have some advantages, in this respect they are not particularly favourable to the development of girls' identity as long as linguistic rules (grammatical, semantic, lexicological) don't progress. (Irigaray, 1993b: 50)

For Irigaray, sexual difference is a political necessity in a culture that is structured on sexual indifference. It is imperative to address the historical and structured subordination of women before sexed subjectivity can be elided, as some poststructural proposals for subjectivity suggest. Hers may be a grand narrative of sexual difference, yet the horizon she faces invokes subjectivity that is multiple and nonprescriptive, and that can account for cultural difference. Becoming engages desire for a future that is not tied to reproducing the structures of the past — regeneration and fecundity are contingent on ethical subjectivity — and it is politically necessary that this be sexed and cultured.

NOTES

1. In "Women the Sacred and Money" and other essays Irigaray (1993c) shows that male privilege rests upon the support of women and the material resources of nature — she draws on the etymological connection between mater and materiality (as does Butler [1994] in "Bodies that Matter") to connect women and nature as both constituting patriarchal sacrifices.

2. In "Of Bugs and Women" Braidotti (1994) describes a proposed distinction between cyclical, discontinuous time (aion), associated with women and linear, recorded time (chronos) of masculinity. She suggests that even the "poststructuralist subject may appear as fragmented and disunited; on a temporal scale [achieves] unity [in the] power to connect and to recollect" (p. 119).

3. See Irigaray's essays "The Universal as Mediation" (1993c) and "Linguistic Sexes and Genders" (1993b).

4. See Levinas (1969: 298).

5. Martin Buber, whom Levinas (1994, chap. 3) addresses in his work, articulates the ethics of the I-Thou relation, but this is based, according to Levinas, on equality, not on absolute alterity.

6. During the writing of this chapter, Michael Peters gave me Derrida's funeral oration, "Adieu," for Levinas. Levinas died in December 1995. My hoped-for response from Levinas to Irigaray now has to be directed through Derrida's words of farewell, "He entrusted to us ... the a-Dieu.... If he no longer responds, it is because he responds in us, — in calling us, in recalling to us: "a-Dieu" (Derrida, 1996).

7. For discussion of Levinas's primacy of ethical difference see Critchley (1992: 225–228).

8. See Irigaray (1993c: 78).

9. Levinas (1969: sec A).

10. In this paper, the other, spelled with a small "o" refers to the general other; Other, spelled with a capital "O" refers to the the specific Other, the Other of absolute alterity who constitutes the Levinasian ethical relation.

11. Levinas uses the term "existent" to refer to the human being that preceeds ontological formation.

12. For detailed explanation see Levinas (1969: 226).
13. From Derrida (1991).
14. Wild (1969: 15) sets out the difficulties of the "neutral englobing system that characterises totalisation and the anarchy associated with individual freedom. The face-to-face, governed by generosity and communication, invokes responsibility for the Other, but not a totalising enclosure in conformity."
15. Bernasconi (1995: 84–85) recognizes that this claim for cultural pluralism in Levinas is problematic. It is implicit by the way in which Levinas uses Hebraic philosophy and theology to bring new consciousness into the Greek philosophical tradition. Levinas does not make a case for cultural pluralism in philosophy.
16. For Burke, C. 'Romancing the Philosophers.' see Hunter, D. (ed) *Seduction and Theory*. Urbana: University of Illinois Press, 1989.
17. For elaboration on essentialism, refer to Schor and Weed (1994: 226–240).
18. See Schor and Weed (1994).
19. "Ontology is the movement of comprehension which takes possession of entities through the activity of labour; it is the movement of the hand, the organ of grasping . . . which takes hold of (prend) and comprehends (comprend) in the virility of its acquisition and digestion of alterity" (Critchley, 1992: 6) and "The hand relating the elemental to the finality of needs . . . confer[s] on it the status of possession. Labour is the very energy of acquisition" (Levinas, 1969: 159).
20. Refer to Waring (1988) and the Milan Women's Bookstore Collective (1990: 6).
21. Braidotti notes "Let us keep in mind . . . that the reference to woman in the process of becoming woman does not refer to empirical females, but rather to topological positions. The becoming-woman is the marker for a general process of transformation: it affirms positive forces and levels of nomadic and rhizomatic consciousness" (1994: 116).
22. Briadotti refers to Helene Cixous's reading of Clarice Lispector: "Cixous connects this faculty to the ability to both give and receive a gift, that is to say, to receive the other in all of his/her astounding difference" (1994: 133).
23. See Whitford (1991a: 162).
24. See Welch (1990).
25. See Whitford (1991a: 93).
26. Derrida theorizes this as that space the interstice, that place or time of the activity of demarkation, the interstice between the in and the out, the process by which differentiation is achieved. This liminal space-time of in-between, he names *differance*.
27. Irigaray (1994) frequently refers to the mythology of Demeter and Kore/Persephone. It is explanatory of the genealogical break in the mother-daughter relation that causes loss of identity and creativity. The restoration of this relation results in creativity and fertility.
28. For essays on language see "Women's Discourse and Men's Discourse," and "Linguistic Sexes and Genders" in Irigaray (1993b) and "The Cost of Words," and "Love of the Other" in Irigaray (1993a).

REFERENCES

Bernasconi, R. (1995). Only the persecuted. In A. T. Peperzak (Ed.), *Ethics as first philosophy: The significance of Emmanuel for philosophy, literature and religion*. London: Routledge.

Bernasconi, R., & Wood, D. (1988). *The provocation of Levinas. Rethinking the other*. London: Routledge.

Braidotti, R. (1994). Of bugs and women: Irigaray and Deleuze on the becoming-woman. In C. Burke, N. Schor, and M. Whitford (Eds.), *Engaging with Irigaray*. New York: Columbia University Press.

Butler, J. (1994). Bodies that matter. In C. Burke, N. Schor, and M. Whitford (Eds.), *Engaging with Irigaray*. New York: Columbia University Press.

Burke, C., Schor, N., & Whitford, M. (Eds.). (1994). *Engaging with Irigaray*. New York: Columbia University Press.

Chanter, T. (1995). *Ethics of eros. Irigaray's rewriting of the philosophers*. London: Routledge.

Cicioni, M. (1989, Summer). "Love and respect, together": The theory and practice of *affidamento* in Italian feminism. *Australian Feminist Studies 10*, pp. 71–83.

Cohen, R. A. (Ed.). (1986). *Face to face with Levinas*. Albany: State University of New York Press.

Critchley, S. (1992). *The ethics of deconstruction: Derrida and Levinas*. Oxford: Blackwell.

Derrida, J. (1996, Autumn). Adieu. P-A. Brault and M. Naas (Trans.), *Critical Inquiry 23*, pp. 1–8.

Derrida, J. (1991). At this very moment in this work here I am. In R. Bernasconi, and S. Critchley (Eds.), R. Berezdivin (trans.), *Re-reading Levinas*. Bloomington: Indiana University Press.

Irigaray, L. (1996). *I love to you: Sketch for a felicity within history*. A. Martin (Trans.). New York: Routledge.

Irigaray, L. (1994). *Thinking the difference: For a peaceful revolution*. K. Martin (Trans.). New York: Routledge.

Irigaray, L. (1993a). *An ethics of sexual difference*. C. Burke and G. Gill (Trans.).London: Athlone.

Irigaray, L. (1993b). *Je, tu, nous*. A. Martin (Trans.).New York: Routledge.

Irigaray, L. (1993c). *Sexes and genealogies*. G. Gill (Trans.).New York: Columbia University Press.

Irigaray, L. (1992). *Elemental passions*. J. Collie and J. Still (Trans.). New York: Routledge.

Irigaray, L. (1985). *This sex which is not one*. C. Porter and C. Burke (Trans.).Ithaca, NY: Cornell University Press.

Irigaray, L. (1981, Autumn). One does not stir without the other. H. Vivienne (Trans.). *Signs* 7(1): 60–67

Levinas, E. (1994). *Outside the subject*. M. Smith (Trans.). Stanford, CA: Stanford University Press.

Levinas, E. (1986a). *Time and the other*. Richard A Cohen (Trans.). Pittsburgh, PA: Duquesne Univerity Press.

Levinas, E. (1986b). The trace of the other. In M. C. Taylor (Ed.), *Deconstruction in context* . Chicago, IL: University of Chicago Press.

Levinas, E. (1981). *Otherwise than being or beyond essence*. A. Lingis (Trans.). The Hague: Martinus Nijhoff.

Levinas, E. (1969). *Totality and infinity*. A. Lingis (Trans.). Pittsburgh, PA: Duquesne University Press.

Milan Women's Bookstore Collective. (1990). *Sexual difference: A theory of social-symbolic practice*. Bloomington: Indiana University Press.

Mortensen, E. (1994). *The feminine and nihilism: Luce Irigaray with Neitzsche and Heidegger*. Oslo: Scandanavian University Press.

Puissi, A. M. (1990). Towards a pedagogy of sexual difference: Education and female genealogy. *Gender and Education*, 2(1): xx23–37

Readings, B. (1995). From emancipation to obligation: Sketch for heteronomous politics of education. In M. Peters (Ed.), *Education and the postmodern condition*. Westport, CT: Bergin & Garvey.

Schor, N. & Weed, E. (Eds.). (1994). *The essential difference*. Bloomington: Indiana University Press.

Waring, M. (1988). *Counting for nothing*. Wellington: Allen & Unwin

Welch, S. (1990). *A feminist ethic of risk*. Minneapolis, MN: Fortress Press.

Whitford, M. (1991a). *Philosophy in the feminine*. London: Routledge.

Whitford, M. (Ed.). (1991b). *The Irigaray reader*. Oxford: Blackwell.

Wild, J. (1969). Introduction. In E. Levinas. *Totality and infinity*, A. Lingis (Trans.). Pittsburgh, PA: Duquesne University Press.

9

Jean Baudrillard: From Marxism to Terrorist Pedagogy
Peter McLaren and Zeus Leonardo

> I just can't breathe in this world of petitioning intellectuals.... I no longer take a position as intellectual. My work now is to make things appear or disappear.
> — Baudrillard, 1993: 182

> History is a strong myth, perhaps, along with the unconscious, the last great myth.
> — Baudrillard, 1994: 47

He made his appearance on the stage sporting a silver jacket with sequined lapels, blue shirt, and glasses that looked too large for his face and that dominated his short frame. The showroom was packed as the performer read for an hour accompanied by the Chance Band. The performer needed no introduction. It was the iconoclastic Jean Baudrillard. Pleased at having won $100 at the slots on his first night at the event, he was captivatingly gloomy and suicidal. The event was called "Chance" and was sponsored by Art Center College of Design in Pasadena. It also featured Chaos theorists, beat poets, a *butoh* dance troupe from Los Angeles, rock bands, performance artists, gamblers, stockbrokers, and new age enthusiasts. Baudrillard was in his element: the professor as lounge-lizard, reading pataphysical texts instead of singing "Feelings."

The work of Baudrillard is vital in understanding the cultures of late capitalism, the parodic, terroristic, and pestilential world of ecstatic nihilism that Georges Bataille (1985) captures in the metaphor of the Solar

Anus and Arthur Kroker and D. Cook (1986) describe as "excremental culture." Baudrillard is the Grand Expositor of the social as corpse, transfiguring through his apocalyptic prose the social into an effigy of a rotting cadaver, its stench and putrescence made all the more beautiful in the ecstasy of its decay. For over two decades Baudrillard's work has transfixed and perplexed several generations of scholars with its heuristic power, its bourgeois indignation and its chilling eulogistic pronouncements about the fate of the postmodern urbanopolis and the vestigial remains of all that is dead. His work represents a sublime connoisseurship of decay. Educators who work in criticalist tradition need to engage current collective arrangements of cultural enunciation that crystallize the subject like a gallstone lodged in the bladder of the social, rendering critical agency hopelessly trapped in metacodes and dominant conventions. Baudrillard's contention that capitalism is part of a larger rationalization process associated with a new type of proliferation of signs, a new type of dissemination of values, and a new type of radical semiurgy associated with cybernetic and semiotic systems, presents a serious challenge to educators working with students who often act as if modern values have been declared dead under the current conditions of hyperreality. We believe that Baudrillard's work, although crucially flawed, nevertheless offers important lessons for educators teaching at a time when the capitalist state is able to overcode machineries of domination and exploitation by molecularizing and particulating the masses while at the same time seducing them to its pulsing flows of fascist desire.

Baudrillard's cultural critique of Western society is a significant contribution to critical theory yet one that remains unpopular. On one hand, Baudrillard's ideas have engaged such critical thinkers as Mike Gane, Kroker, Mark Poster, and Douglas Kellner. Yet for the most part, Baudrillard remains an elusive enigma for many readers, in part because of his iconoclastic tendencies and difficult writing style, specifically in his later books. In Canada a journal is dedicated solely to Baudrillard's ideas and works. As Kroker points out, Baudrillard represents the postmodern scene itself and has reached guru status in some circles as a postmodern theoretician. However, Gane notes Baudrillard's absence from the following important collections (1991b: 47): Joan Miller's encyclopedia *French Structuralism* (1981), John Thompson's *Studies in the Theory of Ideology* (1984), J. Merquior's *From Prague to Paris* (1986), Peter Dews's *Logics of Disintegration* (1987), V. Descombes's *Modern French Philosophy* (1979), or A. P. Griffith's *Contemporary French Philosophy* (1988). For Kroker, Baudrillard reinvigorates Marxism, whereas Kellner criticizes Baudrillard for rejecting Marxism *tout court* in Baudrillard's later works. Clearly, Baudrillard's impact has been felt in the academy.

Baudrillard's eclectic approach to cultural analysis makes a sweep of all the major theoretical frameworks. Marxism, psychoanalysis, feminism, semiotics, structuralism, poststructuralism, modernism, and postmodernism are just some of his hostages. In addition, Baudrillard traces various concepts throughout his corpus, one of them being the fate of the object in society. In the space of this chapter, we will map Baudrillard's engagement with Marxism in his search for a radical theory of contemporary cultural studies. From Baudrillard's structural Marxism (as shown in works like *The System of Objects*) to a break from political economy (for example, *Mirror of Production*) and finally to his announcement of the death of Marxist categories (for example, *Fatal Strategies*), we will assess Baudrillard's relationship with the possibility for a revolution via dialectical materialism. We also will provide textual analyses of Baudrillard's works and appraise his ideas as they contribute to radicalizing social theory, pointing to their limitations. Secondary sources, especially those by Kellner and Gane, will also help synthesize Baudrillard's engagement with and disengagement from Marxism.

Baudrillard's first book, *The System of Objects*, was published in 1968. In it, Baudrillard embarks on his study into the object system. Arguing that one of Marx's limitations was his neglect of consumption, Baudrillard attempts to interpret the meanings people derive through their consumption of objects. Analyzing the evolution of material production, Baudrillard finds that the object's relation with subjects becomes a greater part of daily consumptive practices. This relatively new mode of self-fulfillment takes its form in people's manufactured desires to purchase the latest market object. For instance, Baudrillard writes, "In the United States 90 per cent of the population experience no other desire than to possess what others possess. From year to year, consumer choices are focused en masse on the latest model which is uniformly the best" (1988a: 11). People's social relations with one another no longer are mainly forged at the level of interpersonal relationships but instead are expressed through the objects they own. That is, objects signify subject relations through the objects' differential status. Social relations are relations of objects owned.

At the structural level, purchasing the market object is less about consuming the commodity and more about being socialized into the social order. Baudrillard explains, "But let us not be fooled: objects are *categories of objects* which quite tyrannically induce *categories of persons*. They undertake the policing of social meanings, and the significations they engender are controlled. Their proliferation, simultaneously arbitrary and coherent, to materialize itself effectively under the sign of affluence" (1988a: 16–17). According to Baudrillard, systems of objects are systems of social standings. People traverse the universe of purchasing choices available to them to achieve differentiation from others. This is accomplished through mass production of objects ushering in a new ethic of functionality. In turn, this liberates the object from its traditional association between an idiosyncratic object and its owner. Mass reproduction of the same object alters the owner's relation to the material possession, now seen as something to be manipulated.

According to Baudrillard, social difference is achieved at the level of the object as sign. Baudrillard clarifies, *"In order to become object of consumption, the object must become sign.* . . . It is in this way that it becomes 'personalized,' and enters in the series, etc.: It is never consumed in its materiality, but in its difference" (1988a: 22). The sign code stratifies consumers by assigning prestige to objects through their play on difference from other object forms in the series, together creating what Baudrillard calls ambiance. Objects themselves pose as alibis for the daily consumption of human relations. People do not consume the object they purchase, they consume signs. They buy Nike's "Air Jordans" less for the shoes' utility than for what they signify: that you have the money to buy the shoes or you want the associative function with Michael Jordan. Baudrillard punctuates, "The code is totalitarian; no one escapes it" (1988a: 19). Early in his writing career, Baudrillard develops concepts that will reverberate throughout his prolific academic career. Concepts such as the sign, code, and object are preoccupations that will continue from hereon. In addition, Baudrillard's relationship with structural Marxism becomes obvious. At this stage, Baudrillard underplays more traditional Marxist categories (for example, human labor) in exchange for an emphasis on consumption or social labor.

In *Consumer Society*, Baudrillard continues his critique of the object and consumption. The object form assumes even more significance in its relation to consumers: "We are living the period of the objects: that is , we live by their rhythm, according to their incessant cycles. Today, it is we who are observing their birth, fulfillment, and death; whereas in all previous civilizations, it was the object, instrument, and perennial monument that survived the generations of men" (1988b: 29). People are seen here to survive their objects. This points to the increasing functionality of objects such that they no longer possess the same aura with which previous societies endowed them. Objects owned only exist as long as they are instrumental to the owner. Sentimentality and history become less pertinent because an almost perfect replica of the object can be (re)produced. Baudrillard's fetishism of the object can be seen in this passage. For Baudrillard, the object possesses an aura, a certain vitality that is unmistakably suggestive of humans. In comparison, humans devolve. People become functions of consumer society as they are motivated to purchase more and more objects in order to feel part of the social milieu.

Along with a system of objects comes a system of constructed and conditioned needs and a level of dependency on consumption to fulfill those needs. However, the notion of needs is not as straightforward as rational choice economists would have us believe. Needs arise out of specific modes of production and social organization. Baudrillard reminds us, "Needs are not so much directed at objects, but at values. And the satisfaction of needs primarily expresses an *adherence to these values*. The fundamental, unconscious, and automatic choice of the consumer is to accept the life-style of a particular society (no longer therefore a real choice: the theory of the autonomy and sovereignty of the consumer is thus refuted)" (1988b: 37). Baudrillard incisively reaches a symptomatic reading of consumption at the level of hegemony such that consumers buy into the code of consumption rather than the object itself, into a value system rather than a culture of consumers per se.

However, Baudrillard's model appears too unyielding. It lacks the space for the consumer's relative autonomy and sovereignty. Describing the will to consume as an automatic choice, Baudrillard fails to explain how consumptive choices are mediated by individual consumers and groups (for example, boycotts). Whereas values are to a large degree internal to an individual, subjects experience their consciousness in various ways, some critical and others complacent. Being a consumer does not necessitate conformity. In fact, we prefer a later response to John Kenneth Galbraith where Baudrillard writes, "We are aware of how consumers resist such a precise injunction, and of how they play with 'needs' on a keyboard of objects. We know that advertising is not omnipotent and at times produces opposite reactions; and, we know that in reference to a single 'need,' objects can be substituted for one another" where Baudrillard recognizes consumer resistance and relative power (1988b: 41–42).

In consumer society, consumers are motivated increasingly to make more and more decisions when purchasing objects. This freedom to choose is imposed on the consumer by the code as a duty. Baudrillard expands,

Few objects today are offered *alone*, without a context of objects to speak for them. And the relation of the consumer to the object has consequently changed: the object is no longer referred to in relation to a specific utility, but as a collection of objects in their total meaning. Washing machine, refrigerator, dishwasher, have different meanings when grouped together than each one has alone, as a piece of equipment (*ustensile*). The display window, the advertisement, the manufacturer, and the brand name here play an essential role in imposing a coherent and collective vision, like an almost inseparable totality. Like a chain that connects not ordinary objects but *signifieds*, each object can signify the other in a more complex super-object, and lead the consumer to a series of more complex choices. (1988b: 39)

In a sense, objects can be regarded as possessing their own sociality. Like consumers, objects belong in "imagined communities" (Benedict

Anderson) sedimented at the level of consumer imagination and motivated creativity. Baudrillard continues,

> The arrangement directs the purchasing impulse towards *networks* of objects in order to seduce it and elicit, in accordance with its own logic, a maximal investment, reaching the limits of economic potential. Clothing, appliances, and toiletries thus constitute object *paths*, which establish inertial constraints on the consumer who will proceed *logically* from one object to the next. The consumer will be caught up in a *calculus* of objects, which is quite different from the frenzy of purchasing and possession which arises from the simple profusion of commodities. (1988b: 31)

It is such that objects, in a sense, conspire with one another as a system of signifiers that consumption of individual objects no longer can represent the unit of analysis that figures into purchasing goods. It is this totality of objects in a perpetual play of difference that now constitutes functional compatibility of things and people.

Consumption choices often constrain the consumer into buying ensembles from the same brand so as to maintain compatibility. In some cases, functional compatibility predetermines future purchases: only the same company supplies the required item that will complete the ensemble. Other tactics may be built-in obsolescence or fake improvements that are cosmetic changes in actuality. Consumer needs are atomized, disciplined, and specified to the most minute detail. At this level of decision making, choices are structured like a flowchart where every subsequent decision is already anticipated by the code of consumption. More important, Baudrillard's critique implies a change in social relations. Just as objects become unambiguous in their functional compatibility, likewise subject relations become functional. That is, people with similar object possessions may limit their interactions with other people who own similar objects. In this manner, objects dictate the horizon of relations between people. A change in object relations mirrors a similar effect in subject relations.

Baudrillard's contribution to Marxist discourse comes specifically from the way Baudrillard implicates the code of consumption as the articulation of the mode of production in capitalism. The indoctrination of the social into consumption is analogous to the rural's indoctrination into production throughout the nineteenth century. In effect, consumption and production are intricately linked, the first being the discourse and the second the ideology. Consumption extends the productive forces to invade spheres of life previously thought to be outside of human labor. The code of consumption encroaches on social life at the level of the quotidian. Although the concepts of consumption and production can be discerned as separate processes, they comprise one ideology when considered together: capitalist domination. Baudrillard deconstructs: "It can all be explained only if we acknowledge that needs and consumption are in fact an *organized extension of productive forces*. . . . The truth about consumption is that it is *a function of production.*" (1988b: 43–44). Consumption represents the social cognate of production and a social logic that organizes and controls everyday life. To mimic Steven Best's phrase, this is the "consumption of reality and the reality of consumption" (1995). Welcome to consumer society!

Despite Baudrillard's theoretical rigor, some problems arise from his model of consumption as a social activity. Baudrillard totalizes alienation to the point that consumers fail to discern what is human and what is commodity. The Marxist problematic of revolution becomes less of a possibility in a world where alienation is just a fact of everyday life, where the need to consume is indistinguishable from the need for liberation. Hence, Baudrillard lacks the critical element of subjective agency in his theory of consumption (Kellner, 1989: 18-19). Classes are seen as classes-in-themselves and not for-themselves. Baudrillard highlights no forms of resistance to consumption. Instead, the portrait we receive is an alienated imaginary. Yet the very fact that Baudrillard is writing a critique of consumer society points to possibilities of subverting the code even when using a commodified method, that is, writing a book to be sold.

In a 1981 publication (first translation in English), *For a Critique of the Political Economy of the Sign*, Baudrillard maintains his eye on the problematic of the object in capitalism. Using semiotic Marxist critique, Baudrillard does a wonderful job at introducing a new category to the Marxist notions of use and exchange value: sign value. Baudrillard argues that as consumerism evolves and becomes more complex and abstract, objects begin to signify value as sign form rather than their enjoyment (use) or worth in the marketplace (exchange). Baudrillard explains, "They (objects) no longer 'designate' the world, but rather the being and social rank of their possessor. . . . It is certain that objects are the carriers of indexed social significations, of a social and cultural hierarchy — and this in the very least of their details: form, material, colors, durability, arrangement, in space — in short, it is certain that they constitute a code." Thus, it becomes more obvious that consumption represents a systematization of class differentiation and social classification. Objects in the home, for example, designate "social membership" and their manipulation as the "social tactic" of individuals (pp. 32–37).

Using the foundation established by Ferdinand de Saussure's linguistic semiotics, Baudrillard strips the signifier (linguistic term) from the signified (intended meaning) and the referent (object) and exposes consumption structured at the level of language. That is, Baudrillard's structural method unpacks the culture of consumption as an activity whereby people consume objects as symbols. Objects signify their value through a linguistic structure rather than a practical one. It is here that consumers participate in "conspicuous consumption" (Veblen) or inconspicuous consumption (underconsumption) of goods for their labels and brands, thereby displaying their prestation (Baudrillard, 1981: 30).[1] In an introduction to Roland Barthes's ideas about the object in society, Mike Gane summarizes,

> The problem of understanding the significance of objects is thus one of establishing function, of meaning; or, in other words, there is in the object a struggle between function and a meaning which "renders it intransitive, assigns it a place in what might be called a tableau vivant of the human image-repertoire." ... And then there is a third element, a restoration of the sign to function, into the "spectacle of function," just as it is possible that a sign be transformed into an "unreal function" (e.g. a raincoat that could not function as such). (1991b: 36)

In a similar vein, Best summarizes Marx and Debord's thoughts on the object. Best writes,

> Marx spoke of the degradation of being into having, where creative praxis is reduced to the mere possession of an object, rather than its imaginative transformation, and where emotions are reduced to greed. Debord speaks of a further reduction, the transformation of having into appearing, where the material object gives way to its representation as sign and draws "its immediate prestige and ultimate function" as image. The production of objects simpliciter gives way to "a growing multitude of image-objects" whose immediate reality is their symbolic function as image. Within this abstract system it is the appearance of the commodity that is more decisive [than] its actual "use-value." (1995: 48)

In the age of the sign, image value confounds use and exchange value. Appearance is said to supersede substance. The increasing separation of the social from the agent promulgated by late capitalism infects social relations by promoting the ethic of distinction. This is accomplished through the abstract function of the sign and its displacement of the concrete. Symbolism usurps the reality principle and inaugurates the principle of abstraction.

One strategy of signaling one's social status that consumers employ is redundancy of object signs. For instance, in order to reiterate her differentiation from other people, a consumer emphasizes the television by its spatial placement in the room, the furniture around it, and the protective accessories that shroud it. Objects of consumption circulate like capital for the purpose of social distinction, much like the way language is structured around the prestige of its signs (Kellner, 1989: 21). What results is the simultaneous production of the commodity as sign and the sign as commodity (Baudrillard, 1981: 147). Domination no longer resides primarily in the control of the means of production. Rather, domination can be attributed more to control of the means of consumption. Moreover, this is accomplished at the level of the mode of signification (previously mode of production) in everyday life.

A crucial concept in Baudrillard's analysis is the extension of Marx's concept of commodity fetishism. In a more invidious evolution of a capitalist mode of production, a diversified consumer system serves as an alibi for the productive forces that define capitalism's organizational structure: exploitation of labor and human depotentiation. Kellner explains, "Commodity fetishism thus projects values onto objects that are socially produced, mystifies them and fails to see their social-material underpinnings, just as in pre-capitalist societies individuals fetishized natural objects like trees or the moon as divine or supernatural, failing to see that they were simply products of nature" (1989: 22). Thus, commodity fetishism provides a diversion for the ideological production of things and their concomitant social relations. By endowing commodities with mystical powers, people mystify the process of labor extraction in capitalism. Baudrillard finds Marx's original formulation of commodity fetishism problematic:

All this presupposes the existence, somewhere, of a non-alienated consciousness of an object in some "true," objective state: its use value? . . . By referring all the problems of "fetishism" back to superstructural mechanisms of false consciousness, Marxism eliminates any real chance it has of analyzing the actual process of ideological labor. By refusing to analyze the structures and the mode of ideological production inherent in its own logic, Marxism is condemned (behind the facade of "dialectical" discourse in terms of class struggle) to expand the reproduction of ideology, and thus of the capitalist system itself. (1981: 89–90)

Baudrillard advises,

The term "fetishism" almost has a life of its own. Instead of functioning as a metalanguage for the magical thinking of others, it turns against those who use it, and surreptitiously exposes their own magical thinking. . . . We would have to abandon the fetishist metaphor of the worship of the golden calf . . . and develop instead an articulation that avoids any projection of magical or transcendental animism, and thus the rationalist position of positing a false consciousness and a transcendental subject. (1981: 89–90)

Baudrillard turns the concept of fetishism against itself and some of its uncritical users. He suggests that Marxism's unquestioning acceptance of the concept of labor fetishizes it as a nonideological process and prevents the discourse from reflecting on its own labor as ideological work. In this way Marxism is complicit in reproducing the ideological production of commodities at the level of discourse: theory as labor.

In addition, Baudrillard develops an early movement in his more poststructural critique of the subject as the removed knower. In actuality, he claims, all consciousness (the object included) is alienated in a capitalist mode of production. Achieving subjecthood in capitalism is meaningless if subjects do not question the "actual process of ideological labor." Last, we see Baudrillard's growing disenchantment with Marxism as a sufficiently radical position caught up in the snares of its own productive logic, a tension Baudrillard himself works to resolve throughout his career. By the end of the text, Baudrillard searches for an alternative to production in symbolic exchange, a concept he takes up more fully in following books. His study into the media and communication theories also is beginning to surface.

Baudrillard's semiotic addendum to Marxism revolutionizes and propels Marxist analysis. The insight is uncanny: value at the level of the sign. Nevertheless, some limitations in Baudrillard's model have been pointed out by several key authors. First, while accepting the thesis of the "political economy of the sign," Mark Gottdiener criticizes Baudrillard's semiurgical model (proliferation of signs) for underplaying the persistence of use and exchange value. In short, Gottdiener argues that sign value is the latest child of capitalism in the conditions of postmodernity (1995: 37). Second, the model Baudrillard puts forth underplays the possibility of consumption as a mode of self-valorization. Baudrillard sees consumption as an instrument of capitalist domination and obscures the way consumers purchase goods for their enjoyment and utility. In addition, Michel de Certeau considers the phenomenon of people borrowing (euphemism for stealing) items from work as a form of resistance to the code of consumption (see Kellner, 1989: 28). This is not mainly a question of morality but one of coping with the exploitation of labor for low wages. Some workers even intervene between sales and the market by stealing products from work and selling them to buyers for a fraction of their market price, thereby subverting an otherwise smooth system, or the capitalist imaginary that Baudrillard unwittingly describes. Furthermore, use value still has great implications for certain people who only buy what they need, not what they want. Although this falls under Baudrillard's semiotic thesis that this designates their social difference, buying only what you need suggests the persistence of utility and necessity. Last, poor people who cannot keep up with the Joneses practice what some may call hand-me-downs. To avoid consumption, some people keep their old clothes and knickknacks in hopes of handing down these items to someone else in order that they save money.

John Fiske also offers another interpretation for consumption as a productive activity. According to Fiske, consumption is an outlet for people's need to create some meaning out of everyday life and is never merely an autonomic act of obligation to the dominant ideology.

Although these acts alone are not sufficiently radical, they nevertheless are progressive, oppositional, and rarely unconscious acts (Cook, 1995: 155). Tania Modleski responds critically. Modleski considers Fiske's position, present in some of the Frankfurt School publications as well, problematic because it is the illusion offered by capitalist production that everyone can take part in consumption, that meaning-making through consumption is anticipated by the culture industry (see Cook, 1995: 157). Modleski undermines the cracks and fractures in "the cultural logic of late capitalism" that subjects can seize and appropriate. Fiske's positivity recognizes the shimmers of agency that offer hope for subversion in the face of anomie. However, Modleski brings us full circle to Baudrillard's problematic. To what extent does making the code more tolerable transform social life? Resistance is only critical when transgressive. Otherwise, the code is not threatened. Everyday resistance may only serve to postpone cultural revolution.

Baudrillard's next book, *The Mirror of Production*, continues his engagement with Marxism. More important, it signals Baudrillard's point of departure from political economy. Baudrillard charges that rather than displacing production, Marx replaces one mode of production with another. Therefore, Marx limits the radical direction of his critique by naturalizing the concept of production and merely mirrors capitalism with socialism. Just as Marx prophesied the demise of capitalism, Baudrillard predicts that production itself must be burst asunder. The problem is not the mode of production but the code of production. Baudrillard's eerie description begins like this: "A spectre haunts the revolutionary imagination: the phantom of production. Everywhere it sustains an unbridled romanticism of productivity. The critical theory of the mode of production does not touch the principle of production. All the concepts it articulates describe only the dialectical and historical genealogy of the contents of production, leaving production as a form intact" (1975: 17).

Baudrillard's slicing analysis leaves one agape. He unravels such a seemingly simple and accepted notion, one that had become second nature and common sense to most Marxists. Ideologically embedded in the discourse, production now appears naked and vulnerable. What has previously been assumed as that critical element separating humans from animals, productivity is questioned and blushes like a child caught after years of telling stories: "It is the concept of production, then, which is submitted to a radical critique" (1975: 23).

In perhaps his most didactic prose, Baudrillard scrutinizes one-by-one what he perceives as categories embedded in the ideology of production. The first of these concepts is the law of value. Baudrillard observes, "Failing to conceive of a mode of social wealth other than that founded on labor and production, Marxism no longer furnishes in the long run a real alternative to capitalism. Assuming the generic schema of production and needs involves an incredible simplification of social exchange by the law of value" (1975: 29). By reducing social life and relations to a calculus of value, Marxism fails to subvert the notion that humans do not have to be constituted through the determinacy of the law of value. Instead, people can enjoy the ambiguity of symbolic exchange, which destroys value as its opposite other.

Another important Marxian concept that comes under attack is work or labor. Baudrillard argues that by reducing human fulfillment to labor, Marx foregoes the critique that people may find their potential in other nonproductive endeavors, such as communication, a critique that echoes other critics of Marx, including Jürgen Habermas (Kellner, 1989: 41). Baudrillard continues that in Marx's idealization of the work ethic, Marx makes the error of differentiating between alienated labor and authentic labor. In fact, Baudrillard asserts, *"In this Marxism assists the cunning of capital. It convinces men that they are alienated by the sale of their labor power, thus censoring the much radical hypothesis that they might be alienated as labor power, as the 'inalienable' power of creating value by their labor"* (1975: 31). Baudrillard asserts that labor is a term specifically born under the sign of production. As such, all labor power, whether in a capitalist or socialist economy, is always alienated. He writes, "With German workers the old Protestant ethic of work celebrated in a secular form, its resurrection. Marxism would be that between a religion of the masses and a philosophical theory — not a great deal of difference" (1975: 36). Baudrillard suggests that with production as the doctrine, the opiate of labor can ensure that the proletariat keep the cogs of political economy turning. Even nonwork is easily coopted by the code of production as the negation of work, its repressive desublimation, its mirror. The revolutionary subject no longer resides in the worker, but those out of work, those poor wretches even more alienated than workers themselves. In short, people want work. The radical impetus is to come from elsewhere: in students, people of color, and women (1975: 134). To Baudrillard, labor is no longer axiomatic; its finality has been challenged.

At this point Baudrillard's target is Marx's apparent overreliance on work. Despite its critical analysis of labor, Baudrillard's critique does not explain why certain forms of work appear more alienating than others. Usually, workers who are accorded more autonomy on the job do not react so negatively to their labor. It is uncommon that this particular set of workers take their work home with them. If necessary, they work during their off days (usually weekends) without pay or pecuniary benefits. In contrast, workers with less control over their jobs or who are alienated from human interaction often resist working without pay. In addition, there is a radical separation between workdays and nonworkdays, where nonworkdays become totally associated with leisure or relaxation. In other words, work stops outside of the work place. There may even be a high aversion to any mention of work or its associations. The progression we are suggesting here is that the more alienating the job, the larger its separation from non-work time. Integration between work and life in general is low. This is not to suggest that there is an inherent qualitative superiority of jobs that are more autonomous. However, it suggests that with more control of the labor process, work and everyday life become more congruent. As it is, most workers lacking a critical amount of control over their labor look forward to retirement.

In U.S. schools, because of the currently authoritarian, teacher-centered curriculum, many students resist the very notion of work. They detest classwork, group work, library work, and homework. In Jean Anyon's study of five elementary schools she finds that students trained for the capitalist class practice more self-reliance, are given assignments that challenge creativity, and are in classes that are more intellectually stimulating. Their counterparts, students trained for the working class, practice more procedural drills, are taught to focus on mechanics of learning ("getting it right"), and as a result, struggle against having to do work (1980). She suggests that not only does "schooling in capitalist America" (Bowles and Gintis, 1976) prepare students for different relationships with work, but also that differential amounts of control over student work reflect a similar curve of fulfillment over the work itself. The critical pedagogist Paulo Freire reminds us that "work that is not free ceases to be a fulfilling pursuit and becomes an effective means of dehumanization" (1994: 126). Baudrillard does not account for this gradation of difference among vocations and the element of alienation.

In a reflexive move, Baudrillard charges that Marx's anthropology is caught in its own Western epistemological snares. In fact, this is often the terrorism Marxist ethnographers impose on non-Western subjects. There is no production or its modes and relations, the dialectic movement, scarcity, or surplus in primitive societies. These are all categories associated with political economy and uncritical Marxist anthropologists wreak imperialistic violence on symbolic societies by universalizing these principles. In particular, Baudrillard criticizes Godelier's work on kinship societies where Godelier insists on submitting his analysis to the principles of production. Baudrillard's disgust shines through:

There are no producers; there are no "means of production" and no objective labor, controlled or not. There are no needs and no satisfactions that orient them: this is the old illusion of subsistence economy! . . . Subsistence plus surplus: only the presupposition of production permits this quantitative reduction to additional functions neither of which makes sense in primitive exchange. . . . These acrobatics of the reduction of factors and the remixing "in the dominant" are only conceptual violence. We now know that it is even more destructive than missionaries or venereal disease (1975: 74–77).

Baudrillard takes Godelier and the Marxist paradigm for their insufficient interrogation of their situatedness. In other words, historical materialism is historical. According to Baudrillard, primitive societies espouse no productive concepts and only produce to the point of reciprocal or symbolic exchange, a thesis Baudrillard is opposing to production. Surplus is limited because it institutes uneven power relations by breaking the equilibrious bond of reciprocity. We see here some evidence of the general trend of critiquing the Western world view at the time when *The Mirror of Production* was written. Baudrillard indicts, "The limits of this culture 'critique' are clear: its reflection on itself leads only to the universalization of its own principles" (1975: 89). It is a certain "ethnocentrism of the code" and just as oppressors themselves are not free when oppressing another, a society mistaken about itself is likewise in bondage (p. 107). For Baudrillard, symbolic exchange becomes more important as a point of departure from political economy. The problem of domination is not merely an objectification of the dominated, but an exchange that always involves a violation of reciprocity. The gift requires a counter-gift in order to cancel it and preserve equilibrium. Likewise, production is not only a process of producing something but destroying another (pp. 95–99).

Baudrillard takes his ideas about the gift from Marcel Mauss, later to be systematized by Bataille in symbolic exchange. In a study of Polynesian and Melanesian primitive societies, Mauss writes,

> Many ideas and principles are to be noted in systems of this type. The most important of these spiritual mechanisms is clearly the one which obliges us to make a return gift for a gift received. Refusing to give is like a "declaration of war." . . . No one was free to refuse a present offered to him. Each man and woman tried to outdo the others in generosity. There was a sort of amiable rivalry as to who could give away the greatest number of most valuable presents. . . . The objects are never completely separated from the men who exchange them. . . . Failure to give or receive, like failure to make return gifts, means a loss of dignity. (1967: 5, 40)

Furthermore, these gifts are considered by the people as animate things with power and the spirits of their giver. Later, Bataille appropriates Mauss and creates what he calls a general (or solar) economy (as opposed to political) modeled after the sun and its unwavering gift of energy. Bataille bases his economy on visions of excess, that humans are inclined to waste, expend, and destroy, a model honoring the potlatch Mauss finds in the Polynesian and Melanesian islands (Kellner, 1989: 42).

Bataille's interpretation of the potlatch made a profound impression on Baudrillard, because it signaled for Baudrillard a deep level of reciprocal relations that went beyond the structuralist conception of economic determinism. He links this deep order of reciprocal symbolic exchange to archaic and primitive notions and practices, eventually embracing a symbolic Freud and radicalizing his notion of the death drive that he turns against the whole interpretive machinery of psychoanalysis (Pefanis, 1991). Baudrillard discovers an antieconomic principle of exchange in Bataille's concept of the order of death and its signifying chain: excess, ambivalence, gift, sacrifice, and paroxysm (Pefanis, 1991: 113).

As Baudrillard picks up more speed in his critique of Marxist doctrine, he becomes more dismissive of its potential as a radical alterity. Baudrillard's ideas assume a more apocalyptic tone as he announces the end of certain Marxist categories, like labor, value, and productivity. In what might have been a predictable move, Baudrillard abandons Marxism thenceforth. Kellner considers this "broadside attack and dismissal of Marxism *tout court* unfair and unwarranted." In a deconstructive reading of Baudrillard, Kellner observes that Baudrillard's attempt to eliminate competing theories assumes a capitalistic mode of writing (Kellner, 1989: 53). Baudrillard's pronouncement of the end of political economy does not seem to have sufficient empirical backing. Capital's ability to reproduce itself, circulate, and create new spaces on a global scale contradicts the thesis that capital is on its last legs. The gap between the rich and poor in the United States is still widening and can be attributed to people's relation to the means of production: in late capitalism, finance capital.

Maurice Zeitlin (1989) finds that the U.S. capitalist class maintains its financial domination over the country. He reports that as of 1983, the richest 0.5 percent of all U.S. families, or the "super rich," own 15.3 percent of the net value of all real estate (and 35.6 percent of the commercial real estate), 46.5 percent of the value of all corporate stock, and 77.0 percent of the value of the trust assets owned by all families. The second half of the richest 1 percent, or the "very rich," own another 4.2 percent of all real estate (and 6.5 percent of the commercial real estate), 13.5 percent of the corporate stock, and 5.0 percent of the trust assets. This means that the richest 1 percent of families own over two-fifths of the net wealth owned by every family in the United States. With respect to unearned income (property income, dividends, capital gains, interest, rent, and so forth), or what we will call nonwork, in 1979 people with an adjusted gross income of $20,000–25,000 earned about 90 cents of every dollar whereas those with an adjusted gross income of more than $1 million only earned 14 cents for every dollar they made. This suggests that control of the means of production is not obsolete. Capital is still king. Because the top 1 percent of Americans live in similar affluent neighborhoods, their high property taxes ensure that their children will attend schools with the highest amount of funds and resources, not to mention the cultural network with which they will associate. Zeitlin's findings suggest that work or how we construct pecuniary worth through labor remains as viable today as it has in the past. In addition, Zeitlin contributes to the deconstruction of the myth that poor people are shiftless and lazy. Baudrillard's wholesale rejection of Marxism weakens what is an otherwise insightful problematization of Marxist productive ideology.

In Baudrillard's search for an alternative radical position to Marxism, his turn to symbolic exchange produces a set of books, *Symbolic Exchange and Death* and *Simulations*. In a creative move, Baudrillard outlines a genealogy of three orders of the simulacrum, which, as Kellner (1989: 78) explains, is clearly influenced by Michel Foucault's *Order of Things*. In addition, Baudrillard parallels the evolution of the simulacra with that of the law of value. He writes,

1. *Counterfeit* is the dominant scheme of the "classical" period, from the Renaissance to the industrial revolution.
2. *Production* is the dominant scheme of the industrial era.
3. *Simulation* is the reigning scheme of the current phase that is controlled by the code.

The first order play of simulacrum is based on the natural law of value, that of the second order play on the commercial law of value, and that of the third order on the structural law of value. (1983b: 83)

Before the counterfeit era, the signifier was obligated and always referred to its destined signified. The sign was unambiguous in a caste or cruel society. No peasant could walk around in clothing properly designated for aristocrats. Fashion was nonexistent or heavily restricted. However, during the Renaissance the product counterfeit emancipated the obliged sign. A person could transcend class status to a limited degree by assuming another class's signs. People accomplished this through a natural logic of appearance grounded by the real. During the next stage, the industrial revolution, mass production further emancipated the sign by producing an almost unlimited amount of copies of an original. The series was born under the law of equivalence. An object's existence is owed to its very reproducibility. Labor power itself followed this same logic of producing the equivalent amount of social labor for the series (1983b: 84–86).

In the current era Baudrillard calls simulation, the demarcation between the copy and its original, implodes. In fact, "The very definition of the real becomes: *that of which it is possible to give an equivalent production.* ... At the limit of this process of reproducibility, the real is not only what can be reproduced, but *that which is always already reproduced*. The hyperreal" (1983b: 146–147). The code has not only been realized in its full terror, it has been hyperrealized. Like the DNA double helix, reproduction is doubly simulated to its perfection. Value is accomplished at the structural play of the code as an ideal combinatory model. In

Baudrillard's growing affinity for Nietzsche, Baudrillard cites the German nihilist, "Down with all hypotheses that have allowed the belief in a true world" (1983b: 115). All subjective attempts to capture the real and its companion, the truth, have dissolved into the simulation of the real and the truth. What we get are real effects and truth effects.

In another apocalyptical announcement, Baudrillard declares,

This is the end of labor, the end of production, and the end of political economy.
This is the end of the signifier-signified dialectic that permitted the accumulation of knowledge and meaning, the linear syntagm of cumulative discourse. Simultaneously, this is the end of the use of use value-exchange value dialectic, that which made social accumulation and production possible; the end of the linear dimension of discourse and commodities; the end of the classical era of the sign; and the end of the era of production. (1988c: 127–128)

Effects outrun their causes in the age of the death of linearity and history, an epoch when the model enables the map to generate the territory (Baudrillard, 1983b: 2). In the age of simulation, the reality principle no longer exists; thus the end of the real and its companion, Marxism. The code is complete and engulfs any resistance to it. The alternative is that which is reversible, the indeterminate. It is now the era of complete relativity, of floating signifiers unable to cling onto anything real, and of the inauguration of simulacra. Everything is undecidable as the code neutralizes all values. "Signs ablaze" (Genosko, 1994) and terrorize over social life. Labor becomes a sign among signs. Labor's product no longer maintains any correlation with the actual work that goes into making it. Rather, the type of labor a person does distinguishes her from other laborers as pure sign. There are no means of production because there are no ends of production (Baudrillard, 1988c: 133). In schools, grades do not designate any direct correlation with skill or intellect, but remain, like labor, signs, better yet, simulations of status. They all lie dead in the belly of the code.

Baudrillard's model offers some light on school tests and exams. He writes, "The entire system of communication has passed from that of a syntactically complex language structure to a binary sign system of question/answer — of perpetual test. Now tests and referenda are, we know, perfect forms of simulation: the answer is called forth by the question, it is designated in advance" (1983: 116–117). This implies that school testing communicates very little outside of the code's general terrorism. The educational system applies tests if only to simulate that students have learned something real, that something valuable and meaningful has been communicated to them. In actuality tests only testify to the death of facts; therefore nothing needs to be communicated as such. Tests only serve to point out the general failure of the whole educational system to provide students with a meaningful experience. Testing is more of an instrument to simulate control: a control that is empty because power is now dead.

At this stage in his career, Baudrillard turns his cultural critique toward a dizzying perspective where aleatory forces dominate over social (this is dead, too) life. We could not help feeling slightly inebriated as we read Baudrillard's books from this period. We offer several commentaries. First, Baudrillard's semiological idealism seems to lead him to a certain form of sign fetishism (Kellner, 1989: 62, 100). Second, he uncritically underplays the role of manipulation in the media by suggesting that we are somehow beyond the "society of spectacle," that the mass wants spectacle. As such, Baudrillard's model lacks the power to deconstruct political interests and their sources. Baudrillard leaves control of social processes in the hands of a mystified and disembodied nonentity. By leaving out the actors and architects of policies and control of political discourse, Baudrillard cannot hold particular groups of people accountable for their actions. Meanwhile, Ronald Reagan, Pete Wilson, and Newt Gingrich have a field day. On this point, we prefer Edward Herman and Noam Chomsky's (1993) manipulation theory wherein they expose the media's corporate filters and deconstruct how the media "manufactures consent." By using a framework that takes into consideration social relations and agents and their interests, what we previously referred to as school dropouts may be more accurately termed "push outs" (Fine, 1991).

Third, although the mass's silence, as Baudrillard explains it in *In the Shadow of the Silent Majorities*, may be read as their vengeance in their refusal to participate or vote on the positions being offered, it can be interpreted another way: the general alienation of a mass of people from the political (due) process in the interest of the few. This motivated neglect, of which the mass is complicitous, has real consequences: lack of control over decisions that affect the direction of their lives. This is not to suggest a homogeneous oppressive class (the elite) and a monolithic oppressed class (the mass) of people. Issues of race, class, gender, and culture interlock the indices of privilege and disprivilege. Last, Baudrillard provides no useful model for collective agency or a position of solidarity. In a vertiginous world where people are hyperindividuated, Baudrillard articulates no hope for political projects. What we can look forward to is the perpetual spiral of simulations. Meanwhile, suffering and pain continue.

The metaphysical turn in Baudrillard's writing is clearly the dominant trope that he will maintain hereafter. Not as didactic as his previous works, this period's production concentrates more on effracting conventional discourse. Baudrillard relies more heavily on the poetics of language and less on systematicity or rigor. Having announced the death of multiple key concepts (labor: no longer axiomatic, political economy: the real has been absorbed into the hyperreal, the social: has lost its specificity, and so forth), Baudrillard continues his search for a transgressive theory of cyber culture.

In another book from this period, Baudrillard's victims are psychoanalysis and feminism. In *Seduction*, Baudrillard charges that psychoanalysis is the psychological cognate of production. Obsessed with the production of latent meanings in sexual discourse, psychoanalysis follows its sibling with a political economy of the body. According to Baudrillard, Freudian psychoanalysis has assumed far too much influence, its libidinal economy gaining finality status. Its descendants in Luce Irigaray and others have made destiny out of anatomy. As a theory of appearances, seduction challenges the anatomical depth of psychoanalysis (Baudrillard, 1979: 9). Emphasizing passion and gaming, seduction ruptures Freud's value driven desire, "the body as the material infrastructure of desire" (p. 34). One does not have far to look to find energy as a mode of production of the unconscious and pleasure as either a saving or surplus (Gane, 1991a: 116). The circulation of desire is mimesis of the circulation of capital.

Baudrillard claims that Freud's story is only that, a story. Baudrillard posits the opposite story, that women have been dominant this whole time. Sexual repression, fear of castration, penis envy have all been instituted by men to control women's power, their reversibility. Ironically, men have created their own solution to this problematic through sexual liberation and the male as the bringer of this revolution. However, Baudrillard maintains that women were never oppressed or alienated. This is a male story (1979: 15–20). Sexuality is the masculine's narrative, seduction the feminine's game. However, this must not be confused with the correspondence in sexuality between the feminine and a particular sex, but the feminine as the transversal form of sex, an indeterminate sex (Gane, 1991a: 149). However, Baudrillard admits that women "being closer to the effects to this other, hidden mirror (with which they shroud their image and body) are also closer to the effects of seduction. Men, by contrast, have depth, but no secrets; hence their power and fragility" (1979: 68). Offering seduction as the alternative to or destruction of production, Baudrillard announces yet another set of deaths: meaning, sexuality, and hence, sexism. Feminine theory's problem all along has been its overemphasis on sexual oppression. With the death of the sexual, sexism also will perish.

As a play and challenge to the artifice, seduction welcomes the sexual objectification of women. Baudrillard explains,

Our entire morality condemns the construction of the female as a sex object by the facial and bodily arts. . . . In opposition to all these pious discourses, we must again praise the sex object; for it bears, in the sophistication of appearances, something of a challenge to the naive order of the world and sex; and it, and it alone, escapes the realm of production (though one might like to believe it subjected to the latter) and returns to that of seduction. . . . The feminine was always the effigy of this ritual, and there is a frightful confusion in wanting to de-sanctify it as a cult *object* in order to turn it into a *subject* of production, or in wanting to rescue it from artifice in order to return it to its own "natural" desires. (1979: 92)

In opposition to most feminist theories, Baudrillard suggests that the discourse on women's subjecthood be debunked as another male attempt to institute power over women. With power being everywhere, this only signals that it is nowhere. That is, in response to Foucault, power's ubiquity is its own death (Baudrillard, 1983b). Only objects are seductive through their play on literality and surface; subjects are productive in their irreversible metaphoricalness and depth. Objects consume (in its extreme sense: consummation), whereas subjects create surplus we call meaning (Gane, 1991a: 118). Once again, Baudrillard advances his search for the pure object. The objectification of women's bodies as sex objects implicates, among other things, pornographic activity. Gane clarifies, "It is not sexuality on display in pornography, as many think; it is the absorption of reality into hyperreality. This accounts for so-called voyeurism; it is precisely the breakdown of the sexual scene and the eruption of the obscene. The sexual appears so close to the subject that it confounds itself. It is the end of illusion and the end of imagination" (1991a: 152). To Baudrillard, pornography is sex that is more than sex: hypersex. There is no need to imagine anything; it is all there for you to see, right down to the pores on the skin. "It is the more visible than the visible: the obscene" (Baudrillard, 1990: 55). It is seductive, nothing to be desired, all to be objectified. Psychoanalysis started the big bang that instituted sexuality. It has since imploded, or reversed itself, into the big squeeze. Sexuality has collapsed under its own gravity, unable to supply the energy it needed to survive. Seduction is the void that remains because, as Anthony Wilden might suggest, it is "a dissent of a higher logical type than that to which it is opposed" (Baudrillard, 1988c: 122).

Like symbolic exchange, seduction is a form of gift. One seduces in order to be seduced. One is seduced and is obligated to seduce in return. Seduction is the willingness to perpetuate the game and its stakes to maximal intensity. The pervert is the one who tries to fix the game and stabilize it under a law in order to render it predictable and irreversible. Seduction works by rules and ruses that remain unspoken (Baudrillard, 1988c: 127). Baudrillard clarifies that games are not centered on contingency but obligations and seduction (p. 143). Although seduction is the absence of predictability, it maintains a patterned randomness (p. 138), much like Mandelbrot's chaos theory. The only people oppressed and repressed are those who fail to be seduced.

Baudrillard's attempt to seduce readers into finding a radical departure in his theory of appearances brings into question the whole construction of sexuality, men's hegemonic control over women's bodies, and the tenets of psychoanalysis as an insufficient framework for feminist theory. Because of the exclusivity of his metaphysics in explaining material relations, Baudrillard makes the mistake of assuming that social life will change because we create different stories about men and women. Educators will find it hard to liberate the educational system, its workers, and its students by talking differently about gender relations. Some changes may result from changing the myths we tell one another. However, Freire's reminder that revolutions do not occur just because we create them in our own minds may help ameliorate Baudrillard's otherwise provocative yet antiproductive formulation. A radical theory must have its accompanying action, or theory degrades into mere verbalism. In turn, this action must be directed at objective changes or material relations. Without this crucial pairing, stories may become the opiate of the masses. This ultimately is what is missing in Baudrillard's theory. Seduction offers little, if any, heuristics for action.

Despite its claims to transcend sexuality and sexism, seduction maintains a sexist line of reasoning. Its themes of appearance, objectification of women's bodies, and women as seductresses mystify gender oppression. Baudrillard chooses to eschew the materiality of sexism by creating an elaborate scheme that circumvents his own complicity as a man in sexist relations. For example, take one of Baudrillard's analyses of a story. In the film and novel *The Collector*, after the female character resists her captor for many days, she finally decides to seduce him. In response, the protagonist shuns her and undresses and takes pornographic pictures of her. She becomes ill, falls into a coma, and dies. He places her pictures in his butterfly scrapbook. He buries her in the back yard and the cycle is foreshadowed by his search for a new woman to kidnap. Baudrillard's analysis goes as such:

A need to be loved, but an inability to be seduced. When, finally, the woman is seduced (it is enough that she wants to seduce him) he cannot accept his victory: he prefers to see it as a sexual malediction and punishes her. It is not a question of impotence (it is never a question of impotence). He prefers the possessive spell cast by a collection of dead objects — the dead sex object being as beautiful as a butterfly with florescent wings — to the seduction of a living being who would demand his love in return. (1988c: 122–123)

The focus of Baudrillard's analysis is not the female character's oppression: the forceful kidnap, the psychological torment, and then her death and its objectification. Baudrillard's emphasis is on the protagonist's failure to seduce as if he were the one who has suffered in the exchange. Baudrillard does not problematize the obvious violence that the protagonist perpetrates on her and the violence Baudrillard simulates by neglecting the reality principle.

Indeed, in another piece, "The Obscenario," Baudrillard explains an event involving a feminist, a man inflicted with polio, and himself. During a lecture on seduction, the woman challenges what she considers Baudrillard's sexist discourse. During the exchange, the woman slips the handicapped man's cigarette in and out of his mouth so that he could smoke the butt. Baudrillard labels this event as a sign that the woman is raping him through this "poor [unassuming] wreck." Her revenge was sweet and there was nothing Baudrillard could do about it (Kellner, 1989: 183; Gane, 1991a: 61). Whether the woman was intending to seduce Baudrillard, we cannot tell. What we receive is Baudrillard's imaginary. Yet, if depth is dead, how is it that Baudrillard is able to read into this event when seduction places emphasis on the literal? Does the woman's action literally mean what it signifies for Baudrillard? It would be ridiculous to assume that Baudrillard's actions and description of the event have no structural meaning. Baudrillard's irresponsible use of "rape" returns the reading to the structures of domination. He strips rape of its problems of violence and power. In spite of Baudrillard's desperate attempts to transcend sexuality, he re-presents the event in a sexual-sexist manner with allusions to fornication as she slips the butt in and out of the invalid's mouth.

The Collector is reminiscent of the fable, "Beauty and the Beast," in which the female representative, Beauty, falls in love with her oppressor, the Beast, or the male representative. In light of Baudrillard's analysis of *The Collector*, he would have us believe that as long as seduction is exchanged or returned, women should ignore their beastly counterparts' violence toward them. That is, women like men who mistreat them as long as they are being seduced: the male's imaginary. Baudrillard offers this explanation for the female character's decision to seduce and its outcome: "Perhaps the price paid by beauty and seduction is to be confined and put to death, because they are too dangerous, and because one will never be able to render her what she has given. One can then only reward her with her death" (1988c: 123). Murder as reward? According to Baudrillard, women do not want to be respected or given sovereignty; they want to be seduced. Our current conditions do not call for the cliché of love; it yearns for love that is more than love, love to the nth power: seduction. Baudrillard asserts that love is hot, whereas seduction is cool. Baudrillard's apparent romanticism is confounded by his Nietzschean aristocracy. In fact, the female character's decision to seduce can be explained another way.

In her psychoanalysis of "Story of O," Jessica Benjamin (1988) describes O's quest for subjectivity. In the story, O's masters give her specific instructions to fulfill their will and sexual desires. Using Bataille's Hegelian dialectics of erotic violation, Benjamin explains O's submission as a vicarious attempt to gain subjectivity through her masters' recognition of her as an object: albeit an alienated subjectivity. In turn, the masters' privilege is sustained by O's recognition of her masters' subjective power over her. This points out the problem of submission as well as domination. Benjamin recognizes O's quest for subjective agency inscribed by the discourse of gender domination. Although her analysis does not devote enough attention to the masters' actual violence, Benjamin's insertion of women's participation in their own oppression successfully articulates some of women's unconscious motivations. By focusing on this second element, Benjamin highlights the moments of agency in the complicitous act of women's submission to men.

Consider, too, Baudrillard's explanations of racism. Admittedly, there is a conceptual brilliance in Baudrillard's articulation of violent otherness. He writes: "Racism does not exist so long as the other remains Other, so long as the Stranger remains foreign. It comes into existence when the other becomes merely different — that is to say, dangerously similar. This is the moment when the inclination to keep the other at a distance comes into being" (1993: 129).

Baudrillard notes that racism is an obsession with becoming other. It is a "temptation at the heart of every structural system: the temptation to fetishize difference" (1993: 129). Racism in this view becomes "variations in the order of signs." According to Baudrillard, the Spanish massacred the Indians of the United States because the Indians failed to understand difference. When they allowed themselves to be part of a negotiable otherness, Indians began to practice self-immolation and allowed themselves to die. We disagree with Baudrillard that racism is mere "abreaction to the psychodrama of difference" and that it is an issue that is mainly consigned to the empire of signs. We do not agree that the Indians' "strange collusion in their own extermination represented their only way of keeping the secret of otherness" (p. 133). We do agree with Baudrillard that the European claim to universality located within the humanist virtues of modernity is an underlying feature of racism and that the European colonizers concealed their contempt for and disgust at the Other under the guise of altruism. To claim that the Indians' cruel human sacrifices and alleged religious fanaticism made the Spaniards ashamed of the emptiness of their own Christian faith (and their secular faith in gold and commerce), and provoked them to exterminate the Indians, is, we argue, ludicrous in light of the greater fanaticism and brutality historically detailed in the history of Spanish colonial Catholicism.

We are profoundly disturbed at Baudrillard's suggestion for confronting the racism that has been created on a global basis by universal structural differentiation: to be more racist than racist. Genosko summarizes Baudrillard's position thus:

The primitive societies of the future can only escape extermination if their alterity is essential, radical and singular. This is the utopia which may exist after structural differentiation has been destroyed. Even so, those who carry out such exterminations are also condemned, according to Baudrillard, in the long term by their own systems of extermination. Baudrillard's effort here is to push racism to its extreme in order to destroy it. In order to accomplish this critical task, it is necessary to be more racist than racist (the standard Baudrillardian formula of more x than x remains the same), but without knowledge of the consequences or at least the willingness to turn a "blind eye" to them. In the short term, the effects will be disastrous. In the structural game of differences, all differences are close and nothing is truly exotic; there is neither an Absolute Other nor an incomparable non-structural Difference. These are the dirty secrets of *exotisme*: anti-feminism, anti-egalitarianism, hyperracism and anti-colonialism, but the last only by default. (1994: 135)

Baudrillard's metaphysics reaches its latest apogee in his book, *Fatal Strategies*. Claiming once again that a radical strategy is one that is excentric, Baudrillard aims to replace the revolutionary theory based on the subject with one that is based on the banality of the object. It should be made clear from the outset what Baudrillard means by this. Mimicking Alfred Jarry's pataphysics, Baudrillard clarifies, "when I speak of the object and its fatal strategies I speak of people and their inhuman strategies" (cited in Gane, 1991a: 174). Rejecting what he considers is the banal modernist theory of the determinable subject, Baudrillard inaugurates the revenge of the object, or that which is more banal than banal: fatal. The object strikes back! In a giddy universe of empty forms, Baudrillard outlines his fatal strategy: "The world is not dialectical — it is sworn to extremes, not to equilibrium, sworn to radical antagonism, not to reconciliation or synthesis. This is also the principle of Evil, as expressed in the "evil genie" of the object, in the ecstatic form of the pure object and in its strategy, victorious over that of the subject" (Baudrillard, 1990: 7).

Baudrillard's break from Marxism is completed in his announcement of the subject's death. In fact, Baudrillard contends that the object (Marx's commodity) may have always been the dominant matrix. Like the black hole's event horizon, the subject has passed across the threshold from where it cannot return. This is the event horizon and the horizon of the event, the "pure event" (1990: 17). Today's objective logic swallows everything, even the enlightened subject, and reproduces it as discharge, as pure loss. At this point in Baudrillard's extremism, it is surprising that he does not use the theoretical particle, tachyon. According to theoretical science, tachyon is a particle that exceeds the speed of light. Therefore, tachyons reach their destination (for example, people) even before it registers them. We only feel the spatial effects of tachyons.

According to Baudrillard, we live in cancerous times but there is nothing in this to deplore. During virulent periods, the pedagogical model is the terrorist. To Baudrillard, a self-proclaimed theoretical terrorist, terrorism represents one of the ultimate indeterminate acts. He writes, "We are all hostages, and we are all terrorists. This circuit has replaced that other one of masters and slaves, the dominating and the dominated, the exploiters and the exploited. Gone is the constellation of the slave and the proletarian: from now on it is the hostage and the terrorist. Gone is the constellation of alienation; from now on it is that of terror. it is worse than the one it replaces, but at least it liberates us from liberal nostalgia and the ruses of history. It is the era of the transpolitical that is beginning" (1990: 39).

Baudrillard implies that, like the terrorist, students should take their teachers for hostage and vice versa because it is better to take people as hostage than be taken for one (1990: 40). Terrorists should be appreciated for their random acts of violence, their purposeless goals, and their extremism, a truly fatal strategy patterned after the pure object. There is no meaning whatsoever in schooling but there is everything to challenge.

Kellner's criticism of this stage in Baudrillard's writing is clear and to the point. Kellner writes,

Was his (Baudrillard) word processor (if he has one) taking over his thought processes? Or was his television set controlling his imagination? . . . Desiring sovereignty, he projects sovereignty onto objects. Desiring revenge, he projects revenge onto objects. Supremely ironic, Baudrillard projects objective irony onto objects. Desiring to become a destiny and fatality himself — recall Nietzsche for the psychological roots of this peculiar lust — he ascribes destiny and fatality to objects, and conjures up a fatal universe. Increasingly indifferent to the fate of society and his fellow human beings, Baudrillard ascribes indifference to that supreme object of objects, the masses. Himself impatient, he ascribes impatience to the masses and to the object world. Losing critical energy and growing apathetic himself, he ascribes apathy and inertia to the universe. Imploding into entropy, Baudrillard attributes implosion and entropy to the experience of (post)modernity. (1989: 167, 180)

What can one add to such a critique? If we are to salvage anything from Baudrillard's latest ruminations, it is this: to avoid the ludicrous implications of his theory of the object and against his insistence on the death of metaphors, we may read figuratively his theory of the object's revenge as the strategy of those who have been historically objectified: workers, people of color, women, gay women and men, and so forth. To revolutionize social life, we may reconstitute meaning from the objectified's perspective. To recreate the subject, Baudrillard's pronouncement of the death of the subject becomes the death of the subject *as we have known him*: the banal bourgeois Western male. Knowing this may help us in the task of rethinking the subject as a social agent of transformation.

We agree with Kellner and Best (in press) that the object is not triumphant over the subject in our present culture of the simulacra. Our present social organization is best conceptualized as an intensification of capitalist modernity rather than a wholly new Order of the Hyperreal. Kellner and Best are correct in arguing that Baudrillard's society of generalized economy is an extension of what Kellner has termed "technocapitalism" (1989).

It is at this point that we applaud the attempt by Guy Debord and the situationists to move from the sphere of culture to the arena of everyday life when fashioning strategies of *détournment* in the service of social and political justice. According to Macdonald:

The Situationist notion of cultural politics, unlike some contemporary postmodern arguments for textual politics, clearly understands the limitations that a purely cultural strategy encounters. The point is not to *see politics as a text* or cultural work (and by that very fact, assume that textual play is political play), but to *make politics a textual site* for the creation of freedom and play. This latter emphasis recognizes that while there are important connections between cultural struggles and political practices, agency in one sphere must ultimately be translated into the terms of the other if there is to be a realization of that cultural potentiality. (1995: 107)

Debord's concept of agency is closer to that of Paolo Freire (1994) and suggests a consciously articulable form of praxis grounded in critical self-reflexivity. Although such a praxiological activity begins as micropolitical discourse, and cultural arrangements, it links such struggle to the arena of macropolitical structures.

Insofar as critical pedagogy must be concerned with relationships of power and privilege, including those that specifically structure the relationships of race, class, and gender, it appears that an ethical ideal of social justice is needed, of which little adequate account can be found in Baudrillard's work. In addition, account is needed of the conditions under which a praxis of liberation might be constructed. Consider the absolute cynicism from which Baudrillard articulates his idea of the social, and you will better understand his idea of the dilemma critical educators face: "As for the social, one could say that its obscenity has fully ripened today, like that of the cadaver of which one cannot rid oneself, or more precisely which enters that accursed stage of putrescence. It is at this point, before withering and assuming the beauty of death, that the body passes through a truly obscene stage and must at all cost be conjured and exorcised, since it no longer represents anything, no longer has any name, and its unspeakable contamination invades everything" (1990b: 187).

For Baudrillard, the social is the realm of the obscene; it flows into everything; it assists in the decomposition of the real and the violent submergence of the social into the real. For Baudrillard, there is nothing redeemable about the social, nothing that is worth saving: "Beyond, or short of this terrorist and hyperreal sociality, of this omnipresent blackmail of communication, is there a good substance of the social, an ideality of social intercourse which can and must be liberated? The answer is clearly no: the balance or harmony of a certain social contract has disappeared on the horizon of history, and we are doomed to this diaphanous obscenity of change" (1990b: 190–191).

Seen in this light, we have problems with Baudrillard's injunction against revolutionary praxis and his call for hyperconformity, for absorbing the simulations of the media as a means of simultaneously escaping their terror, and for resisting their regime of truth. The semilogical structure is overwhelmingly impervious to subversion in Baudrillard's account. There is little attention given to how signs are resisted and transformed. The regime of signs is seemingly invincible. Unlike Baudrillard, we do not believe signs to have a life of their own but believe they are connected as much to class struggle as they are to the totalitarian — bureaucratic machineries of state power. We believe that signs must be defamiliarized, decentered, and unsettled, but social relations must also be transformed as part of the struggle over the construction of social subjectivities and the struggle toward socialism. We believe that critical pedagogies are not fully constituted and fully delineated domains of struggle but possess the potential to overthrow the bourgeois state.

We are sympathetic to Felix Guattari's concept of a micropolitics of desire, a form of political struggle that begins from the plurality of partial struggles, a struggle that attempts neither to represent the masses nor to interpret their struggles. It is a micropolitics of desire that does not locate its authority in a transcendent object; its sole object of antagonism is not the bourgeois state. Rather, as Guattari (1995) notes, it centers itself "on a multiplicity of objectives, within the immediate reach of the most diverse social groupings" (p. 230). Centrally ordered movements releasing the serialized masses into the streets are not part of Guattari's revolutionary project. Rather, "the connection of a multiplicity of molecular desires . . . would catalyze challenges on a large scale" (pp. 230–231).

Such a project does not work from an "ideal *unity* which *represents and mediates multiple* interests" (Guattari, 1995: 231). It works instead from a "*univocal multiplicity* of desires whose process secretes its own systems of tracking and regulation" (p. 231). There is no unique objective, no totalizing unity. Rather than grouping the masses according to standardized objectives, there exists the univocality of the masses' desire. We need to recognize that modern fascist democracies depend upon the historical transversity of the machines of desire. A micropolitics of desire sets itself against the totalitarian chemistry of fascism through micropolitical anti-fascist struggle. This is the urgent struggle educators must undertake now and in the years to come. Baudrillard can give us some of the theoretical tools for launching such a struggle, but it is up to us to forge these tools into weapons of war in the fight against capitalist machineries of domination.

NOTE

1. "Prestation," in a footnote by Mark Poster (trans.) "indicates a feeling of obligation to an irrational code of social behavior."

REFERENCES

Anyon, J. (1980). "School Class and the Hidden Curriculum of Work." *Journal of Education*, 162: 25-48.
Batailles, G. (1985). *Visions of Excess: Selected Writings, 1927–1939*. A. Stoekel, with C. R. Lovitt and D. M. Ledie (Trans.). Minneapolis: University of Minnesota Press.
Baudrillard, J. (1994). *Simulacra and Simulations*. Ann Arbor: University of Michigan Press.
Baudrillard, J. (1993). *The Transparency of Evil: Essays on Extreme Phenomena*. J. Benedict (Trans.). London: Verso.
Baudrillard, J. (1990). *Fatal Strategies*. New York: Semiotext.
Baudrillard, J. (1988a). The System of Objects. In Mark Poster (Ed.), *Jean Baudrillard: Selected Writings*. Stanford, Calif.: Stanford University Press.
Baudrillard, J. (1988b). Consumer Society. In Mark Poster (Ed.), *Jean Baudrillard: Selected Writings*. Stanford, Calif.: Stanford University Press.
Baudrillard, J. (1988c). Symbolic Exchange and Death. In Mark Poster (Ed.), *Jean Baudrillard: Selected Writings*. Stanford, Calif.: Stanford University Press.
Baudrillard, J. (1987). *Forget Foucault*. New York: Semiotext.
Baudrillard, J. (1983a). *In the Shadow of the Silent Majorities*. New York: Semiotext.
Baudrillard, J. (1983b). *Simulations*. New York: Semiotext.
Baudrillard, J. (1981). *For a Critique of the Political Economy of the Sign*. St. Louis, Mo.: Telos Press.
Baudrillard, J. (1979). *Seduction*. New York: St. Martin's Press.
Baudrillard, J. (1975). *The Mirror of Production*. St. Louis, Mo.: Telos Press.
Benjamin, J. (1988). *The Bonds of Love: Psychoanalysis, Feminism and the Problem of Domination*. New York: Pantheon.
Best, S. (1995). The Commodification of Reality and the Reality of Commodification: Baudrillard, Debord, and Postmodern Theory. In Doug Kellner (Ed.), *Baudrillard: A Critical Reader*. Stanford, Calif.: Stanford University Press.
Bowles, S., and Gintis, H. (1976). *Schooling in Capitalist America: Education Reform and the Contradictions of Economic Life*. London: Routledge and Kegan Paul.
Cook, D. (1995). Symbolic Exchange in Hyperreality. In Doug Kellner (Ed.), *Baudrillard: A Critical Reader*. Stanford, Calif.: Stanford University Press.
Fine, M. (1991). *Framing Dropouts*. New York: State University of New York Press.
Freire, P. (1994). *Pedagogy of the Oppressed*. New York: Continuum.
Gane, M. (1991a). *Baudrillard's Bestiary: Baudrillard and Culture*. London: Routledge.

Gane, M. (1991b). *Baudrillard: Critical and Fatal Theory*. London: Routledge.
Genosko, G. (1994). *Baudrillard and Signs: Signification Ablaze*. London: Routledge.
Giroux, H. (1993). *Border Crossings*. London: Routledge.
Gottdiener, M. (1995). The System of Objects and the Commodification of Everyday Life: The Early Baudrillard. In Doug Kellner (Ed.), *Baudrillard: A Critical Reader*. Stanford, Calif.: Stanford University Press.
Guattari, F. (1995). *Chaosophy: An Ethico-Aesthetic Paradigm*. P. Bains and J. Pefanis (Trans.). Bloomington: Indiana University Press.
Herman, E., and Chomsky, N. (1993). *Manufacturing Consent*. New York: Pantheon.
Jameson, F. (1993). Postmodernism and the Consumer Society. In E. Ann Kaplan (Ed.), *Postmodernism and its Discontents*. London: Verso.
Kellner, D. (1995). Introduction: Jean Baudrillard in the Fin-de-Millenium. In Doug Kellner (Ed.), *Baudrillard: A Critical Reader*. Stanford, Calif.: Stanford University Press.
Kellner, D. (1989). *Jean Baudrillard*. Stanford, Calif.: Stanford University Press.
Kellner, D., and Best, S. (in Press). *The Postmodern Imagination*.
Kroker, A., and Cook, D. (1986). *The Postmodern Scene: Excremental Culture and Hyper-Aesthetics*. New York: St. Martin's Press.
Macdonald, B. (1995). From the Spectacle to Unitary Urbanism: Reassessing Situationalist Theory. *Rethinking Marxism*, 8(2): 89–111.
Mauss, M. (1967). *The Gift*. New York: W. W. Norton.
Pefanis, J. (1991). *Heterology and the Postmodern: Bataille, Baudrillard and Lyotard*. Durham, N.C.: Duke University Press.
Poster, M. (1995). Critical Theory and Technoculture: Habermas and Baudrillard. In Doug Kellner (Ed.), *Baudrillard: A Critical Reader*. Stanford, Calif.: Stanford University Press.
Tseelon, E. (1995). Fashion and Signification in Baudrillard. In Doug Kellner (Ed.), *Baudrillard: A Critical Reader*. Stanford, Calif.: Stanford University Press.
Zeitlin, M. (1989). *The Large Corporation and Contemporary Classes*. New Brunswick, N.J.: Rutgers University Press.

10

Chantal Mouffe: Pedagogy for Democratic Citizenship
Majia Holmer Nadesan and C. Alejandra Elenes

Chantal Mouffe is a poststructuralist political theorist who is perhaps best known for her advocacy of democratic socialism. Against such classical liberals as John Rawls and against the communitarians, Mouffe argues for the creation of a new political frontier "capable of giving a real impulse to democracy" (1993: 6). As we will demonstrate in this chapter, Mouffe's contribution to this political frontier centers around the role of the individual in democratic politics. Unlike Rawls, who presupposes a universal human capacity for democratic citizenship, and unlike the communitarians who sublate the individual to the community, Mouffe argues that political theorists need to attend to the development of a "radical democratic citizenship" (p. 6). Mouffe sees her project as critical given the state of liberal democratic politics as illustrated by the growing marginalization of many social groups and by the narrowing of options for political representation. Moreover, she contends that the dominant approaches to the current crisis, communitarianism and liberal individualism, are ill equipped to articulate (in theory and practice) the form of democratic politics she endorses.

We believe that Mouffe's view of pluralist democratic politics and, in particular, her view of radical democratic citizenship have important implications for pedagogical theory and practice. In this chapter, we explore the new political frontier of which Mouffe speaks and the role that individual citizenship plays in its articulation and daily enactment. As we will explain, this discussion requires detailed examination of Mouffe's poststructuralist ontology of society, individual agency, and democratic citizenship. After presenting Mouffe's approach to democratic politics, we will explore how critical pedagogy might incorporate Mouffe's insights about subject formation and its relation to democratic citizenship in its efforts to enhance student empowerment and social responsibility.

Given the complexity of Mouffe's approach, we have organized this chapter into the following sections. First, we will explain how Mouffe's theoretical framework, articulation theory, accounts for how individual subjective identities emerge from social discourses. Second, we will explain how Mouffe uses articulation theory to develop an ontology of democratic citizenship. Within this section we will first describe Mouffe's model of pluralist democracy as it is informed by the twin organizing principles (that is, nodal points) of freedom and equality. We will then describe the importance Mouffe places on development of individual subjectivities commensurable with these organizing principles. Accordingly, we focus discussion on her understanding of reflexive agency, a will to act, and respect for adversarial relations. Finally, in the third section we discuss how Mouffe's theory of democratic citizenship might inform pedagogical practice.

ARTICULATION THEORY

Mouffe's social ontology is most fully articulated in her 1985 book with Ernesto Laclau, *Hegemony and Socialist Strategy*. In this book, Laclau and Mouffe deconstruct the Marxist project and rearticulate an approach they term post-Marxist. In this section, we draw upon key terms from this text including articulation, element, moment, and antagonism to unpack their framework for understanding the constitution of social identities.

Laclau and Mouffe (1985) argue that the meanings attributed to linguistic terms, material practices, and subjective identities emerge from the productive power of social discourses. Following Wittgenstein, social discourses are understood as sedimented language practices, that is, games, that render social phenomena intelligible (Laclau & Mouffe, 1985: 108). Each social discourse is delimited by constitutive rules that govern the ways in which that discourse produces meaning. Each social discourse constitutes meanings for terms and practices and produces meaningful social identities for individuals. Social discourses position individuals as subjects (for example, Anglo, female, middle-class) and, in so doing, produce the material conditions and forms of their constitution. However, as we explain, social discourses are not stable and no discourse can completely dominate the social field. Laclau and Mouffe address the concrete processes whereby discourses produce and are transformed by meaning production with the idea of articulation.

Articulation refers specifically to the concrete process whereby social meanings (that is, identities) are constituted, as discursive practices link relational elements. Relational elements (that is, differences) can be linguistic or nonlinguistic signifiers (for example, terms, objects, or practices). Relational elements lack meaning in themselves. They become meaningful only when articulated by a social discourse that enacts their transformation into moments. For instance, the relational elements of worker and manager and the social practices (also relational elements) that determine the organization of the labor process could be articulated in any number of ways. However, for more than 50 years, the discourse of scientific management has dominated the social field within manufacturing in the United States by largely determining what these elements mean. This discourse has material consequences because it predicates the organization of work and, relatedly, the work experiences of those individuals interpellated as workers and those interpellated as managers as moments within the discourse. In effect, an element or signifier (for example, word or behavior) achieves significance as it is discursively constituted as a moment within a particular social discourse.

Laclau and Mouffe's discussion of social elements may lead the reader to question their source. If social elements lack meaning outside of their position as a moment of discourse, then where do they come from? This is an important question because it points to the supplementary nature of meaning. Social discourses are not things but are processes, and every discourse bears the traces of other social discourses. As sets of rules about the production of meaning, discourses are embedded in local social, historical, and cultural contexts. Consequently, a particular discourse, say the discourse of Greenpeace, necessarily draws upon social elements (terms, material signifiers, and so forth) from older discourses and from other, extant discourses (for example, discourses of evolution, secular humanism, animal rights). Accordingly, social elements never really exist as free-standing entities. Laclau and Mouffe simply delineate element from moment to make the point that a particular signifier only achieves significance in the specific social historical context of its production; that is, within the context of its discursive articulation.

For example, take the element homeless. One could trace this element over time to identify its various articulations as moments within specific, historically embedded discourses. Today, this element could be articulated within a Marxist critique of capital, where it would be transformed in relation to its moment or space within that discourse or it could be articulated within a neoconservative discourse, where its space will mean differently. Because an element can never be restricted to a particular discourse, the transformation of elements into moments is always incomplete because their culmination would signal universal fixation of meaning production and, concomitantly, the social system's crystallization.

Lacking necessity or completion, the fixation of discursive articulation is, therefore, fundamentally contingent. Every articulation could be otherwise (Laclau & Mouffe, 1985: 111): "There is no single underlying principle fixing — and hence constituting — the whole field of differences. The irresoluble interiority/exteriority tension is the condition of any social practice: necessity only exists as a partial limitation of the field of contingency. It is in this terrain, where neither a total interiority nor a total exteriority is possible, that the social is constituted. . . . *This field of identities which never manage to be fully fixed, is the field of overdetermination.*" Although the idea of society or any stable identity is rejected, this ontology of difference does not reject partial fixations of the social, partial transformations of elements into moments. Indeed, social discourses themselves rely on some partial fixation of the rules of meaning production.

Those discursive points of partial fixation that manage to arrest the flow of differences by constructing (however incompletely and temporarily) a center are called nodal points (Laclau & Mouffe, 1985: 112). Every discourse possesses a nodal point that serves as the pivotal term affecting how meaning is produced within the discourse (for example, by dictating relations of metaphor and metonymy). As privileged signifiers, nodal points limit the productivity of the signifying chain, thereby enabling communication and the institutionalization of such social discourses as patriarchy, bureaucracy, capitalism, and so forth. An example of nodal points might be the law of the father within a patriarchical discourse or the omniscience of management within the discourse of classical management. Patriarchy and classical management are hegemonic social discourses that for many years monopolized interpretations of such social elements as men, women, workers, and managers. However institutionalized, they are always subject to subversion by the field of discourse "which overflows it" (p. 113).

Although nodal points partially fix the productivity of a particular discourse and the social field, they are ultimately unable to prevent competing discourses from emerging and from rearticulating social elements. This is because Laclau and Mouffe (1985) claim that the meaning of every element (for example, linguistic category and, concomitantly, material practice) is ultimately overdetermined by heterogeneous language practices. Thus, no single complex of language practices, that is, no discourse can fully determine what a particular signifier (that is, element) means. For example, today woman serves as the signifying juncture of numerous competing discourses, each of which attempts to provide a positive space for the term (that is, a moment) within a particular chain of signifiers. However, it is impossible to fix this space across time and space because no single discourse can exhaust what woman signifies; the element itself is infused with the otherness of competing meaning formations. The element, therefore, cannot be fixed but depends upon its appropriation by each act of communication or articulation. Consequently, individuals who occupy the subject position woman are faced with the ambiguities and possibilities that stem from the element's instability.

Antagonism refers to the "final impossibility of any stable difference" (Laclau & Mouffe, 1985: 122). Put differently, antagonism marks the inability of any element to be fully crystallized or sutured as a moment. Although the concept of antagonism bears some similarity to the Marxist notion of contradiction, it does not mean mere opposition and can never be dialectically synthesized into a unitary identity. For example, the elements worker and manager are often situated antagonistically because competing social discourses (for example, labor discourses and probusiness conservative discourses) articulate these elements (as moments) in ways that are incommensurable. In this example, neither the discourse of labor nor the conservative discourse can control the social field by fixing these elements as universal moments because the presence of each discourse marks the limits of the other's power to control the production of equivalences (that is, meaning production): "Insofar as there is antagonism, I cannot be a full presence for myself. But nor is the force that antagonizes me such a presence: its objective being is a symbol of my non-being and, in this way, it is overflowed by a plurality of meanings which prevents its being fixed as a full positivity" (p. 125). Antagonisms name the limits of every objectivity, every attempted presence, and, therefore, "constitute the limits of society, the latter's impossibility of fully constituting itself" (p. 125) and the limits of every social identity to exhaust an individual's experience of his or her personal identity.

Laclau (1990) explains that the ontological undecidability of every structure (that is, partially fixed discourse) has implications for the subjects who occupy its positions. As a discursive space, no subject position is ever completely fixed, or sutured, and is always subverted by its overdetermination (p. 121). An identity may appear fixed or sutured when a particularly hegemonic discourse dominates the social field by virtue of its overdetermination through a multiplicity of practices. For instance, a hegemonic discourse of white supremacy dominated U.S. culture for more than 200 years, although it was and continues to be subject to considerable critique by various counterdiscourses. However, as this example illustrates, even the most hegemonic discourse will ultimately be subject to confrontation or revision. An individual's space for exploration, for creative articulation, is enhanced when formerly hegemonic articulations of their social identity are subject to critique by competing discourses (irrespective of their source). For example, the element Mexican American can be articulated as a moment in any number of discourses. Although recent debates over immigration and welfare reform have been dominated by a neoconservative, nationalistic discourse, the elements Mexican American, immigration, and welfare could be articulated differently as illustrated by the proimmigration essays published in a special edition of the *New Republic* (1993). The embodied individuals who are interpellated as Mexican Americans cannot but be aware of these competing discursive constitutions of their identity and social significance. The very existence of competing discourse destabilizes each articulation of what Mexican American means. However, as developed in this example, the embodied individuals so interpellated have remained silent. Laclau and Mouffe are interested in how the individual makes use of this social polysemy to produce his or her identity by producing his or her own chain of signifiers to articulate concerns, interests, and self-conceptions. Thus, the point of social analysis is not to determine who the social agents are "but the extent to which they manage to constitute themselves" (Laclau, 1990: 36). Beginning with the objective identities of partially fixed discourses, researchers then move to "emphasize the dislocations adulterating their fullness" (p. 36):

It's not a question of "someone" or "something" producing an effect or transformation or articulation, as if its identity was somehow previous to this effect. Rather, the production of the effect is part of the construction of the identity of the agent producing it. It is because the lack is constitutive that the production of an effect constructs the identity of the agent generating it. For example, one cannot ask *who* the agent of hegemony is, but *how* someone becomes the subject through hegemonic articulation. (Laclau, 1990: 210–211)

The subject's identity is not essential as the structural intersection of social structures. Rather, with each articulation (in speech and practice) the subject invokes her or his identity by drawing upon discursive forms but always only partially. The inability to fully determine the identities of self and practice in the terms of a specific discourse has the effect of engendering space for contingency and choice. As Laclau (1990: 42) puts it, discursive dislocation is "the very form of possibility." In sum, every element is overdetermined and overdetermination has the effect of dislocating the presence of every discourse by introducing otherness into the very heart of the system in general and the articulation in particular.

ONTOLOGY OF PLURALIST DEMOCRACY AND DEMOCRATIC CITIZENSHIP

Mouffe uses articulation theory as a framework for critiquing and reconstructing contemporary political theory. Our central concern is her poststructuralist conception of democratic citizenship and its role in her vision of a pluralist democracy. In this section, we will address Mouffe's social ontology of democratic citizenship and its significance for pluralist democracy.

Pluralist Democracy: Freedom and Equality

Mouffe's vision of pluralist democracy is characterized by political struggles over the way "its constitutive values of liberty and equality should be interpreted and ranked" (1995a: 106). Although she regards commitment to these values as critical for democratic processes, Mouffe does not see them as substantive goods. Accordingly, she differentiates herself from the communitarians by arguing that, "What we share and what makes us fellow citizens in a liberal democratic regime is not a substantive idea of the good but a set of political principles specific to such a tradition: the principles of freedom and equality for all" (Mouffe, 1993: 65). This distinction between the good and her relatively abstract conception of political principles ensures that no group can "pretend to have *the* solution" to the problem of interpreting and ranking these values (Mouffe, 1995a: 106).

Freedom and equality are, most basically, social elements whose meanings are contingent upon their articulation as moments within social discourses. Mouffe is not suggesting that any single discourse can or should fix their meanings. Rather, she suggests that democratic politics concerns adversarial relations among social actors as they advocate their interpretations and preferred social identities (that is, subject positions). Although she universalizes the elements of freedom and equality, she sees them as abstract elements requiring continuous discursive articulation to achieve significance: "It is the tension between consensus — on the values — and dissensus — on their interpretation — that makes possible the agonistic dynamics of pluralist democracy. This is why its survival depends on the possibility of forming collective political identities around clearly differentiated positions and the choice among real alternatives" (Mouffe, 1995a: 107). In this sense, Mouffe shares allegiance with the liberal individualists in that she sees political struggles over the meaning, ranking, and implementation of values as vital to democratic processes.

Mouffe deems that many contemporary discourses completely marginalize the social elements of freedom and equality and others subordinate the latter element by privileging the former, individual freedom. To remedy this situation she argues that we must focus our attention on the production of identities that affirm the centrality of these elements. Because identities are ultimately derived from social discourses, Mouffe is implicitly advocating development and advancement of social discourses that utilize freedom and equality as their organizing principles or nodal points. Again, Mouffe is against privileging particular crystalizations of these elements as moments within a single privileged discourse.

Mouffe's view of radical democracy is fundamentally pluralistic. She is interested in the proliferation of social discourses organized around the nodal points of freedom and equality. These discourses will necessarily articulate multiple and even antagonistic formulations of how freedom and equality ought be translated into the realm of everyday practice. Concomitantly, Mouffe recognizes that these discourses will generate a variety of articulations regarding the precise nature of democratic citizenship within democratic politics. In effect, Mouffe does not believe that any final solution should be sought for the transformation of the elements of freedom, equality, and democratic citizenship into crystallized moments. Rather, a pluralist democracy requires consensus only at the level of social agreement about the formal preeminence of the two values while politics concerns their concrete articulation and negotiation. As we shall argue in the next section, the practical success of Mouffe's model of pluralist democracy hinges on development of individual subjectivities committed to these values and their situated articulation in daily life.

Democratic Citizenship: The Significance of Reflexive Agency, Will to Act, and Respect for Adversarial Relations

Mouffe's aspirations for a pluralist democracy rest in the development of subjective identities committed to the dual values of freedom and equality. Moreover, the individuals who occupy these social identities must be able and willing to participate in democratic political processes. However, in accord with her pluralist framework, Mouffe eschews any model that promotes a singular conception of the nature and political orientation specific to these identities. Mouffe's explanation of how political identities are formed around differentiated positions and the significance of this process for democratic citizenship can only be understood in relation to her poststructuralist social ontology.

Articulation theory serves as the theoretical framework for Mouffe's claim that we must "be able to formulate the ethical character of modern citizenship in a way that is compatible with moral pluralism and respects the priority of the right over the good" (1993: 65). Developing this model of citizenship requires that "we urgently need to understand how liberal democratic citizens' identities are created and how solidarity can be fostered among democratic citizens" (1995a: 99). Whereas liberal individualists such as Rawls presuppose autonomous agents able to participate in democratic processes, Mouffe argues that her pluralist view of democratic processes requires social conditions that produce subjectivities that can and will participate in democratic processes. Unlike the liberal individualists, Mouffe is also concerned with the problem of envisaging a *"form of commonality"* that respects both freedom and equality and "allows for different forms of individuality" (1995a: 100, emphasis added). Mouffe's point is that individual freedom cannot be sustained without solidarity on such key issues as equality and respect for social differences.

Mouffe identifies three key conditions necessary for the constitution of democratic citizenship. They include, "reflexive agency," "a will to act," and the ability to "make room for the adversary" (1995a: 102–103). A particular discourse's capacity to contribute to democratic politics can be evaluated in relation to these three conditions. It is critical that all three be met in order for a discourse to satisfactorily address the dual values of equality and freedom. However, as I shall explain, the manner by which a discourse achieves this challenge is always indeterminate and, therefore, open.

Mouffe draws upon Mark Warren's (1988) revisionist reading of Nietzsche in developing the first two conditions. Warren claims that *"Humans are motivated by power as subjectivity,"* meaning "Humans strive to experience themselves as agents, as the cause of effects, and therefore as beings who determine their futures" (Warren, 1988: 9). Warren claims that this power motive (that is, will to act or power) should not be equated with the desire for political domination but rather concerns the meanings that actions have for individuals in terms of "their experiences as agent-unity" (p. 140). Individuals strive for the experience of agency over their actions, the experience of self-determination, or the will to act.

The capacity for individuals to develop a reflexive view of agency is critical for the emergence and development of their experience of will to act (Warren, 1988). In other words, reflexive agency is an essential ground for the experience of self-determination. Reflexive agency is developed as individuals learn to "evaluate their world in terms of their intentions, and at the same time to evaluate those intentions" (p. 10). Warren explains that individuals must learn to reflect on their identities and the core values that make up these identities. In the process of reflection, individuals learn to evaluate their selves and make choices about the kind of self they wish to be.[1] The will to power accompanies the development of reflexive agency because, as Warren puts it, the latter allows individuals to strive for the "self-reflective goal of experiencing the self as agent" (p. 138).

Individuals who fail to develop the capacity for reflexive agency and those who develop this capacity but are unable to externalize their choices experience nihilism. On the one hand, nihilism occurs when individuals' life experiences deprive them of the ability to develop the level of self-consciousness necessary for reflexive agency. Individuals must learn to evaluate critically their beliefs and to reflect upon the grounds of their own and others' actions. In this respect, Warren believes that the capacity for reflexive self-consciousness is achieved rather than given as individuals learn to evaluate the social structures that predicate their identities and value orientations. Agency is not bifurcated from structure but rather derives from reflexive evaluation of how structured discourses produce experience. Nihilism results when individuals are denied the resources or education to reflexively evaluate the conditions that produce their lives.

On the other hand, nihilism also results from the individual's inability to transform into practice his or her interpretations of self and world because of constraining social conditions. In this instance, nihilism occurs when an individual's being in the world cannot be rendered commensurable with his or her knowledge, thoughts, or values leading to a crisis in that person's orientation toward existence, her or his will to act.

Using Warren's framework, Mouffe rejects a view of individuals as autonomous agents and instead focuses on the social conditions that produce subjectivities that experience a will to act and that experience self in terms of reflexive agency. As Mouffe argues, "What is at stake is the constitution of an ensemble of practices that make possible specific forms of subjectivity and individuality" (1995a: 103). Mouffe is concerned that many dominant social discourses and their material instantiation in the form of social institutions preclude individuals from reflecting upon their grounds for action and, relatedly, preclude them from having any real power over their circumstances. Thus, Mouffe argues that we must attend to the social conditions that produce reflexive agency and the will to power in order to avoid the social crisis of nihilism and, concomitantly, to develop a more authentic pluralist democracy.

Discourses can be evaluated in relation to these two components by identifying the ways in which they articulate subject positions for individuals. Analysis might begin by identifying the various subject positions within a discourse. For example, within a discourse of critical pedagogy, one might briefly identify parent, student, and teacher. At an ontological level, these subject positions are simply social elements that are used to signify human beings. All educational discourses will have rules governing the production of these basic elements.[2] However, the rules that constitute these various discourses will vary considerably regarding the kinds of equivalences and differences made across elements and in the kind of nodal points used to partially fix the productivity of meaning.

Within a traditional, authoritarian discourse the element teacher might be borrowed from the discourse of patriarchy. The authoritarian pedagogical discourse would simply substitute the rule of the father as the nodal point limiting the productivity of meaning with the rule of the teacher. So articulated, the moment teacher and its equivalence with certainty, righteousness, and rule would serve as the organizing principle (that is, nodal point) for the discourse. Because all discursive moments are relationally situated, the moment student derives its meaning from its relational situatedness to the moment, authoritarian teacher. In such a discourse, the likelihood is great that these moments will be situated in a hierarchical relationship because authority requires its opposite, less authority or subordination. In this example, the moment student is almost necessarily situated as subordinate because the rules of the discourse (as determined by the nodal point, authoritarian teacher) require that other moments be subordinated.

Although we as teachers might be comfortable affording the teacher authority in some respects, one must consider the degree and scope of authority articulated by the rules of the discourse. How vast is the chain of equivalences the teacher's authority encompasses? Are there moments within the discourse reserved for the student's authority? Can and in what ways may students acquire authority and power within the discourse? More generally, does the teacher's authority contribute to the development of the student's experience of reflexive agency?

Imagine a social discourse whose nodal point was constituted by a desire to develop the student's reflexive agency. There are endless equivalences that can be made with reflexive agency, so what this might mean in practice would depend upon the specific set of rules and equivalences that constitute that particular discourse. However, one challenge that this kind of discourse might hold for Mouffe's model of democratic citizenship concerns such a discourse's implications for the second value, equality.

Beyond developing a will to act and reflexive agency, individuals must also learn to respect one another's differences and value orientations. Mouffe suggests that this might be accomplished by heightening sensitivity to the relational character of all identities and, moreover, by establishing the link between reflexive agency and an abundance of political and social perspectives. As Mouffe (1995a: 105) explains, "in order to live values as one's own, one also needs to perceive what are the limits to the practices that perpetuate those values, i.e., what is their 'constitutive outside,' the 'them' which is the condition of the possibility of the 'we' with its shared values."

Mouffe's point is that recognition that values are, indeed, one's own, requires that we simultaneously recognize those values that are different from our own. Because all identity is relational, we cannot attribute significance to some phenomenon unless we can delimit it from what it is not. One's own values on parenting, for example, only become clear when one distinguishes those values from those held by others. The constitutive outside that Mouffe refers to concerns those social differences that delimit the identities of our beliefs, values, and practices. Therefore, the outside is essentially the condition of possibility for the I and the we. As Mouffe (1995b: 264) puts it, "The existence of the other becomes a condition of the possibility of my identity since, without the other, I would not have an identity."

Recognition of the relational character of identity plays an important role in developing individuals' sense of reflexive agency and will to act. Individuals use others' values to identify and evaluate their own. They learn that their values are contingent upon their world views, or the sum of social discourses with which they identify. By demystifying the source of one's values and, relatedly, by acknowledging their contingent character, individuals develop the capacity to choose among alternatives, to expand their choices for action, and to determine actively their self-identities. Thus, Mouffe (1995b) argues that, "acceptance of the other does not merely consist of tolerating differences, but in positively celebrating them because . . . without alterity and otherness, no identity could ever assert itself" (p. 265). In effect, the possibilities for choice and action are in many respects directly grounded in a multiplicity of heterogeneous discourses.

Moreover, individuals can be encouraged to respect those values that are, at least temporarily, differentiated from their own by stressing the relational character of all social identities and, concomitantly, the contingent character of social discourses. For example, social discourses, such as pro-choice, which advocates abortion rights and pro-life, which advocates prohibition of abortions, clearly differentiate we-them relations. However, the discourse of pro-choice and the discourse of pro-life are both overdetermined by numerous other discourses. For instance, the pro-choice discourse draws upon radical feminist discourses, liberal Protestant discourses, and eugenics discourses. Because these contributing discourses cannot coexist without tension, the discourse of pro-choice is precarious and ever-shifting. The same situation affects the discourse of pro-life. Mouffe hopes that by recognizing that one's social and political alliances are not necessary but contingent individuals will be more likely to respect the very existence of competing articulations, because one never knows where future alliances may lie.

At least in the United States, relations in this example have become transformed from a we-them distinction to a friend-enemy one (Mouffe, 1995a: 105). The pro-choice discourse and the pro-life discourse are antagonistically situated. Their competing articulations of the elements of rights, life, and choice are incommensurable and conflictual. Each discourse threatens the very identities carved out by the other. Thus, neither discourse can recognize the legitimacy of the other or even enter into political dialogue with the other because of their antagonistic articulations of these elements. These discourses have realized the "everpresent possibility of this we/them relation becoming the locus of an antagonism and being transformed into a friend/enemy" (p. 105).

Although Mouffe (1995b) sees such antagonisms as an inevitable component of political life, she argues that politics "consists in domesticating hostility and in trying to defuse the potential antagonism that exists in human relations" (p. 263). Politics is stymied by instances in which such antagonisms cannot be defused. Politics is brought to a halt in situations where a discourse and its adherents reject the basic values — freedom and equality — constitutive of democratic life and, relatedly, when the basic institutions that try to uphold these values are rejected. For instance, when pro-life supporters murder medical providers of abortions or blow up abortion clinics, they forsake politics (at least as defined by Mouffe) by violating the social institutions (for example, free expression, courts, legislative processes) of a democratic society. It is precisely this denigration of politics that must be combated by those individuals committed to the dual values of freedom and equality.

Mouffe's new political frontier is pluralistic rather than relativistic. She argues that "adversaries will fight about the interpretation and the ranking of the values, but their common allegiance to the values which constitute the liberal democratic form of life creates a bound of solidarity which expresses their belonging to a common 'we'" (1995a: 107). In other words, while politics is essentially about struggles over how social existence is organized (1995b), relations among individuals must be mediated at some level by the dual values of freedom and equality or politics ceases to be an open and indeterminate process. Almost paradoxically, solidarity around commitment to these values is necessary to ensure the viability of adversarial, pluralist politics.

Those social discourses that reject these values and violate the democratic institutions that uphold them threaten politics in its entirety. Mouffe urges that threats of this form should serve as a point of common articulation across discourses. In this sense, Mouffe expresses dissatisfaction with the lack of political action that seems to characterize contemporary politics in general and the Left in particular. However, she does acknowledge that this general apathy may very well stem from the social crisis of nihilism. For instance, individuals often feel alienated from the social institutions they produce. At times this alienation is based in actual marginalization and at other times it stems from an inability or unwillingness to reflect critically on the social grounds of action. More activist politics, therefore, cannot occur until individuals are socialized with the capacity for a will to act and reflexive agency. Moreover, in order to ensure respect for the adversary, individuals must be socialized to recognize the contingent and interdependent nature of all social identities. Finally, and relatedly, this socialization must be complemented with efforts to foster common identification with the polysemous social elements of freedom and equality.

Accordingly, in the final section of this chapter we explore how educational theory and practice might participate in the creation of Mouffe's new political frontier. In particular, we develop the role of radical democratic citizenship in this process as it encompasses the three critical components of a will to act, reflexive agency, and respect for the adversary.

PEDAGOGY FOR DEMOCRATIC CITIZENSHIP

Pluralist democracy, according to Mouffe, involves political struggles over how the elements freedom and equality should be interpreted and ranked. Although Mouffe argues that the meanings of these elements should never be fixed as transcendental moments, we know that one of the institutions that does in fact attempt to fix and rank these elements as moments is the school system (see Althusser, 1971). School systems typically invoke and naturalize dominant social discourses that articulate the meanings of freedom and equality in fixed and univocal ways. However, all meanings, and hence all discourses, are subject to subversion. Accordingly, critical and feminist pedagogies have appropriated the elements of freedom and equality and rearticulated them within new chains of equivalences in their efforts to subvert hegemonic articulations of social power and privilege that are often naturalized by dominant social discourses.

Although efforts to democratize educational processes are not new, this chapter contributes to this scholarship by applying Mouffe's theory of democratic citizenship to critical pedagogy in the context of higher education. The examples in this section are drawn from our experiences as faculty members at public universities in the U.S. southwest and midwest regions. The pedagogy for democratic citizenship that we are proposing here recognizes the complexities of classroom practices in relation to the multiplicity of positions that teachers, professors, and students hold. Our pedagogical approach seeks to address the problems that these multiple positions entail in classroom situations. This is a theoretical chapter, but we address pedagogical practice as directly as possible. However, we argue that in order for pedagogical practices to be successful, they must be situationally adapted to their particular social, historical, cultural, and economic contexts. It is impossible to develop pedagogical theories that can address all situations. Indeed, as Mouffe argues, all social discourses afforded transcendental status ultimately run counter to democratic efforts.

Mouffe's theory is significant because it recognizes that discourses and, concomitantly, subjectivities are always processive and are never fully fixed. Articulation theory therefore provides a framework for critiquing pedagogical discourses that attempt to fix the meanings of such social elements as teacher, professor, and student and for developing alternative ways of articulating pedagogical practices.

Reflexive Subjectivity and Will to Power

In order to create or constitute democratic classroom practices, we must recognize that there are a multiplicity of discourses that predicate how classroom activities are enacted and interpreted. Although discourses do not compete directly to control the social field, agents interpellated as subjects by these discourses do vie for the opportunity to dictate the flow of events and the interpretive frames used to make sense of social practices. In this section we provide an example of how social agents compete to articulate various social elements as fixed discursive moments. First, we briefly explore how dominant pedagogical discourses construct the elements of student, teacher, and affirmative action within a chain of equivalences centered around the nodal point rational impartiality. We then suggest why social agents may draw upon these rationalist discourses in their efforts to naturalize or legitimize extant power hierarchies. This example is designed to illustrate the complexities involved with developing democratic pedagogy.

Most educational discourses, including many variants of critical and feminist pedagogy, draw upon rationalist discourses such as classical liberalism and other enlightenment models of subjectivity. Pedagogical practices rooted in such rationalist discourses articulate the element teacher-professor as a rational arbitrator of truth and the element student as an impartial receptacle of knowledge. Thus, the elements teacher and student achieve significance as moments within a chain of equivalences that include impartiality, objectivity, rationality, and transparent truth. Although there are any number of specific pedagogical discourses that invoke this chain of equivalence, they are ultimately united by a common allegiance to the nodal point of rational impartiality.

There are significant and often unexamined consequences that follow from allowing classical liberalism to inform pedagogical theory. For instance, student activities that violate principles of impartiality — activities labeled racist — are typically explained in relation to the student's ignorance and his or her failure to properly assimilate pedagogical practice. Racial partiality, the logic follows, is best eradicated through more extensive pedagogy or application of the law, the ultimate expression of classical liberal rationality. However, what is rarely examined is the role that these pedagogical practices play in reproducing partial behavior. Moreover, similarly unexamined are the vested interests that students and teachers may have in reproducing pedagogical discourses that affirm their personal rationality and impartiality. Consequently, rationalist pedagogical discourses can actually reinforce racial privilege as illustrated by affirmative action.

When affirmative action is articulated as a moment within a rationalist discourse it is likely to be understood as violating other moments of that discourse including merit, individual autonomy, individual rights, and ownership. Affirmative action is, therefore, articulated as partial or as irrational because it cannot be smoothly integrated with rationalist beliefs that individual merit is transparent and reaps its own rewards. Students and faculty articulated as white or as middle-class within dominant U.S. discourses may have a vested interest in invoking rationalist pedagogical discourses, because they have the effect of naturalizing their merit and legitimizing their claims for impartial access to educational resources. These student-faculty agents may find it equally advantageous to label affirmative action as racist, because it can be interpreted as partial within classical liberal discourses, which simultaneously deny class, race, or gender based privileges.

Application of Mouffe's theory of articulation to pedagogical practice suggests alternative ways of addressing inequities in classroom conduct and pedagogy. Drawing upon Mouffe's discussion of reflexive agency, we suggest that pedagogical practices should aim to demonstrate the fundamental contingency of meaning constructs, that is, of discursive structures. This requires that students be encouraged to critically examine the assumptions implicit in dominant discourses and that they learn to recognize the contingent nature of all social articulations. Furthermore, students must learn to evaluate how their identities are constituted through hegemonic articulations. Analysis should focus on identifying the chains of equivalences that constitute their identities as subject positions (that is, as moments) within hegemonic discourses. This kind of analysis will illuminate how relations of power and subordination, privilege and marginalization are embedded in the discursive structures that articulate elements (for example, black, female, working-class) as discursive moments (that is, as subjectivities and partially fixed meanings). All of this entails that the task of progressive educators is not to insist that students become agents (they are already constituted as such), but that they become reflexive agents.

Learning to Make Room for the Adversary

Educational practices, whether liberal, conservative, or progressive, that present subjects and discourses as fixed will preclude development of reflexive agency and will to power and will probably fail to make room for the adversary. Mouffe argues that we must not only attend to the social conditions that produce reflexive agency and the will to power but we must also recognize that in order to constitute ourselves as subjects who are democratic citizens we need to learn to make room for the adversary. Accordingly, a first strategy is to recognize that all discourses can be liberatory or oppressive. There is nothing intrinsic to the relational elements freedom or liberty that causes them to be liberatory or oppressive; what constitutes them as one or the other are the meanings they convey through their articulation as moments within a discourse.

Following is a discussion of an exercise we have implemented that is effective in teaching-learning how to make room for the adversary. We ask students to defend a particular position on abortion regardless of their own views. That is, students must articulate the relational elements pro-choice and pro-life as moments within a discourse in order to constitute their meanings. The classroom is divided into four groups representing groups such as Operation Rescue, Feminists for Life, National Organization for Women, and a radical feminist group. Students are randomly assigned to their groups in order to ensure that some, if not all, learn to understand the position of the other. Each group develops its own position regarding a particular question on abortion. Regardless of what the individual members believe and how they feel, they must articulate the position of the group they represent. Thus, a student who is pro-life might have to defend the most radical position on abortion, or a radical feminist might represent and defend Operation Rescue. Each group makes an uninterrupted 5-minute presentation of its position. After the presentations, the groups debate one anothers' positions. That is, students have to build arguments for and defend the position they represent. The instructor is always the moderator. After most of the crucial points regarding abortion are presented (that is, when life begins, women's right to control their own bodies, life of mother versus life of fetus-embryo-unborn child, funding for abortion and birth control, and so forth), class members can independently represent and discuss their personal standpoints. Through this exercise, the potential that a pedagogy for democratic citizenship has to make room for the adversary is put into practice as students reflect upon the relational similarities and differences that exist across discourses.

Once students start to construct the position they are required to represent, they realize that the only way to constitute meaning is through other discourses. The current debate over abortion was constituted only when medical, scientific, theological, and moral discourses began debating when human life begins. The only way students can construct a position on abortion is to use the various social discourses available. These discourses necessarily construct their own meanings and identities in relation to the other discourses. Put simply, there cannot be a discourse on anti-abortion without a pro-choice discourse, and the pro-choice discourse cannot construct its meaning without the pro-life discourse. The impossibility of constructing an autonomous social discourse becomes very clear. Because in this exercise students are obligated to take the position of the other, this impossibility is concretized. Thus, students themselves begin to see that a discourse they have believed in, and which they have constructed in opposition to the other side of the issue, exists precisely because there is an other discourse. Once this is recognized, the political dimension of the debate over abortion becomes more clear. For instance, a pro-choice student said that after working in a group with a pro-life supporter (the group was representing a moderate position), she had learned to respect the pro-life position. That is, she learned to make room for the adversary by moving beyond the we-them antagonism of most abortion rights discourses.

Learning about the relational embeddedness of each discourse (which is essential to construct and articulate each position) creates the pedagogical space necessary to make room for the adversary. In a very simple way, this exercise helps to demystify the other's position. That is, students have no choice but to understand that discourses are not entities in and of themselves, that they must be related to other discourses, that they do not exist in isolation. This demonstrates that their existence and articulation are necessarily political. In order to understand the other's discourse one does not need to change one's position. Therefore, a pedagogy for critical democracy does not rely on the transmission of knowledge (or only knowledge) to make room for the adversary. In the example given here, students learned to respect the other's position but did not change their minds and were willing to fight and organize to defend their own position. For example, pro-choice students were even more willing to work to maintain the legality of abortion. Knowledge of why people think the way they think, and how related each position is to each other, did not make them change their minds. This pedagogical strategy contradicts the notion that people have their positions because they do not know the other's position. On the contrary, in a democratic society the free exchange of ideas and healthy debate serve to enhance one's position and make room for the adversary.

CONCLUSIONS

Mouffe argues for the creation of a new political frontier "capable of giving a real impulse to democracy" (1993: 6). Crucial to this creation is the role of the individual. In this chapter, we have articulated the crucial role of educators and students in the development of a pedagogy for democratic citizenship based on Mouffe's model of democratic citizenship. Mouffe's model hinges on the development of individual subjectivities that are able and willing to participate in democratic politics. Althusser demonstrated that, historically, schools have prevented the formation of such subjectivities. Therefore, we propose that to ensure a truly democratic citizenship, it is crucial to create pedagogical strategies that cultivate the development of these subjectivities. For this we propose a pedagogy for democratic citizenship that rests in the development of subjective identities committed to freedom and equality. We follow

Mouffe's belief that individual freedom cannot be sustained without solidarity on key issues such as equality and respect for social differences.

For a pedagogy for democratic citizenship what is at stake is to enhance the formation of subjectivities that will make room for the adversary. To accomplish this, these subjectivities must move beyond a will to act and reflexive agency (which, of course are essential). Individuals must also learn to respect one another's differences and value orientations. This must be accomplished by establishing sensitivity to the relational character of all identities and the link between reflexive agency and other social and political perspectives. Our example of abortion rights shows how this might be accomplished in a classroom situation. In our example, students learned to demystify the source of their values (whether liberal or conservative) and to acknowledge the contingent character of such discourses. Students had to understand how they chose their position on abortion from the various discourses available and they had to realize how this understanding actually enhances the maintenance of their own values.

Crucial for a democratic citizenship is the development of subjectivities that understand their own contingency. This democratic project is not about the mere toleration of difference. Rather it is essential to recognize and celebrate these differences, because they are crucial for the development of various identities. Differences, as our example on abortion rights demonstrates, do not necessarily always have to be antagonistic. Differences will exist, and must exist in order for democracy to survive. These differences must be understood as complementary to each other, on an equal footing. We believe that a pedagogy for democratic citizenship can help accomplish this goal.

NOTES

1. Warren is not endorsing a rational view of agency. He does not believe that individuals are autonomous agents. Rather, Warren is taking an existential position by arguing that reflection is always grounded in and presupposes the individual's social, cultural, and economic situatedness.

2. There is a family resemblance among all educational discourses despite the fact that there are wide variations in how the elements teacher, student, and parents are articulated as moments. Even the most radical of critical pedagogies is required to articulate these elements as moments even if they are radically formulated when compared to other, more conservative discourses.

REFERENCES

Althusser, Louis. (1971). *Lenin and philosophy and other essays*. London: Monthly Review Press.

Laclau, Ernesto. (1990). *New reflections on the revolution of our time*. London: Verso.

Laclau, Ernesto, & Mouffe, Chantal. (1985). *Hegemony and socialist strategy: Towards a radical democratic politics*. London: Verso.

Mouffe, Chantal. (1995a). Politics, democratic action, and solidarity. *Inquiry, 38:* 99–108.

Mouffe, Chantal. (1995b). Post-Marxism: Democracy and identity. *Environment and Planning D: Society and Space, 13:* 259–265.

Mouffe, Chantal. (1993). *The return of the political*. London: Verso.

Warren, Mark. (1988). *Nietzsche and political thought*. Cambridge, MA: MIT Press.

Index

Althusser, Louis, 5, 14, 17, 18, 26, 43, 66, 70; biography, 51–52; against economism & humanism, 52–55, 62; epistemological break, 56; *For Marx*, 52; *The Future Lasts a Long Time*, 52; ideological state apparatuses, 49, 57, 58–59; ideology, 58–60; ideology and science, 56; interpellation, 60; poststructural materialist, 49–62; *Reading Capital*, 52
Anyon, Jean, 227
Appel, Stephen, xiii, 18

Bachelard, Gaston, 56, 57, 67, 70
Bakhtin, Mikhail, 19, 87, 88, 93, 94,
Barthes, Roland, 5, 84, 87, 93, 94, 99
Bataille, Georges, 7, 15, 67, 70, 81; *Sur Nietzsche*, 10–11
Baudrillard, Jean, 20, 70, 215; *Consumer Society*, 218; and consumer society, 218–21; and the critique of labor, 226; and cultural critique, 216; *Fatal Strategies*, 138; *For a Critique of the Political Economy of the Sign*, 221–22; *In the Shadow of the Silent Majority*, 232; Marx's anthropology, 227; Marx's commodity fetishism, 223; *The Mirror of Production*, 225; and racism, 237; *Seduction*, 233; sexual objectifiction of women, 233–35; simulacra, 231–32; *Symbolic Exchange*, 230; *The System of Objects*, 217
Beardsworth, Richard, 9
Behler, Ernest, 9
Benjamin, Jessica, 236–37
Bergson, Henri, 154
Bernasconi, Robert, 192
Besnier, Jean-Michel, 11
Best, Stephen, 221
Bion, Wilfred, 32
Blanchot, Maurice, 8, 10, 16, 67, 70
Boler, Megan, xiv, 19
Braidotti, Rosi, 159
Brewster, Ben, 56
Butler, Judith, 153

Canguilhem, Georges, 66, 70
Cixious, HÈlËne, 10
Cook, 216

Davies, Bronwyn, 39

de Beauvior, Simone, 69
Debord, Guy, 222, 240
Deconstruction, 9, 12
De Landa, Manuel, 97
Deleuze, Gilles, 1, 9, 13, 17, 19, 70, 71, 166; alternative figurations for thought, 155–59; *Anti-Oedipus*, 151; Deleuze and education, 149–68; the Deleuzian project, 153–55; and Guattari, 155, 156, 160, 161, 167; lines of flight, 160–62; *The Logic of Sense*, 156; *Nietzsche et la philosophie*, 6–7; rhizomatics, 156, 157, 159–63; and teaching of history and literature, 163–66; *A Thousand Plateaus*, 159, 160
Democracy, 15, 20; and Chantal Mouffe, 245–63; citizenship, 252–58; democratic politics, 245; freedom and equality, 251–52; and Nietzsche, 15; pedagogy for democratic citizenship, 258–63; pluralist democracy (Mouffe), 250–58;
Derrida, Jacques, 4, 8, 10, 13, 15, 17, 70, 71, 153, 191; "The Age of Hegel," 19; deconstructing education policy, 115–20; deconstruction and pedagogy, 104–9, 139; *Groupe de Recherches sur L'Enseignement Philosophie* (GREPH), 108, 128–39; Hegel's *Philosophy of Right*, 121–28; post-Cartesian subjectivity, 125–28; sign of proper name, 124; "Structure, Sign and Play . . . ," 5–6
de Saussure, Fredinand, 5, 36, 93
Descartes, René, 28, 69, 70
Descombe, Vincent, 6, 13
Donato, Eugenio, 5
Dumezil, Georges, 66

Eagleton, Terry, 5, 41
Education, 1; and Althusser, 61–62; and busno-power, 75; deconstructing educational policy (Derrida), 115–20; educational practices, 85; educational reform, ix; educational studies and Lacan, 39–43; educational theorists, 12; face-to-face with (Irigaray), 205–11; Foucault and education, 77–81; and freedom, 65–81; French philosophical curriculum, 69–70; Hegelian curriculum, 129; and imaginative knowledge, 180–81; and Kristeva, 85–99; the pedagogical institution, 128–39; and poststructuralism, 13–18; Prussian system of, 110–15; reform and Hegel, 109–15; role of state in public education, 119; Western liberal education, 75
Elenes, Alejandra C., xiv, 20

Feminism, 19; and Deleuze, 149–68; feminist cautions, 166–68; feminist theory, 194; feminist theory (Baudrillard), 233–36; and Irigaray, 183–211; and serious gossip, 157–59; women becoming subjects (Irigaray), 197–205
Ferry, Luc, 13, 14, 15, 16, 17
Fiske, John, 224
Formalism, 3
Foucault, Michel, 2, 3, 7–8, 13, 18, 19, 42, 103, 150, 151, 160, 162; biography, 65–68; bio-power, 75; care of the self, 74; criticisms of, 78–79; *Discipline and Punish*, 73, 78, 80; freedom as an exercise upon the self, 72–77; governmentality, 72; *Group d'Information sur les Prisons*, 67; *The History of Sexuality*, 73, 74; and the point of philosophy, 68–72; power, 75; power/knowledge, 73, 75; regimes of truth, 77; technologies of self, 73
Frank, Manfred, 4
Freire, Paulo, 227
Freud, Sigmund, 6, 13, 43, 59, 86, 88, 96; Baudrillard's interpretation, 233; *Beyond the Pleasure Principle*, 32; *The Interpretation of Dreams*, 38; Lacan's reading, 25–38
Fritzman, J. M., xiii, 18
Futurism, 3

Gane, Mike, 216, 222

Godelier, Maurice, 227, 228
Guattari, Felix, 241

Habermas, Jürgen, 226
Haraway, Donna, 97
Hardt, Michael, 1–2
Harland, Richard. 4
Hegel, 13, 28, 50, 69, 91, 93, 104, 153, 154; "The Age of Hegel" (Derrida), 108–40; Hegelian dialectic, 7; *Philosophy of Right*, 110, 121–28
Heidegger, Martin, 6, 13, 15, 29, 67, 70, 71, 81, 183, 184; *Letter on Humanism*, 70
Holmes, Lucy, xiii, xiv, 19, 98–99
Hyppolite, Jean, 5, 66, 69

Irigaray, Luce, 16, 17, 20, 153, 166, 167, 183, 233; essentialism, 193–97; an ethics of sexual difference, 192–93; face-to-face with education, 205–11; *I Love to You*, 192; and Levinas, 187, 190, 192; *Marine Lover of Friedrich Neitzsche*, 192; sexual difference, 184–85; women becoming subjects, 197–205, 184

Jakobson, Roman, 5, 38
Jameson, Fredric, 30
Jarry, Alfred, 238

Kant, Immanuel, 9, 13, 20, 69, 70, 81, 179, 180, 181; account of the sublime, 175–78; *The Critique of Judgement*, 177
Kauppi, Niilo, 89, 90
Kellner, Douglas, 216, 229, 239
Klein, Melanie, 40
Klossowski, Pierre, 9, 70, 72
Knowledge: imaginative knowledge, 19, 174–81; institutionalization of, 136; speculative knowledge, 112; three kinds of, 173–74
Kristeva, Julia, 17, 19, 42, 153, 167; *Desire in Language*, 86; and educational practice, 97–99; intertextuality, 92–97; life and work, 86–92; *Revolution in Poetic Language*, 87, 95; *The Samurai*, 87; semanalysis, 90; *Tales of Love*, 87
Kroker, Arthur, 216

Lacan, Jacques, 5, 15, 18; biography, 25–26; and desire, 28–30; and educational studies, 39–43; formation of the I, 33–38; Lacanian psychoanalysis, 32–33, 90; Lacan's seminars, 43–44; metaphor and metonymy, 37–38; mirror stage, 33–35; path of signifier, 35–37; project, 26–27; real, imaginary, symbolic, 30–31; and subjectivity, 27–28; and symbolization, 31–32
La pensée, 68, 14
Large, Duncan, 10
Leach, Mary, xiv, 19
Lechte, John, 89, 91, 92, 96
Leonardo, Zeus, 20
Levinas, Emmanuel, 13, 20, 185, 186, 195; construction of ethical subjectivity, 187–92; *Otherwise than Being*, 206; *Totality and Infinity*, 188
Lévi-Strauss, Claude, 5, 6, 15, 93, 96
Liberalism, 14; autonomous chooser, 75–77; neoliberal theory, 76
Lyotard, Jean-François, xiii, 2–3, 9, 13, 19; the *différend*, 175; and imaginative knowledge, 174–81; *The Inhuman*, 176; *Lessons on the Analytic of the Sublime*, 176; *The Postmodern Condition*, 176; the sublime, 175–78; the unpresentable, 175–76

Macksey, Richard, 5
Marshall, James, xiii, 19, 68; busnopower, 75
Martin, Betsan, xiii, xiv, 20
Marx, Karl, 6, 62, 69, 71, 86, 91, 99; Althusser's reading, 55–60; Baudrillard's critique of labor, 226; Baudrillard's Marxist critique of consumer society, 218–21; classical, 57; commodity fetishism, 223; critique of capital (Mouffe), 247; existential Marxism, 69; Marxism, 20, 51, 88, 93, 216; neo-Marxists, 41;

post-Marxist thought, 155; semiotic Marxism, 223–24; structural Marxism (Baudrillard), 217
Mauss, Marcel, 228
McLaren, Peter, xiii, 20, 40
Modernity, 3
Mouffe, Chantal, 20; articulation theory, 246–50; democratic citizenship, 252–58; and Ernesto Laclau, 246; freedom and equality, 251–52; *Hegemony and Socialist Strategy*, 146; pedagogy for democratic citizenship, 258–63; pluralist democracy, 250–58; poststructuralist philosopher, 245

Nadesan, Majia Holmer, xiv, 20
Nancy, Jean-Luc, 16, 22 n.8,
New Zealand, xiii, 98, 99, 150, 210
Nietzsche, Friedrich, 1, 21, 67, 70, 71, 72, 81, 104, 152, 154, 161; French Nietzsche, 9–13; and poststructralism, 6–13
Nihilism, 253–54
Nuyen, A. T., xiii, 19

Other, 35, 106; and Lacan, 28–29; Levinas and, 186–92

Pedagogy, 20, 39; critical pedagogy, 240; and deconstruction, 106–9; for democratic citizenship, 20; pedagogical discourses, 258; the pedagogical institution, 109; pedagogy for democratic citizenship, 245–63; and the subject and the state, 109–15; teaching history and literature, 163–66; and the teachings of metaphysics, 128–39; terrorist pedagogy, 215
Peters, Michael, 2, 7, 27
Philosophy: analytic philosophy and the question of style, 21 n.1; Anglo-American philosophy, 69; institutional plight, 107; and pedagogical institution, 128–39
Poster, Mark, 4, 79, 216
Postmodernism, 3, 4, 149, 176; postmodern condition, 180; *The Postmodern Condition*, 176
Postmodernity, 3; Postmodern Age of Hegel, 128–39
Poststructuralism, 1, 4, 5, 103, 149, 150, 152, 153, 217; and education, 13–20; Nietzsche and poststructuralism, 6–13; post-critical discourses, 106; poststructuralist ontology of society, 245; poststructuralist philosopher (Mouffe), 245; what is poststructuralism? 1–6
Psychoanalysis, 28, 216; and Kristeva, 86–92, 95; and Lacan, 28–38; Lacanian psychoanalysis, 32–33

Readings, Bill, 205
Renaut, Alain, 13, 14, 15, 16, 17
Rorty, Richard, 180
Roudinesco, Elizabeth, 27, 89, 90
Ryan, Michael, 120

Sartre, Jean-Paul, 69, 70; *Les Temps Modernes*, 71, 72
Schor, Naomi, 194
Schrift, Alan, 11–12, 13, 21
Sollers, Phillippe, 19, 88
Spinoza, 53, 55, 152, 154
Structuralism, 3, 4, 5, 14, 71, 88, 90, 91, 217
Sturrock, John, 4
Subject, 13–17, 91; autonomous chooser, 75; body without organs, 155; constitution of identities, 74; construction of ethical subjectivity (Levinas), 187–92; death of, 27; desiring machines, 155: the education of subjectivity, 121; freedom as an exercise upon the self, 73; interpellation of individual as subject (Althusser), 60; of language, 95; life-writing of the self, 122–25; liquidation of, 16; post-Cartesian subjectivity, 125–28; recreate the, 239; reflexive subjectivity and will to power, 259–60; relational chracter of identity, 256; social agent of transformation, 239–42; and struc-

turalism, 91; subject-Other relationship, 30; subjectivity and Lacan, 27–28; technologies of self, 73; women-as-subjects, 196; women becoming subjects, 197–205; women-becoming-subjects (Irigaray), 184; work upon the self (Foucault), 71
Sublime, 3; Kant's account, 176–77; and Lyotard, 174–79

Tel Quel, 87, 88, 89
Todorov, Tzvetan, 5, 87

Trifonis, Peter, xiv, 19

Warren, Mark, 253–54
Wexler, Phillip, 39
Whitford, Margaret, 194
Wittgenstein, Ludwig, 81, 246
Woolf, Virginia, 165–66

Yale school of criticism, 5

Zeitlin, Maurice, 229
Zizek, Slavoj, 29, 50, 51

About the Contributors

Stephen Appel is a senior lecturer in the School of Education, University of Auckland. His research interests focus on psychoanalytic perspectives in critical education and, in particular, the work of Jacques Lacan. He recently published *Positioning Subjects: Psychoanalytic Perspectives in Education* (1997).

Megan Boler is an assistant professor in education at Virginia Polytechnic Institute and State University. Her research interests encompass feminist theories and cultural studies of the media, and she has contributed to such journals as *Hypatia* and *Cultural Studies*. She has a forthcoming book, which is a cultural history of the discourses on emotion in U.S. education.

C. Alejandra Elenes is an assistant professor of women's studies at Arizona State University West. She is interested in cultural studies and education.

J. M. Fritzman, an assistant professor of philosophy at Northern Illinois University, has research interests in social and political philosophy and in nineteenth- and twentieth-century European philosophy. Fritzman has published articles in such journals as *American Philosophical Quarterly, Clio, Educational Theory, International Philosophical Quarterly, Praxis International,* and *Rhetorica*.

About the Contributors

Lucy Holmes is a lecturer and tutor in art theory at the School of Art and Design, Manukau Technical Institute, Auckland, New Zealand. She is completing her doctorate on the work of Julia Kristeva and its significance for educational theory.

Mary Leach is an associate professor in the College of Education, School of Educational Policy and Leadership, The Ohio State University, in the program area of cultural studies. Her areas of interest are critical, cultural theory and educational and feminist theory. Her work has appeared in such journals as *Harvard Educational Review, Educational Theory*, and *Philosophical Issues in Education*.

Zeus Leonardo is a doctoral student at the Graduate School of Education and Information Studies, University of California at Los Angeles. He has done extensive work on popular culture and the body as pedagogical texts and given seminars dealing with consensus, the politics of language, critical pedagogy, and identity politics.

Betsan Martin is a tutor and part-time lecturer in education at the School of Education, University of Auckland. She is completing her doctorate on the work of Luce Irigaray and its significance for educational theory.

James Marshall is professor of education at the University of Auckland. He has written numerous books and articles on the philosophy of education, including *Michel Foucault: Personal Autonomy and Education* (1996). He edited *Philosophy and Education: Accepting Wittgenstein's Challenge* (1995) with Paul Smeyers.

Peter McLaren is professor in the Graduate School of Education, University of California at Los Angeles. He is the author of numerous books and articles on critical educational theory, including *Cries from the Corridor: The New Suburban Ghettos* and *Life in Schools*. He is also the coeditor with Colin Lankshear of *Critical Literacy: Politics, Praxis and the Postmodern* (1993) and *The Politics of Liberation: Paths from Freire* (1994).

Majia Holmer Nadesan is an assistant professor of communication studies at Arizona State University West. She is interested in the structure-agency relationship as it is developed in social theory and contemporary social philosophy.

A. T. Nuyen is senior lecturer in philosophy at the University of Queensland. His interests include the philosophy of social issues, the philosophy of David Hume and Immanuel Kant, and contemporary French and German philosophy. He has published in numerous international journals, including those in philosophy of education, such as *Educational Theory* and *Journal of Thought*.

Michael Peters is associate professor of education at the School of Education, University of Auckland. His research interests center around educational philosophy and policy, with a particular interest in poststructuralism. He edited the collection *Education and the Postmodern Condition* (1995) and authored *Poststructuralism, Politics and Education* (1996). He is currently working with James Marshall on a book on the work of Ludwig Wittgenstein.

Peter Trifonas is a visiting professor and postdoctoral fellow in social sciences and humanities at the University of British Columbia. His research interests focus on the philosophy of education and curriculum theory. He is currently working on the educational texts of Jacques Derrida.

ISBN 0-89789-485-5

HARDCOVER BAR CODE